GET THE JOB YOU WANT

Includes CD with 200 Resume and Cover Letter Templates

All the information you need to:

Craft a compelling letter and resume

Prepare for any interview

Determine the career that's right for you

Make the best impression every time

Get hired!

Edited by John Berm

Avon, Massachusetts

Published by
Adams Media, a division of F+W Media, Inc.
57 Littlefield Street, Avon, MA 02322. U.S.A.
www.adamsmedia.com

ISBN 10: 1-4405-0484-9
ISBN 13: 978-1-4405-0484-6

Printed in the United States of America.

10 9 8 7 6 5 4 3 2 1

Library of Congress Cataloging-in-Publication Data
is available from the publisher.

This publication is designed to provide accurate and authoritative information with regard to the subject matter covered. It is sold with the understanding that the publisher is not engaged in rendering legal, accounting, or other professional advice. If legal advice or other expert assistance is required, the services of a competent professional person should be sought.

—From a *Declaration of Principles* jointly adopted by a Committee of the American Bar Association and a Committee of Publishers and Associations

Many of the designations used by manufacturers and sellers to distinguish their product are claimed as trademarks. Where those designations appear in this book and Adams Media was aware of a trademark claim, the designations have been printed with initial capital letters.

Contains material adapted and abridged from *The Everything® Get-a-Job Book, 2nd Edition* by Dawn Rosenberg McKay, copyright © 2007 by F+W Media, Inc., ISBN 10: 1-59869-159-7, ISBN 13: 978-1-59869-159-7; *The Everything® Job Interview Book, 2nd Edition* by Joy Darlington and Nancy Schuman, copyright © 2008 by F+W Media, Inc., ISBN 10: 1-59869-636-X, ISBN 13: 978-1-59869-636-3; *The Everything® Practice Interview Book, 2nd Edition* by Dawn Rosenberg McKay, copyright © 2009 by F+W Media, Inc., ISBN 10: 1-60550-050-X, ISBN 13: 978-1-60550-050-8.

Contents

Introduction

THE JOB SEARCH. If the mere words scare you, you'd better get used to them. You will be engaged in this process at least once, but almost definitely more than that, in your lifetime. It is not a pleasant activity, nor is it easy, but it is a reality. It is in your best interests to become as skilled at the job search as you are skilled at anything else you do. You never know when you will have to embark on this journey.

You can have the greatest set of skills and experience, yet finding a job may elude you. Your success is dependent on many factors, some of which are under your control and others not. For example, a bad economy may slow down hiring, making it take longer to find a job. You may be considered too young or too old. There's nothing you can do to change those things, but you can work around them. Employers may frown upon the fact that you are returning from an extended absence from the job market. Again, there's nothing you can do to change that, but you can make the best of it. Regardless of your circumstances, there are things you can do to make yourself as competitive as possible.

First of all, you must make sure you are looking for the right job. If the job you get isn't the right one for you, before too long you'll find yourself back where you started. You must treat your job search like a job in and of itself. You must plan your job-search campaign and stay focused and organized.

Since your resume and cover letter introduce you to potential employers, it is important that they makes a good—no make that a *great*—first impression. Your resume should entice employers to call you in for an interview. Make sure it conveys why you are qualified for the job.

As an astute job seeker, you must utilize all the tools that are available. It is impossible to look for work today without using the web. Learn how to get the most out of your online job search. Once an employer contacts you, it is in your best interests to learn as much about the company as possible. The web is an invaluable tool at this point in the job search as well.

The way you present yourself in a job interview can mean your success or your failure. Your resume and cover letter got you in the door, but your job interview can garner you an invitation to stay. Be prepared for any question an interviewer might ask you. Learn how to get around sticky situations and inappropriate questions. You may breathe a sigh of relief when you finally get a job offer. And you should—it means you were successful at the job search. It doesn't mean you have to accept the offer. You should first determine whether the job is right for you. If not, you may just have to keep going until you find one that is.

This book will take you through the entire job-search process. You will discover how to put together a resume and cover letter that open doors. You will find out where to look for jobs. You will learn how to perform well on job interviews. Finally, this book will teach you how to determine if a job offer is right for you. Good luck and happy hunting.

PART I

Launching Your Job Search

Before you begin your job search, have a clear picture of what you want to do, what you can do, and where you want to do it.

CHAPTER 1

What Job Do You Want?

BEFORE YOU START looking for a job, ask yourself, "What do I want to do?" and "What am I qualified to do?" Your answers to these questions will help you determine how to conduct your job search, or even whether you are ready to start it. You may find that the type of job you thought you wanted isn't the one that's best for you, or you may find out that you don't have the right skills. You may have to reconsider your plans, even continuing your education and training if necessary.

What Kind of Job Do You Want?

One of the biggest mistakes job seekers make is to start looking for a job before they have figured out what career field they want to work in and what job they are qualified for. Before you begin your job search, you must have a clear picture of what you want to do, what you can do, and where you want to do it. You need to define your objectives clearly. Good career planning is essential. Remember, it's not just a job; it's a step in your career.

A Good Match

On a daily basis, you'll spend more time on your job than you spend doing anything else. It's important to know that you'll enjoy the work. If you are thinking about becoming an elementary school teacher, be sure you enjoy spending a great deal of time with children. If you want to be an accountant, ask yourself if you're meticulous and if you like detail-oriented work. If you want to work for a daily newspaper, be sure you can handle a fast-paced, high-pressure environment.

A Job and a Lifestyle

When you choose a career, you are also choosing a lifestyle. If you decide, for example, that you want to be a management consultant for an international firm, it is likely you'll be spending a great deal of your time in an airplane. You'd better like to fly!

You also have to think about where you will have to work. Some jobs exist primarily in certain areas. Do you want a career that would require you to live in a large city? Or would you rather live in a less populated, rural area?

Compensation is another important factor you must consider. Do you feel it is more important to make a lot of money or to be fulfilled by your work?

What will your work schedule be? If you want to have a flexible work schedule, you will have to choose a job that allows for one. Are you willing to work the long hours that are common in certain fields? If not, there are some jobs you shouldn't consider, like most jobs in the legal profession.

Think about how fast you want to advance. Some careers offer a much greater chance than others do to advance quickly. In other fields, the opportunities for advancement are virtually nonexistent. When looking for a particular job in your field, you should also be aware that companies do not all offer the same opportunities for advancement.

Self-Assessment

If you are currently in the process of choosing a career, then a self-assessment is in order. A self-assessment looks at your interests, values, skills, and personality. These factors help determine which careers you will find most satisfying and in which you will be the most successful. Although it's been said that you are what you do, try to think about this phrase reversed: You do what you are. Your personality, likes, dislikes, and values should determine what you do and where you work, not the other way around. Self-assessment is usually done through vocational or career tests that include interest inventories, values inventories, skill assessments, and personality inventories.

Interest inventories let you home in on your interests by presenting you with a series of statements and then asking you whether you agree or disagree with each one. The premise of interest inventories is that people with similar interests will be successful in the same type of work.

Here are some statements you might find on an interest inventory:

- I enjoy playing golf.
- One of my favorite activities is reading.
- I would rather participate in sports than watch sports.
- I would rather watch sports than participate in sports.

A test that focuses on your values will consider the importance to you of different values. Here are some questions you might find on a values inventory:

- Do you enjoy making a difference in people's lives?
- Is having a prestigious job important to you?
- Do you need to have a lot of leisure time to be happy?

A test that assesses your skills will not only ask if you have certain skills, it might also ask if you enjoy using them. Although you may not have the skills you need to work in a particular field, it doesn't mean you shouldn't consider that career for the future—after you've obtained them. Here are some questions you might see on a skills assessment:

- Are you good at working with numbers? Do you enjoy working with numbers?
- Do you pay attention to details? Do you like having to pay attention to details?
- Are you good at working with people? Do you enjoy working with people?

Career-planning professionals have discovered that people with certain personality types are well suited for some careers but not for others. A personality inventory like the Myers-Briggs Type Indicator will look at factors such as traits, motivations, and attitude.

How to Use What You've Learned about Yourself

Now is the time to use what you've learned about yourself to choose a career. The results of your self-assessment will include a list of occupations that are considered suitable based on your personality, values, skills, and interests. Investigate fully each career your self-assessment may have indicated is appropriate for you in order to determine if it is a good match. Once you've done that, your job search will be much more focused and easier; if you try to pursue too many different avenues, you'll only frustrate yourself.

Having a well-developed plan based on objectives you've taken time to think about is easier on you—and will make you a stronger candidate.

Your first course of action when researching occupations is to get some basic information such as job descriptions, working conditions, job and industry outlooks, education and training requirements, and earnings. You can use government resources available both in print and on the Internet to accomplish this. Before making your final decision, get a personal perspective by talking to those working in a particular field.

Job Outlook

Once you've figured out what occupations you would enjoy, you need to figure out which one is the best option in terms of the outlook for that occupation over time. Will there be many job opportunities available or are there more applicants than there are jobs? In addition to considering what the competition will be like to get the job, you must also think about what the competition will be like to advance.

Whatever you do, don't jump into a particular field just because it appears on a list of the hottest careers for this decade. You need to choose a career that is suitable for you based on what you've learned about your interests, skills, values, and personality, and whether it will offer good opportunities for you.

Industry Outlook

You should also look at the industry in which you want to work, keeping in mind that your occupation may allow you to work in a variety of industries. For example, an accountant can work in the timber industry or in the health care industry. The government publishes data on both job outlook and industry outlook.

If an industry is flourishing, it could mean many more exciting challenges and better opportunities—but it could also mean that the industry is going to be in flux for a while. You may have to jump from one company to the next throughout your career. Sometimes it's a good idea to consider careers in industries that are slowing down or maturing, because they're more likely to have greater opportunities for advancement than industries that are booming and flooded with applicants. Sometimes an industry may be doing poorly in one geographical area but well in another. This is no reason to give up on that industry, but you may have to consider relocating.

What Can You Offer Employers?

While it's very important to figure out what a job or industry can offer you, it's also important to spend some time thinking about what you can offer an employer. The first thing you bring is a set of skills that are necessary to do the job. You should have considered your skills during your self-assessment. If not, this is the time to do it. What skills do you have? Are your skills up to date? Are you willing to get some additional training if they are not up to date?

Also think about the attributes you have that do not necessarily fall under the "skill category." For example, will your outgoing personality charm clients? Will your ambition and ceaseless energy drive you to work long hours? Once you've compiled a mental list of what you have to offer an employer, you'll be more confident in your abilities and more prepared to present them when the time comes.

Employers like job candidates who have real interests and a clear direction. They know that if you're interested in a particular industry, company, or job, you're more likely to enjoy the position, perform well, and stay with the company. Employers don't like to hear that you are not at all discriminating and will take whatever job they have available. Stay focused on a particular job function.

Setting Goals

So now you've chosen a career and figured out what you have to offer employers. You must feel relieved. After all, you're on your way to getting a job. Not so fast! Yes, it's true that you have taken a huge step toward getting a job, but your work has only just begun. Getting a job is hard work. The job search is, in fact, a job in itself. As in any job, you must be organized in order to succeed. The first thing you need to do to organize your job search is set goals. A goal is something you want to achieve. There are two kinds of goals: long-term goals and short-term goals.

Long-term Goals

Long-term goals are those that could take three to five years to achieve. Your long-term goals will change over time depending on where you are in your career. If you've chosen to pursue a career for which you must get additional training and education, then a long-term goal might be to get a job in your field after you fulfill those requirements. If you already have all the necessary requirements, a long-term goal may be to advance to a top position in your field.

Short-term Goals

Short-term goals are generally achievable within a few months to a year. Taking the examples from the previous section, if you want to pursue a career for which you need additional training and education, a short-term goal may be finishing that education and training if that can be done relatively quickly, or it may be simply registering for and beginning to take courses. If you already meet the requirements to start working, your short-term goals will include finding a job in your field.

What Employers Are Really Looking For

First-time job seekers may be surprised to learn that employers generally are not looking for candidates with the best grade point averages, who were involved in the most clubs, or scored the highest in sports. They want to find employees who are the best fit for the job. Why? Those candidates will stay the longest.

The average college graduate stays with her first employer for only nine months. Employers have concluded that most new young hires are unrealistic about what entry-level jobs entail and will soon leave in search of something "better." They're right.

This costs companies a lot of money, because training new hires is expensive. It's not surprising, then, that most companies—especially those with training programs—will be interested in whether you're likely to remain in that position.

How can you show a company you won't move on too soon? You must display a true interest in the industry, in the job function itself, and particularly in that employer. Intelligently discussing the company, current trends in the industry, and showing that you are genuinely interested in the job are two great ways to communicate to an interviewer that you're a low-risk hire.

You can also demonstrate commitment by stressing only those extracurricular activities that you have pursued for an extended period of time. You should also choose to highlight those activities from which you developed the most desirable skills. For example, if you want to demonstrate your leadership skills, talk about the organization in which you sat on the board. This shows that you didn't just participate in many different activities, jumping from one to the next. You picked ones in which you could play an active role. If the activity you highlight is one which you spent a lot of time and energy doing and something you made progress in over the years, it will carry more weight than many activities you were only nominally involved in.

Show the employer you are committed to the firm by making it clear that you know what you want. You should show that you have a realistic feeling for what the job entails, that you understand what the pluses and minuses are in the position you're considering, and that you've decided, after making a realistic assessment of the job, that it's something you'd enjoy doing for a substantial period.

Maturity is another factor that employers weigh heavily. Some students or recent graduates, in one-on-one situations with older adults, may not come across as being mature and confident enough for the professional world. Unfortunately, such judgments are often made based on assumptions, but they are sometimes based on an impression made during a job interview. It is up to you to convince the employer otherwise. When on a job interview, make sure you project yourself as a mature candidate who is ready to enter the business community. Practice a firm handshake and learn how to make good eye contact.

Be Professional

It's always important for a job seeker to display a professional demeanor, but this is critical for students and recent graduates lacking work experience. Just as in college you were in the role of student, in this next phase of your life you will be in the role of employee. You must adhere to the standards of communication, appearance, and conduct expected in the workplace. Professionalism is something you need to prove to employers the very first time you make contact with them.

One way you can communicate your professionalism is by presenting a resume and cover letter that follow an acceptable format. Your resume should be printed on paper that is a neutral color and is free of any design. It should be well organized. Your cover letter needs to be well written. It is imperative that both your resume and cover letter be free of grammatical and spelling errors. We discuss all this in much more detail in Part II of this book.

Make sure your career plans are realistic. You have to start somewhere. Accept that most entry-level positions are usually lower paying and less than glamorous. It will probably take you a number of years to achieve your career goals and advance to your ideal job. Consider an entry-level job the first step toward attaining your long-term goals.

You also need to be careful when choosing an e-mail address. Your e-mail address may be the first thing an employer learns about you when you initially contact a company. The e-mail address you use for personal e-mail can invoke any sort of image you want it to—fun, silly, sexy, or whatever you would like people to think of you. The one you use for work-related e-mail, however, should project only one bit of information—that you are a professional adult who is serious about your work. Your name, either first and last name or some combination that uses your initials, is your best choice; for example, *johnbrown@gmail*.com or *jbrown@gmail.com*.

In Part III of this book, we'll discuss how to prepare for your in-person interview and how to make the best possible impression on the hiring manager.

Same Career or New One

If you're re-entering the job market—either after taking some time off or after quitting or being laid off from a previous position—you must decide if you want to continue with the career you had prior to leaving the work force. Did you enjoy the work you did? Will work in this field be compatible with your lifestyle, which may have changed since you last had a full-time job? Has the field changed?

Is it a good one to be in right now, or have job and advancement opportunities dried up? Are your skills up to date?

If you decide to move on to a different field of work, you need to pick one that is suitable for you. The realities of your life—for example, children who need you at home before a certain time—will have an influence on your choices. You may have to find a career that doesn't require late hours in the office or a lot of travel.

Using Your Transferable Skills

An absence from the work force often gives people the opportunity to develop new skills. For example, a parent with children in school may have participated in a parent teacher association. Someone else may have taken the time away from the work force to do volunteer work. Whatever it is you chose to do with your free time, figure out what skills you gained from those experiences. You may be able to use those transferable skills to demonstrate to a potential employer that you have what it takes to work for him.

Perseverance Is Key

Today's job market is competitive. As a job seeker you face many challenges. If you're new to the job market, or returning after a hiatus, things will be especially tough for you. For one thing, technology doesn't wait for anyone. Even a few years of time off is enough time to make you feel out of touch with the latest computer and Internet offerings. This is why you have to throw yourself into the deep end and do whatever it takes to get up to speed. Do research, take classes, build a network of professional contacts, and generally observe what's happening in the field you've chosen.

There will be times when you'll feel overwhelmed, dejected, and unsuccessful. It's likely that you'll suffer at least a few rejections before you get an acceptance, too. But this is all part of the process, and believe it or not, you'll be stronger and more knowledgeable when all is said and done.

If you recognize this fact and keep putting sufficient effort and energy into your job search day after day, you'll greatly increase the number of opportunities open to you and ultimately find the job you deserve. After all, your job search can itself be considered your first full-time assignment. Treat it as such, and you'll reap the rewards.

CHAPTER 2

Plan Your Job Search

PLANNING AND KEEPING TRACK of your job-search efforts will pay off in the long run. A few hours of organizing can save you countless days of unnecessary footwork and can make or break your quest to find a rewarding position. Make a to-do list at the beginning of each day and try to accomplish each of your goals by the end of that day. Keep your desk or work area free of clutter. Use a large appointment book or handheld computer to record all your appointments, names of contacts, and phone numbers. Under each entry, write down all pertinent information. Bring this to each appointment.

Create a chart or similar system that shows where and to whom you've sent your resume. Use it to track whether or not companies have responded and when and if you need to follow up with a phone call.

File away any information about an employer you collect along the way as well as relevant documents like copies of applications, resumes, and cover letters. Hold on to help-wanted ads and copies of job announcements. You never can tell when someone you contacted about a job some time ago will call. While you may have forgotten all about sending an employer a resume a month back, it may have been making the rounds at the office.

Oversized index cards or pages in a binder are another useful way to organize your job search. Keep each contact's name, position, company, address, telephone number, contact method, follow-up date, status, and other important details on individual cards for quick reference. Notes detailing when you called, with whom you spoke, and what responses you received should be included on this card. If you are responding to an advertisement in a newspaper, clip the ad and paste it onto the card, along with the name of the newspaper and the date. If an employer or networking contact gives you her business card, you can staple it to an index card and jot down any other pertinent information. Keep your cards in an index-card box in alphabetical order.

Do Your Homework

In addition, you need to do a little background research. Find out the current trends in the industry and become familiar with names of the major and up-and-coming players. Your industry's trade journal and informational interviews are two terrific ways to find this kind of "insider" information.

If you're a veteran of the field in which you're looking, make sure you keep up with industry trends by talking with your associates, attending your professional association's functions, and reading your industry's trade journals.

Career Tests

Most industries and occupations probably have an organization nearby or a website you can visit. Chances are they also publish some sort of trade magazine or other publication that will give you more insight into a particular line of work. It might benefit you to take a few minutes and investigate an unknown career a bit further.

If you can't find time during the day to meet with a career professional, there are plenty of places online where you can learn more about the kinds of careers that may be right for you. The following websites offer career planning information and will even allow you to take computerized versions of some popular career planning tests:

- Career Perfect: *www.careerperfect.com*
- Experience Network: *www.experience.com*
- My Future: *www.myfuture.com*
- Princeton Review Online: *www.review.com*
- Quintessential Careers: *www.quintcareers.com*

Some people balk at the idea of career tests. It's true that a computer or some premanufactured form or even a career counselor probably won't know more about you than you do. Therefore, you should not rely solely on what these tests or counselors tell you. But be open-minded. If a career test suggests that you would make, say, a fantastic poultry engineer, why not take the time to figure out what such a person actually does?

Informational Interviews

Consider conducting at least one informational interview, particularly if you're an entry-level job seeker or a career changer. An informational interview is simply a meeting that you arrange in order to talk to someone in a field, industry, or company that interests you.

This kind of interview allows you to:

- Examine your compatibility with the company by comparing the realities of the field (skills required, working conditions, schedules, and common traits of people you meet) to your own personal interests.
- Find out how people in a particular business, industry, or job view their roles and the growth opportunities in their business.
- Conduct primary research on companies and industries.
- Gain insight into the kinds of topics your potential interviewers will be concerned about and the methods for interviewing.
- Get feedback on your relative strengths and weaknesses as a potential job candidate.
- Become comfortable talking to people in the industry and learning the industry jargon.
- Build your network, which can lead to further valuable information and opportunities.

To set up an informational appointment, request a meeting, either by phone or by letter, with someone who has at least several years' experience working in your field of interest. Your goal is to learn how that person got into the business, what he likes about it, and what advice someone with experience might pass on to someone interested in entering the field. If you don't know who to contact for an informational interview, ask relatives, teachers, and friends if they know someone.

Tell your contact right away that you'd like to learn more about the industry or company and that you will ask all the questions. Most people won't feel threatened (especially if you assure them you're not asking them for a job) and will usually be willing to help you.

If you tell a contact that all you want is advice, make sure you mean it. Never approach an informational interview as though it were a job interview; stick to gathering information and leads and see what happens. Also, unless you're specifically requested to do so, sending your resume to someone you'd like to meet for an informational interview will probably give the wrong impression.

Now that you've scheduled an informational interview, make sure you're prepared to take the lead. After all, you're the one doing the interviewing.

Prepare a list of questions, such as:

- How did you get started in this business?
- What experience helped you to be prepared and qualified for this job?
- What do you believe is the ideal education and background for a career in this industry?
- What are your primary responsibilities in your current job?
- What do you like most about your job, your company, and your industry?
- What do you dislike most about them? What's been your greatest challenge?
- If you could work with anybody in this field, whom would you want to work with?
- What are typical career path options from here?
- What are the most valuable skills to have in this field?
- What specific experiences helped you build these skills?
- What opportunities do you see in this business?
- What would you say are the current career opportunities for someone with my qualifications in the industry?
- If you were in the job market tomorrow, how would you get started?
- What are the basic requirements for an entry-level position in the industry?
- What would be on a must-read list in your field?
- Where do you see the industry heading in the near future?
- Is there a trade association that might aid me in my job search?
- What things impress you when you interview candidates for positions in this field?
- What would be turn-offs when you interview candidates?
- What critical questions should I expect to be asked in a job interview?
- Do you know of anyone who might be looking for someone with my qualifications?

Always end by thanking the person for her time. Also promise to follow up on any important leads she has provided and to let her know how things turn out. You should also send a thank-you note within one or two days of the informational interview.

Follow up periodically with everyone in your network—even after you get a job. Once you develop a network, it's important not to lose those contacts. You want to translate your informational network into a support network and maintain it throughout your career. (See Chapter 3 for more advice about networking.)

Setting Your Schedule

The most important detail of your job search is setting up a schedule. Of course, since job searches aren't something most people do regularly, it may be hard to estimate how long each step will take. Nonetheless, it's important to have a plan so you can monitor your progress.

When outlining your job-search schedule, have a realistic time frame in mind. If you are searching full-time, it could take two months or more to find a job. If you can search only part-time, it will probably take at least four months. This time frame depends on what the market is like at the time.

If you're unemployed, remember that job seeking is tough work, both physically and emotionally. It's also intellectually demanding work that requires you to be at your best. So don't tire yourself out by working on your job campaign around the clock. At the same time, be sure to keep at it. The most logical way to manage your time while looking for a job is to keep your regular work hours.

If you're searching full-time using several different contact methods, try dividing up each week, designating some time for each method. By trying several approaches at once, you can evaluate how promising each seems and alter your schedule accordingly. Keep in mind that the majority of openings are filled without being advertised.

How Long Should Your Job Search Take?

It is very hard to determine how long a typical job search will take because there are so many factors involved in what is usually a very important life decision. One school of thought suggests that the average job search lasts approximately one week for every $2,000 of income sought. For example, if your goal is a position that pays in the $30,000 range, your search will take approximately fifteen weeks. This is only a rule of thumb; keep in mind that a lot of it is chance, depending on the job market, your personal preferences, and your qualifications and presentation.

If you're like many job seekers, you'll have to contact several hundred companies before you find the right job. If you put tremendous effort into your job search and contact many companies each week, you'll probably get a job much sooner than someone who is only searching casually and sending out one or two resumes a week.

Avoid the trap of letting yourself believe that job searching is easier for everyone else than it is for you. It's all too easy to become frustrated when you aren't seeing immediate results from your hard work. At this stage in the job-search process, it's normal to have self-doubts. Don't let your doubts overwhelm you. Job searching is tough, whether you're a recent college graduate or someone who's been in the workplace for years. Stay with it, work hard, have confidence, and you will get the right job!

Rejection

Again and again during your job search, you'll face rejection. You'll be rejected when you apply for interviews. You'll be rejected after interviews. For every job offer you finally receive, you'll probably have been rejected many times. Don't let rejections slow you down. Keep reminding yourself that the sooner you apply to companies and get those rejections flowing in, the closer you'll be to obtaining the job you want.

Don't let yourself get caught up in what everyone else is doing! Whether you're a new job seeker or a seasoned veteran of the industry, you must demonstrate that in addition to fulfilling the basic requirements, you stand out from the competition and deserve that extra consideration. If you know that a large number of people are trying to interview with just a few highly sought-after companies, don't spend all of your time doing the same. Instead, try to interview at the companies others may have overlooked. Try something different, and you'll be likely to come across several job openings before your competition does.

Go Get Some Experience

Many schools have internship programs designed to give students exposure to the field of their choice as well as the opportunity to make valuable contacts. If you're a student, check out your school's career services department to see what internships are available. If your school does not have a formal internship program or if no available internships appeal to you, try contacting local businesses and offering your services. Often, businesses are more than willing to have an extra pair of hands (especially if those hands are unpaid!) for a day or two each week. Or try contacting school alumni to see if you can "shadow" them for a few days and see what their daily duties are like.

Internships aren't just for students. If you didn't do an internship while still in school, doing one after graduation can still be beneficial and, if you're planning on getting into some of the more competitive fields, practically unavoidable. Advertising, public relations, entertainment, and publishing companies have a history of hiring former interns. Even if your internship doesn't turn into a full-time situation, you'll be well on your way in the field. You'll have made contacts, learned important skills, and added another credential to your resume.

What do you do if, for whatever reason, you weren't able to get experience directly related to your desired career? First, look at your previous jobs and see if you can highlight anything. Did you supervise or train other employees? Did you reorganize the accounting system or boost productivity in some way? Accomplishments like these demonstrate leadership, responsibility, and innovation—qualities that most companies look for in employees. And don't forget volunteer activities and school clubs, which can also showcase these traits.

Conducting Your First Job Search

If you're a student, you can start looking for a job even before you finish school. This is a great time to do preliminary research on your industry and start accumulating contacts. Nonetheless, a majority of students will not graduate with full-time jobs in their chosen fields.

Ideally, for the first few months after graduation, try to look for a job full-time. If you're able to do this, be sure to work from a vigorous, intense job-search plan that allows you to invest about forty hours a week.

Vary your activities a little bit from day to day—otherwise it will quickly become tedious. For example, every Sunday you can look through the classified ads. On Monday, follow up on these ads by sending out your resume and cover letter and making some phone calls. On Tuesday, you might decide to focus on contacting companies directly. On Wednesday, you can do more research to find listings of other companies to contact. Thursday and Friday might be spent networking as you try to set up appointments to meet with people and develop more contacts.

Many graduating students enter the job market thinking that getting a job will be like applying to college. Applying to companies isn't like that at all. Success will not go to the job searcher who invests little effort, becomes discouraged, and takes the first job possibility that comes around. Remember, the time you put into your job search will be time well spent if you make sure all of that effort and energy is going in the right direction.

If you don't have a job secured after a few months, you might also consider finding a part-time position, even if it's not in your field. (Financially, it may be something of a necessity at this point.) With a part-time job, you'll earn some money and gain a valuable sense of personal accomplishment. After some time of tedious searching, you'll probably have dealt with your share of stress; a part-time job will break up your routine and keep you motivated and enthusiastic about your job search. Working part-time also displays initiative and a good work ethic, which is something recruiters like to see.

If you're returning to the job market you may find, when you begin your job search, that things have changed some since you last worked. Take your resume, for example. The last time you looked for a job, you may have used a typewriter to compose your resume. You may have written one resume and sent that out to everyone. Since it's so easy to use most word processing programs now, you can quickly put together separate resumes to target each job for which you are applying.

If you don't have access to a computer that can be used for job-hunting purposes, find one. Several businesses rent out computer workstations by the hour. Most offer high-speed Internet connections. You may spend more than you bargained for if you are there for an extended period of time, though. You may opt to sign up to use a computer at a public library. Many libraries have a number of computers set aside for public use (including some that have Internet access). Call ahead of time to find out the library's policies.

If you've been unemployed for a long time, computers may not have been a big part of your life at work. If your hiatus from work has been short, it's likely that computers were part of your life when you were employed. Even so, technology changes, and you may not be familiar with some of the newer software out there. You may not be as familiar with using the Internet as you could be. If you're not computer literate at all, consider yourself substantially disadvantaged. To be adequately prepared for today's work force, take an introductory computer course. For a nominal fee, community colleges in your area can help you master most commonly used programs, like Microsoft Word and Excel. If you're low on funds, ask your friends for help. There's a PC owner in every bunch, and you're bound to run into one who'll agree to show you the ropes.

CHAPTER 3

Build Your Network

NETWORKING IS A MUCH-USED BUZZWORD in the business arena, yet it is often misunderstood. Networking simply means using your connections to enhance your career and to help others who want to enhance their careers. It is something you should always be engaged in. If you already have a network in place, it will be much easier to access it when you need it—like when you are job hunting.

Why You Should Network

There are many ways in which being part of a professional network can benefit your career. Of course, the first thing that comes to mind is the job search. Some career counselors feel that the best route to a better job is through somebody you already know or to whom you can be introduced. People like former coworkers, friends of friends, neighbors, and even former classmates can turn out to be very helpful in your job search.

There are other reasons to network, too. Members of your network can offer you advice on work-related matters, provide information, hook you up with potential clients, and even help you find potential employees when you need to hire someone. The larger your network, the more opportunities you'll find to get help achieving your goals.

Building Your Network

Building a network can seem like an overwhelming task, especially if you think you are starting without any contacts at all. Well, guess what? You already have contacts—

unless, of course, you've been living in a cave for the last fifteen years. It's likely you have relatives, friends, and acquaintances. Sure, not all of them can personally help you with your career—they probably don't even work in the same field you do—but they haven't been living in caves, either. They have friends and acquaintances they can introduce you to who may be able to help.

Begin your network with as many people whom you know personally as you can. Dig into your personal phone book and your holiday greeting card list and locate old classmates from school. Be sure to approach people who perform your personal business, like your accountant or insurance agent. By the nature of their professions, these people develop a broad contact base.

While you may meet a great contact at your cousin's wedding or your sister's birthday party, these aren't the best places to trade business cards. Luckily, there are events that provide perfect opportunities for networking, such as business seminars, community events, business conferences, fundraisers, and industry trade shows.

Career development experts recommend you build your contact base beyond your current acquaintances by asking each one to introduce you, or refer you, to people in your field of interest. You start off with a few people, and then grow your network from there. If you have fifteen personal contacts and each one introduces you to three additional people, you will now have forty-five contacts. Each one of those contacts can introduce you to others. Before you know it, you'll have over a hundred contacts in your network. Some will be valuable, and some won't be—at least not at the present time. Keep these contacts, though. They may come in handy in the future.

How to Develop Contact Lists

Since the first people you'll draft for your network are probably going to be friends and family members, you don't have to do anything too formal. Generally, you can give them a call or send an e-mail, telling them a little about your career plans, if they don't already know what they are, and asking if they know anyone in your field. It is when you have to begin contacting the friends of friends and family that you must get more formal.

Communicating with a Contact by E-mail

The easiest way to develop a contact list is to send a networking letter by e-mail. You can clearly spell out what your needs are and give the person the opportunity to reply on his own schedule. If you don't know the contact personally or he isn't someone with whom you are familiar, word your correspondence in a businesslike manner. In other words, don't use your addressee's first name (unless you're already on a first-name basis with him) or an overly casual writing style. If you've been in touch with him recently, remind him of this—for example, "It was great seeing you at the Chicago Writers' Convention last month" or "It's been several months since we bumped into each other on that flight to London. How are you?"

Often you'll send a networking e-mail to an addressee to whom you have been referred by a mutual acquaintance. In this case, immediately state the name of the person who referred you, such as "Jean Rawlins suggested I contact you." Ask your new contact for advice about your field, information, or the names of other contacts. Do not ask for a job at this point. Chances are, if your e-mail is politely persuasive, people will be interested in talking with you.

Here's a sample networking e-mail:

Dear Ms. Wilson:

Peter Price suggested I contact you. I am studying to be an accountant, and Mr. Price mentioned that you have worked in this field for the past few years. He thought you would be a good person for me to talk with. I would like to know a bit about the ins and outs of the accounting field. I will be graduating shortly and I'm not sure what area I want to specialize in. If possible, I would like to meet with you to get your advice. In addition, if you know of anyone else with whom I should speak, please let me know.

You can get in touch with me by replying to this e-mail or calling me at (303) 555-5555. Thank you for your time. I look forward to hearing from you in the near future.

Sincerely,

Michael Picard

Communicating with a Contact by Phone

Reaching out to a contact by telephone usually offers something e-mail doesn't—immediacy. You won't have to wait for a reply, and if you don't get one, you won't have to wonder if the recipient is ignoring you or if he didn't receive your message. You may also get the information you are looking for right away, whether that comes in the form of a date for a meeting with this person or the name of another person to add to your list. On the other hand, you may be calling at a bad time, possibly interrupting your contact in the middle of something important. The person on the other end of the line may also feel put on the spot. If you do choose to use the telephone, be polite, be brief, and make your intentions clear.

A good introduction is imperative to getting your networking relationship off to a good start. Aim for a balance of brevity and completeness. Don't simply call someone and say, "Hi, Mr. Pitt. This is George. Linda told me you do quite a business in the stock market. Do you mind telling me about it?"

Write out a short statement, including not only what you want but also who you are. If you waste someone's time, his opinion of you will take a nosedive. So practice your delivery before giving the pitch, and make sure to tailor each one to the situation at hand.

Many people are, at first, a little uncomfortable calling people they don't know and asking for contact names and interviews. You'll be nervous the first few times, but with practice you'll feel much more comfortable and confident making calls. The key is to think about what you're going to say in advance, pick up that phone, and just do it. No one else can network for you. Once you gain some confidence, you'll find that your calls will make a big difference in your job-search campaign.

Communicating with a Contact in Person

Strike up conversations with people you meet at social and business events. While it may be awkward to ask someone what she does for a living, mention what you do, and she may tell you. Lo and behold, the opportunity to add someone to your network may appear out of the blue. The person you're talking to may happen to work in your field, or may know someone who does. While you may find it difficult to ask for help from someone in person, this isn't an opportunity you should pass up. You can ask for help right on the spot, but if this is a social event, you should instead ask for a meeting at a later date. Ask if it would be okay to contact her later and make sure you get an e-mail address or phone number, asking which one she prefers you use.

Business cards, if you keep them simple, are relatively inexpensive to have printed. They are a great way to get your name and contact information circulating. When you meet someone you want to have in your network, instead of scrambling around for a scrap of paper and a pen, hand them a professional-looking business card. Remember to ask for theirs, too.

Developing Your Network Online

The web is a fertile ground for establishing connections for your network. For several years, people have been communicating online with others who share their professional interests by taking part in discussion groups. Online networking services allow you to develop contacts through the web. Some people find participating in message boards or forums on trade association websites to be very helpful.

Online Discussion Groups

There are many online discussion groups on a variety of topics, including those that are career-related. These groups are available through services such as Google Groups (*http://groups.google.com*) and Yahoo! Groups (*http://groups.yahoo.com*). Search for groups in your interest areas, which might include anything from job hunting to current computer technology to the industries you're considering for employment. You will have to register for the group or groups you want to join.

Online Networking Services

Online networking services began as a way for people to establish social networks but are increasingly being used by many to establish business networks. Two business-oriented online networking services are LinkedIn (*www.linkedin.com*) and Ryze (*www.ryze.com*). Here's a general step-by-step look at how online networking services work:

1. You join an online networking service, either on your own or through an invitation from an existing member.
2. You create a personal profile.
3. You invite your contacts, including colleagues and friends, to join your network.
4. Your contacts invite their contacts to join the network.
5. The network grows and grows.

While online networking services can be a great tool, you take a risk anytime you put information about yourself out there on the web. You should exercise extreme caution whenever you reveal anything about yourself online. Most services won't post contact information without your permission, but read each service's privacy policy to make sure. Remember that what you post on the web is out there for public consumption—if you can see something online, so can your current or prospective employer.

This is true of social networking sites such as MySpace and Facebook. It may seem funny to post pictures of yourself partying in your underwear, but more and more employers are looking at potential employees' pages before making a final hiring decision. It's best to be cautious about your posts anywhere on the web.

Trade Association Forums

A great way to network with others in your field or industry is through trade association forums or message boards. Most associations require that you be a member before you are allowed to access the forum. Membership brings you other benefits as well, so it may be well worth the cost. When you post on a forum be sure to follow all the rules, like being polite to other members and respecting people's points of view.

Maintaining Your Network

Building your network is only half the battle. Now you have to monitor and maintain it to be sure that all your hard work does not go to waste. And, of course, your newly arranged network will not be any help to you unless you use it!

Think of your network as an organic being. It will change over time—you will lose contacts and you will gain contacts. Like any living thing, it must be nurtured and maintained. Nurture your network by letting your contacts know you appreciate their help. Send a thank-you note if someone has helped you in any way, including simply giving advice. Not only is this courteous, but that person may be an important business contact for years to come—especially if the individual is active in your industry. Don't let your network sit stagnant. E-mail or call your contacts periodically just to check in with them. If you let your network sit idle, it won't be available to you when you need it. In addition to thanking contacts for any assistance they have provided, you should also offer to help them out whenever possible. You may feel like you're the only one who needs help (and you may not think you have anything to offer), but this is far from the truth. Even though your Aunt Cindy in the fashion industry is not helpful to you in your ambitions to be a lawyer, one of your contacts might be desperately searching for a fashion-merchandising job. Put those two together, and you'll have a solid contact for life.

The Key to Networking

One of the secrets of networking is to simply know what you want—or at least appearing to know what you want. If, when you are making networking calls, you tell your contacts you're interested in the industry they work in and if you sound even somewhat knowledgeable about that industry, that makes you more or less an industry insider.

How do you start? Keep up to date with the industry. Read the trade publications. These are specialized journals and magazines that address the concerns of professionals in a given industry. Virtually every type of business has at least one.

It's Who You Know

Coming out of school, there's a good chance you have a very large social network. "Yeah, a lot of good that'll do me," you may be thinking. "How can my freshman roommate help me with my career?" Your friends probably can't help you with your career directly—after all, they have no more experience than you do. But their parents or other relatives might be in a position to help you. Asking close pals to contact their relatives on your behalf is a most effective way of building a network. Be ready to reciprocate the favor.

Many colleges try to foster relationships between their alumni and their current students. Alumni often look to their alma maters to find qualified candidates to fill positions for which they need to hire. Fraternities and sororities often have gatherings where alumni and current students can get together for the purpose of networking.

Professors can also be a valuable resource when it comes to expanding your network. They probably come into contact with experts from their respective fields regularly and some, particularly adjunct faculty members, may have full-time jobs in their respective fields in addition to teaching. Ask them about their associates. This will help you add to your network.

A Sample Networking Conversation

When talking to a new contact, be sure to drop names that will be meaningful to the person to whom you're speaking. Always let your contact know who gave you his name—for example, "Ally Kendreck suggested I call you." If you've been in contact with a well-known person in the field, make that known, too. As you continue networking, you'll find yourself dropping names of other people in your network. Don't be uncomfortable with this; this is the way it's done.

Here's a sample of what your networking conversations should sound like:

You: Hi, Uncle Ted! It's Emily. As you might have heard, I just graduated from college, and I want to pursue a career in banking. Is there anyone you can think of who might be willing to talk to me about the banking industry and fill me in on some background information?

Relative: I really can't think of anyone in the banking industry—but why don't you call up my attorney, Don Silva. He's not a real close friend, but I deal with him every month or so. He knows a lot of business people, not necessarily in the banking industry, but you never know. Why don't you call him and see if he can be of any help. His number is 555-1234.

You: Thanks, Uncle Ted!

You then call the attorney, immediately identifying who referred you:

You: Mr. Silva, my name is Emily Sampson. My uncle, Ted Giemza, suggested I call you. I'm interested in a career in banking, and I wondered if you might know anyone in that field who might be able to talk to me briefly about the industry.

Attorney: I'm not really sure. Let me think about it a little and I'll get back to you.

Keep the momentum on your side by offering to follow up yourself:

You: That's fine. If you want, I can call you back. If there's someone in the industry you can refer me to or someone who might know somebody else in the industry, I'd really appreciate it.

If a networking contact seems reluctant, you could redirect the conversation:

Attorney: Gee, I do know a few people in the industry, but they're probably not hiring now. . . .

You: That's fine. I just want to talk to someone briefly to find out what's going on in the industry. If you'd like, I can stop by for a few minutes at your convenience so we can meet, and in the meantime maybe you could think of some other names you'd feel comfortable referring me to.

If your contact is hesitant to give any names out without seeing in person that you're a polished, professional individual, you may be able to overcome some of that reluctance by setting up a face-to-face meeting. This technique also gives your contact the opportunity to think of some more names of people he can refer you to.

For Those Returning to Work

When you take time away from the workplace, you should keep your network alive. Sometimes life gets in the way and it isn't possible to do that. There are children to care for if that is the reason you left. There is a business to run if you left to pursue that avenue. There are papers to write and tests to study for if you left work to attend school. You may have had too much to do and networking wasn't something that was high on your list of priorities. There's nothing you can do about it now. What's done is done. All you can do is rebuild your network or build a new one.

Re-establishing Your Network

You can try to re-establish connections with those who were on your network before you left work. Many of your old contacts may be interested in hearing you are returning to work. Send e-mails if you have addresses, or phone your contacts. Remember that some of them may no longer be at the same jobs they were at previously. You can try to track them down by asking other members of your network acquainted with those contacts if they know how to reach them.

You can also try using a search engine, like Google, to look for your long-lost contacts. In addition to helping you locate them, you may be able to learn what they are doing now. You can use what you learn about an individual as an icebreaker when you make your phone call—for example, "I heard you were just elected to the executive board of the AMA. Congratulations!"

Making New Connections

You may have to build your network from scratch entirely, or at least make some new connections to bulk it up a bit. Spending time away from the workplace probably means you were spending your days elsewhere. If you took time away from work to be a stay-at-home parent, your personal network may now include people you met on the playground, other parents at your child's school, or those with whom you worked on volunteer projects. If you were a student during your time away from work, look to your professors for contacts, as was discussed earlier in this chapter. If you left the workplace to start your own business, your customers may now be candidates for your network.

CHAPTER 4

Marshal Additional Resources

IN ADDITION TO the contacts you make by networking, there are a number of other possible leads on jobs you must develop and nurture. Some of these will be easy to spot; others may take a bit more digging.

Employment Services

Employment services fall into four basic categories: executive-search firms, employment agencies, counseling services, and executive-marketing or -outplacement firms. There are also important distinctions among the organizations listed within each basic category. We'll conduct a more extensive examination of employment services in Chapter 6, but here's a brief survey.

Executive-Search Firms

Have you ever heard the term "headhunter" used in relation to a job search? What's really being talked about are executive search firms. If you're considering using one, here's a summary of what they are, what they do, and whom they're for. Essentially, there are two types: those that operate on retainer for their client companies, and those that operate on a contingency basis, meaning that they receive payment only when a successful search is concluded.

These firms aren't for everybody. Executive-search firms handle only experienced executives, focus only on positions in the higher salary ranges, and generally don't specialize in any particular industry. They're always hired and paid by the employer, and they're just as likely to contact and recruit candidates who aren't even looking as those who are currently in the job market. Search firms are interested only in executives with successful, proven track records in jobs that directly apply to their clients' needs. For this reason they often file the names of tens of thousands of possible candidates for placement.

After receiving an assignment a search firm will go through its own records and through other sources, then limit its search to a few hundred names, depending on the position being filled. Then, after studying the backgrounds of these candidates and discussing them with sources in the industry, the firm narrows its choices to a few dozen candidates. Finally, the firm will present the strongest candidates to its client. If you're an experienced executive, you may want to send your resume to one or more executive search firms, but don't bother to follow up with a phone call—and don't expect an interview unless your background happens to match the firm's current needs.

These organizations aren't licensed, so if you decide to go with an executive-search firm, make sure it has a solid reputation. You can find names of search firms by contacting the following:

ASSOCIATION OF EXECUTIVE SEARCH CONSULTANTS (AESC)
230 Park Avenue, Suite 1549
New York, NY 10169
(212) 949-9556
www.aesc.com

AMERICAN MANAGEMENT ASSOCIATION (AMA)
Management Services Department
1601 Broadway
New York, NY 10019
(212) 586-8100
www.amanet.org

Don't let an executive-search firm become a critical element in your job-search campaign—no matter how encouraging it may sound. Continue to seek out your own opportunities actively and keep all of your options open.

Employment Agencies

Much more common than headhunters are general employment agencies. These can be divided into private agencies and state-government agencies. State agencies place a much wider range of people, including many hard-to-place, low-skill workers, although they do place others as well and shouldn't necessarily be ruled out as a valuable resource. More often, though, job seekers looking for professional positions will have better luck with private employment agencies.

In some states private employment agencies can charge job seekers a fee, but the employer pays the vast majority of these agencies. Typically, employment agencies charge the employer a fee based on a percentage of the new employee's first-year salary.

A word of caution: Unfortunately, a few less-than-ethical employment agencies have done a great deal to tarnish the reputation of the entire industry. Some firms, especially those specializing in lower-end placement—for secretarial and office help, for example—are notorious for running ads for openings that don't exist, and for pitching fictional candidates to employers. Because placement fees can run in the $1,500 to $2,000 range, even for a secretarial position, some agencies feel pressure to push a job seeker to take a position they know the person won't enjoy. Another danger sign: If your agency tries to have you stop by the office both before and after job interviews, odds are they're actually trying to monopolize your time. Naturally, once you've signed on, they don't want you to go to another agency (or, for that matter, find work on your own).

If you're unsure about a particular agency, keep in mind that employment agencies must be licensed by the state in which they operate. Some states can give you the number of business complaints that have been lodged against an agency. The vast majority of employment agencies place great importance on their reputation. Companies that engage in shady business practices generally aren't around long before they're exposed, and tend to get forced out of business. To play it safe, though, review the following list before choosing an agency:

- Find out when the company was founded. If it's been around awhile, chances are you're dealing with a reputable, established company.
- Consider choosing an agency that specializes in your profession. In general, these agencies are more likely to be reputable because they operate in only one industry—and bad word of mouth can travel quickly. Employers in certain high-demand fields rely heavily on specialized employment services to find good candidates. These fields include banking, finance, advertising, data processing, health care, insurance, publishing, retailing, sales, and a variety of technical industries.

  Like executive-search firms, specialized employment agencies aren't particularly interested in people with little or no experience in the industry, or in those thinking about switching careers. But because these agencies fill fewer senior-level positions than do executive-search firms, a specialized employment agency will probably be interested in trying to place you if you're a professional with, say, five to ten years of relevant experience in the industry.

- Find out if the agency belongs to a national or regional professional organization. The industry's most notable national organization is the National Association of Personnel Consultants (NAPC). Thousands of agencies across the country belong to this group; members are required to follow the prescribed business practices of the organization, known as the Standards of Ethical Practice, and the NAPC Code of Ethics.

If you decide to register with an agency, your best bet is to find one that's recommended by a friend or associate. Barring that, you can find names of agencies in the yellow pages or by contacting the following:

NATIONAL ASSOCIATION OF PERSONNEL SERVICES
10905 Fort Washington Road, Suite 400
Fort Washington, Maryland 20744
(301) 203-6700
www.recruitinglife.com

After you've selected a few agencies (three to five is best), send them your resume and cover letter. Make a follow-up phone call and try to schedule an interview. Be prepared to take a number of tests (vocational, psychological, and other) on the day of your interview.

Above all, don't expect too much. Only a small percentage of all professional, managerial, and executive jobs are listed with these agencies, so they're not a terrific source of opportunities. Use them as an addition to your job-search campaign, but focus your efforts on other, more promising methods.

Career-Counseling Services and Executive-Marketing Firms

Counseling services are even more diverse than employment agencies. Many nonprofit organizations—colleges, universities, and private associations—offer free or very inexpensive counseling services. For-profit counseling services, on the other hand, can charge a broad range of fees, depending on their services. Services include:

- Individual career counseling
- Internship programs
- Specialized workshops in areas such as resume and interview preparation, and aptitude and interest testing.

You can find them listed in your local phone book, or write to:

NATIONAL BOARD FOR CERTIFIED COUNSELORS
3D Terrace Way
Greensboro, NC 27403
(336) 547-0607
www.nbcc.org

Executive-marketing firms, or outplacement firms, are sometimes confused with career counselors. The distinctions are important, though: a career counselor will teach you how to conduct your own job search; an executive-marketing firm will conduct a search for you. (Executive-marketing firms can also be confused with executive-search firms. For the most part, executive-search firms work for client companies, not for the job seekers whose resumes they keep on file.) If you're considering an outplacement company, check it out carefully. Some of these firms charge upwards of $3,000 and do little more than circulate your resume. Many will promise you the moon and stars but won't guarantee results. Best bet: check with the local Better Business Bureau and ask for information on the firm.

Alumni-Placement Offices

These services are now part of many universities and colleges. They function basically as a clearinghouse for interested companies attempting to match job-seeking alumni to their needs. Although most are not well supported, either financially or with staff, they shouldn't be overlooked as a source. If your school doesn't offer placement services, try to take advantage of the membership listings many alumni associations make available, as they can serve as a valuable source for contacts.

Professional Associations

Many of these organizations have established placement services for members' use. Companies, either via the association's mailings or through society meetings, put your resume in a referral system for review. Employers use some of these services quite extensively. Contact these associations directly to inquire if they offer any employment services.

Even if a particular association doesn't offer placement services, it's still a valuable resource. Many professional associations have annual meetings or hold conferences and seminars, which are great opportunities for making contacts and keeping abreast of industry trends. For a comprehensive nationwide directory of professional associations, check your library for the *Encyclopedia of Associations* published by Gale Research.

Online Databases

Below, you will find a directory of helpful online databases. Some allow you to conduct free searches, while others require users to buy a subscription. The list is broken down into two parts—the first being those sites that are specifically geared to job seekers, and the second being information services that may also be helpful in your research on a particular company or industry.

Career-Related Online Databases

CAREERBUILDER

Offers company listings, classifieds, and more.
(866) 438-1485
www.careerbuilder.com

FEDERAL CAREER OPPORTUNITIES

Lists federal jobs across the U.S. from GS5 to SES levels. The online system is updated daily, and job information may also be accessed through a newsletter updated every two weeks.
(703) 281-0200
www.usajobs.com

HOTJOBS

An online career network providing job listings and career advice.
www.hotjobs.com

MONSTER.COM

An online career network providing job listings and career advice.
(800) MONSTER
www.monster.com

For Company and Industry Research

THE BUREAU OF LABOR STATISTICS
www.bls.gov

DUN'S ELECTRONIC BUSINESS DIRECTORY
www.dnb.com

DOW JONES FACTIVA
www.factiva.com

GALE RESEARCH GROUP
Publishes a broad range of databases including Gale Digital Archives and Gale Reference Library.
www.galegroup.com

HOOVER'S ONLINE
(800) 486-8666
www.hoovers.com

LEXISNEXIS
www.lexisnexis.com

STANDARD & POOR'S ONLINE SERVICES
www.standardandpoors.com

Managing Your Most Important Resource: Time

Job searches aren't something most people do regularly, and so it may be hard to estimate how long each step will take. Nonetheless, it's important to have a plan so that you can see the progress you're making.

When outlining your job-search schedule, you should have a realistic time frame in mind. If you'll be job searching full-time, your search will probably take at least two months. If you can devote yourself only part-time, it will probably take at least four months.

You probably know a few people who seem to spend their whole lives searching for a better job in their spare time. Don't be one of them. Even if you can search only part-time, give the effort your whole-hearted attention. If you've got a job and don't feel like devoting a lot of energy to finding a new one right now, then wait. Focus on enjoying your present position, do your best, and store energy for when you're really ready to begin your job search.

If you're currently unemployed, remember that job hunting is tough work physically and emotionally. It's also intellectually demanding work that requires you to be at your best. So don't tire yourself out by working on your job campaign around the clock. At the same time, you must be sure to discipline yourself. The most logical way to manage your time while looking for a job is to keep regular working hours.

If you're still employed, job searching will be especially tough; don't work yourself to the point where you show up for interviews looking exhausted, or where your current job begins to suffer. On the other hand, don't be tempted to quit the job you already have! Employers prefer hiring applicants who are already working somewhere. The long hours are worth it. If you're searching for a job while you have one, you're in a position of real strength.

If you're searching full-time and have decided to use several different contact methods, divide each week, allotting time for each method. For instance, you might devote Mondays to answering newspaper ads, because most of them appear in Sunday papers. You might devote Tuesday and Wednesday mornings to developing your contacts and calling a few employment services. You could spend the rest of the week contacting companies directly. This is just one plan that may or may not work for you.

Combine Methods

By trying several methods at once, you'll make your job search more interesting, and you'll be better able to evaluate the potential of each method, altering your schedule accordingly. Take care, however, not to judge the success of a method simply by the number of interviews you obtain. Positions advertised in the newspaper, for instance, are likely to generate many more interviews per opening than are unadvertised positions. But there are far more of the latter.

If you're searching part-time and decide to try several different contact methods, we recommend that you try them sequentially. You simply won't have enough time to put a meaningful amount of effort into more than one method at once. So estimate the length of your job search, then allocate so many weeks or months for each contact method you'll use.

If you're expected to be in your office during the day, then you have an additional problem to deal with. How can you work interviews into business hours? And if you work in an open office, how can you even call to schedule interviews? You should make every effort to keep up both performance and appearance on your present job, so maximize your use of the lunch hour, early mornings, and late afternoons for calling. If you keep trying, you may be surprised how easy it is to reach a particular executive after office hours. Often you can catch people as early as 8 A.M. and as late as 6 P.M. Jot down a plan each night on how you'll be using every minute of your precious lunch break.

Lunchtime Interviews

Your inability to interview at any time other than lunch just might work to your advantage. Set up as many interviews as possible for your lunch hour and schedule them to take place at a mutually convenient restaurant. This will go a long way toward creating a relaxed rapport with the interviewer. (Who isn't happy when eating?) But be sure the interviews don't stray too far from the issue at hand.

Lunchtime interviews are much easier to obtain if you have substantial career experience. People with less experience often find no alternative to taking time off work. If you have to take time off, take time off, but try to do so as discreetly as possible. You might want to take the whole day off to avoid being too obvious about your job search, scheduling two to three interviews on the same day—but no more. It's very difficult to maintain an optimum level of energy for more than three interviews in one day. Explain to the interviewer why you might have to juggle your interview schedule—he or she should be impressed with the consideration you're showing your current employer by minimizing your days off, and will probably appreciate the fact that another prospective employer is interested in you.

If you're searching for a job—especially part-time—you must get out there and do the necessary tasks to the best of your ability and get them over with. Don't let your job search drag on endlessly. Finally, remember that all schedules are meant to be broken. The purpose of a job-search schedule is not to rush you to your goal but to help you map out the road ahead, and then to evaluate periodically how you're progressing.

CHAPTER 5

Looking for a Job Online

ACCORDING TO THE business management research organization Conference Board in their Help-Wanted Online Data Series reports, there were over two million jobs posted on Internet job boards as of April 2006. Given this staggering statistic, the web should be part of everyone's job search. From major job-search sites to smaller niche sites, you can do almost all of your job hunting online. You can even find tools to aid you in your job search, like fax services and free e-mail accounts.

Major Job-Search Sites

It doesn't matter what type of work you do; if you are looking for a job, there's a good chance you will find one that interests you on one of the major job-search sites. These sites are also called job banks. Employers in all industries post jobs on these websites. Those looking for work can search for jobs by keyword, location, or job category. Job seekers can often apply for jobs online or get further information on where to send their resumes.

Why You Should Visit the Major Job Banks First

If you were looking for a pair of shoes, would you first go to a tiny shoe store with a limited selection or would you turn to a big store with a large selection from which to choose? Most people would turn to the big store with the idea that they would be more likely to find something they wanted when there was more to choose from. Looking for a job on a major job bank is similar to shopping in that big store. You will find more jobs listed on those sites and therefore you will be more likely to find one for which you qualify.

CHECK OUT CORPORATE WEBSITES

You can often find job listings on corporate websites. Look for links to "Careers" or "Jobs." If you can't find a link on the front page, look for a link to "About the Company." Once you get to that page, you may see a link to job openings.

Which Job-Search Sites Should I Use?

There are several big job-search sites, but the biggest four are Monster (*www.monster.com*), CareerBuilder (*www.careerbuilder.com*), Yahoo! HotJobs (*www.hotjobs.com*), and America's Job Bank (*www.americasjobbank.com*). You don't have to choose just one, since you can use all of them for free. It's only a matter of finding the time to sit down and look at the jobs listed on each one.

MONSTER

You can search for a job on Monster without registering. However, if you want to take advantage of some special features, you should register. For example, to apply for a job through Monster, you must register. Registered members may also build a resume online that is searchable by employers. If you are a member you can also set up a job search agent by indicating the type of job you want along with its desired location. You will receive search agent results when there is an appropriate match. You can also save a search as an RSS feed, or news feed. Using a news-feed reader, you can receive updates on jobs that match your specifications.

MONSTER IS NUMBER ONE

Monster is the number one job-search site, according to TopJobSites.com (*www.topjobsites.com*), a company that ranks the top job-search sites on the web in terms of page views and popularity. Also according to TopJobSites.com, Monster lists over 800,000 jobs and 130,000 employers.

CAREERBUILDER

CareerBuilder is another very large and very popular job-search site. Through its partnership with several large newspaper publishers, CareerBuilder provides job listings from many local markets. Employers may also post listings to this site.

Anyone can search for jobs on CareerBuilder, but if you want to apply to any of them online, you must sign up to be a member. Membership also allows you to upload a resume or build one online. Your resume, if you wish, will become part of a resume database that employers can search. You can use your resume when you apply for jobs online. Members can set up job alerts by specifying certain criteria. CareerBuilder will send you these job alerts by e-mail.

YAHOO! HOTJOBS

Search-engine powerhouse Yahoo! is the parent company of HotJobs. When you search for a job on Yahoo! HotJobs, your results will include jobs employers have posted on this site, as well as jobs listed on other sites across the web. In this sense, HotJobs is a hybrid of a job-search site and a job search engine. Job search engines will be discussed later.

Taking full advantage of its search-engine experience, HotJobs has some unique search capabilities. For example, once you begin your search, you can refine it by using the HotJobs Guided Search tool. You can limit your search to jobs that have been posted today or over the past two days, seven days, or 30 days. You can also narrow your search by company, experience required, or location. In addition to these criteria, you can have your results show only those jobs that have been posted by employers as opposed to staffing firms.

NEW BEFORE OLD

You want to apply for newer job listings before you apply for older ones. Jobs that have been listed for a while may already have a glut of candidates applying for them, or those jobs may have been passed over because they are in some way undesirable.

If you want to apply for a job online, you will need to become a registered member of Yahoo! If you have ever signed up for any other Yahoo! service you are already a member (you just need to remember your username and password). You can upload or create a resume that you can choose to make searchable by employers. You can also block specific companies from viewing your resume. HotJobs will send you alerts when jobs that fit your criteria are posted.

AMERICA'S JOB BANK

One of the largest job-search sites is America's Job Bank. This site is administered by the U.S. Department of Labor. It comprises job postings submitted by employers as well as by state labor departments. Job seekers can search America's Job Bank by job category, keyword, and location.

If you sign up for an account with America's Job Bank, you can create and post your resume online. It will be put into a database that employers can search. You can also set up job scouts that will alert you, by e-mail, of job openings that meet your specifications.

CAREER ONESTOP

Use the CareerOneStop Online Coach feature on America's Job Bank to help you with your job search. This service will help you search for jobs, find unemployment information, identify and upgrade your skills, and locate career advancement tools.

Job Search Engines

When you use a general search engine like Yahoo!, Google, or Ask.com to do a search about something, it looks for information on the web. It combs through thousands of websites to find what you are looking for. Job search engines work in much the same way that general search engines do. You put in your search terms, usually the type of job you want and the location, and the job search engine will look through job listings on a variety of websites. Three popular job search engines are Indeed (*www.indeed.com*), SimplyHired (*www.simplyhired.com*), and Jobster (*www.jobster.com*).

Indeed

According to information on the website, Indeed includes all the job listings from major job boards, newspapers, associations, and company career pages. After you search using your initial terms, you can then refine your search further by selecting key phrases, company names, location, and job type—for example, part-time, full-time, or temporary.

OTHER TOOLS

Next to each job listing on Indeed, you will see a link that says "more actions." Clicking on that link will reveal a set of links to useful tools including a Google search on the company, a map, and general salary information for that job title.

Anyone can search Indeed, but if you become a member you can set up job alerts that will be sent to you by e-mail when jobs that match your criteria are posted. You can also save your searches in order to run them again without having to type in all the terms. Membership also lets you save individual job listings. You can then add notes, visible only to you, to each listing. This can help you stay organized.

SimplyHired

SimplyHired claims to list "thousands of jobs from job boards, classifieds, and company sites." This site allows you to narrow down your search by setting up filters. You can refine your search by job type, company, required education, or the date the job was posted. You can also ask this search engine to only display jobs with employers that appear on a ranked list, such as the *Fortune* 500.

Signing up for a SimplyHired account gives you access to services similar to those offered by Indeed. For example, you can save your searches and set up e-mail alerts. You can also save individual jobs, rate them, and type in notes about them.

Jobster

Jobster works like the other job search engines listed here as far as its search function is concerned. The similarities end there. The first noticeable difference is that when you do a search, the results page tells you how long ago the job arrived on Jobster and what job bank it came from. When you return to the website, Jobster remembers your previous searches—updated results appear on the front page. You must have cookies enabled in your web browser for this to occur (use the Help feature of your browser to learn more about cookies).

Signing up for MyJobster lets you create a profile that highlights your skills and qualifications. You can choose whether or not to make your profile public. You can also set up job alerts to notify you, by e-mail, about new job openings that match your criteria. The biggest difference between Jobster and its competitors is the networking opportunities it can help facilitate. Jobster operates on the premise that employers are more likely to hire candidates whom their employees recommend. In addition to listing job opening from job banks and company websites, Jobster has client companies for which it also lists job openings. If you know someone who works at one of these companies (or if you know someone who knows someone), you can ask that person for a referral. Once Jobster has that referral, it is passed along to the hiring team at the company. You can also receive "Insider Alerts" about other job openings with that employer.

Niche Job-Search Sites

Niche job-search sites are those that focus on a particular industry or field. While the large job-search sites and the job search engines provide a broad base of job openings, these more specialized sites allow you to focus on your particular field of interest. The job search engines may turn up some of the jobs posted on these job lists, but they are still worth looking at.

PROFESSIONAL JOURNALS

Professional journals often list job openings. You should be reading the ones for your field anyway. If the journal has a website, visit it to see if they have job listings. You may have to subscribe to the journal in order to access them.

TopJobSites.com (*www.topjobsites.com*) lists the most popular niche job sites. The fields covered by those sites include law, finance, engineering, human resources, and communications. What should you do, though, if your field isn't covered by one of these sites? The About.com Job Searching page has a huge list of job banks arranged by career field: *http://jobsearch.about.com/od/jobsbycareerfieldaz/a/topsbytype.htm*. You can also visit the website of the trade or professional associations for your field.

Using Resume Banks

Many of the job-search websites mentioned above let you upload your resume or create one online. Your resume then gets put into a database that employers may search when looking for job candidates. Some of these services allow you to keep your resume private, or at least invisible to employers you specify. Why would you choose to do this? Let's take this likely scenario: you are looking for a new job without your current employer's knowledge. You upload your resume to one of these services. Your boss has to fill a job opening and decides to look for candidates on the same site to which you just uploaded your resume. Now, wouldn't that make for an awkward situation?

KEEP PRIVATE INFORMATION . . . PRIVATE

If you do decide to make your resume public, make sure you can keep your personal information—address and phone number—private. That is information you don't want to make available to the world at large.

All of that said, posting your resume to a resume bank or other job-search site can be a big help to you as a job seeker. Someone may contact you from out of the blue to see if you are interested in a particular opportunity. These opportunities may not always be exactly what you're looking for, but this is still a good way to become more educated about your options and to reach a broader "audience." Keep an open mind. You never know; an option you might never even have considered may turn out to be the perfect choice for you.

Government Jobs

Government jobs have a reputation for being stable and for having excellent benefits. That is why many people turn to this venue, also called civil service, when looking for work. Whether you are looking for federal jobs or for jobs in local governments, you can easily access job openings on the web.

Federal Job Listings

USAJOBS (*www.usajobs.opm.gov*) is the official job-search website of the United States government. All vacancies in every federal government agency are listed here. You can do a basic search by keyword, job category, and location. You can also search for jobs within specific agencies or by Occupational Series (all federal jobs are assigned a series number). Additionally, you can specify a salary range when you search for a job.

To create an online resume you must become a My USAJOBS member. Membership also allows you to apply for jobs online. As you can with the other job-search sites, you can create automated job alerts.

SHOULD I PAY A FEE FOR GOVERNMENT JOB LISTINGS?

No. Beware of websites and other companies that charge a fee for government job listings. Access to this information is available to anyone who wants it, free of charge. The only fees you may encounter are application and exam fees charged by the government entity with which you are applying for a job.

U.S. Postal Service

You can find some jobs with the U.S. Postal Service listed on USAJOBS. However, Postal Service employees are not considered federal workers. For a more extensive list of Postal Service jobs, you should visit the U.S. Postal Service website: *www.usps.gov*. You can look for mail processing jobs and corporate jobs. You can also apply for exams, a necessary evil if you want all but a corporate job with the U.S. Postal Service.

Local Government Jobs

Many local governments, including states, counties, and cities, have their own websites on which they list, among other information, job openings. There are also several websites dedicated to local government employment. One of these sites is *www.govtjobs.com*. You can search through job categories for a position or you can use the search box to specify a job title. Another website on which to search for local government jobs is Careers In Government (*www.careersingovernment.com*). Search for jobs by selecting a job category, organization type, location, and salary.

Online Tools to Assist You in Your Job Search

Conducting a job search is almost like running a small business. You have a product to sell (yourself). You have an advertising campaign, which consists of your resume and other job-search tools that will get your name out there. Just as you would if you were running a small business, you are going to need some tools to help you with the demands of your job search.

You will need a personal e-mail account, since you never want to use your work account for your job search. Many employers will ask you to send your resume by fax. If you don't have a fax machine, you will run up quite a bill faxing resumes from your corner drugstore or print shop. What about receiving phone messages from employers when you aren't available to take calls? Do you want to change your home voicemail message to make it sound more formal, or would you prefer to have a voicemail service dedicated to your job-search campaign? Fortunately, there are web-based resources that provide many of these services.

Free E-mail

Is your only e-mail address your work account? Or does the personal e-mail address that you use to communicate with your friends not sound very professional (for example, *honeybabe@email.com*)? You should never use your work e-mail account for your job search, nor should you use an address that sounds less than professional. You can set up a free e-mail account dedicated specifically to your job-search campaign. You will put this address on your resume, cover letters, and anywhere else you are asked to put contact information.

Google offers free e-mail accounts through their Gmail service. You can store an almost unlimited number of e-mail messages on their server. You can also get a free Yahoo! e-mail account. Other free e-mail services are AIM (*www.aim.com*) from AOL (you don't need to subscribe to AOL), MSN Hotmail (*www.hotmail.com*), and Inbox.com (*www.inbox.com*).

Fax Services and Voicemail

Web-based fax services let you send and receive faxes online. You can send faxes as e-mail attachments. Generally, you will be faxing documents that are saved as files on your computer, so it's just a matter of attaching the file to an e-mail message. You can even send a scanned document by saving it as a file and attaching it to an e-mail message. When you use one of these services, you also receive faxes as e-mail attachments. These services give you a local or toll-free telephone number.

MaxEmail (*www.maxemail.com*), eFax (*www.efax.com*), and jConnect (*www.j2.com*) are web-based fax services. They all charge a monthly fee and a small fee per fax. If you only need to send and receive faxes during your job search, it may not be worth buying and setting up a fax machine. This type of service will fit your needs.

MaxEmail, eFax, and jConnect also offer voicemail services for an additional fee. Messages are sent to you as e-mail attachments. MaxEmail and jConnect also let you listen to your messages over the phone, which is great if you are away from a computer.

CHAPTER 6

Using Employment Services

MANY PEOPLE TURN TO temporary agencies, permanent employment agencies, or executive recruiters to assist them in their respective job searches. At their best, these resources can be very valuable—it's comforting to know that someone is putting his wealth of experience and contacts to work for you. At their worst, they're more of a friend to the employer or to more experienced recruits than to you personally. For this reason, it's best not to rely on them exclusively. Employment services fall into several categories, each of which is described here.

Types of Employment Services

There are several types of employment services you may encounter in your job search. There are temporary employment agencies, contract services firms, and permanent employment agencies. Each one serves a different purpose, but all have the primary goal of finding qualified candidates to fill job openings. Most employment services work on behalf of the employer. Generally, it is the employer who will pay them, so beware of agencies that ask for a fee before they will place you.

Temporary Employment Agencies

Temporary, or "temp," agencies can be a viable option. Often they specialize in clerical and support work, but it's becoming increasingly common to find temporary assignments in other areas, like accounting or computer programming. Working on temporary assignments will provide you with additional income during your job search and will add experience to your resume. It may also provide valuable business contacts or lead to permanent job opportunities.

Temporary agencies often advertise in the help-wanted sections of newspapers. You can also find them listed in local telephone directories.

GO TEMPORARY

Temporary work appeals to people for a variety of reasons. It can be a wonderful way for a recent college graduate to gain much-needed experience. Those who like variety might find that temping is just what they need. Parents who want flexibility in work hours might also benefit from temporary jobs.

Contract Services Firms

Firms that place individuals on a contract basis commonly receive job orders from client companies for positions that can last anywhere from a month to over a year. Most often, contract services firms specialize in placing technical professionals, though some do specialize in other fields, including clerical and office support. Most contract services firms don't charge a fee to the candidate. For more information on contract services, visit Contract Employment Weekly at *www.ceweekly.com*.

Permanent Employment Agencies

Permanent employment agencies are commissioned by employers to find qualified candidates for job openings. The catch is that their main responsibility is to meet the employer's needs—not necessarily to find a suitable job for the candidate. This is not to say that permanent employment agencies should be ruled out altogether. Permanent employment agencies specializing in specific industries can be useful for experienced professionals. However, they're not always a good choice for entry-level job seekers. Some will try to steer inexperienced candidates in an unwanted direction or offer little more than clerical placement to experienced applicants. Others charge a fee for their services—a condition that job seekers should always ask about up front.

DON'T TAKE A JOB YOU DON'T WANT

Some employment agencies are looking to fill positions as quickly as possible. These agencies are interested only in what work you can do, not what work you want to do. To them a job seeker is simply a commodity from which they hope to earn money, in the form of a commission or fee from an employer. As long as you stay at a job for a specified length of time, they will earn their money. If you are not interested in a particular job, speak up.

Some permanent employment agencies dispute these criticisms. As one recruiter puts it, "Our responsibilities are to the applicant and the employer equally, because without one, we'll lose the other." She also maintains that entry-level people are desirable, saying that "as they grow, we grow, too, so we aim to move them up the ranks."

Finding an Agency

If you decide to register with an employment agency, your best bet is to find one recommended by a friend or associate. As mentioned previously, you can find local employment agencies advertised in the help-wanted sections of local newspapers. You can also find them listed in local telephone directories. Of course, you can always search for employment agencies on the web. One website that lists agencies is the American Staffing Association. Go to *www.americanstaffing.net* where you can search by type of agency, location, and occupational category.

Once you gather names and phone numbers of several employment agencies, it's time to make contact with them. Call the firm to find out if it specializes in your area of expertise and how it will go about marketing your qualifications. After selecting a few agencies, send each one a resume with a cover letter. They will probably ask you to send it via e-mail, so be sure to read Chapter 11, which will help you design an electronic resume.

CONTACTING AN AGENCY

Making contact with an agency is no different than making contact with an employer. You should always be professional whether you are contacting an agency on the telephone, in person, by mail, or by e-mail. Treat them as you would a potential employer. If you are visiting an agency, even just to drop off a copy of your resume, dress professionally.

Make a follow-up call a week or two later and try to schedule an interview. Above all, don't expect too much. Only a small number of all professional, managerial, and executive jobs are listed with these agencies. Use them as an addition to your job-search campaign, not as a centerpiece.

Executive Search Firms

Also known as "headhunters," executive search firms seek out and carefully screen (and weed out) candidates, typically for high-salaried technical, executive, and managerial positions (although lower-salaried positions are handled by many such firms as well). Executive recruiters are paid by the employer; the candidate is generally not charged a fee. Unlike permanent employment agencies, they often approach candidates directly, rather than waiting for candidates to approach them. Some prefer to deal with employed candidates.

WHAT IF A RECRUITER CALLS ME AT WORK?

Since executive recruiters often prefer to work with those who are currently employed, they usually contact people at work. That can make for an uncomfortable situation if your boss, or anyone else, is hovering nearby. If you are interested in working with the recruiter, ask him if you can return the phone call at a later time. Then do so on a break or lunch hour using your cell phone and not an office phone.

Whether you're employed or not, don't contact an executive search firm if you aren't ready to look for a job. If a recruiter tries to place you right away and finds you aren't really looking yet, it's unlikely he will spend much time with you in the future.

Types of Executive Search Firms

There are two types of executive search firms—retainer-based and contingency-based. Essentially, retainer firms are hired by a client company for a search and paid a fee by the client company, regardless of whether a placement is made. Contingency firms receive payment from the client company only when their candidate is hired. The fee is typically 20 to 35 percent of the first year's salary, with retainer firm fees at the higher end of that scale, according to Ivan Samuels, president of Abbott's of Boston, an executive search firm that conducts both types of searches.

RETAINER FIRMS

Generally, companies use retainer firms to fill senior-level positions, with salaries over $60,000. In most cases, a company will hire only one retainer firm to fill a given position, and part of the process is a thorough, on-site visit by the search firm to the client company, so the recruiter can check out the operation. These search firms are recommended for a highly experienced professional seeking a job in her current field.

Confidentiality is more secure with these firms, since a recruiter may use your file only in consideration for one job at a time, and most retainer firms will not freely circulate your resume without permission. This is particularly important to a job seeker who is currently employed and insists on absolute discretion. If that's the case, make sure you don't contact a retainer firm used by your current employer.

CONTINGENCY FIRMS

Contingency firms make placements that cover a broader salary range, so these firms are preferable for someone seeking a junior or midlevel position. Unlike retainer firms, contingency firms may be competing with other firms to fill a particular opening. As a result, they can be quicker and more responsive to your job search. In addition, a contingency firm will distribute your resume more widely. Some require your permission before sending your resume to a company; others ask that you trust their discretion. Inquire about this with your recruiter at the outset, and choose according to your needs.

BE UP FRONT ABOUT RELOCATING

It's common for recruiters to try to match job seekers with jobs in other states. For example, recruiters in Boston sometimes look for candidates to fill positions in New York City, and the reverse is true as well. If you are not interested in relocating, be up front with the recruiter from the start so she can look for local jobs only.

Finding an Executive Recruiter

Look for executive recruitment firms that specialize in your field of interest or expertise as well as generalist firms that place people in a variety of fields. You don't need to limit yourself to firms in your geographic area, as many firms operate nationally or internationally. Once you've chosen the specific recruiter or recruiters to contact, keep in mind that they are working for the companies that hire them, not for you. Attempting to fill a position—especially among fierce competition with other firms—means your best interests may not be the recruiter's only priority. For this reason, contact as many search firms as possible to increase your chances of finding your ideal position.

Making Contact with an Executive Recruiter

A phone call is your first step. Speak with a recruiter and exchange all relevant information. Find out whether they operate on a retainer or contingency basis (or both), and ask some brief questions, if you have any, regarding the firm's procedures. Offer the recruiter information about your employment history and the type of work you are seeking. Make sure you sound enthusiastic and assertive, but not pushy. The recruiter will ask you to send a resume and cover letter, probably by e-mail.

Occasionally the recruiter will arrange to meet with you, but most often this won't occur until she has received your resume and found a potential match. James E. Slate, president of F-O-R-T-U-N-E Personnel Consultants, advises that you generally should not expect an abundance of personal attention at the beginning of the relationship with your recruiter, particularly with a large firm that works nationally and does most of its work over the phone. You should, however, use your recruiter's inside knowledge to your best advantage. Some recruiters will coach you before an interview, and many are open to giving you all the facts they know about a client company. Names of executive recruiting firms nationwide can be found in *The Directory of Executive Recruiters* published by Kennedy Information. This directory is also available online for a fee.

Contacting an Executive Search Firm

Although executive search firms actively recruit candidates for client companies, don't let this discourage you from contacting them. A well-crafted cover letter can alert an otherwise unknowing recruiter to your availability. Remember, this is your chance to shine. Highlight your most impressive accomplishments and attributes and briefly summarize all relevant experience. If you have certain preferences, like geographic location, travel, and salary, mention them in your cover letter. Generally, if executive search firms are interested, they'll call you, so keep your closing succinct. Here's a sample of a "cold" cover letter to an executive search firm:

1441 Pistash Park
Flandreau, SD 57028
March 4, 2009

Heidi Button
Director
First Search Corporation
1140 Main Street
Chicago, IL 60605

Dear Ms. Button:

During the past ten years I have worked in the liability insurance field, in positions ranging from transcriber to senior field claims representative. Currently, I am seeking a new position with an underwriter or a corporate liability insurance department with a need for expertise in claims settlement, from fact-finding analysis to negotiation.

I am hoping that among your clients, one or two may be looking for someone knowledgeable in the area of corporate liability insurance. If so, I would like to explore the opportunity. I can be reached at (605) 555-5555.

I look forward to hearing from you.

Sincerely,
Jennifer-Anne Kelly

Outplacement Services

Outplacement services, also called outplacement counseling services or employment marketing services, charge a broad range of fees depending on the services they provide. These include career counseling, outplacement, resume development and writing, interview preparation, assessment testing, and various workshops.

CHECK REPUTATIONS

If you decide to work with an outplacement firm, choose wisely. Fees range from hundreds to thousands of dollars! Get recommendations from trusted friends and acquaintances. Ask the firm for references. Don't be afraid to ask to interview the person with whom you would be working, before you hire the outplacement firm. As results are not guaranteed, you may also want to check on a firm's reputation through the local Better Business Bureau.

While employers pay employment agencies and executive recruiters, job seekers pay an outplacement service (often thousands of dollars) to help them find a job. These companies will send out letters, make phone calls for you, and basically do the things you should be doing. If you go out and do it yourself, not only will you save money, you'll gain important experience and probably make invaluable contacts.

Community Agencies

There are many nonprofit organizations that offer free or inexpensive job counseling services. Many nonprofit organizations—colleges, universities, public libraries, and private associations—offer free or inexpensive counseling, career development, and job placement services. Often these services are targeted to a particular group—for example, women, minorities, the blind, and the disabled—although there are also agencies that are available to the general public. Many cities and towns have commissions that provide services for these special groups. The United States Department of Labor also offers job placement services through One-Stop Career Centers located throughout the country. You can search for a local center by visiting America's Service Locator on the web at *www.servicelocator.org* or by calling 1-877-US-2JOBS.

Employment Services for Students and Recent Graduates

If you're just starting out fresh from academia, don't expect headhunters to help you out. Executive search firms are paid by employers, and your lack of professional experience puts you straight into the unprofitable bin. Consider this resource later on down the line, once you've added some kick to your resume.

Permanent employment agencies are probably more your speed at this career juncture. The reputable agencies are usually compensated by employers, so if you're asked to pay up front, run for the door.

Temporary agencies are a great way to get in on the corporate ground floor; just make sure you request placement with a company specializing in your area of interest. Once so installed, you can make all the right contacts while watching for a more upscale position to become available.

TEMPORARY DOESN'T MEAN SLOPPY

Treat a temporary assignment just as you would a permanent one. That means be on time, dress professionally, and take your work seriously. Even though you may not end up with a permanent position at this company at this point, you don't know what will happen in the future.

Outplacement services, which were discussed earlier, can be costly and may be unnecessary. A lot of the work they do, you can do yourself. You need only be diligent, ambitious, and organized. Turn to your college placement office first. The services are probably free to you, and the people who staff those centers are experts at working with recent graduates. Nonprofit agencies, also discussed earlier, can be a wonderful resource for you.

CHAPTER 7

Researching Companies

FINDING INFORMATION ABOUT a prospective employer should be on your "must do" list before you set off on any job interview. Learning about the industry the company is part of is also imperative. Taking the time to do this research will benefit your job search in several ways and it could help you get the job you desire. Follow the steps laid out here as you go about the task of gathering company and industry information.

Why You Need to Do Company Research

In the business world, corporations spend significant amounts of money on competitive intelligence. Competitive intelligence involves gathering information about the company's clients, competitors, and the industry in general. Large companies often maintain research departments, or libraries, where professional librarians do this work. Before a company goes out and tries to woo a new client, the research department will learn as much as it can about that client and the industry of which it is a part. This will help the company compete more effectively with the other companies that are pursuing the client. Take your cue from those companies. While you won't, of course, be able to hire a staff of researchers, you should spend some time and energy researching prospective employers. There are several reasons you need to do company research. You want to be able to intelligently discuss the company and the industry on a job interview. Because you did the research, you will know what you are talking about. You will also be able to ask the interviewer meaningful questions about the company. For example, if your research tells you that the company is about to introduce a new product, you might ask if you will be involved in that product introduction (yes, ask the question as though you know they will hire you!).

If you get a job offer, the information you gathered about the company while doing your research will help you decide whether you should accept it. Your research will help you learn about a company's financial health. You will feel comfortable accepting an offer from a company that is financially sound versus a company that is teetering on the edge of bankruptcy.

SHOW YOU'RE SERIOUS

One reason for doing company research is simply to demonstrate to the employer that you have taken the job interview seriously, just as you will take seriously any project you are assigned. Don't be afraid to show off what you learned through your research.

What Information Do You Need?

Before you begin your research, you need to establish goals. Begin by listing the questions you want to answer. Here is a list of some important questions you should be able to answer by the time you finish your research.

- What does the company do—what products or services do they sell?
- What industry is the company part of?
- Who are the company's customers or clients? Are they big companies, small companies, or individuals?
- Does the company have any subsidiaries?
- Does the company have a parent company?
- Who are the company's leaders?
- Where is the company's corporate headquarters?
- Does the company have regional locations? Where are they?
- Is the company publicly or privately held?
- Who are the company's competitors?
- How does the company rank in its industry? Is it considered a big player, a small player, or somewhere in the middle?
- What are the company's sales and profits trends?
- What are the company's plans for the future?
- Has the company been in the news lately? If so, why?
- What other companies are in the industry?

You should be able to answer these questions for many companies. However, information about some companies will be more readily available than for others. Publicly held companies, those that have shareholders (also called stockholders), are required to release a great deal of information to the government. Finding information on them is as simple as locating a copy of their annual report, which will be discussed later in this chapter. Privately held companies, by contrast, aren't required to release much information to the public. It could take much more digging to find what you are looking for.

Step One: Getting Started

Once you have determined what questions you want to answer, you can begin your research. This guide will help you stay organized as you proceed through the task of finding information about your prospective employer.

Keep a separate folder for each company on your list. This can be either a paper folder or an electronic one that you store on your computer. The first page in your folder should include basic information about the company: the location of the company's headquarters and regional offices, its parent company, the names of its subsidiaries. Subsequently you will gather information about the company's products and services and its leadership team. You will obtain financial reports as well. Finally, you will look for current news about the company.

You will need access to the Internet to do most of your research. If you don't have a computer or Internet service at home, find out if your local library has computers for public use. If they don't, find a friend who is willing to let you use his computer.

Step Two: Find the Company's Website

Most companies have websites. That is the first place you should look for information about your prospective employer. You will usually find a wealth of information there. It is almost like walking into the company's offices and saying "Tell me about yourself." A corporate website is also the "face of the company"—it conveys its personality, or at least the personality it wants to share with the public.

CHECK OUT THE WEBSITES

Most industry trade groups and professional associations have websites. You can learn a lot about an industry by looking at these sites. If you don't know the name of the association for the industry in which you want to work, look in *Gale's Encyclopedia of Associations*. This annually updated publication is available in many public libraries. There is also an online version, Associations Unlimited. If your library subscribes to it, you may be able to access it from home. Keep reading to learn more about library resources.

Use a search engine, such as Google or Ask.com, to find a company's website. Type the company's full name into the search box. Use lowercase letters. For example, search for "xyz group incorporated." If you can't find it under its full name, try searching for a name by which the company is commonly known. The company's name will usually appear in the URL (Uniform Resource Locator), which you may know as the web address. You should also try searching for the parent company, if you can't find a website for a subsidiary.

Once you are on the company's website, begin clicking around. You will usually find a link that directs you to information about the company. Hint: Look for links that say "About XYZ Company" or "About Us." Try to find a link to company news (these links may be called news, press releases, media relations, or press room). You will even find a link to jobs or careers. This can be very helpful if you need a detailed job description. Larger companies may have links to their subsidiaries on their websites. You can often find a company's annual report on its website.

WHAT IS AN ANNUAL REPORT?

An annual report is a document that most publicly held companies must make available to their shareholders. It contains financial information about the company as well as information about key personnel and newsworthy items, such as new product introductions.

If you had no luck hunting down a company's website, there are still other resources to try. Let's move on to the next one—company directories.

Step Three: Look in Company Directories

You will probably learn more about a company from its website than from a company directory, which is just a compilation of basic facts about many different companies. A company directory, in book form, is generally arranged alphabetically, much like an encyclopedia or dictionary. Many of these directories are available online and can be searched using the internal search engine on that site. By using these directories you will be able to learn what industry a company is in, what products and services they sell, where their regional offices are located, and who their parent company is.

Many online company directories charge a fee before they will grant a researcher access to their information. These are called proprietary databases, but you might also see them referred to as electronic databases or directories. You may be able to access these databases through your public library or through your college library at no charge if that institution has a subscription. Many libraries even allow their patrons remote access to the proprietary databases to which they subscribe. That means you can enter the directory through your library's website with your library card number and a username and password. Call the reference desk of your library to find out what resources they subscribe to and how to access them.

FREE DIRECTORIES

There are some free directories available on the web. One example is Hoover's (*www.hoovers.com*). You can use Hoover's to find basic information about public and private companies. There is a fee if you want to see more information than that. For example, the free service will give you an overview of a company, a few names from its leadership team, and some key dollar figures. If you want anything additional, you will need to pay a fee. The good news is that, at the time of this writing, Hoover's offers a "Hoover's Lite" subscription to students and job seekers.

Step Four: Obtain Annual Reports

As mentioned earlier in this chapter, another good resource for company information is an annual report, which many companies publish on their websites. Unfortunately, only publicly held companies are required to publish annual reports. The U.S. Securities and Exchange Commission (SEC) requires most companies that have stockholders to send those stockholders annual reports. If you can't find an annual report on a prospective employer's website, you can call the company's investor relations department to ask them to send you a copy of the latest one. You don't even have to identify yourself as a job candidate—corporations send these reports to anyone who requests them.

BE UP-TO-DATE

You always want a company's most recent annual report. A company has a few months to file its annual reports following the end of its fiscal year (which isn't necessarily the same as the calendar year), so there may be a time lag between the date of the financial data contained in an annual report and the date the report is published.

In addition to sending shareholders annual reports, companies also file a more detailed version of this report with the SEC. It is called a Form 10-K. They also file quarterly reports, called Form 10-Qs, with the SEC. You can search for company filings on the SEC website, *www.sec.gov*. Bear in mind, though, that these reports can be difficult to understand for those not well versed in reading financial statements.

Step Five: Get the Latest News

Once you've gathered all the basic information you can about the company, you'll want to find out what's happening with the company now and what has happened in the recent past. You'll want to look for newsworthy information about the company. This could include new or anticipated product introductions or changes in key personnel. It may even include some negative news, such as lawsuits filed against the company or financial problems that company may be experiencing.

You should look for news about the company that occurred during the past year, with a focus on the most recent news. These newsworthy items may have shown up in newspapers, magazines, and business journals. It would be an enormous (and probably an impossible) task to search through these publications individually to find the information you need, even though many have websites on which they archive past issues. Fortunately there are several tools that will help expedite this process.

Searching for News on the Web

Google, Yahoo!, and Ask.com all have news sections that you can use to find current headlines about a company (or any topic). Click on the "News" link located on the front page of any of these search engines. Once you get to the news search page, you simply type in your search term (the company name, for example), just as you would if you were doing a regular search. The only difference is that the search engine looks through news sources rather than regular websites. Topix, *www.topix.com*, is a search engine devoted exclusively to news.

Since news occurs continuously, there is a chance that something can happen after you've done your search. All the search engines mentioned above are updated throughout the day, and the news headlines you find on them could be only minutes old.

BLOGLINES

Bloglines.com is a free web-based news-feed reader. You can subscribe to feeds from news sites and blogs and use them to create a personal page on Bloglines. You can choose to share your page with others or you can keep it private.

If you want to keep track of breaking news for your company—and you should—you can subscribe to a news alert, which you may also see referred to as a news feed. A news alert will let you know, by e-mail, when there is breaking news on the topic you specify. A news feed sends current headlines to a news-feed reader or news aggregator. (This will be covered in more detail later.) Google and Yahoo!

offer alerts through both e-mail and news feeds, while Topix only offers a news feed. In any of these search engines, you simply do a search for your topic and then look for a link to "news alerts." Provide your e-mail address and specify how often you want to receive alerts, and you're set.

Subscribing to a news feed is a bit more involved, but it isn't difficult to do. First you must sign up for a news-feed reader or an aggregator. You may also see this referred to as an RSS (rich site summary) reader. This is a type of software that collects news feeds to which you subscribe. A few of these are web based—you access them through a website using a personal username and password. There are other types of news-feed readers available, but we will focus only on the web-based ones here. Once you've signed up for a news-feed reader, you can subscribe to a web feed on one of the news search engines described previously. After doing your search, click on the orange button that says either XML or RSS. For a good primer on RSS and news feeds, read the article "What Is RSS?" (*www.whatisrss.com*).

Business Databases and Newspaper Indexes

There is one major drawback to news search engines. All of them only post news from the last thirty days. Since, ideally, you should get news that occurred during the entire year, you must look to other sources. One source is a business database. Business databases are usually available by subscription only. Fortunately, most public libraries subscribe to them and allow their patrons access. Check with the reference librarian at your library to find out which databases they have available. Then find out if you can use them at home, through the library website, or if you must use them at the library.

Your library may subscribe to one or more of the following databases: General BusinessFile ASAP from Gale, Predicasts PROMT, Mergent Online, and Business Source Premier from EBSCO. You should also look in a national newspaper index, particularly one that lists articles from the *New York Times* and the *Wall Street Journal*. A good one is EBSCO's Newspaper Source.

Press Releases

Press releases are another good source of company information. When a company has news it wants to share with the public, very often it issues a press release. It will send the press release to various news organizations that may or may not choose to publish the information. PR Newswire distributes press releases on behalf of public relations professionals. You can search for press releases by company on PR

Newswire's website: *www.prnewswire.com*. You can also search for press releases about various industries on this website.

Blogs

Blogs, shorthand for weblogs or web logs, are online journals or diaries. Although in the past they have been frequently associated with teens writing about the details of their daily lives, they have come into their own as a place to post continuously updated information on a variety of topics. There are blogs that focus on every topic you can think of.

Companies use blogs to help make the public aware of the latest news about their products and services. Employees maintain these corporate blogs, often writing about their areas of expertise.

BLOG LIST

The *Fortune* 500 Business Blogging Wiki, which can be found at *www.socialtext.net/biz-blogs/index.cgi*, lists blogs maintained by employees of *Fortune* 500 companies. All blogs listed on this site are open to the public. There is also a link to the Global 1000 Business Blogging page, which lists blogs from large companies that aren't in the *Fortune* 500.

While some companies encourage their employees to post information to official company blogs, there are many unofficial blogs floating around the web. Those blogs are where you might find information employers might not want the public to see. For example, ex-employees might post unfavorable comments about the companies for whom they worked. You may learn something by looking at these blogs, but remember not to believe everything you read.

In addition to learning about prospective employers by reading blogs, you can also learn a lot about various industries. Many trade and professional associations publish blogs. One way to find out if your trade or professional association publishes a blog is by going to their website. If they do have a blog, you might see it right on their front page, or you might see a link to it on the menu. You can also find blogs published by people who work in different industries. Those who write those blogs often are the movers and shakers in their fields. If you want to know what's going on in an industry, reading a blog is often the best way to do it.

SELECT WHICH BLOGS TO READ

It seems that a lot of people have a lot to say! There are many blogs out there but your time is limited. So, how do you figure out which industry blogs you should be reading? Ask people who work in the industry in which you are looking for a job. They should know which blogs are "must-reads" and which you can skip.

You can search for blogs in several ways. Technorati.com (*www.technorati.com*) is a blog search engine. Use the "Blog Finder" tool to search in Technorati's directory of blogs. Many of the standard search engines have blog-search tools. Try Google's Blog Search (*http://blogsearch.google.com*) or Ask.com's blogs and search (*www.ask.com/?tool=bls*) to find blogs about the industries or companies for which you need to find information.

To keep up with the latest postings on a blog, you can subscribe to its RSS news feed. You would use a news-feed reader or aggregator, as described earlier. You can use the same one you use to read feeds from news sites,. Click on a link that says "subscribe" or on an RSS or XML button on each blog you want to subscribe to.

CHAPTER 8

Looking for a Job Under Difficult Circumstances

THE JOB SEARCH IS HARD ENOUGH under normal circumstances, but what should you do if you have to look for a job under an unusually difficult or awkward circumstance? Let's say, for example, you're still working. You will have to schedule interviews around your work schedule and you will have to keep your job search from your current employer. Other difficult circumstances include a long-distance job search, returning to work after an absence from the job market, looking for a job when you don't have work experience, and coping with a long-term job search.

Job Hunting While You're Still Employed

Job searching while you're still employed is particularly tiring because it must be done in addition to your normal work responsibilities. Don't overwork yourself to the point where you show up to interviews looking exhausted or start to slip behind at your current job. On the other hand, don't be tempted to quit your present job! The long hours are worth it. Searching for a job while you have one puts you in a position of strength.

Making Contact

If you must be at your office during the business day, you have additional problems to deal with. How can you work interviews into the business day? And if you work in an open office, how can you even call to set up interviews? Obviously, you should keep up the effort and the appearances on your present job. Maximize your lunch hour, early mornings, and late afternoons for calling. If you keep trying, you'll be surprised how often you can reach the executive you're trying to contact during your out-of-office hours. You can frequently catch people as early as 8 A.M. and as late as 6 P.M.

DON'T JOB SEARCH FROM WORK

Do not use your work telephone for job-hunting purposes. You also shouldn't send e-mail from your work computer. Employers often monitor e-mail and phone calls. Use your cell phone during breaks and lunch hours to make any job-search-related calls. Send and receive e-mail from your home computer using a personal address rather than your work address. Most potential employers will understand that there are times during the day when you can't be reached, and they will probably appreciate the fact that you don't want to job hunt on your current employer's time.

Scheduling Interviews

Your inability to interview at any time other than lunch might work to your advantage. Set up as many interviews as possible for your lunch hour. This can create a relaxed atmosphere, but be sure the interviews don't stray too far from the agenda. Lunchtime interviews are easier to obtain, however, if you have substantial career experience, and these are usually not standard practice for filling entry-level positions.

Often, you will find no alternative to taking time off. Try to take the whole day off in order to avoid being blatantly obvious about your job search, and try to schedule two or three interviews for the same day. It's difficult to maintain an optimum energy level at more than three interviews in one day. Explain to the interviewer why you might have to juggle your interview schedule. He should honor the respect you're showing your current employer by minimizing your days off and will probably appreciate the fact that another prospective employer is interested in you.

SHOULD I DROP EVERYTHING TO GO ON A JOB INTERVIEW?

No, you shouldn't drop everything to go on a job interview. If you are currently working, you are responsible to your current employer. Your future employer will understand if you tell her you must schedule your interview around your current job and will take that as a sign that you take your work seriously.

References

What do you tell an interviewer who asks for references from your current employer? Just say that while you're happy to have former employers contacted, you're trying to keep your job search confidential and would rather that your current employer not be contacted until you have a firm offer. Offer to provide a list of previous employers who can provide a reference for you.

You must let someone know if you have given her as a reference. You don't want a phone call from your potential employer to catch her off guard. While it may be that your reference simply isn't expecting the call, the employer may interpret it to mean he isn't confident providing a reference for you. Furthermore, once a potential employer has asked for your references, be sure to forewarn or remind those references that they may expect to receive a phone call soon.

Be Discreet

The days when employees dedicated their entire careers to a single employer are long gone. It's expected that people will change jobs several times during their careers, and it could be unwise to leave a position without having something else lined up. You shouldn't feel obligated to inform your current employer you're job searching until you're ready to give your notice. Revealing this information too soon could cost you your job. Remember, employers would rather lose you at their convenience than at yours.

To ensure that your job search is kept quiet, avoid telling any of your coworkers or colleagues of your plans. This may sound obvious, but it's a mistake that's too often made—at the expense of the job seeker. Gossip flows very freely in most workplaces, and before too long your news will reach your boss.

If You're Fired or Laid Off

Being fired or laid off is demoralizing. Your self-confidence may be very low at the moment. Remember that you're not the first person and won't be the last one to go through this traumatic experience. In today's changing economy, thousands of professionals lose their jobs every year. Even if you were terminated with just cause, don't lose heart. Try to keep your confidence up. Your positive attitude will be a key element in helping you get your next job.

Severance and Unemployment Compensation

A thorough job search could take months, so be sure to negotiate a reasonable severance package from the company you are leaving, if possible. Make sure you know what benefits, particularly health, you still have. Also, register for unemployment compensation immediately. Look in the government listings in your telephone directory to find out where your local unemployment office is. Don't be surprised to find other professionals collecting unemployment compensation—it's for everyone who has lost her job.

CONTINUING YOUR INSURANCE COVERAGE

The Consolidated Omnibus Budget Reconciliation Act, better known as COBRA, allows you to continue to participate in your employer's group health insurance plan by paying for the policy out-of-pocket. Your company's human resources or benefits department should be able to provide you with the proper paperwork.

Follow a Plan

Don't start your job search with a flurry of unplanned activity. Start by choosing a strategy and working out a plan. Now is not the time for major changes in your life. If possible, remain in the same career and in the same geographical location, at least until you've been working again for a while. On the other hand, if there aren't jobs available in your field, you may consider making a change now. If you had planned to make a career change prior to losing your job, you could also consider doing it now. Don't, though, make a change in the heat of the moment.

Expect the Inevitable Question

Avoid mentioning you were fired when arranging interviews, but be prepared for the question "Why were you fired?" during an interview. Be honest, but try to detail the reason as favorably as possible and portray what you've learned from your mistakes. If you're confident one of your past managers will give you a good reference, tell the interviewer to contact that person. Don't speak negatively about your past employer. The person with whom you are interviewing is more likely to identify with him, and doing this will reflect poorly on you. Try not to sound particularly worried about being unemployed. If you were laid off as a result of downsizing, briefly explain this, being sure to reinforce that your job loss was not due to performance.

Finally, don't spend too much time reflecting on why you were let go or how you might have avoided it. Do try to look at the situation honestly, and if you think you made some mistakes along the way, plan to find ways not to repeat them. Think positively, look to the future, and be sure to follow a careful plan during your job search.

Planning Your Finances

In addition to being stressful, looking for a new job can be costly. Expenses relating to your job search, in addition to everyday living expenses, can mount to a formidable sum in the face of a reduced income. Following are some guidelines to help you make this aspect of your job search somewhat smoother.

- Find out about your company's severance pay policy.
- File for unemployment benefits.
- Extend your health insurance.
- Find out if your company offers outplacement services.
- Assess your financial fitness.
- Make a detailed list of your income and assets, including income from part-time, temporary, and freelance work, unemployment insurance, severance pay, savings, investments, spouse's income, and alimony.
- If you can't meet your expenses, ask your creditors for a reduced payment schedule.
- Establish a realistic budget and monitor it regularly.

You may not think about your monthly expenses until you suffer a financial hit, like job loss. If you lose your job, make a detailed list of your expenses, separating them into three categories: priority one, priority two, and priority three. Priority one expenses should include the essentials: rent/mortgage, utilities, groceries, car payments, and job-search expenses. Priority two and three expenses should include items that can be sacrificed temporarily. Total your estimated expenses in each category.

Long-Distance Job Hunting

As if finding a job isn't tough enough, long-distance job hunting can be even more difficult. The ideal way to apply for a job in another city is to move there first, although this is not a viable option for everyone. Many people can't move to a new city unless they already have a job lined up. Others are open to moving to several locations and will choose which one after they are hired. Job searching long-distance is possible, but you should explain to potential employers immediately that you are willing to relocate to that particular area.

When planning to move, there are several steps you can take to make the transition as smooth as possible. First, call or write to the chamber of commerce in the city (or cities) to which you want to relocate. Subscribe to a local newspaper, check for job postings online, and sign up with local employment agencies. Inform your networking contacts of your plans and ask them for any leads or suggestions they can give you in this new location. Do they know of anyone who works in that area who can give you suggestions? Also, be sure to check with your national trade or professional association. Most large associations offer members access to a national network. Contact the national office for a list of chapters in your new city.

RESOURCES FOR YOUR RELOCATION

There are several websites that can help you with relocating to a new city. For example, RealEstateJournal.com (*http://homes.wsj.com*), from the *Wall Street Journal*, links to several helpful resources including one that profiles over 300 metropolitan areas, another that provides statistical information about school districts, and a few that help you with financial matters related to relocating.

Compare Costs of Living

What may be considered a high salary in one part of the country may be considered low in another. You must know what the cost of living is for the city to which you want to move and what the comparable salary should be. If you move from an area of the country where the cost of living is high, the salaries in that area will be high as well. It's not like you'll have a lot of disposable income floating around—you will use what you earn to pay your expenses. Likewise, don't be taken aback by what may look like a low salary. Your expenses will probably be lower as well.

COMPARE COST OF LIVING

You can compare costs of living between two different cities using tools that are available online. Using the Salary Calculator at Homefair.com (*www.homefair.com*), input your salary, your location, and then the place to which you want to relocate. This tool will calculate how much you will need to earn in your new city. The Cost of Living Comparison Calculator on Bankrate.com (*www.bankrate.com/brm/movecalc.asp*) takes it one step further. In addition to comparing incomes, it also gives a detailed list comparing expenses.

Returning to Work after an Absence From the Job Market

Many people, usually women, make the decision to stay home for a few years while raising their children. Others take time off from work to care for an elderly parent.

Most don't take this decision lightly because they know the effect it could have on their careers. Several years out of the work force can mean several more years trying to get one's career back up to where it was before they left.

Keep Up with the Field

Stay-at-home parents, or anyone who takes a hiatus from work for whatever reason, have an obligation to keep up with the field they plan to return to "someday." You can do this by maintaining membership in professional or trade associations, reading relevant literature including journals and newsletters, and keeping your network alive. Take continuing education courses to help you keep up with a changing set of requirements in your field. Don't discount the value of taking a part-time job in your field. It will allow you to keep your skills sharp and up-to-date.

PROFESSIONAL ASSOCIATIONS

Attend meetings of professional and trade associations. While it may be expensive to attend a national conference of one of these organizations, many have local chapters. Attending meetings of these chapters is generally quite affordable. It is a great way to make contacts with others in your field and will help you keep up with current trends.

Discussing Your Absence

A potential employer will undoubtedly make note of an extended gap in employment on a resume and inquire about it on a job interview. You shouldn't make excuses for your time away. You made a decision that was right for you and your family and you should be proud of the fact that you did so. You can briefly state your decision to take time off, but don't dwell on it. What you should do is stress the fact that you kept up with things while you were gone. Be ready to talk about new trends in your field. Tell the employer how you've enhanced your skills while away from the workplace. Talk about any classes you took or professional meetings you attended.

Lack of Work Experience

Whether you are new to the job market or new to a particular field, you will have to deal with your lack of experience. You can't create a resume full of jobs in your field if you haven't had any! What you can do is make any experience—work and otherwise—count in your favor.

Be ready to let a potential employer know about the things you've done that are related to the skills he wants. If one of the requirements of the job for which you are interviewing is the ability to work on a team, talk about sitting on the board of directors of a campus organization, or about working on a team cleaning up your local park. If strong organizational skills are needed, discuss the time you were on the committee that planned the high school yearbook. Remember that experience doesn't only come from paid employment. It also doesn't only come from paid work in a particular field. Part-time jobs count, too. So if you worked closing shift at a fast-food joint, you were part of a team that was responsible for making sure everything was cleaned up at the end of the day.

KEEP A JOURNAL

This is another time when a journal comes in handy. If you don't do so already, start keeping a record—a journal or just a book with jotted notes—of all the experiences you have that relate to your preferred career field. The act of cataloging these items will help you remember their details, and you'll always be able to review your notes before an interview to refresh your memory.

Long-Term Job Search

When the job market is tough, finding work can take a very long time. It can take months or even a year or more to find employment. While you may have started off with a very positive attitude, you may not have one after spending a significant amount of time facing rejection. Unfortunately, your negative attitude may sabotage your job search. You may feel so unenthusiastic that you won't feel like putting forth your best effort. Your attitude will be visible to employers who may be reluctant to hire someone who doesn't look like she has enough energy to get the job done. Changing your attitude isn't easy though. Here are some tips to help you stay positive:

- Don't be so hard on yourself. Remember, you aren't the only one in this situation.
- Stay in shape. Exercise can be a great way to relieve stress, and you will look better, too.
- Eat well. It's easy to get into bad eating habits when under pressure.
- Set aside some time each day to do something that makes you feel good.
- Spend time with people who make you feel good about yourself.

- Volunteer. Not only will it be gratifying, it may give you some valuable experience.
- Learn a new skill.
- Be supportive of someone else going through a tough time.

Following these tips or doing anything you can think of to help you feel better about yourself will revitalize you. Your self-esteem will get a much-needed boost. This self-confidence will be evident to prospective employers when you go on job interviews. Best of all, you will also have more energy to put into your job search, and that can really pay off in the end.

PART II

Crafting Your Resume and Cover Letter

Creating your resume is an opportunity to identify the positive things about very important aspects of your life.

CHAPTER 9

What Kind of Resume Should I Write?

DURING THE YEARS that the "resumes any way" attitude prevailed, authors echoed the belief that there is no one perfect resume. This mentality made it difficult for resume writers to find the focus necessary to present themselves successfully on paper. In this chapter we'll look at creating resumes your way, following a methodical approach to creating successful resumes.

The Seven Key Steps to Writing a Resume

Gaining focus and creating a strong, content-rich resume is easy when you follow these seven simple steps:

1. Review as many resume samples as you can. Look over old versions of your own resume, and ask friends and associates if they'd mind letting you take a look at theirs. This book includes many samples of many different resumes, designed for many different fields. You can also find a wide range of resume samples on the web.
2. Analyze those resumes. Think about what makes them work (or not work). Effective elements might include things like format, content, typeface, and the order of information.
3. Identify your job objectives and your target audience. This doesn't mean you need to include a career objective on your resume. It does mean that you need an understanding of the field you plan to pursue. Be sure you know the proper terminology, the job functions that will make you valuable, and how to present yourself as a viable candidate.

4. Perform an inventory of your qualifications and achievements. Knowing yourself and being confident in your abilities is key to creating a powerful resume.
5. Analyze your competencies and capabilities as they relate to your job goals and your chosen field. This is another aspect of the "know yourself" mantra. How do you see yourself contributing to this field? Remember your unique value proposition and identify what makes you the most desirable candidate for the job you seek.
6. Draft your resume and critique it. Compare your draft to the samples you've analyzed and admired. How does it compare in terms of format, content, and order of information? Fix those elements you see that can be stronger. Proofread it carefully, and after you're sure it's perfect, ask a friend to look it over.
7. Make plenty of copies, and distribute your resume whenever appropriate. Try sending it by e-mail to several friends. See if any of them have trouble opening up the document or if your layout or fonts become altered.

The Resume Your Way

If there is no perfect resume, how can you hope to create a document that all employers would want to see? The answer comes from a change in emphasis. Stop thinking about resumes any way, designed to present yourself as you think an employer would want to see you. Start writing resumes your way.

A good resume presents your past achievements as well as the assets and capabilities that qualify you for this new job. As you get better at communicating your qualifications, you will approach the job of writing your resume with confidence. The seven steps to success are good guidelines, and they should inspire confidence. But before you start writing, it is also a good idea to understand the different types of resumes and the purposes they serve. The following sections describe some traditional types and formats of resumes.

Chronological, Functional, and Combined Resumes

Chronological resumes present information in reverse chronological order, starting with the present and working backward. Students and recent graduates usually list education first, and all other job seekers list experience first. They traditionally use one-word headers to identify content sections. As you've read and heard again and again, they are usually no longer than one or two pages in length.

Functional resumes present candidate skill sets and discussions independent from job descriptions, if those descriptions are included at all. In this resume type, skill listings come before all other content. Such summaries tend to be lengthy, presented with hope that some broadly chosen phrases might stick in the minds of readers and encourage interviews. In this model, it's employers, not the job seekers, who define the job being sought. Most resume guides recommend functional formats for career changers or for those who are keeping their options open, while the chronological format is usually recommended for all others.

Combined resumes contain skill or qualification profiles, like the functional format, but they also incorporate the chronological format by presenting work history, educational background, and other content in reverse chronological order.

Be careful about using a functional resume. Almost all inquiries to prospective employers reveal that this format is ineffective and difficult to review. According to studies and polls, the pure functional resume format is the least preferred. To strengthen your functional resume, link each of your job skills to a particular position or responsibility. Tell your prospective employer where and how you used your skills.

Targeted and Customized Resumes

Recent resume guides use words like *targeted* and *customized*. Targeted resumes include either a branding statement or a clear objective and/or description of professional goals. They are aimed at a specific job opening and allow you to address your skills and qualifications in regard to the position.

Like targeted resumes, customized resumes are often created for a specific job title or employer, particularly when you know the desired skills and hiring criteria. These are the most powerful resumes because they speak directly to potential employers.

Many large employers now use software programs to help them sort through the volume of resumes they receive. A targeted approach will help your resume appear in keyword searches done by recruiters or the services they employ. Post a targeted resume on job boards; recruiters often search the boards for potential job candidates.

Combinations, Permutations, and Confusion

Some guides advise you to include all the schools you attended. Some suggest you include only those schools where you were conferred a degree. Many books and articles emphatically suggest that you list courses, while as many others strongly urge you not to because your potential employers will already have a good idea of what courses someone with your major took.

Some suggest you present all scholarships and honors, no matter how small, because the longer the list, the more impressive it is to potential employers. Still others encourage you to present a selected list of scholarships and honors. But when it comes to grades, everyone agrees: Only include good grades and averages!

Advice regarding experience is equally conflicted. Some say describe all jobs—no matter how small—in active terms, in hopes that some of those verbs will catch a prospective employer's eye. Others state with conviction that you should only include impressive jobs. Should you list volunteer and community service experience? Some say yes, but some say no; the same goes for personal interests. In years past, the phrase "References available upon request" indicated the standard close of the resume. Some resume professionals now omit this phrase and see it as unnecessary.

The Modern Resume Your Way

As you focus on your chosen career field and articulate your abilities, your resume writing and your job search will be inspired. A resume that projects "me and my goals" will strengthen the rest of your job search; it will also have an impact on the outcome. Keep your goals firmly in mind; they will enhance the power and purpose of your resume. Plan and implement strategic actions.

Goal setting is critical to all resume-writing and job-search efforts. Overall, goal development and articulation are the most crucial components of resume writing and your comprehensive job search.

State-of-the-Art Documents Focused on You

A resume that focuses on you makes you the central figure in the resume-writing and job-search process. You must clarify and articulate your goals on paper but also in person. If anyone asks how you created such an effective resume, you can tell them you place a high value on your career goals and have a good understanding of what will mutually benefit you and your employer.

No single resume format is specifically required by any particular field. The samples presented in this book are aimed at many popular fields. It's up to you, the job seeker, to establish your targets and create or update the formats you deem appropriate.

Samples shown in this book illustrate techniques for building a stronger resume, including the following:

- Headlines or objective statements that clearly project focus. Well-crafted headlines advertise the nature of your content and reinforce your stated job goal or career focus.
- A comprehensive summary of qualifications section, including appropriate terminology and field-focused verbs and nouns, which projects a knowledge of self as well as a knowledge of the field (and is critical for keyword searches).
- Information is presented to highlight the most important information first rather than chronologically.
- Relevant courses, academic accomplishments, and other pertinent activities are listed briefly.
- Descriptions of work experience appear under headlines in order of significance. They project your capabilities and industry knowledge, as well as your accomplishments.
- Left-justified and text block formats are easy to e-mail and to upload into PDF-based resume banks and job board sites.

When you're reviewing these resume samples, examine those that match your field(s) of interest, but don't limit yourself. Review all the samples, and pick out the formats and contents you'd like to model. Be analytical and curious.

Your background may be different from the fictional Chris Smith, whose qualifications are presented over and over, but you and Chris are not in competition. Avoid focusing your resume on the faceless employers who will be reading it. Project your knowledge of field and functional goals. Focus on you, because when you do get the interview, the hiring manager will use your resume to establish a dialogue. Your resume must say everything important to help you get the offer.

The best resumes use headlines rather than headers. They include qualifications summaries, lists of courses and projects, and highlights of specific accomplishments. The best resumes use field-focused terminology and present information in order of importance.

The College Graduation Benchmark

The people who most need resume guidance are those who have little or no experience preparing a resume. Many of those who find themselves in the market for their first "real" job belong in the college grad category.

New job candidates usually hope that a large quantity of data will overcome any issues of quality. Anxious about what recruiters want to see and hoping that something in their arsenal will get them interviews, they include everything. Myths about recruiters seeking well-rounded individuals inspire this kind of unfocused volume. Ironically, candidates are actually screened with narrow, rather than diverse, criteria. Reviewers of college resumes are mostly on the lookout for field-focused majors, high grade-point averages, and pertinent internships.

An Internet poll of more than 500 top entry-level employers revealed that hiring employers ranked a student's major as most important (42.8 percent), followed by interviewing skills (25 percent), and internship experience (15.9 percent).

Second-semester seniors are either inspired by reactions of recruiters during the fall, or they become anxious and pessimistic because few recruiters responded favorably to their resumes. Those with goals matching the fields and functions that recruiters are looking for often use the same resume and reactive strategies through the spring semester and beyond.

Those whose goals do not match recruiters' needs, and those who cannot express their goals, get very anxious around commencement time. This anxiety often inspires unfocused, multipurpose resumes or leads to procrastination that lingers well past commencement day.

Approximately 30–50 percent of college graduates keep looking for a job after commencement. About 15–25 percent did not set goals or start their job search before graduation. For these candidates, like anyone else looking for a new job, it's important to work through the seven steps to resume success. The assessment and research steps are particularly effective for gaining and projecting focus. This is critical; a complete, effective job search mirrors the candidate's knowledge of qualifications and field-specific competencies.

College graduates are commonly confused by misunderstood job-related data and statistics. Many feel that the top students take all the good jobs, with nothing left by commencement. In reality, recruiting seasons are on-campus anomalies. In the real world, the job search goes on well after June. Many, many candidates get their jobs three to six months after they graduate.

Here are a few common questions among recent or soon-to-be graduates:

How do I make my resume stand out?

Answer ▶ Flawless spelling, punctuation, and sentence structure. Use an appealing visual format. Emphasize professionalism. Write strong content that plays up work experience while in school, internships, coursework, and extracurricular activities, as well as any honors.

What if I don't have related experience or education?

Answer ▶ Emphasize the contributions and skills you can make or possess that are universal to all employers, and focus on transferable skills such as coordinating events, customer service, computer skills, or budget planning. Find the common thread between what you've done and what you want to do. Talk to a professor or mentor to see if they can help you bridge any relevancy gaps based on their knowledge of the workplace.

Should I include education or experiences from high school?

Answer ▶ If you are an entry-level grad, it is permissible to do so if you were a stellar student who received awards or scholarships or held officer titles in school clubs or community groups. Otherwise, focus on college experiences.

When and how do I present my most significant work experience?

Answer ▶ Lead it off directly under the "Employment" heading, but recent grads need to list education first. Use descriptive keywords that illustrate actions taken and any important on-the-job achievements.

If I had one very relevant course and project, how do I highlight both, or either?

Answer ▶ It can be set off under "Education" as "Thesis" or "Case Study." Treat it like a work experience.

If I haven't been successful getting an interview, should I change my resume?

Answer ▶ Probably—or maybe your methodology. Ask for critical feedback from any senior-level business professionals you know. See if anything strikes them as problematic. Compare your resume to others on the web. Assess whether you are being proactive enough in your approach or are just being a passive job seeker, waiting to be called.

My GPA in my major is higher than my cumulative average. Should I include it?

Answer ▶ Include a GPA in your major or overall GPA only if it is 3.5 or above. Otherwise, leave it for discussion at the interview should it come up. More than any other kind of job candidate, if you are a soon-to-be or recent graduate, you must work hard on identifying and articulating your goals. Identify and analyze what you learned in the classroom and beyond. Pick out your most significant courses, labs, and projects, and present those in terms of their potential for making you valuable and effective on the job. Focus your resume and your search for a job or internship on your academic achievements, but don't forget to analyze what you've learned in terms of your personal exploration and your choice of a career field.

Intern Candidates

About 75 percent of college students use resumes in their search for an internship. Internships are difficult to define. In general, an internship is more sophisticated than a summer job. There are both paid and unpaid positions. Some internships offer academic credit, while others are more project-focused, offering the opportunity to build skills and explore a field of interest. Some internships are promoted through large, well-publicized, and structured programs, and others are identified through networking and self-initiated efforts.

Internships are growing in importance. Students in search of an internship should use their resumes to project their curiosity, competence, and awareness of the field.

As college students become more sophisticated about their career aspirations, internships have grown in importance and popularity. A 2007 poll by MonsterTrak showed that 78 percent of college students plan to complete one or more internships before interviewing for their first job.

Just like any other job candidate, those seeking internships must project focus, since competition is high. You're probably looking for an internship to get a deeper knowledge of your field of interest, but—in an ironic twist—you need to project focus and some familiarity with the field before you can get that internship. Do that on your resume!

First Jobs

Many college grads do not get their dream jobs right away, nor do they usually start out on a clearly defined career path. Often, these young men and women lack the focus to begin their true career development or to implement a goal-directed job search. So, naturally, they find transition positions.

These positions include a variety of experiences. Some people plan to enter graduate school, so they seek something meaningful to do. The jobs can be for experience or adventures, such as the Peace Corps, Americorps, Teach for America, or a job teaching English in another country. The job might also be something practical, such as a retail sales job, just for a paycheck. Still others might be in positions unrelated to their majors, but are with a well-known employer and offer name recognition and prestige. No matter what the position is, the resume must support and inspire a first step onto a true career path. In these cases, it is best to avoid the reverse-chronological format, as experience is still limited and the format will make it difficult to project any sense of goal or focus. It's most important to present your potential and identify your goals for the future. Here are common questions that new job seekers ask:

If what I am doing now has nothing to do with my goals, how and where do I present my experience?

Answer ▶ Spend some time on self-assessment. Find some commonality between your goals and current or past experience. If there is no connection, employers will not view you as qualified for their opening. Consider taking additional coursework with your goals in mind. Or, take a step back and go for a lower-level job in the area of your goal to gain some credible work history.

What about education; specifically, my major?

Answer ▶ Build this up as it applies to your job target. Show how your education and recent training will be advantageous to the new employer.

Do I highlight what I have been doing for the past few years?

Answer ▶ Yes—but focus on specific responsibilities that are similar in scope or typical of what you will be doing in your new job. What can you bring to this position that others cannot?

Where and how do I present my most recent experiences?

Answer ▶ Any job candidate except a recent college graduate should place work experience above education, near the top of the resume and/or a qualification summary. Follow the examples in this book on formatting and presentation.

If I wasn't given enough responsibilities to yield achievements, how do I leverage my current job?

Answer ▶ Surely, something you did makes you proud—what is it? Did you streamline a process? Did you generate more reports than your predecessor? Did you volunteer for any committees? If you think you haven't had any notable achievements, you need to re-examine your work and the challenges you've faced. Almost all employment experiences can be positioned to showcase the job seeker in some way. Additionally, consider your present employer's reputation. A position with negligible responsibilities at a company that is a household name may generate interest simply because of the kind of environment or leadership interaction you faced on a daily basis.

Candidates seeking their first jobs must focus their resumes, job-search correspondence, and interviews on the qualifications they already have and those they will need to succeed in the future. Your objective must be presented clearly and supported with powerful summaries of your qualifications. Focus here is critical. You must use the resume-writing process to identify and articulate your goals. Working through the first five of the seven steps will help. You must abandon the attitude of leaving your options open if you're going to focus on future goals.

Beyond Entry Level

Some people take their first steps (or giant leaps) on their career paths right after they graduate. Two or three years later, they're ready for more responsibility. Job advice from career centers is easy to come by for college seniors, but sound guidance is much less accessible later on. Entry-level workers, those with two to five years of experience, can become confused and anxious; as with anyone, fear of change plus fear of focus yields procrastination and anxiety.

Some recent graduates seek change in a subconscious effort to recapture their college experience. In college, you got to choose your courses. Your life changed from semester to semester, always offering something new. As a new member of the work force, either seeking promotion or a new position, you must decide what is driving you. Do you miss the cyclical changes of academic life or are you motivated by ambition and the need to develop your career?

Steps four and five of the resume-writing process encourage you to analyze your accomplishments so far and to assess your capabilities. This proactive approach is positive. It motivates you to present your experience dynamically, in terms of what you've accomplished. As you consider your past achievements, your performance potential for the future becomes clearer.

Resumes for All

Whether you're called an hourly worker, nonexempt personnel, or—more traditionally—a blue-collar laborer, you may be working in an administrative, food-service, customer-service, or manufacturing position. People in these fields often do not create or update resumes that reflect their potential for continued success. Too often, when it's time to look for a new job, they depend upon applications, references, or word of mouth. Everyone needs and deserves a powerful resume. Word of mouth can be translated into words on paper, creating an effective resume that mirrors capabilities and projects a clear future focus.

People at the other end of the professional spectrum are also often guilty of overlooking their resumes. In most cases, those we call senior management have old, vague resumes or no resume at all. Though they're responsible for large operations and organizations and generally supervise many others, these people may not be as ready for the job search as they should be. However, with our culture focusing more and more on career advancement and reinvention of self, many senior leadership professionals are taking the time to keep their resumes current in anticipation of being recruited or finding new ways to use their talents and enjoy meaningful job satisfaction.

Anyone, on any rung of the job-success ladder, should use the resume-writing process to identify and articulate their goals. No matter how diverse your interests or background, creating a powerful resume will enhance your focus and effectively project your qualifications and commitment for your future performance.

Resumes Between Generations

As baby boomers age and Gen X and Gen Y advance within the workplace, it is important that the generations understand each other's skills and strengths as denoted by their resumes. The younger millennials tend to like electronic resumes, and some do not even possess paper versions.

On the other hand, baby boomers may feel more comfortable with printed resumes, and might be reluctant to post their resumes online or unsure how to format their resumes for readability by computer users. Each generation must be sure that their resume can be understood and appreciated by the other, even though the mindsets of each group might differ.

According to the U.S. Bureau of Labor Statistics, more than 25 percent of the working population will reach retirement age by 2010, resulting in a potential shortage of nearly 10 million workers. The number of people who are over age fifty-five will increase by 73 percent by 2020, while the number of younger workers will grow only by 5 percent. This means it will be a candidate's market, with employers competing hard for talent.

Baby boomers must be sure that their resumes don't date them unnecessarily or to their detriment. They can't keep adding to a resume that was originally written twenty years ago. If you're guilty of this, it's time for a rewrite. Go online and review newer job descriptions, even for some of your old titles. Update your terminology. Industry speak is critical for keyword searches and to demonstrate you have kept pace with your field. Have you included jobs that have no bearing on your current position or the one you desire? Go back only as far as your current employment objectives, and use the rule of relevancy to determine which jobs to highlight.

If you've been with one employer for many years, separate your tenure by positions and changes in responsibility. Remember, one resume doesn't fit all. It may be necessary for you to have two or three different versions, each with a different focus. Maintain several formats to accommodate different users: a standard Microsoft Word-formatted resume, a PDF version for downloading, and a plain text version to paste into an e-mail message.

Gen Xers and Gen Yers tend to hold more jobs with more employers than baby boomers. You might need to communicate the reason behind your multiple moves to the baby boomer hiring manager, who could perceive your job hopping as restlessness rather than growth. Millennials, who use text messaging and casual e-mails as a way of life, need to remember to be more formal in their approach to prospective employers by watching their use of abbreviations. Not everyone knows web speak such as PTMM for "please tell me more" or NRN for "no reply necessary."

The Video Resume

The latest trend in the employment marketplace is the video resume. These presentations waver between homemade versions from job seekers equipped with web cams and movie-making software to versions that are professionally produced by videographers, executive search firms, or special video resume services. While the popularity of such resumes is growing, they remain uncharted territory for most job hunters and employers, many of whom are wary of the potential discrimination based on race, age, or other factors that would not be obvious from a more traditional resume.

You can view a variety of video resumes online by doing a simple search. Be sure to view several samples before creating your own so that you have a good idea of what works and what doesn't and whether this format is a good fit for you.

Many of them seem a little bit like infomercials, but it is usually the individual's overall appearance and comfort level speaking on camera that give some candidates leverage in their job hunt.

Eighty-nine percent of employers said they would watch a video resume if it were submitted to them, with the primary reason being to better assess a candidate's professional presentation and demeanor. Only 17 percent admitted to actually having viewed this kind of job-search technology. No doubt the usage of video resumes will continue to grow as technology permeates all facets of our workplaces, but just like the traditional resume, you may want to have several versions depending on your target audience.

What can you convey in video that would not be possible in print? Are you truly making yourself a more desirable candidate on screen or will your credentials be better represented in a traditional format? Be careful not to get caught up in a trend that isn't advantageous to your personality or skill set.

You don't want your video resume to seem like a bad TV audition. However, if you are comfortable on camera, speak well, and have good stage presence, a video resume may give you a leg up on the competition. Tips for preparing an effective video resume:

- Dress as though you were going to the interview
- Talk into the camera; make good eye contact
- Smile and speak clearly, without pauses, and not too fast
- Introduce yourself by your first and last name
- Outline your skills, experience, education, and what you can contribute
- Eliminate background noises or other distractions
- Keep it short—two to three minutes maximum
- Conclude with a thank you and your contact information

Some of the major job boards and specialty sites now have sections for you to upload your video. You can also create your own page and link to your video resume. Have others screen it to get their opinion. If the reaction is favorable, include a link for viewing on your e-resume.

The Vitae Alternative

For professors, physicians, and scientists, resumes are not enough to present accomplishments and experiences. Vitae, or curriculum vitae, are comprehensive documentations of academic and employment performance. Still, it isn't a bad idea for these professionals to prepare a powerful resume that encapsulates their goals and abilities on a single page.

Don't be confused or delay your response if someone asks for a vita. Unless you are seeking positions outside the United States or within special fields, respond to requests with your resume. If applying overseas, create a vita by adding information including date of birth, sex, height and weight, marital status, and all educational experiences, including high school.

Even though vitae are usually lengthy documents listing publication citations, research projects, presentations, affiliations, and educational and training experiences, they don't have to be passive collections of data.

The same qualities that make for a powerful resume—self-knowledge, goal focus, and clear statement of objectives—also apply to a quality vita.

CHAPTER 10

Write a Great Resume

RESUME WRITING IS NOT as difficult as many believe. Creating your resume is an opportunity to identify the positive things about very important aspects of your life. The process can be simplified to seven easy steps, discussed in the previous chapter, that you can use to update or create resumes in just a day. Here they are again:

1. Review samples.
2. Determine format, content, and order of information.
3. Identify objectives and target your audience.
4. Inventory your qualifications and achievements.
5. Analyze your competencies and capabilities.
6. Draft and critique your resume.
7. Duplicate it, post it, and distribute it.

Reviewing Samples

Break out the pens, highlighters, and sticky notes and start examining the samples that appear in the next section of this book. Analyze them like the knowledgeable and focused job seeker you are. Instead of thinking critically, identify the qualities you like.

The first thing employers and recruiters do when they want to fill a position is to list the qualifications the job requires. They list these traits in order of priority, according to which are essential, which are optimal, and which are merely desirable (or optional).

Once the employer decides on the qualities he or she is looking for—such as capabilities, areas of expertise, character qualities, employment history, and educational background—candidates are encouraged to apply, screened, and, ultimately, interviewed and selected. Sometimes job descriptions and postings include detailed qualification criteria. More often, however, these preferences are expressed vaguely in broad descriptions. It is helpful to understand the employer's perspective, and it is a good idea to review other resumes. Just remember, this is your resume. You, and not anyone else, are responsible for success.

No matter how inaccurately they express their defined criteria, employers are always aware of them. Employers review resumes and cover letters, conduct interviews, and make their offers with those qualification criteria clearly in mind. In particular, they use written profiles of their desired qualifications for keyword scanning and behavioral interviews.

While the job seeker might wish otherwise, employers almost never share detailed qualification criteria, nor do they thoroughly analyze the resumes they receive. The employer is not responsible for digging through a mass of poorly organized, badly written resumes to find the perfect job candidate. As the job seeker, you are responsible for conveying your goals, objectives, and a clear sense of job purpose. You must create a powerful resume that mirrors your qualifications and follow that up with an interview that impresses the employers with your capability to perform the job.

Format, Content, and Order of Information

Pick out your two or three favorite sample resumes. Examine them from top to bottom. Here are some basic questions to consider:

- What first impression does the resume generate? How is it formatted?
- What appears first on the page?
- How does the resume identify the candidate? Does it include a street address, an e-mail address, and a phone number?
- Does the resume include a brief yet effective objective and a qualification summary?
- Does the resume present educational information before or after a qualification summary? Before or after experience? How will you present this information?
- How does the resume order information about the candidate's work history, qualifications, and objectives?
- Does the resume use as few lines as possible, reserving most of the page for critical content?

- Does the resume use columns, with dates on the left and descriptions on the right, or a block format?
- Are headlines centered or left justified?
- Does relevant information appear under clearly phrased and focused headlines?

You may have been told that it was bad to write in books, but in this book you should write your response to the sample resumes as you review them. Anyone's first response to a resume is often purely visual; therefore, as you read, note the ways in which you can give your resume a greater visual impact.

Look at the answers to these questions, and let them guide your resume writing. The resumes you selected jumped out at you for a reason, and you can use the aspects you like to form your own resume.

Formatting Basics

The font you choose is the key to a well-formatted resume. Fonts should be traditional, easy to read, and common. You don't want to create a beautiful resume in some obscure font that will be replaced on your reviewer's computer by an automatic bad font substitution (probably destroying all your careful line spacing and other formatting work as well).

For headlines, increase the font size two points at a time until the headline is emphasized but not disproportionate. You can highlight important elements with CAPITALIZATION, ***boldface,*** and *italics,* as well as with indentations, line spacing, and bullet points. At one time, e-mailed resumes had to be formatted so they could be easily scanned. Today, PDF is more common. PDF, or portable document format, is a file format that anyone can read using special viewing software (free from software maker Adobe).

Most current word-processing systems let you save documents directly as PDFs. Your software should explain how you can do this. The beauty of PDFs is that they allow you to use more creative formatting, such as graphics.

Just keep in mind that a cluttered page will confuse your reader; use only those elements that help you present yourself effectively. Consistency is the key to readability and effectiveness. Resumes are rarely read very thoroughly at all. Most employers say they review each resume for less than a minute before keeping it live or filing it. You want employers to be able to pick up important information just by scanning your page. Review the samples for illustrations of effective and not-so-effective highlighting techniques.

The Best Fonts and Point Sizes for Resumes

Book Antiqua, 9-Point
Book Antiqua, 10-Point
Book Antiqua, 11-Point

Century Schoolbook, 9-Point
Century Schoolbook, 10-Point
Century Schoolbook, 11-Point

Garamond, 10-Point
Garamond, 11-Point

Palatino, 8-Point
Palatino, 9-Point
Palatino, 10-Point

Times, 9-Point
Times, 10-Point

Times New Roman, 9-Point
Times New Roman, 10-Point
Times New Roman, 11-Point

Identify Yourself

Maybe you don't need an eye-catching logo, but you do need to begin your resume consistently. Letterhead is the best and easiest way to do this. You can design your own very simply, using the features in any word-processing program. Letterhead features your name on the first line.

Letterhead includes your full mailing address, the telephone number(s) where you can be reached during business hours, and your e-mail address. By the way, lose any cutesy or gimmicky e-mail monikers like Partyallnight@ or Muscleman@; it's hard to take such names seriously. Set yourself up with a free address at a major search engine to keep your job search correspondence easier to track. This keeps it separate from your personal e-mail or your work e-mail.

Never use a current employer's e-mail address. You don't want your prospective employer to think (or know) you aren't giving 100 percent to your job while you're working. Also, take the time to review your voicemail messages on the phone numbers you include on your resume, both home and cell. While you're in the job market, refrain from music, clever hellos, or other weird greetings. Try not to think of this formality as stifling your personality, but rather as improving your chances for getting the interview.

The point is to make it as easy as possible for your reader to recognize you and to contact you with minimal effort. Use the same letterhead for all your job-related documents, including cover letters, thank-you notes, or submissions of reference information. This is also part of creating your personal brand.

Summarize Yourself

Targeted resumes use qualification or achievement summaries to present objectives and goals. Summaries follow or even replace the statement of objectives, depending on what you learn in your self-assessment and goal research (steps four and five). Sometimes these sections come at the end, providing the resume with a solid bottom line.

Putting Your Experience in Order

The best resumes present the job seeker's most significant experiences first. Entries are grouped under headlines. They include undergraduate and graduate degrees, specialized training, and work history. Education can come at the top, as the first or second category, or last. Candidates with plenty of valuable on-the-job experience generally list that first, saving the bottom of the page for a summary of their education.

Most recent graduates put their education at the top of their resumes. Your academic achievements may be significant, but you should think about where and how you want them to appear. Don't list education first just because you think you should; you might make important work history, projects, and other achievements look less important by bumping them farther down the page.

Academic achievements and honors can be presented in a bulleted list. To figure out what belongs on this list, think about courses, papers, and projects with special relevance to this field. You might also have pertinent extracurricular or community experience. In general, these activities should follow your education and employment entries. Most good resumes do not have a personal interests section. Include yours only if you're sure it emphasizes your goals and qualifications in the field.

Identify Your Objectives and Your Audience

This critical step is too often overlooked. You *must* identify your objectives and your target audiences. What do you aim to achieve with your resume? Answer that question, and you will define your goals. You must also define, as best you can, who will read your resume. Your reviewers belong to the field. They use particular words, phrases, and other field-focused terminology when they talk about their work. By using the proper language, you project the sense that you can do the job.

Your resume should clearly state your career objectives, but not necessarily with a designated career objective line. Instead, the content of your resume should convey the career objective. Too often old-fashioned career objectives were pure fluff. They were vague or did little to enhance the job seeker's qualifications or goals. Look through the samples in this book.

When a sample resume includes a career objective line it is very targeted, meaning it clearly focuses on a specific field and, within that field, on a certain job function.

Inventory Your Qualifications and Achievements

Why do so many resume-writing and job-search guides ask you to list your ten most significant achievements? The answer has to do with the power of positive thinking. With your greatest achievements in mind, you are more likely to think about—and represent—yourself as a valuable job candidate, full of potential.

It's not so easy to draft a summary of your qualifications, and don't worry if it takes some time. Start by asking yourself this question: What skills have I demonstrated in the past that will make me valuable in my chosen field in the future? Think of problems you have solved, instances of collaborative teamwork, or projects you managed with great success.

The best way to pick out your important achievements is to think in terms of the job or field you're aiming to enter. Freeform lists of random accomplishments are not as effective. You don't want to rely on your reviewer to figure out or analyze the significance of anything in your resume; it's your job to make your value clear.

Achievement summaries are the heart of any good resume. That's what makes a resume content-rich. They should be enough to convince the reviewer of your commitment, your qualifications, and your obvious value.

It's important not to skimp on the time or energy you put into summarizing your past accomplishments; to a potential employer, your past has everything to do with the future.

Analyze Your Competencies and Capabilities

It may be physically impossible to look backward and forward at the same time, but the world of resume writing follows different rules. Great resumes reflect past achievements and, via qualifications summaries, look ahead to future roles and responsibilities. You are not limited to talking about what you have achieved in the past. Instead, your resume is the perfect platform to express your confidence and competence in tackling the future.

Drafting and Critiquing Your Resume

Your first draft should be inspired by the sample resumes you've reviewed and analyzed. They will probably influence your choice of content and the order of your information. Let them. Later on, you can go back and determine the best order of presentation, and omit unnecessary entries.

Resume Software

You'll find plenty of resume-building software to tempt you as you create your draft. Resist the temptation and use a basic word-processing application. Most, like Microsoft Word, come with resume templates. While attractive, these lock you into a format, and that can limit how you present yourself. Also, prospective employers have seen these templates used over and over. You might eliminate yourself from consideration just because a hiring manager dislikes a particular format. Give yourself the greatest control over your resume by starting with a blank page.

The Internet has hundreds of listings for professional resume writers. Do your best to resist! Your resume is your responsibility; nobody can present you better than you can. If you are still dissatisfied with your finished product, you may consider a professional resume writer. Your drafts will be a good basis for your consultation with an expert.

The First Draft

As you put your first draft together, don't worry about keeping it to any particular length. If anything, it is better to start long and edit it down later. Write as spontaneously as you can. Don't rewrite as you go; that's a sure way to inhibit your creativity and there will be plenty of time for rewriting when your draft is complete.

Your finished resume should be concise. If it is still longer than one page after your best editing efforts, so be it! Employers do read two-page resumes as long as they are well organized, with the most important information on the first page. The one-page resume rules are part of the old way of job hunting.

When drafting, aim just to get the information down. Jot descriptive phrases to help you capture your thoughts quickly. You don't have to use articles (*the, an, a*), and you can leave the pronouns out. It's unnecessary to say, "I completed the survey" in a resume—"completed survey" gets the point across. Without shocking your English teacher, you can feel free to use sentence fragments.

Reviewing the Draft

Begin your critique only when you have a complete draft in hand. Some people like to see their resume on paper, and they edit with the old red pen technique. Others revise and edit onscreen. Work the way you're most comfortable, being sure that your method helps you polish your draft to perfection.

Critiquing does not mean criticizing. Your revisions are meant to transform your resume into its most powerful form. Be positive. Make immediate changes as you need to, and be prepared to make future changes as your job search progresses.

Mass Production, E-mail, and Distribution

At one time, people worried about things like typesetting and having a clean ribbon in the typewriter. Then it was a good laser printer, picking the right paper, and finding matching envelopes. That eventually moved into fax machines and now e-mail. Each era comes with its own advantages and pitfalls.

Most of your resumes will probably go out via e-mail or be posted to the web, though you will still need a printed version as well. In either case, it's important to make a good first impression. Make your resume effective with a strong format, very simple graphics (as long as they contribute to your statement), and an attractive design.

Most resumes are created or updated using word-processing software and duplicated on paper using quality printers and photocopiers. It's best to use standard portrait orientation (with the resume reading top to bottom on the page), and while you've probably seen creatively formatted resumes—horizontal style, foldouts, or brochures, for instance—it's really best to stick with the standard.

For paper copies, use a top-quality laser printer or photocopier, and use bond or linen paper. White, ivory, natural, and off-white are your best color options. The content and format of your resume will make your document stand out; the color of your paper does not matter. If you have your resumes copied, get extra paper and matching envelopes. Use the same paper for your cover letters and other correspondence. Brand yourself; a professional image contributes to your marketability.

CHAPTER 11

Writing Your Web Resume

RECRUITING THESE DAYS could just as easily be called e-cruiting. Resumes today are e-mailed, sent as attachments, posted to job boards or websites, or uploaded to resume banks. You must be able to transmit your resume electronically so that a reviewer can open it easily without jeopardizing your content or layout. After that, your concern, as usual, is with quality. No matter who (or what, in the case of a database search engine) opens your resume, it must be clear that you are goal-oriented and qualified for the job. This chapter describes how to create a resume suitable for the technology that dominates today's job market.

Uploading Your Web Resume

Many employers use the Internet to list their job postings. Some use their own corporate websites. (For example, the *Everything*® book publisher, Adams Media at *www.adamsmedia.com*, has an Employment link on its home page.) Many also use targeted recruiting sites, where the website organizes and displays an employer's opening or advertisement and also makes sure qualified applicants come to the employer's attention.

The process of uploading a resume from your personal computer is simple. Websites walk job seekers through the process step by step. The process may vary a little, but in all cases you are using your Internet connection to send the electronic file containing your resume directly to an employer or to the job board's online job bank.

File Format for the Web Resume

Uploading is easy, and it is a very effective way of making your resume easily available to many potential employers. However, the electronic file that contains your resume must be in the correct format. Your uploaded resume is useless if the database can't store it or your recipient can't open and read it.

All online job banks specify the file format you should use. The following are some common formats:

Microsoft Word. Almost everyone in almost all professional fields uses Microsoft Word. This is the application most preferred by hiring companies and job boards. If you create your resume using another software application, see if your software has the option to save your file as a Word document.

PDF. PDF files retain the formatting of the original file, and they tend to not get corrupted in their travels across the Internet. You can create a PDF from almost any file format. PDFs cannot be edited or altered, making them a good way of keeping your content exactly as you created it. They are created through Adobe software, which you can download for free.

Web page input. Some job banks ask you to create a resume by filling in the fields of a resume form. In this case, you are not really uploading a file at all. The information you enter into the various fields gets saved directly into the job banks' database. Instead of storing resume files, this database contains the information directly.

No matter what format you use, you should do a quality check before uploading your file:

1. Make sure your resume file can be opened, and that it is formatted correctly. Word files can be corrupted, and PDFs can substitute fonts and change things like font size or margins. Do not assume that just because you saved the file or created the PDF that it will meet your requirements.
2. Name your file correctly. Check the requirements of the job bank: They might have a system for naming files. In general, your filename should be short and descriptive.
3. If you are filling in a web form, take your time entering your information in the fields. Keywords here are essential. You might need to edit your resume, aiming to keep things short while using as many keywords as possible.
4. Test it yourself. E-mail your resume to several friends or family members and ask them how it looks on screen, and ask for a sample printed version to review yourself.

Keywords Are Essential

Many job seekers upload their resumes to web job banks or job boards. These are true web resumes, sometimes referred to as e-resumes. The potential employer only sees this electronic version, only printing a paper version at his or her own preference. Often, before any human being lays eyes on these web resumes, they are subject to review by a search engine. This tool is loaded with certain keywords that the employer has defined as critical to any applicant's qualifications. Regardless of your abilities, if your qualifications summaries or general content does not use these keywords, it is likely that you'll never make even the first cut.

Here is where your research pays off. In defining your goals and drafting your resume, you learned the terms and phrases used in your chosen field. When possible, in your statement of objectives, you should name a particular title that you know is used in your field. The verbs you use to describe your qualifications and experience should mirror those terms as closely as possible.

Here are two statements of objectives that could be used for the same resume. See which one would yield the more fruitful keyword search:

- ***Objective:*** Position designing logos and graphics for state-of-the-art websites.
- ***Objective:*** Position as Web Designer for software design firm, using skills in XML, DTML, streaming video, Flash animation, Oracle database design, and website maintenance.

Chances are that you are uploading your resume into a job bank in answer to a specific job posting. The smartest thing to do, therefore, is to compare the job description to your resume. Does your resume, particularly your qualifications summary section, contain the key verbs, terms, and phrases used in the job description? If this job description is short or vague, search the web for other descriptions of similar jobs. You will notice that they use a common vocabulary to define job functions and desired qualifications.

Check the rules of the online job boards. Most allow you to regularly update your resumes. When you do an update, take the time to upload it so all potential employers always see the best and most accurate depiction of your job skills.

Keep an Inventory of Keywords

As you continue to search out new job postings, you will learn new industry-specific ways of phrasing your qualifications and summaries. Rather than rewriting your resume every time you find a new, more appropriate term, keep a list. Update your resume when you have a collection of these terms. In this way, your update will not only be more efficient in terms of time, you may come up with better ways of phrasing whole sections instead of changing a word at a time.

E-mailing Your Web Resume

Some job postings ask you to e-mail your resume directly to a contact person. The process here is very simple: Your e-mail message is your cover letter, and your resume gets included as a file attachment. An e-mail cover letter should be short and direct. The first line should state your purpose ("I am writing in response to your posting for an experienced Web Designer"). Any subsequent text should state your qualifications bluntly ("I have five years of freelance experience designing websites for independent movie studios, sometimes using GoLive and Adobe Design software but mostly writing my own code to incorporate movie clips and other complex elements").

How Much Information Should I Include in My E-mail?

It's a good idea to say what made you respond to this posting ("I use links to your site to give our visitors access to real-time industry news, and I would love the opportunity to work for you"). E-mails are quick and informal by nature. You know from experience that an overwritten e-mail is hard to read. Be polite, but don't be stuffy. Be specific so that the recipient knows it is not generic.

E-mail Etiquette

In this case, the question of file formats is particularly important. Pay attention to the stated format requirements, and do not bother submitting a resume that doesn't meet them. You may think PDF is much better than Word, but if Word is what the contact person requests, he or she will not appreciate your substitution, and it immediately signifies that you don't take direction well.

The common question with an e-mailed file of any kind is whether the recipient got it in a legible form. If your resume file is huge, with graphics or other special features, it will take a long time to transmit and to open. Nobody appreciates being made to wait, so for e-mailed resumes, it's a good idea to keep things very simple. Regardless of your care, file attachments do sometimes get mangled. That gives you an automatic excuse for a follow-up. Ask the recipient to let you know if your file did not come through. Take the opportunity to slip in another quick selling point. There's no harm in sending a follow-up, as long as it is very brief and not demanding in any way.

Addressing the E-mail

Job postings often ask you to reference a job number in your subject line. Be sure you include this information, as it is unlikely your e-mail (or resume) will reach its destination without it. Most job postings include a link to the contact person's e-mail. All you have to do to address your e-mail properly is to click on the link. You must also use a personal address, however, in your cover e-mail. Online job postings are notorious for giving little to no information about the contact person.

Sometimes all you have is an e-mail address and no name at all. Use whatever information you have. If you don't have a contact name, start the letter immediately after the address, using no salutation at all.

Web-Based Research and Job Search

The web is full of all the information you could ever need to know about your chosen career. Chances are that your dream job is out there somewhere—if only you could find it. In doing research on the web, the best place to start is with what you know. It doesn't matter whether you start off in the exact right place. The web is a job seeker's paradise because it is so easy to follow any trail in whatever direction you choose. Here's an example. We'll let our web designer friend Chris Smith take a quick look around the Internet to see what's happening in the working world.

1. Chris is just beginning a job search, so he starts at his favorite all-purpose search engine (we'll say that's *www.google.com*).
2. Chris types in his chosen job title, "web designer," in the search field and narrows the search just a little by adding "employment."
3. The Google search engine returns nearly 2 million websites that are related somehow to the phrase "web designer employment." Some of these sites belong to other web designers looking for employment. Chris ignores these for now, although later they might be a good way of networking with others in his field. He wants actual job postings. He doesn't have to look very hard to find them. The second link on the page lists a job board specializing in web designer and other graphic-oriented opportunities. These are sometimes known as niche job boards.

4. In the next five minutes, Chris finds the following information, just by clicking links that look promising:
   - Dozens of job postings for web designers, containing plenty of keywords.
   - Several big job boards or niche sites specific to graphics and web professionals. These contain not only job postings for web designers, they give Chris an idea of what companies are hiring, what industries in his part of the country are seeking web designers, and what qualifications employers currently expect. Some job postings include a salary range. But these are not often reliable, so Chris clicks around a little and finds salary statistics on an employment-related government website, as well as on salary sites.
   - Sites of individual companies with pages devoted to current openings, all with contact people listed.
   - Online forums and blogs maintained by people just like himself, experienced web designers of all kinds. Their discussions cover topics ranging from "Freelance Survival" to "Making It Big in the Corporate World."

These are the results of a real web search, using these keywords, conducted during a coffee break. As you can imagine, the key to getting useful information from the web is knowing when to stop. Five minutes can easily yield more information than anyone could use in a week; one page links quickly to another. The web is a huge, chaotic haystack of information. But as long as you don't worry yourself about hunting for one in particular, you'll find more needles there than you can possibly use.

Vistas for a Web-Based Job Search

Here are a few avenues for beginning your online job search: Check with your local librarian to see whether your state or geographic region sponsors a job bank or whether individual listings can be found online. Check the websites of companies in your chosen field or marketplace. Use a web search engine to visit the three current major job boards: *www.hotjobs.com*, *www.monster.com*, and *www.careerbuilder.com*. Your local newspaper may also list its help wanted ads online. Online listings are usually much easier to search than the printed version.

Reactive and Proactive Web Strategies

It is easy to think of the web as a giant fishing pond. You, as the job seeker, have a certain kind of bait on your pole, and you dangle your line in hope that the right fish is out there, waiting to bite. This is a reactive job-search strategy, where you react to postings and try to model yourself as the best candidate for the job. Sometimes that's all it takes, but a truly effective job-search campaign incorporates proactive techniques as well.

You have already begun using the web in a proactive manner. When you research your chosen field, for instance, to find the websites of the top companies, you are engaging in proactive research. Maybe the company you would most like to work for has several postings that are close to what you're looking for, but nothing that you feel qualified to apply for. You plan to keep checking back, but in the meantime why not write a quick e-mail to the contact person listed for that job. Tell him or her of your interest. Explain briefly how you believe you could be a real asset to the company. Close by saying you will keep in touch, and do it.

The 2009 User's Choice Awards, compiled from an online poll by the Internet recruitment site *www.weddles.com*, named thirty favorite job boards as chosen by job seekers and recruiters. Among them were *www.careerbuilder.com*, *www.theladders.com*, *www.monster.com*, *www.net-temps.com*, and *www.vault.com*. Another proactive technique on the employment e-frontier is a twist on our old favorite, networking. Online forums and bloggers cover almost any topic imaginable. They are easy enough to search out (try Yahoo!'s egroup listing, at *www.groups.yahoo.com*) and to join. You may not get any job offers, but you are likely to learn a lot about your chosen field and the function you hope to perform in it.

Job Board Giants and Niche Sites

The job seeker who fails to make use of the Internet's most popular job boards and niche sites is doing his or her job search a major disservice. These Internet resources have become a major source of recruiting for almost all employers.

A job board is a website that lists job postings by employers and resumes offered by job seekers. Although each site has different methodologies, both the employer and the candidate can identify good prospects based on their need. Some job boards are generic and offer a wide range of employment opportunities by industry, job title, location, and earnings.

Job Board Giants

At the time of this writing, the three most popular general job board giants are: *www.monster.com*, *www.careerbuilder.com*, and *www.hotjobs.com*. You can visit *www.topjob*

sites.com for an up-to-date ranking of job boards that are categorized under General, College, Executive, Diversity, Niche, and International.

Many job seekers choose to set up a search agent at the boards, which means they are regularly e-mailed openings that match a specific criteria according to parameters they set up for themselves. If you see a position that appeals to you, click the link that allows you to reply to the opening and send your resume. Do not rely on the job board or the employer to find you on the site, even if you have a resume posted there. Be proactive and go after the openings that seem the best match for your skills and career goals.

Niche Sites

The niche sites are exactly as they sound and are typically sites that are devoted to an industry, earning capacity, or geographic region. Some popular niche sites include:

www.absolutelyhealthcare.com
www.allretailjobs.com
www.jobs4hr.com
www.talentzoo.com (this last one for advertising and media professionals).

If you want to make your job search more focused, you might find greater success with the niche boards.

Online Networking

Social networking sites on the Internet are changing how people communicate and gain information about employers and job candidates. Sites such as *www.myspace.com*, *www.friendster.com*, *www.facebook.com*, *www.jobster.com*, *www.ryze.com*, and *www.linkedin.com*, to name a few popular resources, provide personal web pages and personal and professional information about individuals, which can include their job titles and where they work.

Online networking is very proactive and means you actively seek out and introduce yourself to someone who might work at a company you aspire to be part of. You can also seek people with a certain title to learn more about their professional duties or their company and perhaps give you an inside edge on getting your foot in the door at their firm.

Estimates regarding how many resumes are stored on or transmitted via web-based resources vary. Some believe that the numbers of resumes stored in resume banks and connected to postings via mega job-search sites doubled each year over the past five years. While actual totals are difficult to confirm, almost all agree that millions of resumes are stored annually and tens of thousands are transmitted by e-mail daily.

Typically, you can join a social networking site on your own, or someone already a part of the network invites you to join. Joining simply means you set up a profile viewable to others who then have the opportunity to contact you as well. Social networking sites that are not business oriented often showcase an individual's hobbies and lifestyle. Be careful what you include on such sites since many employers now go to these sites to see if a candidate is profiled there. On some occasions, individuals have included inappropriate photographs or comments that may reflect poorly on their consideration for employment. Be careful what you include on such sites, since you do not want to be blind-sided by digital dirt. Additionally, do yourself a favor and Google your name. Simply type your name into the search engine and see if you or others with your name show up. You can remove anything of your own that might jeopardize your search. This also allows you to discover if there are others with your name that might be mistaken for you if an employer goes through this same process.

Blogging

Blogs are online journals. Some bloggers write about their lives, some about their jobs, and still others write about interests or simply the mundane. You can go to *www.blogger.com* to read blogs and gain a better understanding of their wide scope and subject matter. For job-search purposes, you might visit a blog site and read what someone has to say about your anticipated line of work or a prospective company as an employer. Recruiters sometimes search blogs to target candidates with special interests or expertise in a specific field. The same way some people like to read a daily column or someone else's diary, blogs have loyal fans, and the community of bloggers continues to grow. Again, if you choose to maintain a blog, be sure that what you write won't jeopardize your chances of getting the job you want. You never know who will be reading it!

CHAPTER 12

Sample Resumes

Chris Smith
178 Green Street
St. Louis, MO 63130
(314) 555-5555
csmith@e-mail.com

PROFESSIONAL EXPERIENCE:

MARCA INFRARED DEVICES, St. Louis, MO
Manufacturers of infrared sensing and detecting devices.

2004–Present **Administrator**

Control, track, and maintain engineering personnel status, capital expenditures, and perform budget support for engineering departments.

- Automate weekly labor reports to calculate effectiveness and utilization and report against plan.
- Automate calculation of vacation dollars used in engineering budget planning.
- Automate capital equipment planning cycle.
- Act as capital expenditure liaison for all of engineering.
- Maintain engineering personnel status and monitor performance to plan.
- Perform year-end close out on all engineering purchase orders.
- Control, track, and maintain all contractor and consultant requisitions.
- Cross-train in library functions involving documentation ordering and CD ROM usage.

2003–2004 **Documentation Control Clerk**

Controlled, tracked, and maintained all changes to engineering documentation.

- Trained personnel in status accounting function and audit performance.
- Downloaded engineering and manufacturing tracking files from mainframe to Macintosh.

2000–2003 **Documentation Specialist**

Controlled, tracked, and maintained all changes to engineering documentation.

- Generated parts lists and was initial user of computerized Bills of Material.
- Directed changes in material requirements to material and production control departments.

1998–2000 **Configuration Management Analyst**

Controlled, tracked, and maintained all changes to engineering documentation.

- Chaired Configuration Review Board.
- Presented configuration status reports at customer reviews.

1997–1998 **Inside Sales Coordinator**

- Served as first customer contact.
- Directed customer calls and customer service.
- Maintained Literature files and processed incoming orders.

EDUCATION:

B.S. – Biology, Washington University 1997

Chris Smith
178 Green Street
Pocatello, ID 83204
(208) 555-5555
csmith@e-mail.com

SUMMARY OF QUALIFICATIONS:

- Over 12 years experience in inventory control management.
- Strong background in customer service.
- Excellent interpersonal skills.

EXPERIENCE:

J.C. RIVINGTON & CO., Pocatello, ID
(An Employee-Owned company since 1985)
Manufacturer/Distributor of premier quality Photo Frames.

2005–Present VICE PRESIDENT Inventory Management/Administrative Services
Monitored the Production/Distribution/Inventory Control Systems, and the Import Purchasing, Product Costing Department. Managed the Distribution, Electronic Data Processing, and Communications Departments.

2001–2005 DIRECTOR Inventory Control/Materials
Managed/Controlled the Production/Inventory Control System including finished goods, Work-In-Process, and Raw Materials, translating Sales Forecasts into production/inventory budgets and plan. Directed and monitored the Purchasing Department, both domestic and foreign purchases including goods purchased for resale. Chaired weekly Production Meetings to set/communicate priorities to Plant, Warehouse, Purchasing, and Customer Service managers. Designed/computerized a Product Costing System initially utilized as a marketing tool.

1996–2001 MANAGER Inventory Control/Materials
Performed Production/Inventory Control managerial functions of Finished Goods, Work-In-Process, and Raw Materials to meet company inventory investment objectives, to provide even production budgets on factory floor, and to meet agreed upon targeted levels of customer service.

1992–1996 OFFICE MANAGER
Supervised, directed, and coordinated Customer Service/Order Department, Communications including Word Processing, Switchboard, and Mail Room, Data Processing, Credit and Collection, Accounts Payable and Accounts Receivable Departments. Established company newsletter.

EDUCATION:

Northwestern College, Orange City, IA
Master of Business Administration, 1992

Iowa State University, Ames, IA
Bachelor of Science in Management, 1990

CHRIS SMITH
178 Green Street
Mesa, AZ 85203
(602) 555-5555
csmith@e-mail.com

Summary of Qualifications

- Strong management background; owned and operated a successful interior design store for nine years.
- Experience in delegating authority; managed retail staff of six, and later performed volunteer work with countless children and adolescents.
- Superior training/teaching skills; patient and supportive, having years instructional background in crafts, swimming, sports, CPR, cooking, etc.
- Communicate well with children.
- Strong team player; enthusiastic attitude motivates increased productivity in others.

Experience

Girl Scouts of America, Mesa AZ — 2003–Present (Part-time)
Brownie Troop Leader, ages 10-11
Lead weekly troop meetings; work with girls towards achievements of merit badges in camping, cooking, sewing, and crafts. Organize monthly overnight trips to local campgrounds. Teach practical first aid techniques and CPR. Facilitate discussions on personal safety when unaccompanied by an adult; teach girls methods of dealing with unsolicited attention from strangers, peer pressure, drug and alcohol abuse, and eating disorders. Organize annual cookie drive; profits garnered support Girl Scouts across America in both their performance of community service and their journey towards personal growth.

Weight Watchers, Mesa, AZ — 2002–Present (Part-time)
Meeting Leader
Educate and motivate members toward healthy lifestyle changes. The topics change weekly and range from healthful eating habits and exercise to behavior modification techniques. Manage cash and bookkeeping for each meeting.

Baroque Backdrops and Design, Mesa, AZ — 1993–2002
Business Owner/Manager (Interior design company)
Performed all aspects of retail and office management, sales, purchasing, closet and space design, estimates, planning, installations, inventory control, brochure designs, and text publishing. Maintained office and inventory control on a Macintosh.

Community Involvement

Parks and recreational department, Mesa, AZ — Spring 1999–Present
Coach girls' softball team, ages 12-14

Saint Martha's Church Choir, Mesa, AZ — 2005–Present
Play organ for three services every Sunday morning

CCD Instructor, Mesa, AZ — 2002–2003
Taught Catholic doctrine to elementary school children in preparation for Sacrament of First Communion.

Education

Stonehill College, Easton, MA
B.A. Early Childhood Education, 1988

CHRIS SMITH
178 Green Street
Aberdeen, SD 57401
(605) 555-5555
csmith@e-mail.com

OBJECTIVE:

To contribute acquired teaching skills at the Secondary Level.

EDUCATION:

SIOUX FALLS COLLEGE, Sioux Falls, SD
Master of Science in Education (January 2006)
Bachelor of Science in Biology (May 2001)

CERTIFICATION:

South Dakota, 9–12 Secondary

RELATED EXPERIENCE:

8/05 – Present
DOWNEY HIGH SCHOOL, Aberdeen, SD
Student Teacher
Assist in the teaching of ninth grade Earth Science. Plan curricula for laboratory experiments and lead post-lab discussions. Administer weekly quizzes. Confer with parents and teaching staff.

9/02–2/05
HAVEN HILLS HIGH SCHOOL, Sioux Falls, SD
Student Teacher
Assist in the preparation of instructional materials for tenth grade Social Studies class. Help teach and evaluate students. Advise students regarding academic and vocational interests.

OTHER EXPERIENCE:

7/02–Present NORTHERN LIGHTS PUBLISHING CO., Sioux Falls, SD
Freelance Editor

5/00–7/02 Administrative Assistant

MEMBERSHIPS:

Big Sister Program
Volunteer Tutors of Sioux Falls

CHRIS SMITH
178 Green Street
Juneau, AK 99801
(907) 555-5555
csmith@e-mail.com

PROFESSIONAL EXPERIENCE
A position in public relations in which to apply interpersonal, organizational, and conceptual skills.

SUMMARY
- Over twenty years experience in public relations.
- Proven ability to plan and supervise major special events.
- Knowledge of all aspects of media relations.
- Skilled educator and public speaker.

RELATED EXPERIENCE

2005 to Present
ALASKANS FOR A CLEANER WORLD, Juneau, AK
Public Relations Coordinator
- Contribute time and creative services to non-profit organization
- Plan and supervise special events
- Organized first annual "A Breath of Life" Walk-a-thon, raising over $15,000
- Handle all aspects of media relations
- Educate public about environmental issues
- Speak at local schools to encourage environmental awareness

2004 to Present
MT. JUNEAU MEDICAL CENTER, Juneau, AK
Coordinator, Department of Neurosurgery
- Promote department, oversee public relations
- Coordinate all communications for medical and non-medical activities with department
- Serve as liaison between administrations of two hospitals, physicians, and nurses
- Educate in-house staff, patients, and families on techniques, equipment, and related subjects

UNRELATED EXPERIENCE
UNIVERSITY HOSPITAL, Anchorage, AK
Staff Nurse, Surgical Intensive Care Unit, 2003 to 2005

PRESENTATIONS AND LECTURES
Have given over 25 presentations and lectures to various schools, hospitals, in-house staff, and professional associations

COMPUTER SKILLS
Word, Excel, Photoshop, Quark

EDUCATION
UNIVERSITY OF ALASKA, Anchorage, AK
Bachelor of Science degree in Nursing, 2002

CHRIS SMITH
178 Green Street
Cheyenne, WY 82009
(307) 555-5555
csmith@e-mail.com

Objective:
A position in Food Service in the public school system.

Related Experience:

Jameson Homeless Shelter — Cheyenne, WY
Weekday server. Act as liaison between homeless and national food distributor, securing special requests and unanimously favored items.

St. Bernadette's Parish — Cheyenne, WY
Coordinate annual bake sale; provide approximately ten percent of the bakery items sold.

Brady Family — Cheyenne, WY
Act as live-in nanny for eight-year-old twin boys; duties include the preparation of their meals and snacks on a regular basis.

Lion's Club Carnival — Cheyenne, WY
Work the concession booths at annual carnival each June; prepare and serve such items as fried dough, sweet sausage, pizza, and caramel apples; maintain a receipt record of profits for event administrators.

Conduct informal cooking classes out of the Payne Community Center kitchen on a weekly basis.

Awards:
Award-winning country style cook.
Placed first in national fruit-based pie competition.
Won cash prize for best pot roast recipe, *Reader's Digest.*

Education:
Cheyenne Community College, Cheyenne, WY
Associate's degree, Home Economics

Interests:
Gourmet cook, Little League softball coach, avid gardener

References:
Available upon request.

Chris Smith
178 Green Street
Clarksville, TN 37044
(615) 555-5555
csmith@e-mail.com

OBJECTIVE
A challenging position in the field of sales and electronic publishing.

SUMMARY OF QUALIFICATIONS

- More than fifteen years of Art Director/Buyer and graphics design production experience in the publishing field; extensive knowledge of typesetting, budgeting, and scheduling.
- Excellent interpersonal, communication, and managerial skills; adept at coordinating and motivating creative artists to peak efficiency.
- Aware of cost management and quality control importance on all levels.
- Self-motivated; able to set effective priorities and meet tight deadlines.
- Productive in fast-paced, high-pressure atmosphere

PROFESSIONAL EXPERIENCE

2002–2006 NO CONTEST GRAPHICS, Nashville, TN
Owner/President, Art Director/Buyer
Coordinate operations, 12-member production staff, freelance desktop publishers and illustrators. Maintain overview of works-in-progress to produce optimum efficiency. Provide advice to personnel in designing materials to appropriately meet client needs; conceptualize product; delegate staff to make decisions. Commission freelance agents by utilizing nationwide illustrator four-color manuscripts using watercolor illustrations, photography, or graphics. Act as liaison between executive personnel and staff. Budget each project; motivate artistic staff and typesetters to meet projected deadlines and remain within cost-efficient parameters. Projects include: greeting cards, care package kits, magazine fragrance inserts, cereal boxes, toy packages, coloring books (cover and contents), holographic bumper stickers, and retail store signs and logos.

2000–2002 NEW JERSEY LITHOGRAPH, Newark, NJ
Head of Typesetting and Design Department
Supervised staff in design and execution of print materials for commercial printer.

EDUCATION

CENTENARY COLLEGE, Hackettstown, NJ
A.S. in Technical Illustration, 2001

ART INSTITUTE OF NEWARK, Newark, NJ
Certified in Graphic Design, 1989

CHRIS SMITH
178 Green Street
La Jolla, CA 92093
(619) 555-5555
csmith@e-mail.com

OBJECTIVE

A position utilizing my experience in recycling and developing environmentally conscious programs.

SUMMARY OF QUALIFICATIONS

- Acquired the first recycling permit in the City of San Diego for ferrous and non-ferrous metal, aluminum, high-grade paper, and plastic.
- Developed profitable pilot program for community and industrial recycling.
- Recovered non-ferrous and precious metals from waste solutions, photo and electrical scrap.
- Conducted research and formulated chemical process to liquefy Styrofoam in reusable plastic.

EXPERIENCE

2002 to 2006 CALIFORNIA RECYCLE RENEGADES, INC., San Diego, CA
Owner/President
Established First Aluminum Recycling in San Diego. Developed programs for expansion from ferrous and non-ferrous metals to high-grade paper, aluminum, and plastic. Conducted pilot program; formulated a network in Sable Park and Briody Hills for voluntary recycling. Provided containers biweekly for aluminum, glass, and newspaper. Picked up and processed material, sending check for proceeds to community associations.

EDUCATION

University of California, Riverside – Bookkeeping
M.A. Business Administration 2000

University of California, Berkeley
B.A. Environmental Science 1998

AFFILIATIONS

Member of Pacific Community Association

REFERENCES

Available upon request.

CHRIS SMITH
178 Green Street
Lawrence, KS
(913) 555-5555
csmith@e-mail.com

FREELANCE PRODUCTION

Writer/Producer/Director/Editor: Training videotape for Child Services of Squaw Valley. Incorporated; tape is designed to instruct current and prospective members of the Council on Children in the most effective and efficient conductance of board functions (2006).

Writer: Series of short videotapes on recreational drinking use for Social Science Research and Evaluation, Incorporated. Program depicts strategies teens may use to avoid problems associated with drinking; to be shown in high schools throughout Kansas. Worked as Camera Operator during production (2006).

Producer/Writer/Editor: Two PSA's for the Kansas Commission for the Deaf, to be aired throughout the state of Kansas (2005).

Camera Operator/Editor: *Missing Buttonholes,* 4th program to be used by Kansas State University's Broadcast Journalism Department (2005).

Producer/Writer/Assistant Editor: Volunteer Recruitment PSA for Specialized Ambulatory Care Clinic, Wichita, KS (2004).

EDUCATIONAL BACKGROUND

KANSAS STATE UNIVERSITY, Manhattan, KS
Master of Science Degree in Broadcasting

- Concentration, Television Production and Writing
- Assistant Director: *Dinnertime Mind Dance* for Cablevision of Lawrence (2005)
- Grade point average: 3.4/4.0
- Awarded $2,000 scholarship from School of Public Communication (2004)

REFERENCES

Excellent references available upon request.

Chris Smith
178 Green Street
Fort Worth, TX 76114
(817) 555-5555
csmith@e-mail.com

SPECIAL SKILLS

Experienced and competent with Mac and PC systems. Solid communications skills in person and by phone. Possess strong work ethic and enthusiasm. Strong organizational skills.

EMPLOYMENT

Copywriter/Service Director
WDDE Radio Station, Fort Worth, TX 2005–present

- Compose copy for advertisements and promotions.
- Edit client copy, client newsletter and executive correspondence.
- Communicate with clients and listeners by phone.
- Produce commercials.
- Organize and oversee copy and taped spots.
- Delegate on-air personalities for recording.
- Coordinate technical aspects of on-air programming.

Claims Coder
Texas Mutual Inc., Dallas, TX 2003–2005

- Process claims reports and encode data to computer system.
- Review and revise reinsurance files.
- Conduct inventory.
- Balance daily accounts for each computer system.

Mathematics Tutor
University of Dallas, Irvine, TX 2001–2003

OTHER EMPLOYMENT

Graduated Dave Erickson "Public Speaking" course, 2005
University of Dallas, Irvine, TX, 2003, Graduated Summa Cum Laude
Bachelor of Science degree in Education, Minor in English

- Member of Kappa Kappa Gamma Honor Society
- Dean's list four years

SPECIAL INTERESTS

Volunteer at MiCasa, a Dallas Battered Women's Shelter
Surfing, Window Shopping, and Canoeing

REFERENCES AVAILABLE UPON REQUEST

CHRIS SMITH
178 Green Street
Sumter, SC 29150
(803) 555-5555
csmith@e-mail.com

Objective:
An editing position within a major publishing house.

Summary of Qualifications:

- More than seven years of writing/editing experience.
- Adept at managing multiple responsibilities simultaneously.
- Experienced at delegating authority and motivating others to ensure efficiency and productivity.
- Computer knowledge includes Excel, Microsoft Word, InDesign, and Photoshop.

Work Experience:

Editor-in-Chief, Renegade Magazine
Sumter, SC
Selected submissions, edited and wrote headlines for submissions and columns, laid out page, recruited columnist, trained associates from 2004-2006. Frequent copyediting and research.

Associate Editor, Modern Daze Magazine
New York, NY
Wrote articles for both the magazine and its associated newsletter, *Disembodied Voices.* Edited features and department articles from 1998-2002. Read and critiqued assigned articles from contributing editors.

Copy Editor, Heathcliff's Garden Magazine
Boston, MA
Edited news stories, wrote headlines, assisted with layout of page, occasionally solicited advertising and helped with distribution from 1994-1996.

Other Experience:

Writer, professional musician, world traveler.
(Details available upon request.)

Military

Army Corporal (honorable discharge).

Education:

University of Richmond, Richmond, VA
Bachelor of Arts, English, 1985
Le Student Roma, Rome, Italy
Intensive study of Italian language and culture, 2005

CHRIS SMITH
178 Green Street
Kankakee, IL 60901
(815) 555-5555
csmith@e-mail.com

EXPERIENCE

K.T. BIRCHWOOD AND SONS, Chicago, IL
Senior Accountant, December 2005–Present
Responsible for G.I. processing reporting, initially for six companies, also bank reconciliation, etc. Involved in preparation for Chapter 11 filing (2006), subsequent reporting requirements, also handling account receivables and internal audits.

ESSEX COMPUTER, LTD., Glasgow, Scotland
Assistant Financial Accountant, 2002–2005
Maintained the general ledger system; oversaw the preparation of the month-end and year-end financial reports, audit reports, budgets, and variance analysis of the monthly financial package for submission to U.S. headquarters. Maintained capital assets, depreciations schedules, and reconciliation of bank accounts. Maintained the operation of the accounts payable system with vendors, also involved in the set-up and modification of a new computer system. Experience using micros, primarily Multi-plan and Lotus. Member of steering committee; selected a new general ledger package, which is currently used at this facility.

S.G.R., LTD., Glasgow, Scotland
Temporary Accountant, 2001–2002
Maintained and reconciled all bank and investment accounts. Performed inventory control. Involved in inter-company accounting with foreign subsidiaries.

UPSCALE ENTERPRISES, Glasgow, Scotland
Accounts Assistant, 1998–2001
Performed all bookkeeping functions of company; creditors (including foreign currency), contract payments, debtors, payroll, management accounts, profit and loss by flight reports, budget, and costing.

EDUCATION

COLLEGE OF COMMERCE, Glasgow, Scotland
Certificate in Business Studies, 1998–2000
Major: Accounting

NOTHERN ENTERPRISE OF CERTIFIED ACCOUNTANTS, Glasgow, Scotland
Exempt-Level I, have passed subjects in Level II.

PERSONAL

Work permit.

Chris Smith
178 Green Street
Vancouver, WA 98665
(206) 555-5555
csmith@e-mail.com

CAREER OBJECTIVE
To secure an **Administrative/Supervisory** position in the Human Services field.

SYNOPSIS
Self-starter with involved style of leadership. Excellent communicator with the ability to elicit interest, enthusiasm, drive, and energy using a common-sense approach. Adept at sizing up situations, analyzing facts developing alternative courses of action in order to achieve, even exceed desired results.

QUALIFICATIONS

- Extensive supervisory experience.
- 6 years counseling up to 120 soldiers with subsequent referrals when necessary.
- Exceptional training and instructional skills.
- Strong administrative and organizational abilities.
- Relevant course work in college and U.S. Army professional training.
- Bilingual: English and Spanish.

EXPERIENCE

1998–2006 U.S. ARMY **Squad Leader/Training NCO**

From initial tour of duty to honorable discharge, details have included military driver, senior gunner, squad leader, acting platoon sergeant, and training NCO.

- Command inspections and training 120-Main Air Defense Battery with an 18-hour worldwide mission in the 7th ID (L.).
- Trained and targeted career progression for soldiers on staff.
- Directly responsible for the discipline, training, morale, and quality of life of one particular soldier.
- Accountable for training records, personnel performance, strength reporting, and weight control.
- Liable for personnel processing, NCO Evaluation Reports, evaluations, awards, in/out processing, legal actions, and orders.

AWARDS

- Army Service Medal
- U.S. Defense Medal
- Four Army Good Conduct Medals
- Four Officer Development Ribbons

EDUCATION

Farmville High School, Farmville, VA
Graduate Diploma, 1998

Chris Smith
178 Green Street
Wise, VA 24293
(703) 555-5555
csmith@e-mail.com

OBJECTIVE An entry-level position in Human Resources.

SUMMARY OF QUALIFICATIONS

- Trained in basic computer skills.
- Developed interpersonal skills; excellent mediation abilities.
- Proven supervisory abilities; deal equitably with all levels.
- Function well independently and in a team environment.
- Adapt easily to new concepts; adept at handling multiple responsibilities.
- Extensive experience in training; able to explain procedure and garner significant results within a brief time span.
- Charismatic, assertive personality; skilled at commanding the attention of others.

WORK HISTORY

1998–Present ARMY NATIONAL GUARD, Richmond, VA
Assistant Section Coordinator, Sergeant/ E-5
Coordinate training of soldiers, creating schedules, overseeing adherence to rules, assisting in directing operations.

2005–Present BENNIE WARD'S STYLE SHINDIG, Winchester, VA
Sales Associate
Provided customer assistance. Acknowledged as one of top salespeople; consistently met/exceeded sales goals.

2002–2005 MARTELL BLUE SECURITY SERVICES, Salem, MA
Security Shift Supervisor
Handled employee ID checks; secured building; ensured other site call-ins. Worked independently on on-site assignments.

1999–2002 VIRGINIA SAMARITAN ASSOCIATION, Charlottesville, VA
Fundraiser
Utilized telephone techniques to raise funds for organizations.

1996–1998 FIRST NATIONAL BANK OF LEXINGTON, Lexington, VA
Teller
Processed withdrawals and deposits; tallied vault moneys.

EDUCATION RICHMOND JUNIOR COLLEGE, Richmond, VA
Associate's degree in Management Science
Major: Business Administration

REFERENCES Furnished upon request.

CHRIS SMITH
178 Green Street
Johnson, VT 05656
(802) 555-5555
csmith@e-mail.com

OBJECTIVE

To join a dynamic sales staff with a firm that has a need for a highly motivated representative skilled in retail markets.

SUMMARY OF PROFESSIONAL EXPERIENCE

- Four years of substantial experience in positions as Sales Representative, Retail Sales Manager, and Warehouse Manager with a major retail and wholesale organization.
- Assumed responsibility for divisional sales from $1.4 million to $2.1 million within one year.
- Hands-on experience in sales, inventory control and promotion of chemicals, furniture, clothing, and seasonal products.
- Skilled in developing special merchandising effects to increase product visibility and sales.

WORK HISTORY

Raintree, Inc.
Seasonal Specialty Stores, Raintree Industries, Johnson, VT
Retail Manager (Part-time) (2005-Present)

- Hire, train, schedule, and supervise a highly productive staff of 11, selling and promoting a diverse product mix.
- Develop, implement, and expand seasonal merchandise and presentations for year-round sales. Greatly expanded product knowledge and sales through use of in store-video and other image equipment.
- Select and purchase all billiard equipment and accessories.
- Prepare inventory projections, work on sales promotions (in-store and chain-wide). Excellent consumer base resulting in strong repeat business.
- Maintain financial control of all debts/credits.

Wholesale Warehouse Manager (Part-Time) (2004-2005)

- Supervised a staff of 6 and controlled all aspects of shipping and receiving. Directed fleet scheduling maintenance as well as building maintenance control and security for this facility.

Sales Representative (Part-Time) (1997-2004)

- Increased all aspects of wholesale pool and supply and accessory business. Control of expanding sales and sales force. Established new sales and accounts within New England area.

EDUCATION

Cornell University, Ithaca, NY
B.A. Business Administration, 2003

CHRIS SMITH
178 Green Street
Casper, WY 82604
(307) 555-5555
csmith@e-mail.com

OBJECTIVE
An Engineering position in the field of Electro-Optics.

WORK EXPERIENCE

2005–Present JT Technology — Casper, WY

ASSISTANT ENGINEER
- Provide engineering support to various senior and electro-mechanical areas.
- Solve engineering-related problems for production department; assist through direct observation, positive communication, and dynamic interaction between production floor and test engineering management.
- Perform equipment and component testing; troubleshoot malfunctions; assist engineers with special projects and with department support tasks as required.
- Monitor current developments in the engineering fields for possible practical applications.

2002–2005 Charles Technology Corporation — Casper, WY

ASSISTANT ENGINEER
- Supervised various test-engineering projects that required operating specialized equipment, documenting test results and making reports of findings to engineering management.
- Implemented software/hardware modifications and engineering changes requested by company clients.
- Assisted senior engineers with projects and performed support duties as needed.

2000–2002 Dishwashers, Etc. — Green Bay, WI

APPLIANCE TECHNICIAN
- Made household and commercial service calls to troubleshoot malfunctions and engineering changes requested by company clients.
- Assisted senior engineers with projects and performed support duties as needed.

EDUCATION

Associate's of Science Degree in Electronic Technology, 2002
Green Bay Community College, Green Bay, WI
GPA 3.5/4.0

ACTIVITIES

New York Marathon
Placed 5th, Wheelchair Division – 2005

CHRIS SMITH
178 Green Street
Arkadelphia, AK 71923
(501) 555-5555
csmith@e-mail.com

OBJECTIVE

To contribute extensive experience and administrative skills to a part-time teaching position.

EXPERIENCE

ARKANSAS PUBLIC SCHOOL SYSTEM

1996 to 2002 **Principal-Retired**
RODHAM ELEMENTARY SCHOOL Arkadelphia, AR

- Oversaw all operations for entire school.
- Supervised and evaluated teachers and teaching assistants.
- Developed curriculum for mainstream and special needs children.
- Directed staff meetings, oriented new administrative and teaching staff.

1989 to 1996 **Principal**
HOPE CLINTON JUNIOR HIGH SCHOOL Arkadelphia, AR

- Directed and facilitated all operational procedures.
- Developed curriculum and supervised staff.
- Created and implemented educational program enhancements.
- Directed staff meetings, informed staff of district-ordered changes.

1987 to 1990 **Teaching Assistant Principal**
NOAH JUNIOR HIGH SCHOOL Arkadelphia, AR

- Served as acting principal and directed operational processes.
- Assisted and supervised teaching staff.
- Interfaced with parents/teachers for educational program development.

1979 to 1987 **Teaching Assistant Principal**
DAMON ELEMENTARY SCHOOL Conway, AR

- Assisted principal in the coordination of educational programs.
- Purchased books and various educational aids.

1968 to 1979 **Teacher**
CONWAY JUNIOR HIGH SCHOOL Conway, AR

- Instructed students in math and science.

EDUCATION

JOHN BROWN UNIVERSITY, Siloam Springs, AK
Master's degree: Education, 1992
Bachelor of Arts degree: History, 1959

CERTIFICATION

State Teacher Certification

CHRIS SMITH

178 Green Street
Fairfax, VA 22030
(703) 555-5555
csmith@e-mail.com

SKILLS

Research
General office skills
Writing
Excel
Microsoft Word
Access

WORK EXPERIENCE

Legal Assistant
Parnell & Swaggert
Fairfax, VA 2006–Present
Responsible for corresponding via courier, telephone, letter, and facsimile with clients, attorneys, Secretaries of State, U.S. Dept. of State, and foreign associates in matters of intellectual property law, primarily trademarks. Meet with clients regarding applications/registrations of trademarks and direct either U.S. Commissioner or foreign agent how to proceed. Other duties include: compiling information from other Parnell & Swaggert branches, paying our debt notes and billing clients.

Legislative Intern
Office of Senator Fisher
Fairfax, VA Summer 2006
Responsible for correspondence, involving casework. Assisted Labor and Human Resources Committee Judiciary Sub-Committee, and Fund for a Democratic Majority. Projects included research, writing; covered hearings and wrote memos.

Legislative Aide
Office of Senator Florio
Washington, D.C. Summer 2005
Responsible for overseeing communications between Senator Florio and the general public.

EDUCATION

George Mason University, Fairfax, VA
B.A., Law and Society, 2006

HONORS AND AWARDS

Oxford Honor Scholar
Who's Who Among Students, 2004
Student Government Award

CHRIS SMITH
178 Green Street
Raleigh, NC 27611
(919) 555-5555
csmith@e-mail.com

OBJECTIVE:
A long-term position in administration.

SKILLS AND QUALIFICATIONS:

- Five years Accounting, Financial and Administrative experience.
- Computer knowledge includes PC and Mac.
- Outstanding communications and organizational skills.

EXPERIENCE:

11/06–Present CARMICHAEL ENTERPRISES, Raleigh, NC
Accounting Clerk/Data Entry
Temporary Position
Prepare and maintain all general ledger accounts, records, and files. Input data on various computer systems, including PC and Mac.

6/06–10/06 CHAVEZ INVESTMENTS, Winston-Salem, NC
Customer Service Representative
Temporary Position
Responded to questions and assisted shareholders in regards to their stocks, bond, equity and money markets accounts, as well as tax questions. Approved check disbursement and utilized PC.

11/00–6/06 JOHN HANCOCK LIFE INSURANCE CO., Boston, MA
Purchasing Clerk
Temporary Position
Maintained general supply inventory levels and purchased general supplies and specialty requested items and materials. Negotiated price and coordinated delivery with various vendors. Prepared purchase orders. Assisted in other administrative activities.

4/02–12/04 SCANLON CORPORATION, Chapel Hill, NC
Residential Counselor
Assisted and counseled mentally retarded and emotionally disabled adults in reading, math, personal hygiene, and motor skills.

OTHER EXPERIENCE:
Other temporary assignments have included: Receptionist, Order Entry Clerk, Switchboard Operator, Proofreader.

EDUCATION:
Clydeston Business School Certification, 2006
Kennedy High School Graduate, 2002

CHRIS SMITH
178 Green Street
Myrtle Beach, SC 29577
(803) 555-5555
csmith@e-mail.com

OBJECTIVE

To apply skills obtained through experience in supervision of Parking Facilities to the position of Assistant Manager of Parking Facilities.

SUMMARY

- Proven abilities have resulted in the rapid advancement to a supervisory position.
- Self-motivated, people-oriented, consistently responsible.
- Familiar with all prerequisite functions of maintaining a smooth-running Parking Facility.
- Sworn Deputy Sheriff, Birchwood County.

EXPERIENCE

1998–Present **SPORTS AUTHORITY ROLLINS AIRPORT,** Lexington, SC

2003–Present **SUPERVISOR OF PARKING FACILITY**
Oversee collection of all moneys. Maintain public relations and customer service. Resolve all problems. Administer work schedules, payroll, assignments of duties, and various other functions. Attend to snow removal. Represent Port Authority at scheduled court appearances.

2002–Present **PRESIDENT OF LOCAL CHAPTER OF NAGE**
Represent all cashiers and attendants. Settle all problems pertaining to Parking Facilities. Negotiate contracts.

2000–2003 **ASSISTANT SUPERVISOR/CASHIER**
Assisted supervisor. Collected all parking fees. Achieved high standard of customer relations.

1998–2001 **ATTENDANT**
Patrolled and maintained cleanliness standards of Parking Facility. Assisted customers.

OTHER EXPERIENCE

Skilled carpenter's helper; advanced to highest skilled fish cutter within one year and then elected shop steward. (Total experience, 4 years.)
Truck driver, class 2 license to Lead Bartender/Beverage Manager/Assistant Manager. (Total experience, 6 years.)

REFERENCES

Furnished upon request.

Chris Smith
178 Green Street
Troy, MI 48098
(313) 555-5555
csmith@e-mail.com

OBJECTIVE:
To fully utilize over ten years of experience in investment accounting within an allied field.

SUMMARY:
Experience in monitoring money flow in money market funds and mutual funds, as well as calculating the yield for various money market accounts, and pricing mutual funds.

EXPERIENCE:

GERGEW SERVICE COMPANY Troy, MI
Senior Money Market Accountant 2002–Present
Determined daily available cash, calculated daily yields and dividends. Posted general ledger. Reconciled trial balance accounts. Acted as liaison between fund traders and custodian banks. Prepared audit schedules. Assisted in training new personnel.

Mutual Fund Accountant 1999–2002
Functions included daily pricing of common stock and bond funds, accruing and reconciling interest and dividend accounts, reconciling trial balance accounts and daily contact with bankers to obtain stock and bond quotes.

TIMBERCREST COMPANY Boston, MA
Assistant Supervisor 1996–1999
Prepared schedules for fund audits. Prepared reports for fund managers. Assisted fund accountants with month-end trial balance reconciliation. Trained new personnel.

Fund Accountant 1994–1996
Manually priced funds and posted journals and ledgers through trial balance. Heavy daily contact with brokers.

OTHER QUALIFICATIONS:
Licensed Michigan Real Estate Broker, 1993

EDUCATION:
Waterford High School, Waterford, MI
Graduated 1992

CHRIS SMITH
178 Green Street
Loretto, PA 15940
(814) 555-5555

OBJECTIVE

An accounting position offering the opportunity to utilize my professional financial expertise, extensive business expertise, and ability to interact with senior management and with the business community on a worldwide basis.

SUMMARY OF QUALIFICATIONS

- **Accountant** and **Administrative Manager** of medium-sized motor components manufacturing and distribution company serving national and international markets.
- Hands-on expertise with firm of certified Public Accountants and Auditors.
- **Certified Public Accountant** and **Auditor.**

PROFESSIONAL EXPERIENCE

2003–Present **LISMORE SHIPPING CO., LTD.,** Loretta, PA
Accountant

- Managed, developed, and maintained all aspects of finance, accounting, foreign exchange dealings, marketing, and data processing of company and its overseas offices in London and New York.
- Controlled budget, cash flow, and capital expenditure.
- Reviewed, analyzed, and evaluated finances and securities pertaining to advance and shipping for client base of about 200.
- Established and maintained close relationships with bank executives, auditors, and attorneys, ensuring compliance with all regulatory bodies.

1998–2003 **RABINO PRODUCTS,** Meadville, PA
Accountant

- Developed and implemented corporate and project-oriented financial strategies.
- Provided financial overview and leadership for all major operating considerations and activities, including development of business and profit plans.
- Controlled line management for all accounting, production costing, EDP, and financial functions.

1996–1998 **MANNINGS, DAVE, AND BOND,** Pittsburgh, PA
Auditor

- Audited private companies, listed companies, partnerships, and individual businesses.
- Prepared financial statements and schedules.

EDUCATION

UNIVERSITY OF PENNSYLVANIA, Philadelphia, PA
Bachelor's degree, with major in Accountancy, Marketing, and Business Finance, 1996

CHRIS SMITH
178 Green Street
Newark, NJ 07102
(201) 555-5555

OBJECTIVE

Seeking a position in administrative support where acquired accounting skills will be advanced.

WORK EXPERIENCE

5/04 to Present

BETTY LOU'S LINGERIE, Newark, NJ
Accounts Payable/Payroll Department
Light typing, filing, and other general office duties. Key in bills on a PC and print all checks for six different offices. Assist in payroll preparation by calculating all time sheets and related duties.

2001 to 2004

DYNAMO DANCE SUPPLIES, Newark, NJ
Accounts Payable
Set up all invoices to match purchase orders for input into computers. Added up all invoices to match check amounts. Responsible for filing, sorting mail, and general office duties.

1999 to 2001

LEDA AND THE SWAN PET SITTERS, New Brunswick, NJ
Administrative Coordinator
Acted as cashier, light typist, bank depositor, and key punch operator. Handled filing and accounts payable/ receivable. Heavy customer contact.

COMPUTERS

Most PC and Mac applications, including Microsoft Word, Excel, FileMaker, Internet Explorer

SPECIAL INTERESTS

Camping, fishing, and jogging.

REFERENCES

Furnished upon request.

CHRIS SMITH
178 Green Street
Birmingham, AL 35294
(205) 555-5555

OBJECTIVE

A challenging position within the fields of Tax Accounting or Investment.

SUMMARY OF QUALIFICATIONS

- Thorough knowledge of individual income, employment, and excise tax laws and regulations; IRS Service policies; and selected tax forms. Experienced in preparation of individual and employment tax returns. Proficient accounting, bookkeeping, and problem-solving skills.

EMPLOYMENT HISTORY

10/04 to Present — **Taxpayer Service Representative**
INTERNAL REVENUE SERVICE — Birmingham, AL
- Individual income and businesses.
- Explain various IRS bills and notices to taxpayers and set up installment agreements.
- Maintain knowledge of current IRS tax documents, enforcement policies, forms, laws, notices, regulations, Service organization, and policies.
- Develop understanding of "tiered" interview techniques to determine taxpayer's ability to pay outstanding tax obligations.

1/04 to 5/04 — **Intern**
PRICE, PATTON, AND TATE — Atlanta, GA
- Posted trades and performed general office and receptionist duties.

Summer 2003 — **Sales Intern—China Department**
JAKES DEPARTMENT STORE — Selma, AL
- Provided customer service and resolved consumer and departmental complaints.
- Created displays and initiated sale of merchandise.
- Controlled inventory and trained employees.

Summer 2002 — **Ticket Salesperson**
BUDGE BUS TOURS — Montgomery, AL
- Maintained bookkeeping records, deposited currency, and resolved customer complaints.
- Commended for achievement of second highest ticket seller in twelve years.

EDUCATION

ARMSTRONG STATE COLLEGE — Savannah, GA
Bachelor of Arts degree: Management, May 2004

COMPUTERS

Proficient with most PC and Mac applications.

CHRIS SMITH
178 Green Street
Albuquerque, NM 87140
(505) 555-5555

OBJECTIVE

A challenging career opportunity in Accounting/Bookkeeping.

SUMMARY OF QUALIFICATIONS

- More than eighteen years experience in Accounting/Bookkeeping.
- Able negotiator/liaison, dealing with professionals, clients, and staff.
- Accurate, organized, and aware of importance of meeting deadlines and maintaining smooth workflow.
- Computer literate.

EXPERIENCE

CHUTES AND LADDERS DAYCARE CENTER, Albuquerque, NM

Agency Bookkeeper 5/06–Present

Handle cash disbursement, verify vendor invoices, and generate weekly checks. Administer General Ledger, fund coding and checkbook maintenance for agency accounts. Record transactions; maintain up-to-date bank balances. Prepare/post disbursements and monthly invoices to state and municipal contractors.

Voucher Bookkeeper 6/05–5/06

Processed current/outstanding for reimbursement for over 300 providers (3,000 payments). Dealt with underpayment/overpayment and rate changes; verified adjustments requests against payment history; issued/recorded advance payment checks. Ensured immediate update of computerized fiscal files and accounts payable to meet rigid deadlines schedule. Assisted providers; verified payments for auditors. Oversaw part-time staff.

Assistant Bookkeeper 4/01–6/05

Supervised current/outstanding invoice payment approval, computerized data input, invoice verification, posting to Ledger, and dispatching checks.

SAWYER REALTY TRUST, Las Cruces, NM

Part-time Bookkeeper

Recorded rent payments, paid banks/vendors, reconciled bank statements.

EDUCATION

NEWBURY JUNIOR COLLEGE, Boston, MA

Associate's degree in Accounting, 1999

CHRIS SMITH
178 Green Street
Seattle, WA 98122
(206) 555-5555

EMPLOYMENT HISTORY

January 2004 to Present

THE ATHENA GROUP, Seattle, WA

Manager of Finance

Manage a group of three associates responsible for producing financial reports, all aspects of budgeting a $51 million office, A/R, A/P, petty cash, expense reports, revenue collection, and monthly closing for an office of 284 associates. Responsible for producing systems that generate the necessary financial information to determine our profitability. Systems track accrual profit, cash profit, expenses by sub-groups, and a new cost accounting systems.

- Upon hiring into this position in July of 2007, had written off $3 million of unbillable or uncollectable business. The office posted a 0% profit. Currently looking to make a 5% accrual profit for this fiscal year.
- Designed a billing tracking system to allow team managers to determine where they stood on a monthly basis for revenue collection. The system projects where the team is in accordance with where they need to be in order to meet the goal of 5%.

Systems Analyst, Finance and Administration

Systems analyst for a network of ten users. Administered COBRA software application—health care/dependent care reimbursement system.

- Assisted in implementing new health care system. Installed remote connection for offsite claims processing.
- User liaison for billing system in place in forty offices throughout U.S. and Canada. Designed training materials, performed on-site training, troubleshooting via telecommunications.

Sept. 2002 to Jan. 2004

FANFARE INTERNATIONAL, Tacoma, WA

Programmer/Analyst/Consultant

- Provided large utility client with database software to track political campaign contributions. System provided feedback on how campaign contributions were distributed versus the way "supported" legislators voted on key issues.

EDUCATION

Longfellow University, Wordsworth, MA
Master's degree in MIS, anticipated December 2009

Barley College, Sioux City, IA
Bachelor of Arts in Economics, 2002
Minor in Computer Science

COMPUTERS

Languages: HTML, Perl, SQL, C++
Applications: Microsoft Word, Excel, FrameMaker, Photoshop
Operating Systems: Mac OS, Windows NT, UNIX
Hardware Platforms: PC and Mac

CHRIS SMITH
178 Green Street
Salt Lake City, UT 84117
(801) 555-5555

OBJECTIVE

A challenging position in the Business/Financial area.

SUMMARY

- Developed interpersonal skills.
- Self-motivated and able to function well in high-stress atmosphere.

EXPERIENCE

7/02–Present **THE MORMON BANK,** Salt Lake City, UT
Loan Servicer, Commercial and Real Estate Loans
Prepare customer billing and weekly/monthly reports; resolve customer problems. Set up/maintain customer legal and credit files. Record and adjust income in General Ledger. Process loan payments into computerized system. Maintain tax and insurance Escrow accounts; remit payments to respective institutions. Review loan documents. Responsible for general Portfolio management.

2/01–12/01 **ISLAND OF JAMAICA,** Negril, Jamaica
Cooperative Officer
Responsible for promotion and supervision of cooperative Societies, mainly Commercial Credit Union.

11/98–12/01 **RICHARD'S RESTAURANT,** Montego Bay, Jamaica
Manager
Managed daily retail store functions. Supervised staff and inventory control. Maintained Accounting System; ensured viability and profitability of business.

9/93–9/98 **ISLAND OF JAMAICA,** Education Department, Negril, Jamaica
School Teacher
Instructed children ages 10–13 in Mathematics, English Language, Reading, Social Studies, and History.

VOLUNTEER POSITIONS

Appointed by government to local government administration; Member of Village Council, 5/98–12/01.

EDUCATION

UNIVERSITY OF LIMBURG, The Netherlands
General Certificate in Education
Courses in Cooperative Principles, General Accounting, and Financial Management.

REFERENCES FURNISHED UPON REQUEST.

CHRIS SMITH
178 Green Street
St. Paul, MN 55105
(612) 555-5555

CAREER OBJECTIVE To secure a Senior Level position as Payroll Manager.

EXPERIENCE

2005 to Present

JASMINE HEART, INC., St. Paul, MN
PAYROLL MANAGER
Management of multi-state payroll for 150 shops in North America and ten shops in Canada for well-known apparel and home décor company.

- Act as systems administrator for combined Human Resources and Payroll System (produce 5,500 W-2s and 200 T-4s).
- Act as liaison between Finance, Human Resources, corporation executives, and outside vendors.
- Monitor all payroll tax liabilities, filings, journal entries, accounts payable, and wire transfers for direct deposits.

Accomplishments

- Continued operations of payroll department in Newark, New Jersey, while simultaneously re-establishing department in new St. Paul headquarters.
- Coordinated entire department move to new headquarters and oversaw all human resources payroll-related issues.
- Identified programming errors in Human Resources Payroll System; directed and oversaw corrections.

2001 to 2005

ADAGIO LEASING, INC. Mankato, MN
PAYROLL MANAGER
Supervised department team of seven. Coordinated a $40 million payroll for 3,000 employees.

- Managed and controlled eighteen separate multi-state payrolls with eight weekly union- and non-union payrolls and nine biweekly payrolls.
- Acted as interface liaison for all payroll coordination and assimilation for executive level financial departments and Internal Human Resources.

Accomplishments

- Allocated six months to correct, organize, and implement eighteen separate payrolls.
- Converted existing manual-worksheet system to full online computerized system.
- Revised procedure for customer audits of Adagio records, thus increasing revenue.

EDUCATION STATE UNIVERSITY OF NEW YORK AT CORTLAND—B.S., EDUCATION 2003.

COMPUTERS ADP online payroll system, Excel, LAN, Windows, Mac, and PC

CHRIS SMITH
178 Green Street
Loretto, PA 15940
(814) 555-5555

PROFESSIONAL EXPERIENCE

DEVONSHIRE EQUIPMENT, INC., Loretto, PA 2005–Present

Staff Auditor

- Plan, identify, and test controls; present findings and recommend actions to management.
- Assist in the audits of New England; Northwest; New Jersey; Washington, D.C.; Southeast; and Great Lakes Districts, as well as U.S. Areas General Ledger Group.

BILL CHESTNUT & COMPANY, Greensburg, PA 2003–2005

Staff Auditor

- Participated in audits of $4 billion bank, major manufacturing company, mutual fund, software distribution company, and large, urban transportation company.

GROVE CITY COLLEGE, Grove City, PA 2002–2003

Tutor/Instructor, Introduction to Financial Accounting

- Formulated, administered, and graded exams.
- Tutored individuals in a self-paced course.

LONDON COMMERCIAL BANK, London, UK 2001

Intern

- Conducted over fifty onsite investigations of firms with assets up to $2 million; assessed "fair" valuation of assets.
- Assisted evaluation of $80 million brewery.
- Identified potential bank investments by analyzing financial statements and determining written reports to financial officer.

EDUCATION

Mercyhurst College, Erie, PA
M.B.A., 2005

Grove City College, Grove City, PA
B.A., Economics, 2003

EXPERIENCE

Available on request.

Chris Smith
178 Green Street
Stanford, CA 94305
(415) 555-5555

Experience: **Stanford Law School**

1/06–Present **Administrative/Research Assistant**
Provide support for legal, doctoral candidate. Coordinate manuscript production phases. Research changes in case law pertaining to "Mechanisms of the Supreme Court and Human Rights."

12/05–present **Administrative Assistant**
Edit Stanford Law School journal. Provide administrative support to Editor-in-Chief.

9/05–1/06 **Administrative/Research Assistant**
Utilize database, periodical governmental reports for country-specific research on legal, economic, and political issues. Manage manuscripts from production through publication.

Fall 2005 **Special Events Coordinator**
Organized Annual Stanford Law School Alumni Conference.

Education:

2005 **Michigan State University**
BA: International Politics and History.
Studied in Madrid, Spain, Fall 2005.

Skills: Computers—Microsoft Word.
Languages—Fluent in Spanish; working knowledge of French.

Interests: Travel, swimming, inline skating, surfing.

References: Available upon request.

CHRIS SMITH
178 Green Street
Erie, PA 16541
(814) 555-5555

Objective:
To provide efficient and effective administrative support.

Experience:

2004–Present *Redmond Computer, Inc., Erie, PA*
Administrative Assistant to the Chief Executive Officer
Coordinated and prioritized the daily activities of the Chairman of the Board. Performed the administrative functions in support of the CEO. Required an in-depth knowledge of the company, the industry, the financial community, the investors, the customers, the educational community, etc. Interfaced and assisted in the preparation for the Board of Directors meetings. Recorded and distributed the minutes of management meetings.

2001–2004 *Steppenwolf Associated, Pittsburgh, PA*
Administrative Assistant to the President and Chief Executive Officer
Prioritized the daily activities of the CEO. Set up and maintained a "tickler system." Composed and edited correspondence on behalf of the President.

1997–2001 *Jasmine Rain Inc., Beaver Falls, PA*
Administrative Assistant to the Chief Operating Officer
Interacted on behalf of the COO in sensitive customer and employee relationships. Recorded and distributed minutes of the Management Committee. Maintained and distributed monthly department reports.

Education:

2000–Present University of Pennsylvania Continuing Education Program: Management, Business, Computer Skills, and Marketing. French and Italian. Cutler College: Computer Literacy, Shorthand Refresher, and Medical Language.

Computers:

PC. Word Processing. Proficient in most PC software.

CHRIS SMITH
178 Green Street
Cohasset, MA 02025
(781) 555-5555

OBJECTIVE

A position as a File Clerk in a progressive organization.

SKILLS

Typing 70 wpm accurate
Spreadsheets
Word Processing

EMPLOYMENT

January 2006–Present
Brigham and Women's Hospital, Boston, MA
File Clerk. Type; maintain patient filing system.

September 2005–January 2006
ProTemps Employment, Quincy, MA
Clerk/Typist. Responsible for typing, filing, and general office duties.

May 2004–September 2005
Cohasset Cleaners, Cohasset, MA
File Clerk. Performed clerical duties; processed mail, daily reports, and correspondence; retrieved, updated, and corrected files.

EDUCATION

2004–2005
The Burdett School, Boston, MA
Courses in Typing, Filing, Word Processing, Computers (PC: Microsoft Word, Excel, and Access).

References available upon request.

CHRIS SMITH
178 Green Street
Providence, RI 02903
(401) 555-5555

CAREER OBJECTIVE

A technical/administrative support position in inventory analysis.

BACKGROUND SUMMARY

A dedicated, conscientious individual with a solid background in inventory control. Demonstrated ability to identify, analyze, and solve problems. Knowledgeable in all facets of inventory control. Experienced in data entry. Proven ability to work independently or with others. Work well in a fast-paced environment. Organized. Excellent attendance record.

CAREER HISTORY

SULLIVAN DATA SYSTEMS, Providence, RI
Inventory Control Analyst (2001–Present)
Inventory Control Clerk II (1997–2001)

- Analyzed, investigated, and resolved inventory discrepancies identified through section inputs and daily cycle count procedures.
- Served as a principal consultant on plant inventory systems.
- Assisted in reviewing and revising physical inventory procedures.
- Coordinated and assisted in conducting physical inventories.
- Created and maintained computerized filing systems. Generated reports from files.
- Assisted in liquidation of excess and used computer equipment.
- Trained new departmental personnel on data entry procedures using a CRT.
- Demonstrated knowledge of Microsoft Word, Excel, and other software applications.
- Created and maintained daily, monthly, and yearly reports for upper management.
- Conferred with management on a daily basis.
- Coordinated projects with coworkers at multiple plant sites.

EDUCATION

Roger Williams College, Bristol, RI, 1983–1987

CONTINUING EDUCATION

Sullivan Data System
ISO 9000 Awareness Training (International Standardization Organization)
QWG (Quality Work Group)

CHRIS SMITH
178 Green Street
Wayne, NE 68787
(402) 555-5555

OBJECTIVE

To contribute developed skills to a challenging Office Manager/Secretarial position with a progressive organization offering opportunities for growth and advancement.

SUMMARY OF QUALIFICATIONS

- Nearly twenty years office experience including knowledge of typing and word processing.
- Self-motivated; able to implement decisions and set effective priorities to achieve both immediate and long-term goals.
- Bilingual—Spanish and English.
- Excellent communication skills, both oral and written.
- Proven interpersonal skills, having dealt with a variety of professionals and clients.

PROFESSIONAL EXPERIENCE

2006–Present EMERSON ASSOCIATES, Wayne, NE

Office Manager

Arrange logistics for office expansion and relocation. Establish office procedures and systems. Actuate/implement filing systems, client billing system, and bookkeeping. Order supplies; maintain inventory. Handle word processing and receptionist responsibilities.

1997–2006 RUNNING FAWN HOUSING COMMISSION, Primrose, NE

Administrative Assistant

Functioned as principal support staff person to Executive Director, providing comprehensive administrative and clerical support services. Organized and managed work schedule. Coordinated communication flow with commissions, staff, Mayor's Office, public and private officials, and the general public. Prepared Director's scheduled events; organized and presented information in a useful format. Administered workflow.

1992–1997 COMMISSION ON JEWISH AFFAIRS, Table Rock, NE

Administrative Assistant

Management of office included: typing, recording minutes at commission meetings, handling incoming calls, assisting general public, and maintaining office supplies. Coordinated information release to press, legislators, and interested individuals.

1989–1992 PAULA SHELL HOSPITAL, Broken Bow, NE

Personnel Assistant

Provided administrative support to Personnel Recruiter and Personnel Representative. Screened applicants, checked references, and scheduled interviews. Prepared candidates for typing tests. Answered incoming calls. Typed all office materials and correspondence.

Receptionist

Utilized Word Processor. Greeted and screened applicants.

CHRIS SMITH
178 Green Street
Laramie, WY 82071
(307) 555-5555

QUALIFICATIONS:

- Over twenty-five years Secretarial/Administrative experience.
- Skills: Typing (65 wpm), Dictaphone, multilane phones/switchboard, ten key (110 kspm) digital DECmate computer, bookkeeping, credit checks, and statistical typing.
- Extensive business experience including accounting firms, legal firms, financial firms, insurance companies, transportation companies, medical environments, government agencies, and nonprofit groups.
- Offer common sense, ability to take initiative, quality orientation, and the ability to see a job through.
- Outstanding communications skills . . . Extremely hardworking and dedicated.

EMPLOYMENT: MARSTON CONVENT, Laramie, WY, 2003–Present
Receptionist
Answer phone, greet visitors, and provide information, tours, and literature. Record and monitor thank-you notes for all received donations. Perform light typing, filing, and word processing.

WYOMING PUBLIC TELEVISION, Laramie, WY, 2002–2003
Telemarketer
Solicited donations. Monitored the ordering of informative pamphlets, placards, buttons, T-shirts, etc.

RINALDO RANCH, Laramie, WY, 1998–2003
Secretary
Provided word processing, customer relations, and some accounts payable processing. Implemented new system for check processing; increased prompt payment of client bills.

WOMANPOWER INC., Laramie, WY, 1990–1998
Secretary
Acted as liaison between public and CEO.

STATE HEALTH COALITION, Laramie, WY, 1980–1990
Statistical Typist
Prepared health record documentation of infectious disease patients at State hospital. Managed training of new hires.

EDUCATION: TRAINING, INC., Boston, MA, 1980
An office careers training program in bookkeeping, typing, reception, word processing, and office procedures.

ST. JOSEPH'S ACADEMY, Portland, ME
High School Diploma

CHRIS SMITH
178 Green Street
Melrose, CT 06049
(203) 555-5555

OBJECTIVE

To apply skills attained through experience and education to an entry-level position in the field of travel.

STRENGTHS

- Self-motivated and goal-oriented.
- Proven abilities in organization and communication.
- Perform well in high-stress atmospheres.
- Highly developed interpersonal skills, having worked cooperatively with a variety of professionals.
- Experienced traveler.

EDUCATION

Assertiveness Training Courses, The Burke Program, 2006

Computer Programming Workshop
Certified, 2007

University of Bridgeport, Bridgeport, CT
B.A., Public Relations, 2005

WORK EXPERIENCE

TICKET AGENT, Davis Harwin Tours, Ivoryton, CT — 2006–Present
Resolved all customer needs. Arranged travel schedules. Handled incoming cash.

MACHINE OPERATOR, Carlisle Sand Inc., Melrose, CT — 2004–2006
Duties include sorting and metering mail.

CASUAL DISTRIBUTION CLERK, U.S. Post Office, Hartford, CT — 2002–2004
Set up mailroom and appropriate forwarding of packages and mail.

MENTAL HEALTH COUNSELOR, Mystic, CT — 1999–2002
Counseled, supervised, and evaluated clients. Arranges special events for youths.

RECEPTIONIST, Warbell Realty, Hartford, CT — 1998–1999
Serviced clients. Arranged appointments. Handled incoming calls. Dealt with general office functions.

REFERENCES

Available on request.

CHRIS SMITH
178 Green Street
Waukesha, WI 53186
(414) 555-5555

EDUCATION

University of Massachusetts, Amherst, MA
Bachelor of Arts in English, 2005

College of Humanities and Fine Arts, Boston, MA, 2000–2001

TELEVISION PRODUCTION

2004 to 2008 WTOR EDUCATIONAL FOUNDATION, Worcester, MA

Producer

Produced:

Three contract series (twenty half-hour programs for each) for U.S. Marines and Stanford University Commission on Extension Services: "Ideologies in World Affairs," "Computer Science I," and "Computer Science II."

"Fighting Mad"—series of two-hour-long group therapy sessions conducted by Dr. Paula Hershey, Hamline University.

"The 21-Inch Classroom"—History, Geology Pilot

"Bob Bersen Reviews"

Writer/produced:

Half-hour promotional videotape selling ETV for the University of Massachusetts, Amherst.
Half-hour promotional videotape selling ITV for the 21-inch Classroom.

REFERENCES

Available upon request.

CHRIS SMITH
178 Green Street
Swannanoa, NC 28778
(704) 555-5555

EDUCATION

WAKE FOREST UNIVERSITY, Winston, NC
Master of Arts, Print Journalism, May 1999

SHEFFIELD UNIVERSITY, Sheffield, UK
History Degree, June 1998
Literature Degree, June 1997

PRINCETON UNIVERSITY, Princeton, NJ
Summer Program in Anthropology, 1996

EXPERIENCE

2006–Present LE RECORD DU JOUR
French Daily Newspaper

Responsible for writing stories and features on local affairs for the Cultural and the National Sections. Assignments completed on deadline. Travel extensively throughout France and topical point of interest stories. Have been awarded six GLOBE journalism awards for international reporting. Broke several high-profile stories.

1999–2005 TOKYO RECORD
Japanese Daily Newspaper—English Edition (second largest in country).

Responsible for writing stories and features on social and political issues throughout the country.

SKILLS

Microsoft Word, Excel
35mm Photography
½-inch Videotape
Super 8 Movies
Fluent in French, English, and Spanish

PERSONAL DATA

Writing fiction and poetry (novel is pending publication). Traveled extensively throughout the world.

Letters of reference and writing samples will be furnished upon request.

CHRIS SMITH
178 Green Street
Birmingham, AL 35244
(205) 555-5555

EXPERIENCE

BANKS AND SON, INC., Birmingham, AL
Senior Editor, Reference (10/06–Present)
Responsible for the evaluation and acquisition of general trade reference titles. Assessed the profitability of projects and negotiated contracts.
Involved in all aspects of publishing process from development and editing to productions, publicity, and marketing.
In-house editor for institutional authors such as the American Library Association and the *Vintage Motorcycles* newsletter.

ROMANCE NOVEL-OF-THE-MONTH CLUB, INC., Kinsey, AL
Associate Director (5/04–10/06)
Evaluated fiction and nonfiction manuscripts.
Managed all club titles in terms of pricing and inventory, and initial, backlist, and premium uses.
Responsible for Club sales budgeting and estimating.
Supervised ten employees.

Managing Editor (1/99–5/04)
Deputy Editorial Director of the British division.
Evaluated manuscripts.
Scheduled new and backlist titles in the RNMC News and in Club advertising.
Supervised two employees.

ILL-FATED KISSES, Selma, AL
Editorial Director (1/95–1/99)
Supervised the design and production of titles for two continuity programs.
Responsible for identifying, developing, and/or acquiring poetry and artwork.

EDUCATION

New York University, New York, NY, 1999.
Completed twelve credits in the Masters in Publishing Program.
Courses included Publishing Law, Finance, and Subsidiary Rights.

Pace University, New York, NY, 1998.
B.S. degree, Magazine Journalism.
B.A. degree, English Literature.

CHRIS SMITH
178 Green Street
Pullman, WA 99164
(509) 555-5555

OBJECTIVE:

Publicist position at ABC Corporation.

EXPERIENCE:

CNBS TELEVISION, *Confrontations*, Pullman, WA 2006–Present
Production Assistant
Book main guests and panelists. Generate and research story ideas. Conduct video research. Edit teases for show. Organize all production details for studio tapings. Troubleshoot equipment malfunctions. Monitor lighting and TelePrompTer. Coordinate publicity ads in local newspapers.

BARSTOW COMPANY, Seattle, WA 2004–2006
Publicity Assistant
Publicized new books and authors. Assisted in booking media tours (TV, radio, and print). Wrote and designed press releases. Fulfilled review copy requests. Conducted galley mailings and general office work.

WNBN-TV, Tacoma, WA 2003–2004
Production Intern
Assisted producers of a live, daily talk show. Researched and generated story ideas. Pre-interviewed possible guests. Logged tapes. Went out on shoots and wrote promotional announcements. Produced five of my own segments for the show.

THE BENEDICT COUNCIL, UNIVERSITY OF WASHINGTON, Seattle, WA 2002–2003
Promotional Assistant
Implemented promotional campaign for concerts on campus. Wrote and designed promotional advertisements. Initiated student involvement with program.

THE CHERRY HAIKU, INC., Seattle, WA 2001–2002
Art Assistant
Responsible for paste-ups/mechanicals. Operated Photostat camera; coordinated logistics for photo shoots. Participated in "brainstorming" sessions with creative team.

EDUCATION:

UNIVERSITY OF WASHINGTON, Seattle, WA
B.A. Cum Laude, May 2003
Major: Communication
Minor: English

CHRIS SMITH
178 Green Street
New Haven, CT 06511
(203) 555-5555

STRENGTHS AND QUALIFICATIONS

- High levels of enthusiasm and commitment to a successful sales, marketing, or communications career.
- Strong leadership qualities; able to schedule priorities and perform/delegate accordingly to effectively accomplish tasks at hand.
- Working knowledge of both written and verbal Japanese and French.
- Broad perspective of Japanese people, culture, and customs, as well as Japanese-American diplomatic relations.
- Computer literate in most popular software, including Microsoft Word, Excel, Quark, and Computer-Aided Design (CAD).

JAPANESE-AMERICAN RELATIONS

Served as liaison between Japanese diplomats and the Japanese-American Relations Group and with the Japanese press during Prime Minister's stay.

Translated correspondence and filed inquiries from the Japanese population in the Boston business community.

Organized travel itineraries for Japanese officials visiting the New England area.

SALES/MARKETING/ENTREPRENEURIAL SKILLS

Founded International Resumes, a company designed for the creation of English and Japanese resumes, and ran it from 2003–2005.

Designed and circulated posters, banners, and invitations in order to introduce the Japanese community to New England.

EDUCATION

Yale University, New Haven, CT
M.A., East Asian Studies, expected to be received June 2007.

Harvard University, New Haven, CT
B.A., Psychology and Japanese Studies, May 2003.

EMPLOYMENT HISTORY

2006–Present	**Technical Writer/Junior Programmer**	Universal Programs, Inc., New Haven, CT
2004–2005	**Assistant to the Japanese Ambassador**	Japanese Embassy, Washington, D.C.
Summers 2002–2003	**Sales Representative**	Carlisle's Inc., West Hartford, CT
1999–2000	**Marketing Representative**	A.M. Keegan & Company, Easton, MA

CHRIS SMITH
178 Green Street
Indianapolis, IN 46205
(317) 555-5555

SUMMARY OF QUALIFICATIONS

- Experienced in the general planning and detailed execution of projects.
- Have written numerous in-house company documents including program proposals, five-year plans, research reports, and executive correspondence.
- Participated in marketing teams which conceived, wrote, and produced direct mail campaigns and support materials for a sales force.
- Flexible in assuming a leadership role, collaborating with colleagues, or supporting a department head or executive.
- Have written and edited over 200 audio-visual scripts and 100 related booklets for science, mathematics, and social studies education.

PROFESSIONAL EXPERIENCE

Writing/ Editing

Writer/Editor
FREELANCE EMPLOYMENT, 2005–Present, Indiana State.
For Business: Wrote numerous planning, policy, and procedural documents; produced in-depth reports which required extensive research and analysis; wrote letters and memos for executive signature.

For Science Education: Wrote clear, accurate audio-visual programs for students; developed useful, informative support materials for educators.

Management/ Publishing

The Ruby Shoes Press, Terra Haute, IN
Editorial and Development Manager 1994–2005

- Began as freelance writer and progressed to the management of company's audio-visual editorial and production.
- Refined and administered annual budget of $300,000 for development of new programs.
- Recruited and supervised ten in-house editors and an average of thirty freelance writers, artists, and producers.
- Conceived, scheduled, and produced over 120 audio-visual programs and an equal number of teaching guides.
- Collaborated on marketing plans for all audio-visual products. Delivered presentations of new products to sales force.
- Developed award-winning programs that ranked among the company's bestsellers.

EDUCATION

NEW YORK UNIVERSITY, New York, NY
Master's degree in English, 1993

- Teaching Fellowship, 1992–1993

COLUMBIA UNIVERSITY, New York, NY
Bachelor of Arts degree in English, 1989

- Minors in Biology and Chemistry.

COMPUTERS

Windows, Microsoft Word, Quark, and InDesign.

CHRIS SMITH
178 Green Street
Huntington, WV 25701
(304) 555-5555

OBJECTIVE

To contribute relevant experience and educational background to the position of **Computer Programmer/Software Engineer.**

SUMMARY OF QUALIFICATIONS

- Proficient in the design and implementation of program enhancements, including an online message system, database repair/troubleshooting utilities, and a release system to update clients on the current version of software.
- Demonstrated ability in the provision of client support services.

EXPERIENCE

6/2004 to Present **Senior Programmer—Patient Scheduling System**
TESSERACT CORPORATION Huntington, WV
A privately owned software company specializing in the needs of the health care industry.

- Design and implementation of new system enhancements.
- Sole development of new generator product. Designed file structure and conducted actual coding based on functional specification requirements.

3/2003 to 6/2004 **Programmer/Analyst**

- Installed software for new clients and provided onsite support.
- Developed online message system for members of the programming group.
- Instituted utilities that aided in the detection and evaluation of client bugs and made repairs to the client database.
- Supported existing clients and resolved critical issues/problems in a timely fashion.

EDUCATION

MARSHALL UNIVERSITY, 2005 to Present Huntington, WV
Enrolled in Graduate Mathematics program (Part time)

WEST VIRGINIA UNIVERSITY, 2000 to 2004 Morgantown, WV
Bachelor of Science degree: Computer Science Engineering

COMPUTERS

Programming Languages: Java, PHP, ASP.NET, C++, Visual Basic.NET, CGI/Perl, HTML, XML.
Databases: SQL Server, Oracle, Access
Hardware: PC, Mac, UNIX

REFERENCES FURNISHED UPON REQUEST

CHRIS SMITH
178 Green Street
Albuquerque, NM 87104
(505) 555-5555

CAREER SUMMARY

An experienced professional with expertise in the design and development of multi-user database management systems running on a Local Area Network. Skilled in LAN management and user training.

BUSINESS EXPERIENCE

JEFFERSON MANUFACTURING, CORP., Albuquerque, NM — 2003 to Present

Documentation Development Coordinator

Analyze, develop, and maintain application software for engineering LAN. Provide training and user support for all applications to LAN users. Maintain departmental PC workstations including software installation and upgrades.

- Reduced data entry errors and process time by developing a program which allowed program managers to submit model number information online.
- Replaced time-consuming daily review board meetings by developing a program which allowed engineers to review and approve model and component changes online.
- Developed an online program which reduced process time, standardized part usage, and which allowed engineers to build part lists for new products and components.

Computer Systems Analyst — 1999 to 2003

Responsibilities included database management systems analysis and design, workstation maintenance and repair, and LAN management.

- Reduced process time and purchasing errors by developing an online program, which allowed the purchasing department to track the status of all purchasing invoices.
- Developed a purchase order entry program for the purchasing department, which improved data entry speed and reduced the number of data entry errors.

LAFAYETTE, INC., Albuquerque, NM — 1994 to 1999

Engineering Technician III

Prototyped and tested new PC products, drawing schematics, and expediting parts for these new PC products. Designed and coded multi-user database management software for engineering use.

- Expedited the parts for twenty-five or more telecommunications terminal prototypes. Built, troubleshot, and transferred those prototypes to various departments for testing.

EDUCATION

Associate's Electronics Engineering Technology, University of Notre Dame, 1994

Continuing education training courses include, Advanced Digital Electronics, C Language Hands-On Workshop, Visual BASIC Programming, and Structured Analysis and Design Methods.

COMPUTER EXPERIENCE

PC Systems and Architecture, Tape Backup Systems, Local Area Networks, MS Windows, Excel, Access, Visual BASIC, Oracle, and SQL Language.

CHRIS SMITH
178 Green Street
Sunset, SC 29685
(803) 555-5555

OBJECTIVE

A position as a computer operations analyst.

SUMMARY OF QUALIFICATIONS

- More than eighteen years computer experience.
- Dedicated professional; set effective priorities to achieve immediate and long-term goals.
- Self-motivated; able to implement decisions to ensure smooth workflow.

EXPERIENCE

LARCHMONT MUTUAL, Sunset, SC
Operations Analyst, 2006 to Present
Translate information requirements into logical, economical, and practical system designs for large systems; cooperate with users and Senior Operations Analyst. Evaluate corporate requirements; investigate alternatives to identify/recommend best design. Prepare flowcharts; synthesize gathered information and present in logical/manageable components. Write detailed specifications; coordinate system testing; develop practical solutions to problems. Prepare associated documentation, user manuals, and instructions for complete operation of system. Assist junior personnel.

Support Technician, 2000 to 2006
Maintained/monitored Financial Information Services Equipment: PC system and printers.

Senior Quality Reviewer, 1993 to 2000
Scrutinized percentage of claims processed to ensure correct coding of claims; reported statistical errors.

Data Entry Clerk, 1991 to 1993
Processed Data Entry; required knowledge of Medicare operational guidelines and Medical Terminology.

CHRIS SMITH
178 Green Street
Olympia, WA 98505
(208) 555-5555

Employment Experience:

Pisces Data Systems, Inc.—July 2000 to Present.
Olympia, WA

Pre-Sales Technical Support:

Support the Eastern Area sales staff, which averages about five reps. Work closely with the sales reps to formulate and implement sales strategies. Working with prospects to understand business problems and propose appropriate technical solutions. Write and deliver technical product presentations. Develop and deliver customer product demos. Design proposed system configuration and write proposals.

Key Achievements:

Managed large data migration effort. Designed and implemented an open-systems migration plan. This effort included: system installation and configuration, development of file migration utilities, conversion of in-house code, conversion of over 50,000 files, and developing and delivering system-administrator and end-user training.

Education:

Washington State University, Pullman, WA
B.S. in Management Information Systems, 2000

Programming Languages:

Perl, C++, Visual Basic

Operating Systems:

UNIX, Linux, Windows NT, Windows Server 2000, Windows Server 2003

Hardware Experience:

PC servers and workstations
Sun workstations
Macintosh

Professional Awards:

MissionCritical Professionals Excellence Award, 2003
MissionCritical Sales Analyst of the Month, 2005

CHRIS SMITH
178 Green Street
Appleton, WI 54912
(414) 555-5555

SUMMARY OF ACCOMPLISHMENTS

- Set up the interfacing of mini computer to PC in order to archive daily receipts onto optical disks.
- Created a device for a new disk system, and developed a new operating system to handle the new driver.
- Qualified all of Devlin software onto a new computer system.
- Built a new method of handling orders into the system.
- Rewrote accounts receivable program system to handle long-term notes.
- Suggested an improvement in board revectoring at Price Computer, which was later implemented.

EMPLOYMENT HIGHLIGHTS

2004–Present **Systems Analyst** DEVLIN INDUSTRIES, Appleton, WI
Create or change programs; generate new reports and new ways of retrieving information in and out of the computer; responsible for making system more efficient.

2003 **Typesetting Operator** OSHKOSH NEWS, Oshkosh, WI
Interim position with tasks that covered production of all type for several area newspapers.

2000–2003 **Production Assistant** PRICE COMPUTER, Madison, WI
Worked in Production Department on board repair, board revectoring, equipment assembly, and basic production on electronic manufacturing.

PROFESSIONAL AFFILIATIONS

MADISON COMPUTER SOCIETY, ASSOCIATION OF COMPUTING MACHINERY

EDUCATION

MILWAUKEE SCHOOL OF ENGINEERING, Milwaukee, WI. Two Bachelor of Science degrees: Computer Science/Systems and Applied Physical/Astronomy. Graduated, January 2000.

COMPUTER LITERACY

Hardware: PC, Mac, Unix, E-mail Servers, Data Servers and Storage.
Language: C++, Perl, Visual Basic, Java.
Systems: MS Windows, Mac OS, Linux, UNIX.

Chris Smith
178 Green Street
Chapel Hill, NC 27514
(919) 555-5555
csmith@e-mail.com

EXPERIENCE:

6/06–Present UNIVERSITY OF NORTH CAROLINA, Chapel Hill, NC
Archivist
- Handle daily operations of College Archives, including: cataloging, photo indexing, and reference services.
- Manage school records.
- Work with alumni and local community to expand collection.
- Organize annual alumni weekend events and displays.

9/04–5/06 **Technical Services Librarian**
- Maintained and updated catalog.
- Oversaw retrospective conversion of bibliographic data in preparation for implementation of online catalog.

9/02–8/04 MUSEUM OF SOUTHERN HISTORY, Chapel Hill, NC
Library Assistant
- Transferred newspaper clippings to microfilm.
- Cataloged Civil War era monograph collection.

EDUCATION:

University of North Carolina, Chapel Hill, NC
Master of Science in Library Science, 2004

Wingate College, Wingate, NC
Bachelor of Arts in English, 2000

MEMBERSHIPS:

Southern Personal Computer Users Group
- Program Committee, 2003–2005
- Board of Directors, 2005–Present

ACCOMPLISHMENTS:

Received “Alumni Appreciation Award” for organizing 2008 reunion.

CHRIS SMITH
178 Green Street
Delaware City, DE 19706
(302) 555-5555
csmith@e-mail.com

EDUCATION:

University of Delaware, Newark, DE
Bachelor of Arts, 2008
Major: Early Childhood Education; GPA in Major: 3.5/4.0

CERTIFICATION:

Delaware State K-5

TEACHING EXPERIENCE:

Head Teacher: City Child Care Corporation, Delaware City, DE
September 2006–Present
Taught educational and recreational activities for twenty children, ages five to ten years, in a preschool/play care setting. Planned and executed age-appropriate activities to promote social, cognitive, and physical skills. Developed daily lesson plans. Observed and assessed each child's development. Conducted parent/teacher orientations and meetings. Organized and administered various school projects.

Teacher: Little People Preschool and Day Care, New Castle, DE
June 2005–August 2006
Taught educational and recreational activities for children, ages three to seven years, in a preschool/day care setting. Planned, prepared, and executed two week units based on themes to develop social, cognitive, and physical skills. Lessons and activities were prepared in Mathematics, Language Arts, Science, and Social Studies. Observed and assessed each child's development and followed up with parent/teacher discussions.

Student Teacher: Rolling Elementary School, Newark, DE
January–May 2005
Taught and assisted a kindergarten teacher in a self-contained classroom of twenty-eight students. Planned and instructed lessons and activities in Mathematics, Science, and Social Studies.

Teacher's Aide: YMCA Day Care Center, Wilmington, DE
June–August 2004

Teaching Intern: Freud Laboratory School, Newark, DE
January–May 2003

Teaching Intern: Green Meadow Elementary School, Newark, DE
January–May 2002

Teaching Intern: Delaware State College Day Care Centers, Dover, DE
October–December 2001

CHRIS SMITH
178 Green Street
Echo, Oregon 97826
(503) 555-5555
csmith@e-mail.com

OBJECTIVE

A teaching position with an established university seeking the services of a highly commended educator, with total capacity in the teaching and translation of French.

TEACHING EXPERIENCE

Teacher of French Literature and Language: 2006–Present
Smith College, Northampton, MA

Professor of French Language: 2005–2006
Faculty of Literature and Human Science, University of Vermont, Burlington, VT
- Continually active in all aspects of the education process and administration.

Head of French Language Department: 2000–2005
College of Translation, Pratt University, Brooklyn, NY
- Teaching, Translation, French and Persian Literature, Art, History.
- Full curriculum—all aspects of administration—public service.

Professor of French and Persian Language and Literature: 1995–2000
College of Translation, New York University, New York, NY
- Teaching, Translation, French and Persian Literature, Art, History.
- Full academic schedule—research, writing, public service.

Educational Advisor: 1993–1995
Stoughton High School, Stoughton, MA
- Full academic schedule—active in school affairs.

EDUCATION

Ph.D., Harvard University, Cambridge, MA: 1990
- French Literature

M.A. *(Highest Honors),* Hood College, Frederick, MD: 1988
- French Literature

B.A. *(Highest Honors),* University of Illinois at Chicago: 1986
- French Literature

Chris Smith
178 Green Street
Norwood, MA 02062
(781) 555-5555
csmith@e-mail.com

EDUCATION:
Simmons College, Boston, MA
M.S., Library Science, Graduated Cum Laude 2004.

Northeastern University, Boston, MA
B.S., Computer Science, Graduated 1998.

AREAS OF EFFECTIVENESS
- Analysis
- Research
- Numerical Ability
- Troubleshooting Skills

EXPERIENCE
BOSTON PUBLIC LIBRARY, Boston, MA 2003–Present
Systems Coordinator
- Ensure all PCs are up and running on a 24-hour basis.
- Troubleshoot, run codes, keep systems operating smoothly.
- Train librarians and library staff on use of systems.
- Provide instant access to newsprint publications on microfiche; maintain terminals.
- Assist librarians to develop materials to aid the public.

THOMAS CRANE LIBRARY, Quincy, MA 2000–2003
Computer Assistant
- Assisted Systems Coordinator in maintaining all PCs and Mac computers.
- Ensured smooth running of all UNIX systems.
- Assisted librarians and public in the use of PCs and Mac computers.

PROFESSIONAL AFFILIATIONS
- Library Technicians of Boston.

CHRIS SMITH
178 Green Street
Williamsburg, VA 23185
(804) 555-5555
csmith@e-mail.com

OBJECTIVE

A challenging HIGH SCHOOL ADMINISTRATIVE position.

PROFILE

- Offer Master's Degrees in School Administration and Biology/Immunology enhanced by fifteen years of teaching and student guidance experience combined with a ten-year corporate Marketing and Management background.
- Facilitator of the Discipline Committee. Initiated, organized, and orchestrated numerous class trips and education expeditions with durations of up to two weeks.
- Self-started with strong planning, controlling, organizing, and leadership skills. Consistently meets deadlines and objectives; works well under pressure.
- Articulate and effective communicator with proven ability to work with diverse populations of students at a variety of academic levels. Consistently maintain excellent relations with students, parents, faculty, and administration. Works well as part of a team or independently.
- Task record for identifying complex administrative problems; resourceful in developing and implementing creative solutions resulting in increased productivity with enhanced sensitivity to costs and efficiency.

EDUCATION

MASTER OF SCIENCE IN SCHOOL ADMINISTRATION, 2006
College of William and Mary—Williamsburg, VA

MASTER OF SCIENCE IN BIOLOGY/IMMUNOLOGY, 2000
James Madison University—Harrisonburg, VA

MASTER OF SCIENCE IN SCIENCE EDUCATION/ENVIRONMENTAL SCIENCES, 1996

BACHELOR OF SCIENCE IN BIOLOGY, 1980
Drew University—Madison, New Jersey

(continued)

PROFESSIONAL EXPERIENCE (continued)

HEAD TEACHER 1998–Present
The Adams School Williamsburg, VA
Responsible for planning, developing, preparing, and implementing an effective science curriculum, management, and student assessment. Devise and prepare daily lesson plans, materials, teaching aids, and demonstrations to effectively convey critical concepts and factual knowledge in Biology, Physical Science, Physics, Earth Science, and Oceanography. Develop engaging daily classroom presentations; assign work projects; review and discuss lesson objectives and class performance. Stimulate and motivate students by generating excitement and enthusiasm; encourage exploration of new concepts, joy in learning, and pride in performance. Provide clear explanations, creative approaches, and extra tutoring as required. Compose and administer exams and grade student performance. Advise and counsel individual students in academic areas and on aspects of student life. Communicate with parents on their child's progress, fostering excellent professional relations. Interact positively with faculty members and administrators. Provide educational leadership through serving on committees and executing special projects to further high educational standards.

HIGH SCHOOL TEACHER 1997–1998
West Harris High School Harrisburg, VA
- Presented Biology and Physical Science classes at the high school level.

MIDDLE SCHOOL TEACHER 1996–1997
Reede Middle School Harrisburg, VA
- Taught an Earth Science curriculum to eighth grade students.

TEACHER 1991–1993
Melbourne Academy Madison, NJ
- Instructed students in Biology, Marine Biology/Ecology.

LICENSES AND CERTIFICATIONS

VIRGINIA * NEW JERSEY PERMANENT CERTIFICATION IN BIOLOGY, CHEMISTRY, EARTH SCIENCE, AND PHYSICAL SCIENCE.

CHRIS SMITH
178 Green Street
Rochester, NY 14623
(716) 555-5555
csmith@e-mail.com

WORK EXPERIENCE:

SANFORD CORPORATION, Rochester, NY 1998-Present

Chemical Process Modeling Engineer

Carbon Dioxide Process Simulator

- Applied knowledge of thermodynamics; reactor design; phase separation; fluid compression and expansion; process control to complete simulation from preliminary coding.
- Wrote operations manual.

Computer Models for Hydraulic Devices

- Researched, designed, coded, and tested detailed models for submersible centrifugal and hydraulic pumps.

Drilling Control Simulators

- Revised and developed computer models for oil well simulation.
- Utilized knowledge of fluid mechanics, mathematics, and computer programming.
- Wrote operations manuals.

SKILLS:

- Extensive research experience; quantitative and qualitative analysis of dynamic systems, inorganic chemistry.

EDUCATION:

Bachelor of Science in Chemical Engineering, May 1997
Rochester Institute of Technology, Rochester, NY
Honors: Magna cum laude graduate, member of the Engineering Honor Society of America.

MEMBERSHIP:

American Society of Chemical Engineers. Student Chapter Vice President, 2007-Present

PERSONAL:

Willing to relocate.

CHRIS SMITH
178 Green Street
New London, NH 03257
(603) 555-5555
csmith@e-mail.com

PROFESSIONAL OBJECTIVE

A leadership position supporting product development or engineering utilizing knowledge of electrical, electronic, and mechanical design.

BACKGROUND SUMMARY

Progressive engineering management experience from project manager, group leader, section manager, to engineering manager over four sections and forty people. Responsible for consumer product development from inception to discontinuance covering mechanical, electromechanical, and electrical design.

PROFESSIONAL EXPERIENCE

The C. Marlowe Company, New London, NH
Engineering Manager 2001–Present

- Created International Technical Engineering responsible for technical coordination and support to multiple global manufacturing sites.
- Created Alpha Test Engineering responsible for creating preproduction engineering prototypes for global marketing use. Planned, hired, and trained the staff, provided for procurement, logistics, facilities, and capital equipment.
- Managed $0.6 million in expense budget +$2–9 million in preproduction engineering prototypes per year. Provided definition input to all proposed products as well as resource allocation, scheduling, planning, control, problem reporting, and solving support.
- Developed major portions of the Quality documentation system for Engineering to comply with ISO 9000.
- Participated in Engineering Documentation Control conversion from manufacturing to stock, from assemble to order. The first product under this system had 700,000 planned configurations.

The Kipling Company, Wolfeboro, NH
Product Design Engineer 1996–2001

- Oversaw design engineering for over 200 consumer and PC products, both in assembled form and in kit form.
- Prepared and monitored expense and capital budgets.
- Prepared cost feasibility studies, analysis of design, and product financing.
- Monitored product safety and regulatory compliance and product cost and development schedule.
- Responsible for adding $9 million of new product revenue out of $90 million total business.

EDUCATION

- New Jersey Institute of Technology, Newark, NJ
  Bachelor of Science, Electrical Engineering, 1995

CHRIS SMITH
178 Green Street
Broomfield, CO 80021
(303) 555-5555
csmith@e-mail.com

OBJECTIVE: A challenging position in facilities engineering, project engineering, or engineering management.

EXPERIENCE: Facilities Engineer—Breckenridge Company, Broomfield, CO (2001–Present)

Supervise all phases of maintenance and engineering for this specialty steel company, which employs 800, and covers a 60-acre facility.

- Direct multi-craft maintenance, utilities, engineering, and construction departments.
- Supervise staff of 100 people and ten supervisors in all phases of maintenance and engineering.
- Plan and install maintenance program and directing all improvement and/or new construction projects starting from studies for justification to project start-up.
- Represented the company as general contractor on project and saved approximately $4 million of the original estimates submitted by outside contractors.
- Direct technicians and supervisor on the design, construction, and maintenance of equipment and machinery.
- Established standards and policies for testing, inspection, and maintenance of equipment in accordance with engineering principles and safety regulations.
- Prepared bid sheets and contracts for construction facilities and position.
- Full responsibilities for a budget of approximately $10 million annually.
- Extensive involvement in labor relations with various trades.

Project Engineer—Gibraltar Corporation, Loveland, CO (1997–2001)

- Planned and implemented modernization program including the installation of bloom, billet, bar, rod, and strip mills as well as the required soaking pits and reheating furnaces.
- Directed a multi-craft maintenance force of approximately 250 craftsmen and supervisors.
- Planned and installed a maintenance program which reduced equipment down-time and increased C/P/T savings substantially.

ASSOCIATIONS: Member of American Iron and Steel Engineers Association.

EDUCATION: University of Colorado at Boulder, Boulder, CO
B.S., Mechanical Engineering, 1997.

CHRIS SMITH
178 Green Street
Troy, NY 12180
(518) 555-5555
csmith@e-mail.com

Experience

MDK Incorporated, Troy, NY
Product Engineer (12/06–Present)
Engineer for cable products designed for high-speed applications. Responsibilities include product extension, electrical analysis, release of proposals and products, approval of tools and dies, resolving manufacturing problems, quality assurance, and interacting with customers.

Engineering Analyst (2/05–11/06)
Corporate staff member responsible for electrical engineering computer software packages used internationally. Provided consulting, support, and training of electrical analysis software used to design interconnects. Developed software interface. Evaluated new software packages. Administered UNIX environment and specified optimal configurations for engineering packages.

Development Engineer (9/03–2/05)
Designed computer board-to-board connection specializing in the electrical characterization of the interface. Provided computer modeling to determine capacitance, inductance, impedance, effective dielectric, propagation delay, and crosstalk for multiple conductors. Performed laboratory testing of samples using oscilloscope, TDR, and spectrum analyzer. Used CAD software to represent 3D models of connector proposals and construct mechanical layout.

Engineer Trainee (Summer, 2003)
Worked with development engineering group. Designed and performed procedure to test filtered connector's response to load conditions.

Computer Experience

Operating Systems: UNIX, Linux, Windows
Languages: C++, Java.
Software: Many PC- and Mac-based applications.

Education

Master of Science in Engineering anticipated, August 2007
Rensselaer Polytechnic Institute, Troy, NY
Currently pursuing an advanced degree in computer and electrical engineering.

Bachelor of Science in Electrical Engineering December 2002
Hofstra University, Hempstead, NY

Associate of Arts in Engineering May 1999
Elmira College, Elmira, NY

CHRIS SMITH
178 Green Street
Mantua, NJ 08051
(609) 555-5555
csmith@e-mail.com

OBJECTIVE: To utilize skill in administration, management, and personnel toward further responsibilities in professional administration.

SUMMARY OF QUALIFICATIONS:

- Experience with financial administration of retail sales and service operations.
- Management of high-volume retail operations. Includes supervision of merchandising, asset management, customer service, and maintenance. Effect creative marketing programs and maintain compliance with corporate procedure.
- Skill in direction and development of individual and team personnel. Responsible for training, schedule, and motivation of staff personnel.

EXPERIENCE:

Assistant Store Manager **1998 to Present**
LORAX SUPERMARKETS Woodbury, NJ

- Responsible for control and administration of financial transactions in retail environment. Includes control of cash flow and expenses, internal audit and protection of corporate assets, and establishment of seasonal budgets.
- Manage schedule and procedure of over 175 personnel. Directly supervise all customer services, lottery sales, display merchandising, maintenance, sanitation, and employee training.
- Received awards for best cash variance and payroll percentage. Set goals and adjust departmental budgets by sales projections. Perform internal audits, control expenses, and protect assets.
- Worked part time 1998–2002. Promoted to Assistant Manager in 2005.

COMPUTERS:

Microsoft Word, FileMaker, Excel

EDUCATION:

Bachelor of Science in Business Management **2002**
STOCKTON STATE COLLEGE Pomona, NJ

VOLUNTEER:

Reader Program at Children's Hospital, Red Cross Blood Donor, Youth Tutor League.

REFERENCES:

Available upon request.

CHRIS SMITH
178 Green Street
Helena, MT 59601
(406) 555-5555
csmith@e-mail.com

OBJECTIVE

A senior administrative position which would take advantage of twenty years of varied, in-depth background.

CAREER SUMMARY

Executive primarily skilled in banking operations and data processing systems. Strong background in retail banking, marketing, planning, budgeting, and P & L management. Demonstrated record of developing and implementing solutions to multidimensional complex operational problems.

EMPLOYMENT

Calliope Savings Bank, Helena, MT **2006–Present**
PRESIDENT/CEO
Originally hired as Executive Vice President and subsequently elected President/CEO in June of 2007.
Company provides check processing, consulting, and other services to forty banks. Developed and conducted corporate planning strategy meetings. In addition to having overall responsibility for operations, also responsible for financial management and P & L for the company, which presently employs sixty-five people and processes 30 million checks per year. Company turned profit within two years of start up. Developed data processing delivery system analysis; recommendations were adopted by ten banks.

The Prudent Savings Institution, Billings, VT
VICE PRESIDENT—HEAD OF BANKING DIVISION **2004–2006**
Under the direction of Chairman of the Board, responsible for administrating, planning, and directing retail banking activities. Conferred with senior management and recommended programs to achieve bank's objectives.

VICE PRESIDENT—MARKETING **2002–2004**
Administered and directed marketing activities of the bank. Organized and planned actions impacting on various publics supporting banks' markets. Worked with the divisions and outside agencies to develop plans which supported division's objectives. Supervised the following; liaison with advertising and public relations firms; the development and sales of bank services to various businesses; and development and control of the advertising and public relations budgets.

(continued)

EMPLOYMENT (continued)

VICE PRESIDENT—SAVINGS DIVISION **1999–2002**

ASSISTANT VICE PRESIDENT—SAVINGS DIVISION **1995–1999**

PROGRAMMER **1992–1995**

EDUCATION

Bowdoin College, Brunswick, ME
B.A., English, 1988

Colby College, Waterville, ME
M.A., Finance, 1992

SPECIAL EDUCATION

Graduate School of Savings Banking
NAMSB—Carroll College 1995

Management Development Program—NAMSB
University of Montana 1997

Marketing School
Rocky Mountain College 1999

Various courses in: Economics, Finance, Law, Public Speaking, Speed Reading, and Banking.

PROFESSIONAL ACTIVITIES

Contributor, *Hiking for Stress Relief*
Contributor, *Horizons in Corporate Clout*
Rocky Mountain College 2001–2007
Assistant Professor of Business, University of Montana

HOBBIES

Hiking, jogging, and mountain climbing.

CHRIS SMITH
178 Green Street
Fort Bragg, NC 28307
(919) 555-5555
csmith@e-mail.com

PROFESSIONAL BACKGROUND

2003 to Present — DEPARTMENT OF DEFENSE, Logistics Division, Supply Branch, Ft. Bragg, NC
Commodity Manager, inventory Control

- Supervise staff of ten; train, schedule, evaluate, and delegate responsibilities—monitor work done and give final approval upon completion.
- Coordinate procurement and delivery of military supplies including electronics, modules, boards, guidance systems, tanks, aircraft, weapons, petroleum products, and spare parts.
- Receive bills of lading and resolve discrepancies with original orders.
- Input receipt of materials into database and monitor inventory.
- Interpret government rules and regulations regarding ordering and receipt of supplies; ensure proper application of all other procedures and policies.
- Review damaged item listings, determine whether to repair, and ship to repair shop.
- Complete financial paperwork ensuring orders are within budgetary requirements.
- Complete paperwork for inventory, shipping, purchasing, accounting, and end-of-month reports.
- Received awards for "Outstanding Performance," 2005, 2006.

2000 to 2003 — NATIONAL GUARD, Raleigh, NC
Communications Supervisor

- Coordinated all communications and electronic suppliers for the North Carolina National Guard.
- Trained, scheduled, evaluated, and motivated as many as forty workers.
- Developed and implemented innovative system for ordering supplies and tracking inventory control.
- Input data and monitored inventory via computerized system.
- Forecasted, prepared, and monitored expenditures of operational budget.

EDUCATIONAL BACKGROUND

Asheville High School, Asheville, NC, 2000.

TRAINING

Supply Systems; Storage Management; Logistics Organization; Equal Opportunity; Application of Management Improvement Techniques for First Line Supervisors; Procurement; Financial Management in Stock Control Systems; Management of Materials Handling Equipment.

CHRIS SMITH
178 Green Street
Dunnellon, FL 34433
(813) 555-5555
csmith@e-mail.com

OBJECTIVE

A position requiring comprehensive product management, product/protocol development, and clinical research/nursing skills to obtain FDA product approval.

EXPERIENCE

Estrade, Inc., Dunnellon, FL — **October 2006–Present**
Product Manager

- Provide a comprehensive coordination of all product development activities, from research to market; fulfill the ultimate objective of a commercially marketable product.
- Devise, implement, and evaluate training and educational materials for providers of ALT services.
- Follow up on the continuous assessment and evaluation of product application needs and ALT provider needs through collaboration with multidisciplinary team (clinical research, process development, research and development, and regulatory affairs).
- Assist in the strategic planning for the development of further applications for ALT and the adaptation of cell processing techniques for other clinical indications.
- Assemble and manage multidisciplinary project teams for product development of each application of ALT.
- Prepare and present the clinical aspects of protocols to physicians' investigative groups.

Manager—Clinical Services — **October 2004–September 2006**

- Developed, managed, and provided ongoing evaluation of clinical training and staff development plans for use in fifteen company-operated outpatient treatment centers and participating clinical research facilities throughout the country.
- Participated in the hiring, orientation, and technical training of clinical personnel. Provided ongoing assessment of clinical performance including annual performance evaluations.
- Designed and implemented Clinical Quality Assurance/Quality Improvement Plans for use in company-operated outpatient treatment centers.

St. Theresa's Hospital — **July 1998–September 2004**
Staff RN

- Provided primary nursing care of critically ill pediatric patients in a tertiary care facility. Responsible for patient and family education, discharge planning, and home care placement.

EDUCATION

Boston College, Chestnut Hill, MA
***Bachelor of Science degree—Nursing,* 1998**

COMPUTER LITERACY

Windows, Microsoft Word, Outlook, ACT. Work with systems consultants on the design and implementation of data management systems including remote access.

CHRIS SMITH
178 Green Street
Poughkeepsie, NY 12601
(601) 555-5555
csmith@e-mail.com

OBJECTIVE

A position as a Medical Assistant or related position of responsibility where there is a need for clinical as well as administrative experience.

SUMMARY OF QUALIFICATIONS

- Over five years of experience as a Dental Assistant and Medical Receptionist in direct patient care and patient relations.
- Honor Graduate as Medical Assistant from National Education Center.
- Sound knowledge of medical terminology and clinical procedures.
- Certified in: First Aid, Cardiopulmonary Resuscitation, Electrocardiography.
- Additional experience as Receptionist/Secretary with an executive search/management consulting firm, financial management company, and realty firms.

HEALTH CARE EXPERIENCE

Dr. Herbert Dickey, M.D., Brooklyn, NY **2005–Present**

- Perform accounts payable/receivable.
- Schedule patients for appointments.
- Prepare patients for surgical procedure; record temperature and blood pressure, insert intravenous units, and administer sedatives.
- Provide postoperative care; record vital signs every ten minutes until consciousness; establish patient comfort; provide necessary information to patients regarding new medications/possible side effects.

Drs. William and Joseph Janell, New York, NY **2004–05**

- Began as Dental Trainee, advanced to Dental Assistant.
- Sterilized instruments, processed X-rays, scheduled appointments, and maintained patient relations.

Externship
Internal Medicine Associates, Brooklyn, NY **2005**

- Multidisciplinary practice, including gastroenterology, rheumatology, endocrinology, and cardiology.
- Took vital signs, performed urinalysis, EKGs, and blood chemistries. Maintained patient charts.

EDUCATION

State University of New York, Binghamton, NY
A.S. Biology

COMPUTERS

Microsoft Word, Excel

CHRIS SMITH
178 Green Street
Atlanta, GA 30350
(404) 555-5555
csmith@e-mail.com

WORK EXPERIENCE:

Dietitian
Ellsworth Hospital, Atlanta, GA **2006–Present**
- Confer with medical and multidisciplinary staffs.
- Prepare nutritional care plans.
- Interview patients.
- Maintain and document patients' medical records.
- Instruct patients and their families.
- Perform miscellaneous duties as a member of the hospital support team.

Dietary Aide
Bentley Nursing Home, Atlanta, GA **2005–2006**
- Assisted in preparation of patient food trays.

Office Assistant
Morehouse College, Atlanta, GA **2004–2005**
- Served as Receptionist for main office.

Library Assistant
Morehouse College Library **Summer 2004**
- Worked in circulation and periodical sections.

EDUCATION:

Morehouse College, Atlanta, GA
B.S. degree, 2005
Major: Consumer and Family Studies
Minor: Sociology

RELEVANT COURSES:

Human Nutrition; Family Financial Decision-Making; Professional Preparation; Principles of Food I and II; The Four Food Groups; Interpersonal Communications; Social Psychology; Human Relations.

INTERNSHIP:

Dowdell County Extension Service, Atlanta, GA (Fall 2004)
- Wrote weekly food advice column, "Eat Up!"
- Developed chart and gave presentation on the major nutrients.

CHRIS SMITH
178 Green Street
Hoxie, KS 67740
(913) 555-5555 (work)
(913) 555-5555 (home)
csmith@e-mail.com

OBJECTIVE:
Seeking a position as a TECHNICIAN/COORDINATOR that utilizes my skills and experience.

EXPERIENCE:

2005–Present KANSAS GENERAL HOSPITAL, Topeka, KS
Medical Media Technician Coordinator, 2002–Present
Coordinate, set up, and implement media services for hospital personnel and BU Medical School students and faculty. This includes supervising 3–8 Media Technicians. Complex medical and educational photography, processing, and slide-reel set-up. Set-up and direction of medical videos and video equipment. Set-up, operation, and demonstration of medical equipment to medical students. Diagnostic troubleshooting, coordination, and problem-solving. Departmental troubleshooting and problem-solving. Conduct Hematological and Seratological medical testing. Work closely with undergraduate and graduate medical students, interns, faculty, physicians, and hospital staff.

Laboratory Supervisor
Coordinated laboratory operations, including media technology, analysis of test results, reporting, and record keeping. Troubleshot and resolved departmental problems.

2002–2005 **Laboratory Technician**
DAMON CORPORATION, Shawnee Mission, KS
Conducted hematology and serology testing, as well as test sample photography. Recorded, analyzed, and communicated results to physicians, patients, and their families.

1999–2002 **Media Research Technician**
MAYFARB INSTITUTE, Wichita, KS
Produced synchronized audio and slide programs on medical and medical-educational topics. Conducted career research. Served as a reference and research guide for institute staff and Harvard Medical School affiliates.

EDUCATION:

B.A., Media and Communications, 1999

References Available Upon Request.

CHRIS SMITH
178 Green Street
Cherry Fork, OH 45618
(513) 555-5555
csmith@e-mail.com

SUMMARY OF QUALIFICATIONS:

Intensive Care Unit

- Working closely with recently graduated interns at major metropolitan trauma certified hospital.
- Accurate reporting and recording of lab values with follow-up medical treatment.
- Recognizing life threatening arrhythmias and means of treatment for patients placed on cardiac monitors.

Post Anesthesia Care Unit

- Caring for arterial lines, monitoring BP and MAP, drawing arterial blood gases and other labs, and interpreting and reporting abnormal values to physician for medical management.
- Providing specialized nursing and medical care in seventeen-bed unit for anesthetized patients following surgical procedures in the operating room.
- Calculating and recording cardiac output SVR and cardiac indexes.

EDUCATION:

UNIVERSITY OF CINCINNATI, Cincinnati, OH
Bachelor of Science in Nursing (1999)

MUSKINGUM COLLEGE HOSPITAL, New Concord, OH
Trauma Certificate (2006), Critical Care Course (2004)

EXPERIENCE:

OHIO STATE UNIVERSITY HOSPITAL, Columbus, OH
Staff Nurse, Post Anesthesia Care Unit and Trauma Unit
(10/05–Present)
Night Charge Nurse, making assignments and utilizing on-call nurses when necessary. Trauma certified for major trauma unit in the City of Columbus. PACU often turned into ICU for patients unable to get an ICU bed in high crime area location. Experience in treating patients recovering from surgery for gunshot and stab wounds.

Staff Nurse, Medical Respiratory Intensive Care Unit

VIRTUE HOSPITAL, Dayton, OH
Nursing Internship, Medical-Surgical Unit (8/03–10/05)
Nurse's Aide (7/02–8/03)

REFERENCES:

Excellent references available upon request.

CHRIS SMITH
178 Green Street
Providence, RI 02903
(401) 555-5555
csmith@e-mail.com

PROFESSIONAL EXPERIENCE

2006–Present VISITING NURSE ASSOCIATION OF PROVIDENCE, Providence, RI
Supervisor of Specialty Home Health Aides
Supervised forty HHAs who care for pediatric patients with HIV.

2003–2006 **Reimbursement Specialist,** Northeast and Providence District Offices
Managed and evaluated all clinical documentation for Medicare and all third party related Medicare payers. Worked in cooperation with managers, clinicians, patients' accounts, and clerical staff to ensure quality documentation.

2000–2003 **Staff Nurse**
Provided skilled nursing assessment of primary patients and family needs. Utilized appropriate resource personnel and agencies in a collaborative effort to provide continuity of care to patient and family. Worked with liaison nurses to discharge patients to home with appropriate services and realistic expectation of third party reimbursement payers.

1999–2000 RHODE ISLAND PARAMEDICAL REGISTRY, Providence, RI
Visiting Nurse
Responsible for the home care of chronically ill children to give the primary caretakers physical and emotional respite.

1998–1999 THE CHILDREN'S HOSPITAL, Cranston, RI
Staff Nurse in cardiovascular/surgical intensive care unit. Provided surgical and medical management of critically ill children in collaborative effort with medical team. Supported parents and provided discharge teaching for comprehensive home care utilizing primary nursing.

1995–1997 KINGSTON HOSPITAL, Kingston, RI
Staff Nurse in pediatrics with charge responsibilities for a twenty-bed ICU. Provided surgical and medical treatment for children ages 3–17 years. Incorporated levels of development and psychological needs in teaching discharge goals. Counseled parents about disease process and child's needs.

EDUCATION

SALVE REGINA COLLEGE, Newport, RI, B.S. in Nursing; Graduated 1994.
Summer Externship, Rollins Hospital, Orlando, FL, 1993.

CHRIS SMITH
178 Green Street
Lafayette, LA 70504
(318) 555-5555
csmith@e-mail.com

PROFESSIONAL EXPERIENCE

2004 to Present **Pharmacist**
ZERTEX ALLIED HEALTH SERVICES Lafayette, LA
- Review and fill prescriptions and enter orders in computer.
- Coordinate total intravenous therapy program for nursing homes.
- Supervise staff and conduct purchasing procedures.
- Provide consultation for patients and nursing home staff on drug therapy and regulations.
- Simultaneously coordinate hospital and retail pharmacy services.

2002 to 2004 **Pharmacist**
BEAUCHAMPS HOSPITAL New Orleans, LA
- Dispensed drugs to and counseled inpatients and outpatients.
- Advised professional staff regarding drug information, interactions, etc.
- Trained new technicians in pharmacy computer operations.
- Assisted in decentralization of pharmacy services.
- Distributed unit doses, prepared intravenous and chemotherapy admixtures.
- Assisted in inventory control and performed various related duties.

2000 to 2002 **Clinical Pharmacy Clerkship**
VETERAN'S HOSPITAL Baton Rouge, LA
- Worked with team of physicians and other health professionals on rotation through various hospital departments.

1999 to 2000 **Pharmacy Extern**
CUPID'S PHARMACY Natchitoches, LA
- Assisted in the provision of pharmacy services, including: dispensation of medications, advising patients on usage of prescription and nonprescription drugs, monitoring patient profiles for interactions, medication compliances, inappropriate therapy, etc.
- Assisted in the processing and pricing of third-party prescription reimbursement claims.

EDUCATION

Bachelor of Science degree: Pharmacy, 2000
TULANE UNIVERSITY New Orleans, LA
Louisiana Registered Pharmacist #34217
Georgia Registered Pharmacist #36954

PROFESSIONAL DEVELOPMENT AND AFFILIATIONS

Member—Louisiana Society of Hospital Pharmacy.

CHRIS SMITH
178 Green Street
Providence, RI 02918
(401) 555-5555
csmith@e-mail.com

EDUCATION

Brown University, Providence, RI
Master of Education in Human Development and Reading, 1997
Cape Town University, Cape Town, South Africa
Bachelor of Arts with Honors in Speech Pathology and Audiology, 1994

PROFESSIONAL EXPERIENCE

2001 to Present — ST. CHRISTOPHER'S HOSPITAL, Providence, RI
Clinical Supervisor, Bennet Hospital Satellite Speech and Language Program

- Started and directed Speech and Language Program under aegis of Bennet Hospital.
- Market program; designed brochure, performed on radio talk shows, administer all advertising.
- Provide in-service consultation to hospital staff, students, various agencies, and organizations.
- Hire, supervise, orient, instruct, and discipline employees, graduate students, and clinical fellows.
- Conduct quality assurance; appraise performance.
- Evaluate, diagnose, and treat inpatients/outpatients, adults/children with variety of communication disorders.
- Provide supportive and educational counseling.
- Develop policies and procedures, perform various managerial and administrative tasks.
- Perform Speech, Hearing, and Language screening.
- Develop augmentative communication systems for non-verbal population.
- Conduct aural rehabilitation for elderly.

1998–2001 — BENNET HOSPITAL, Providence, RI
Staff Speech-Language Pathologist, Speech, Hearing, and Language Center

- Evaluated, diagnosed, and treated inpatients/outpatients, adults/children with variety of communication disorders including: apraxia, aphasia, dysarthria, head injury, fluency, voice, neurological impairments, language, mental retardation, phonology, laryngectomy, dialectical variances, hearing impairments, cleft palate, and cerebral palsy.
- Ran preschool language group.
- Participated on Stroke Team.
- Provided in-service consultation to staff and agencies.

1995–1998 — PRIVATE PRACTICE, Cape Town, South Africa
Speech Pathologist

- Assessed, diagnosed, and treated adults and children exhibiting variety of communication disorders.
- Conferred with physicians and schools.
- Provided supportive/educational parent counseling.

CHRIS SMITH
178 Green Street
Marylhurst, OR 97036
(503) 555-5555
csmith@e-mail.com

OBJECTIVE

To obtain a position as an Animal Health Technician.

EXPERIENCE

PIAGETTI ANIMAL CARE CLINIC Marylhurst, OR
Neonatal Intensive Care Nurse 2003–Present

- Monitor patients and schedule work, personnel, and supplies.
- Perform pre- and post-operative care and emergency care.
- Collect and ship blood samples.
- Organize labs for veterinary students and for clinical instruction.
- Monitor ventilation and vital statistics of premature and critically ill animals.
- Collect blood, perform intravenous and arterial catheterization. Intubation of endotracheal and nasogastric tubes.
- Member of Emergency Ventilation Team.

Surgery Staff Nurse 2004–2006
Administered pre- and post-operative surgical care.

- Prepared animals for surgery.
- Administered antibiotics.

Rotating Staff Nurse 2003–2004

- Assisted clinicians and students in treatment of patients.
- Room nursing: pre- and post-operative management of patients.

CERTIFICATIONS

Licensed Animal Health Technician, 2003
Veterinary Medicine, University of Portland, 2005
Applied Dentistry for Veterinary Technicians, 2005

EDUCATION

University of Oregon, Eugene, OR
B.A. Animal Health Technology, 2002

University of Portland, Portland, OR
A.S. Animal Health Technology, 2000

CHRIS SMITH
178 Green Street
Portales, NM 88130
(505) 555-5555
csmith@e-mail.com

CAREER SUMMARY

A Human Resources Manager with extensive experience in maximizing corporate, team, and individual performance through progressive human processes. Diversified generalist experience in strategic human resource planning, employee relations, employment, compensation, training, and organizational development.

CAREER HISTORY

BANK OF NEW MEXICO, Portales, NM
Compensation Manager (2006-Present)
Managed the Compensation and Payroll functions, including Job Analysis, Salary Administration, Employee Payroll, and Personnel Records. Utilized the job evaluation system and implemented a total HRIS conversion.

Compensation Representative (2004-2006)
Provided employee relations support and consultation to three departments. Specific activities included development, implementation, and administration of compensation function. Responsible for all compensation activities, including position analysis and evaluation, benchmarking, salary surveys, and merit budget recommendations.

Employment Manager and Employee Relations Counselor (2003-2004)
Developed recruitment sources, college programs, internal staffing, outplacement, and provided employee counseling. Interpreted personnel policies for employee effectiveness.

M-N-M PLACEMENT AGENCY, Santa Fe, NM
Placement Counselor (2003-2004)
Recruited, screened, and placed candidates for permanent positions. Advertised, interviewed, and placed candidates for temporary assignments, as well as generated new business activity through cold sales calls.

EDUCATION

UNIVERSITY OF NEW MEXICO, Albuquerque, NM
B.A. Political Science, 2004

PERSONAL

Willing to relocate.

REFERENCES

Available upon request.

CHRIS SMITH
178 Green Street
Franklin, IN 46131
(317) 555-5555
csmith@e-mail.com

PROFESSIONAL BACKGROUND

PERSONNEL MANAGER
Cronin Construction, Franklin, IN
July 2006 to Present

- Adjust Human Resources policy to needs of expanding company.
- Develop Human Resources goals and objectives.
- Manage Human Resources budget.
- Handle employee relations.
- Direct employment and recruitment efforts.
- Manage company benefits and compensation.
- Compile statistics for employee benefits handbook.
- Assist in development of training programs.

PERSONNEL ADMINISTRATOR
Moschella Management Corporation, Franklin, IN
July 2004 to July 2006

- Initiated affirmative action program.
- Compiled policies and procedures manual for Human Resources Department.
- Coordinated recruitment program with agencies and attended job fairs.
- Created advertising campaign for recruitment program.
- Developed and packaged new employee orientation.
- Implemented additional benefits, i.e., tuition reimbursement and employee referral program.

MANAGER OF PERSONNEL/PAYROLL
Purdue University School of Management, West Lafayette, IN
May 2003 to June 2004

- Supervised administrative and technical support staff.
- Interviewed, hired, and terminated personnel.
- Negotiated salaries, budgets, and business plans.
- Analyzed and resolved personnel grievances.

ASSISTANT MANAGER
Atwood Industries, Beloit, WI
September 2001 to May 2003

- Hired and terminated personnel; handled salary negotiations.
- Implemented billing and credit procedures (accounts payable and receivable).
- Served as liaison among client companies, East Coast office, and Home Office.

NOTABLE ACHIEVEMENTS

Developed and managed Human Resources role as company grew from 140 to 275 employees.
Completed course work in media presentations and computer applications (Excel, Microsoft Word, PowerPoint).

EDUCATION

Bachelor of Arts degree in English, 2001
Beloit College, Beloit, WI

CHRIS SMITH
178 Green Street
Boise, ID 83725
(208) 555-5555
csmith@e-mail.com

OBJECTIVE A position in recruiting with a progressive, expanding firm offering growth potential within the organization's structure. Willing to relocate and/or travel.

ACCOMPLISHMENTS

- Established excellent relationships with employment agencies from California to Massachusetts; increased quantity and quality of resumes received by 200%.
- Developed monthly mailer directed to agencies.
- Implemented new administration procedures, increasing clerical productivity by 95% and reducing personnel department overhead by 30%.

EXPERIENCE Professional Recruiter—TAB/GTK Corporation, Boise, ID
August 2006–Present

- Recruit sales and marketing support personnel.
- Plan and execute field recruiting trips to major cities, seminars, career centers, conferences, and universities.
- Design and implement college recruiting programs.
- Establish and maintain working relationship with select employment agencies.
- Prepare statistical reports relating to department expenditures and provide recommendations for eliminating excessive cost and overhead.
- Assist in the development of employee communication programs.

Personnel Manager—Bannen Boot Company, Syracuse, NY
May 2004–August 2006

- Established first complete personnel program including developing all procedures, records, programs, sources of hire, and all administrative functions related to the recruiting and hiring of personnel.
- Established a child-care service in-house.
- Worked on human relations problems arising with the introduction of newly established standards and work procedures.
- Developed new employee orientation programs including visual aids and prepared tests.
- Developed and maintained employee recreation program, music and PA system, bulletin boards, etc.

EDUCATION

Syracuse University, School of Communications, Syracuse, NY
B.S. degree, Public Relations, 2004. Minor: Sociology.

CHRIS SMITH
178 Green Street
Daytona, FL 32114
(904) 555-5555
csmith@e-mail.com

OBJECTIVE

Executive-level position in Human Resources Management.

PROFESSIONAL EXPERIENCE

Vice President, Human Resources
Ann Davis Laboratories, Inc., Daytona, FL 2006–Present
Direct a staff of eight in the design and delivery of HR programs and services for the $175 million biotech/pharmaceutical business.

- Operated at Executive Staff Level in directing the business and resolving organizational issues.
- Changed existing Personnel Department into a streamlined HR department with bottom-line accountability.
- Recruit difficult to fill positions in an extremely competitive recruiting environment. Reduced turnover by 15%; managed cost per hire to below 30% for exempt hires.
- Introduced new performance compensation program—structure development, management guides and training, distribution curve, common reviews, and new survey participation. Formulated management incentive programs. Reconstructed field operations incentive program which greatly improved performance/morale.
- Formulate and administer new HR policies; employee suggestion system and opinion survey; various other employee motivational and communication programs.

Director, Human Resources
Olsen Laboratories, Inc., Sebring, FL 2001–2006

- Directed large staff (forty-five–seventy-five) in providing all HR services and programs to the Corporate Headquarters organization.
- Introduced and directed a corporate centralized employment function operating as an in-house sourcing unit to reduce costs and streamline operations.

Corporate Compensation Manager
McCormick, Inc., Tampa, FL 1996–2001

- Directed worldwide compensation programs including manufacturing facilities in the United Kingdom for the European sales force.

EDUCATION

M.A., Organizational Communications, Flagler College, St. Augustine, FL, 1997
B.A., Liberal Arts, University of Miami, Miami, FL, 1995

CHRIS SMITH
178 Green Street
Sabattus, ME 04280
(207) 555-5555
csmith@e-mail.com

OBJECTIVE:

A challenging and responsible position in Law Enforcement, Criminal Justice, or related field where my education, experience, and capabilities can be fully realized.

EDUCATION:

BANGOR POLICE ACADEMY, Bangor, ME
Act 120 Certificate with 90% average (2002)

CERTIFICATIONS:

- NRA, shotgun and firearms; Monadnock PR 24; VASCAR plus.
- CPR First Aid.

EXPERIENCE:

2005–Present **MAINE STATE PRISON,** Lewiston, ME
Correctional Officer
Responsible for control of fifty prisoners. Conduct population counts, cell checks, and searches. Supervise dinner and yard duty. Monitor prisoner visitation. Issue money orders for prisoners. Assignments have included escorting special prisoners and serving as outside hospital guard. Prepare and file incident reports.

2004 **BIDDEFORD POLICE DEPARTMENT,** Biddeford, ME
Part-Time Police Officer

2003 **SOUTH PORTLAND POLICE DEPARTMENT,** South Portland, ME
Part-Time Police Officer
Responsible for routine patrol, issuing criminal arrest citations, and testifying in court.

2000–2002 **FIRST FEDERAL SAVINGS BANK,** Cape Elizabeth, ME
Security Guard

VOLUNTEER:

Volunteer Firefighter; Cape Elizabeth Fire Co.

CHRIS SMITH
178 Green Street
Palos Heights, IL 60445
(312) 555-5555
csmith@e-mail.com

SUMMARY OF QUALIFICATIONS:

- Emergency Medical Technician and volunteer firefighter.
- Able to remain calm and take control in emergency situations.
- Have held numerous elective offices.

EDUCATION:

DEERFIELD COMMUNITY COLLEGE, Deerfield, IL
Emergency Medical Technician, 2003.

Certified by the Illinois Department of Health.
Illinois Association of Arson Investigators Certificate, Forensic File Photography.
Chicago Electric Company Fire Academy.
Gas and Electric Firefighting, 1989–90.
Deerfield Fire Academy, Firefighting I, II, III, 1988–89.

TRINITY VOCATIONAL-TECHNICAL SCHOOL, Deerfield, IL
Communications Technician, 1989–91.
Photographic Technician, 1988–89.

WORK EXPERIENCE:

1988–Present **PALOS HEIGHTS FIRE COMPANY**—Life Member
Firefighter, Emergency Medical Technician

- Ambulance Lieutenant, 1993, 2005—conduct training drills.
- Ambulance Captain, 1994.
- Ambulance Auxiliary Secretary, 1994.
- Photographer, 2002–Present.

2004–Present **INTERNATIONAL FIRE PHOTOGRAPHERS ASSOCIATION**

1988–Present **DEERFIELD FIREMAN'S ASSOCIATION**

1994–1998 **MIDWEST AMBULANCE,** River Forest, IL
Assistant Manager/Crew

- Scheduled ten full-time and eight part-time Emergency Medical Technicians for emergency and hospital transportation of patients. Serviced Burn Center at River Forest Medical Center.

CHRIS SMITH
178 Green Street
Sundance, WY 82729
(307) 555-5555
csmith@e-mail.com

OBJECTIVE

A position in security.

PROFESSIONAL EXPERIENCE

FIELDSTONE BANK — Sundance, WY
Bank Guard — 2006–Present
- Responsible for ensuring safety and security of customers, bank employees, and bank assets.

WILLOW MEAD ART MUSEUM — Wolf, WY
Security Guard — 2004–2006
- Responsible for patrol, surveillance, and control of facilities and areas.
- Maintained reports, records, and documents as required by administration.

CITY OF ROCK SPRINGS POLICE DEPARTMENT — Rock Springs, WY
Property Clerk — 2002–2004
- Responsible for security, transfer, and storage of personnel effects/properties as evidence in trial and court cases.

CITY OF GILLETTE SCHOOL DEPARTMENT — Gillette, WY
Transitional Aide — 1998–2002
- Responsible for ensuring safety of students and security of school property at Madison Park High School.

THUNDERBEAT CONSTRUCTION — Crowheart, WY
Weigher of Goods/Track Foreman — 1997–2000
- Weighed materials and supervised track construction at University of Wyoming.

PINEDALE & SONS — Miami, FL
Mason — 1995–1997
- Performed variety of duties including masonry, stucco, finishing work, and foundations for general contractor.

EDUCATION

UNITED STATES COAST GUARD, Miami, FL
Certificate, Interactive Query Language, 1995.
Certificate, Advanced PMIS, 1994.
Certificate, Coast Guard WP School, 1993.
Winter Park High School, Winter Park, FL 1993.

CHRIS SMITH
178 Green Street
Danville, KY 40422
(606) 555-5555
csmith@e-mail.com

OBJECTIVE

To acquire a **Legal Secretarial** position, preferably, but not limited to, Civil Litigation or Criminal Law, where my experience and commitment to excellence will be fully applied.

SUMMARY OF QUALIFICATIONS

- Fifteen years experience as a legal assistant/secretary in civil litigation.
- Ten years part-time experience in general practice.
- Computer literate: PCs and Macs.
- Notary Public.
- Supervisory skills, delegate and distribute workload evenly among secretarial staff.

HIGHLIGHTS OF LEGAL EXPERIENCE

2004–Present LAW OFFICES OF LANGSTON & GREY, Lexington, KY **Legal Secretary**
Responsibilities include organizing pre-deposition conferences with doctors, attorneys, and involved parties; handling, canceling, and rescheduling; setting up motions for court hearings; trial papers and schedules; researching files for necessary documentation and proofreading; notarizing legal documents.

1994–2002 THEODORE F. LOGAN, Danville, KY **Legal Secretary**
Part-time evening duties involved court and client scheduling, typing legal documents, drafting wills, letters, and complaints in general practice law office.

1990–1993 CUMBERLAND INSURANCE, Lexington, KY **Secretary**
General secretarial tasks; typing correspondence and reports, filing, and phones.

EDUCATION

CENTRE COLLEGE, Danville, KY Paralegal Studies, 2003–2004
Also participated in Communications Skills Workshop for Paralegals.

DANVILLE COMMUNITY COLLEGE, Danville, KY
Relevant training and coursework in legal issues and computers.

PERSONAL

Baseball, cooking, and travel.

CHRIS SMITH
178 Green Street
Jackson, MS 39217
(601) 555-5555
csmith@e-mail.com

PROFESSIONAL EXPERIENCE

2002–Present OLIVER, FIELDING, & OLIVER, Jackson, MS
Legal Assistant

- Provide paralegal services to attorneys in residential real estate sales within Mississippi and surrounding states.
- Monitor transactions from start to final settlement statement; order and review titles, obtain plot plans and municipal lien certificates, research background, and work successfully against deadlines.
- Prepare loan documents.
- Determine outstanding utility and tax bills.
- Ensure completion of mortgage payments by previous owners.
- Serve as liaison for clients, banks, and attorney; schedule meetings, identify documents necessary for all parties.
- Coordinate all post-closing functions, complete title insurance forms, send final payments to banks and municipalities, and disburse funds.
- Maintain constant communication with all parties involved throughout the entire process.

1996–2002 HALPERN INSURANCE AGENCY, Jackson, MS
Subrogation Clerk, 2001–2002

- Negotiated payments with attorneys on Third Party Liability cases; reviewed medical records.

Operator, Third Party Liability Dept., 2000

- Provided subscriber information to customers, assisted in completion of questionnaire.

Senior Clerk, Hospital Claims Dept., 1996–1999

- Reviewed claims, made payments for patients with nerve and mental disorders.

EDUCATIONAL BACKGROUND

BELHAVEN COLLEGE, Jackson, MS
Certificate in Paralegal Studies

- Introduction to Paralegal, American Legal System, Criminal Law, Litigation, Utilization of Legal Materials, and Real Estate Law.

HALPERN INSURANCE Courses:

- Legal Terminology, Contractual Terminology, Mathematical Skills.

SKILLS PC literate, word processing, and typing (55 wpm).

CHRIS SMITH
178 Green Street
Baltimore, MD 21210
(410) 555-5555
csmith@e-mail.com

PROFESSIONAL EXPERIENCE

2000 to Present JOHNS HOPKINS UNIVERSITY POLICE DEPARTMENT, Baltimore, MD
Patrol Officer

- Protect life and property on and about the campus of Johns Hopkins University.
- Uphold laws and codes of the state of Maryland and Johns Hopkins University.
- Patrol on foot and via automobile; utilize strong observational skills.
- Cooperate with other law enforcement agencies; act as Deputy Sheriff, Essex County.
- Maintain community relations; give seminars on drunk driving.

1998 to 1999 BUCKMAN ASSOCIATES, Bethesda, MD
Head of Security

- Managed all aspects of security for hotels and adjoining properties.
- Hired, terminated, scheduled, supervised, and evaluated personnel.
- Provided all policing functions with emphasis on defusing potentially violent situations.
- Cooperated extensively with Baltimore and Bethesda Police Departments.
- Promoted from starting position as Patrol Officer.
- Received standing offer of return for emergency or full-time employment.

1993 to 1997 TOWN OF ROCKVILLE POLICE DEPARTMENT, Rockville, MD
Patrol Officer

- Performed all aforementioned policing functions.
- Oversaw proper use of Chapter 90 sheets and citations.
- Interacted and communicated with town officials.
- Kept records; maintained data.

EDUCATION AND TRAINING

Graduate, Baltimore Police Academy, 2000
Graduate, Rockville Police Academy, 1993

CERTIFICATIONS AND LICENSURES

- License to carry firearms.
- Emergency Medical Technician, National Certification.
- Certification in radar usage.

REFERENCES

Available upon request.

CHRIS SMITH
178 Green Street
Wise, VA 24293
(703) 555-5555
csmith@e-mail.com

PROFESSIONAL EXPERIENCE

2003 to Present — **WCVT-TV (NLC-Channel 3),** Wise, VA

Account Executive/Sales Department 2005–Present

- Established and maintained new and existing corporate accounts representing more than $1.5 million in new clients.
- Initiated and developed marketing strategies and target grids for the second ranked TV station in fifth largest market for effective sales programs/promotions.
- Aided with potential clients in developing effective marketing strategies and programs.

Associate Director/Sales Manager 2004–2005

- Production Department Stage Manager for Noon, Five O'Clock, and News at Ten newscasts, all public affairs programs, editorials, and news cut-ins.
- Assembled sets and operated chyron machine.

Production Intern 2003

- Wrote hard news, feature stories, scheduled and interviewed guests.
- Researched materials and packaged tapes for production.
- Operated TelePrompTer.

2001–2003 — **UNIVERSITY OF VIRGINIA**, Charlottesville, VA

Producer, Television and Radio Station WNUV-Channel 62 2002–2003

- Responsible for researching materials for mini-documentary.
- Scheduled and interviewed guests for round-table discussions.
- Wrote and edited scripts and edited master tape.

Production Assistant 2001–2002

- Performed as camera technician, stage manager, and chyron operator.
- Assembled lighting and audio equipment.

EDUCATION

RANDOLPH-MACON WOMAN'S COLLEGE, Lynchburg, VA
B.A. degree, Communications/Mass Media 2004
Magna Cum Laude. Concentration: Economics and Afro-American Studies.

HONORS/AFFILIATIONS

Recipient, Virginia Chapter, National Association of TV Arts and Science Award. National Achievement Award. National Association of Women Journalists. National Association of Media Workers.

CHRIS SMITH
178 Green Street
Nashville, TN 31210
(615) 555-5555
csmith@e-mail.com

OBJECTIVE

A challenging career in Advertising.

PROFESSIONAL EXPERIENCE

2006 to Present — USA OLYMPIC PUBLICATIONS, Nashville, TN
Advertising Manager
- Sell advertising space for a publication distributed at Olympic Conventions. Sell rental contracts for booths at trade shows, etc.
- Design fliers and brochures as part of promotions for conventions and trade shows. Handle other promotional work as assigned.
- Initiate, organize, and promote trade show for Tennessee merchants and for others interested in area trade and commerce. Contact merchants to rent booths, send promotional materials to buyers, and contract for media advertising.
- Coordinate and secure facilities and services for trade show project of approximately $150,000.

2004 to 2006 — *GOOD MORNING NASHVILLE NEWS,* Nashville, TN
Executive Secretary to the Advertising Manager
- Prepared statistical analysis of advertising lineage for use in assessing competitive ranking.
- Typed, answered the Call Director, and performed general secretarial duties for sales personnel as assigned.
- Provided resource contact and encouragement to States Staff.

2001 to 2004 — DEPARTMENT OF SOCIAL SERVICES, Memphis, TN
Legal Secretary
- Handled correspondence, telephones, and general secretarial work, as well as light research.

1999 to 2001 — RYE BROOK COMPANY, Madison, TN
Typist
- Typist of documents usually 40 to 50 pages long; compiled and typed statistical information for analyses.

INTERESTS Rock climbing, gardening, '70s trivia.

REFERENCES Furnished upon request.

CHRIS SMITH
178 Green Street
Terre Haute, IN 47804
(812) 555-5555
csmith@e-mail.com

OBJECTIVE

A position that will further develop my superior marketing skills.

EXPERIENCE

Marketing Assistant, The Art Lover's Institute
Indianapolis, IN 2/06–Present

- Temporary position assisting the Manager of Public Information on the exhibit "Proud Triangles: Gay Life in America."
- Executed the distribution of exhibit posters and organized the development of displays merchandising products to promote the exhibit at local retailers.
- Coordinated press clippings and releases about the exhibit.

Assistant Box Office Manager, Terre Haute Performing Arts Center
Terre Haute, IN 6/05–1/06

- Managed daily operations for a staff of twenty operators responsible for customer service and the sale of all tickets in a theater seating 5,000.
- Compiled all financial statements on a daily and monthly basis for each performance in the theater averaging ten performances per month, including daily deposits and revenue from outlet sales on secondary ticketing systems.

Gallery Assistant/Window Exhibit Coordinator, Jim Cannon's Art Implosion
Bourbon, IN 5/04–6/05

- Developed marketing plan for fine art prints and coordinating notecards.
- Developed client base and serviced accounts.
- Coordinated special events relating to current exhibits, opening receptions, and artist signings. Handled press releases.

EDUCATION

Valparaiso University, Valparaiso, IN
Bachelor of Arts, 2006
Arts Administration with a concentration in marketing and communications.

SKILLS

Proficient with many Mac and PC applications, including: InDesign, Word, Excel, and Access.

CHRIS SMITH
178 Green Street
Salt Lake City, UT 84102
(801) 555-5555
csmith@e-mail.com

OBJECTIVE

To contribute exceptional sales ability, account management, and communications skills to a challenging Sales Representative position.

SUMMARY OF QUALIFICATIONS

- Thorough knowledge in the provision of sales services, account acquisition, and management; consistent enhancement of product and industry knowledge; reactivation of dormant accounts; and the development of successful sales techniques.
- Consistently meet and exceed sales quotas.
- Accumulated over six years experience within a major hardware/software company.

EXPERIENCE

2/06 to Present **Sales Representative**
GRASSVILLE SYSTEMS Salt Lake City, UT

- Sell computer hardware and peripherals to corporate accounts and dealer channels.
- Acquisition new accounts; maintain and reactivate existing accounts. Coordinate cold calling; process orders and sell service accounts.
- Devise solutions for customer computer needs and after-sales support.
- Sell PC desktops and laptops.

7/04 to 1/06 **National Sales Representative**
NIMBUS COMPUTERS Provo, UT

- Acquired new accounts, maintained and reactivated existing accounts.
- Instituted solutions for customer computer needs and after-sale support.
- Sold Macintosh and PC desktop and laptop systems.

12/01 to 6/04 **Sales Associate**
SUEDE BOGGS COMPANY Salt Lake City, UT

- Facilitated promotional activities, dealt with customers.

EDUCATION

NEW HAMPSHIRE COLLEGE, Manchester, NH
Bachelor of Arts: Communications, May 2002.

COMPUTERS

IBM, Macintosh

Chris Smith
178 Green Street
Saint Petersburg, FL 33713
(813) 555-5555
csmith@e-mail.com

OBJECTIVE

A position in inside sales, preferably in the telecommunications industry.

QUALIFICATIONS

- Outstanding selling and closing capabilities with proven track record.
- Excellent listener; patient and sensitive to clients' needs.
- Calm under pressure; meet deadlines; meet all sales quotas.
- Proven problem-solving skills.

EXPERIENCE

2006–Present
ESP Telecommunications, Saint Petersburg, FL
Telemarketing Professional
Cold called residential consumers, discovered their domestic/international calling needs, recommended programs. Consistently achieved at least 125% of sales goals.

2005–2006
Kaybee Education Group, Miami, FL
Marketing Assistant
Cold called high-school and college students selling diagnostic college and graduate school entrance exams.

2004–2005
Bill Wonka Quality Car Wash, Cambridge, MA
Bookkeeper
Performed bank reconciliations, trial balances, and general ledger.

AWARDS AND ACCOMPLISHMENTS

- Inducted into national club of Top Ten Percent, 2005.
- Awarded Golden Ring Award for meeting sales goals throughout 2006.

EDUCATION

Quincy College, Quincy, MA
B.S., Finance, 2004

COMPUTERS

Excel and Microsoft Word, InDesign

CHRIS SMITH
178 Green Street
Conyers, GA 30208
(404) 555-5555
csmith@e-mail.com

EXPERIENCE:

Shockley Associates, Inc., Conyers, GA
Publisher of *Anarchists in Love Comedy Magazine*
Vice President of Marketing 2006–Present
Manage all corporate day-to-day operations, including production, distribution, sales, marketing, and administration.

- Increased annual sales by 10% while achieving net profit margins in excess of 35%.
- Strengthened company management structure by recruiting key personnel for production, distribution, and accounting operations.
- Saved $70,000 annually and improved production schedule by switching printers.
- Reduced accounts receivables to average of thirteen days.
- Improved effectiveness of distribution operation through daily contact with distributors and stores.
- Capped growth in production staff through aggressive work flow management.

Barton, Quivers, and Spunk, Athens, GA
Testing and Consulting Firm
Vice President 2002–2006
Responsible for the strategic, sales, and business management of the company's publications operations.

- Doubled annual division sales to $2 million in 2002; increased sales by 400% in five years.
- Created $400,000+ in annual ad placements for parent company at no cost.
- Increased total advertising pages 30% over two years, versus 30-40% decreases for competitive publications.
- Built technical seminar business from scratch to $275,000 in annual revenues; developed seminars.

Edgewild Laboratories
Pharmaceutical Manufacturer
Marketing Representative 2000–2002
Sold proprietary pharmaceuticals and OTC medications in hospital and pharmacies.

- Doubled annual sales in two years, from $200,000 to $400,000.
- Achieved 110% of budget in first year.

EDUCATION:

New York University, New York, NY
M.S., Marketing, 2000

PERSONAL:

Willing to relocate.

CHRIS SMITH, Ph.D.
178 Green Street
Wellborn, TX 77881
(409) 555-5555
csmith@e-mail.com

OBJECTIVE

A position as a Chemist utilizing my education and experience with microcomputer systems in a laboratory setting.

PROFESSIONAL EXPERIENCE

Menden Corporation, Bryan, TX
Chemist I—Instrumentation and Computer Science (2006–Present)
Developed laboratory microcomputer systems for instrument automation and custom and specialized instrumentation/test equipment. Programmed technical applications on various microprocessors, minicomputers, and mainframe systems.

- Engineered a patented design and coordinated construction of ten particle size instruments for Quality Control and Research saving $150,000 over commercial alternatives while providing improved performance and reliability. Received Award for Technical Excellence.
- Designed and built a continuous viscometer detector for gel permeation chromatography to provide absolute molecular weight and branching data. Design was later commercialized by Cook Associates.

EDUCATION

Texas A&M University, College Station, TX
Ph.D., Chemistry, Anticipated, 2012

Baylor University, Waco, TX
M.S., Chemistry 2006

Austin College, Sherman, TX
B.S., Chemistry 2004

CHRIS SMITH
178 Green Street
West Hartford, CT 06117
(203) 555-5555
csmith@e-mail.com

OBJECTIVE:
To use extensive experience in recombinant DNA technology to help solve molecular biological problems.

EXPERIENCE:

2000–2005 RESEARCH ASSISTANT
New England Cancer Institute, Hartford, Connecticut
Performed DNA sequence analysis, S1 Mapping, plasmid and miniprep DNA purifications; made plasmid constructions.

1992–1999 CHEMIST
Drew Chemical Co., Hartford, Connecticut
Developed chemical synthetic procedures and isolation schemes for various nucleotides, nucleosides, and their derivatives.

1988–1991 GRADUATE STUDENT
Department of Physiological Chemistry, University of Connecticut, Storrs, Connecticut
Developed biochemical procedures for study of ribosome structure with respect to the RNA component.

1984–1987 RESEARCH ASSISTANT/TECHNICIAN
Department of Chemistry, Western Connecticut University, Danbury, Connecticut
Researched fungal cell metabolism; isolated plant alkaloids and their bacteria; performed various organic syntheses.

EDUCATION:
Master of Science—Physiological Chemistry, 1991
University of Connecticut, Storrs, CT

Bachelor of Science—Chemistry, 1984
Fairfield University, Fairfield, CT
Emphasis in the field of biochemistry.

CHRIS SMITH
178 Green Street
Ayer, MA 01432
(508) 555-5555
csmith@e-mail.com

OBJECTIVE

To acquire a career continuation in **farm management** including animal husbandry.

AREAS OF EXPERTISE

- ✓ Animal Husbandry/Livestock
- ✓ Crop/Produce
- ✓ Lambing/Foaling
- ✓ Dairy Production
- ✓ Accounting

PROFESSIONAL EXPERIENCE

2003–Present La Grange Farms, Ayer, MA
FARM MANAGER
Responsible for the operation of a livestock and produce farm; its marketing and accounting tasks; selling beef, lamb, and produce to supermarkets, restaurants, and roadside vegetable stands.

1990–2003 Cory-Copia Farms, Lexington, MA
ASSISTANT FARM MANAGER
Handled all livestock, dairy cows, and goats; assisted in lambing season checking for newborn foal diseases and malformations. Raised lambs and hens; baled and sold hay.

1985–1990 Pleasure Acres Farm, Brigham, KY
FARM HAND
Grew up on family owned and operated dairy and livestock farm; baled hay, collected eggs from hens, milked cows; assisted in the birth of cows and horses; assisted father and uncle in marketing meat and dairy produce to restaurants, supermarkets, and local dairies.

EDUCATION

Bunker Hill Community College, Charlestown, MA
Business Management Certificate 2002

Lexington Community College, Lexington, MA
A.S., Animal Husbandry 1994

CHRIS SMITH
178 Green Street
Felda, FL 33930
(407) 555-5555
csmith@e-mail.com

OBJECTIVE

A challenging career as a Forest Ranger where environmental and horticultural experience, education, and skill, combined with motivation and a commitment to our forests; will be utilized and advanced.

EXPERIENCE

FOUNTAIN OF YOUTH NATIONAL PARK — Felda, FL
Manager, Agrarian Development — 1999–Present

- Monitor and evaluate areas of agriculture, timber/forestry, and agrarian-based industries.
- Provide consultations to U.S. Wildlife Department with regard to national and regional objectives and priorities.
- Examine all aspects of forestry/timber credit, marketing, labor, and productivity, with strict adherence to territorial logging and replacement of new pine and oak shoots.
- Generate field support for project budgetary controls on lumber projects; negotiate pricing and products with mill contractors.
- Extensive involvement in environmental protection of forests, land, fisheries, and wildlife activities.
- Document existing state of forest destruction and increase public awareness through public relations; conducted start-up group of concerned citizens and schoolchildren through field trips, lectures, films, and videos.

MYLES STANDISH STATE FOREST — Plymouth, MA
Manager, Planning and Development — 1992–1999

- Performed case studies on marketing forest and public recreation areas, including inefficiencies concerning fisheries, wildlife, fire prevention/firefighting techniques, and cost of educating both public and private sectors.
- Appraised financial and economic projects for expanding public recreation areas with feasibility studies; monitored water supply, drainage and irrigation, flood protection, and ground water.

U.S. PEACE CORPS—SALIM ABBAS RESERVATION — Malaysia
Case Worker—Forester — 1989–1991

- Evaluated areas of lumber, fisheries, and wildlife; examined and planned turf management.

EDUCATION

University of Massachusetts — Amherst, MA
M.S., Forest/Plant Science and Management — **1998**
B.S., International Agriculture — **1989**

CHRIS SMITH
178 Green Street
Manchester, NH 03102
(603) 555-5555
csmith@e-mail.com

PROFESSIONAL OBJECTIVE

A challenging and rewarding position as a Laboratory Assistant in the field of Molecular Biology.

EDUCATION

NOTRE DAME COLLEGE, Manchester, New Hampshire
Master of Science degree in Microbiology, 2005

ST. ANSELM COLLEGE, Manchester, New Hampshire
Bachelor of Science degree in Biology, 2006

- Dean's List.
- Natural Sciences Department Award.
- Senior Class President.
- Named to *Who's Who in American Colleges and Universities.*

EXPERIENCE

ST. ANSELM COLLEGE, Manchester, New Hampshire
Laboratory Assistant to Microbiology Department Head, 2005–Present

- Prepare all media and cultures for microbiology classes.
- Order supplies for department, monitor inventory.
- Act as informal tutor, help other students.

DURHAM MEDICAL ASSOCIATES, Durham, NH
Laboratory Technician for four doctors, 2004–2005

- Initiated running of laboratory; organized equipment and materials.
- Ran tests for patients, reported on same-day basis.
- Ordered supplies; maintained inventory.

REFERENCES

Available on request.

CHRIS SMITH
178 Green Street
Bar Harbor, ME 04609
(207) 555-5555

OBJECTIVE:

To secure a position as a Meteorologist at an International Airport or for Local Television.

EXPERIENCE: MAINE OCEANOGRAPHIC INSTITUTE, Bar Harbor, ME

Meteorologist **2002-Present**

- Analyze and interpret data gathered by surface and upper-air stations, satellites, and radar, and those effects on the surface and subsurface of the ocean and coastline; prepare reports and forecasts.
- Prepare special forecasts and briefings for air and sea transportation, fire prevention, and air pollution.
- Observe and record weather conditions, including upper-air data on temperature, humidity, and winds using weather balloon and radiosonic equipment.

WAYN-TV, Bar Harbor, ME

TV Meteorologist/Announcer **2006-Present**

- Weekend TV weather forecaster and announcer for local cable TV.
- Broad-based knowledge of TV broadcasting and forecasting weather for seasonal climate conditions affecting Bar Harbor tourism and/or natural disasters that affect the harbor's special ecosystem.

PORTLAND AIRPORT, Portland, ME

Meteorologist **2002-2004**

- Part-time and on-call emergency situation staff member at small airport.
- Observe and record weather conditions utilizing weather balloon and radiosonic equipment.
- Prepare specific, timely forecasts for air transportation.
- Assist in forecasting for hurricanes, northeasters, and natural disasters.
- Conduct pilot briefings.

EDUCATION: CORNELL UNIVERSITY, Ithaca, NY

B.S. and M.S. degrees in Meteorology **2000, 2002**

Excellent References Available On Request

CHRIS SMITH
178 Green Street
Dillon, MT 59725
(406) 555-5555
csmith@e-mail.com

OBJECTIVE

To contribute acquired skills to a retail position.

SUMMARY OF QUALIFICATIONS

- Developed interpersonal skills, having dealt with a diversity of professionals, clients, and staff members.
- Adept at cashiering and reconciling cash.
- Proven communication abilities—both oral and written.
- Function well independently and as a team member.
- Self-motivated, able to set effective priorities to achieve immediate and long-term goals and meet operational deadlines.

EDUCATION

BURDEN JUNIOR COLLEGE, Missoula, MT
Major: Criminal Justice B.A. Candidate, 2007

WORK HISTORY

YOUR STORE, Dillon, MT 2006–Present
Cashier
Provided customer and personnel assistance. Handled cash intake, inventory control, and light maintenance. Trained and scheduled new employees. Instituted store recycling program benefiting the Dillon Homeless Shelter.

RONDELL IMAGE, Helena, MT 2005–2006
Data/File Clerk
Assisted sales staff. General office responsibilities included data entry, typing, and filing invoices.

TARPY PERSONNEL SERVICES, Bozeman, MT 2004–2005
General Clerk
Duties included shipping and receiving, and filing invoices.

TELESTAR MARKETING, Great Falls, MT 2003–2004
Telephone Interviewer
Conducted telephone surveys dealing with general public and preselected client groups in selected demographic areas. Required strong communication skills.

REFERENCES

Furnished upon request.

CHRIS SMITH
178 Green Street
Marion, IN 46952
(317) 555-5555
csmith@e-mail.com

PROFESSIONAL EXPERIENCE

2005–Present **LATITIA GREEN ACADEMY,** Marion, IN

Instructor

- Provide instruction to all levels in cosmetology theory and practical applications.
- Develop lesson plans in all subjects; administer tests; give demonstrations.
- Motivate and counsel twenty-student classes; evaluate tests and performances.

2002–Present **LE SALON DESIREE,** Lafayette, IN

Owner/Operator

- Hairdresser/Cosmetologist performing all relevant functions.
- Arranged for promotion of business and maintained good customer relations.

1998–2002 **DYE HEALTHY SALON,** Muncie, IN

Hairdresser

- Performed hairdressing, manicuring, skin care, hair coloring, and hair styling.

1997–1998 **BORELLI MORALIO SALON,** Lisbon, Portugal

Hairdresser

- Provided hairdressing, skin care, facials, permanents, and hair coloring.

1995–1997 **ZACHARY DRAKE'S SHOP,** Lisbon, Portugal

Hairdresser

- Serviced customers with hairdressing, manicuring, skin care, facials.

EDUCATION

WINNIFRED ACADEMY, Muncie, IN; Completed Cosmetology course work. Received License #1 (#1372), 1999.
BONNY LASS BEAUTY ACADEMY, Lisbon, Portugal; Completed one-year course in Cosmetology, 1995.

PERSONAL

Bilingual in English and Portuguese. Managed a grocery store in Lisbon, Portugal, for three years.

REFERENCES

Furnished upon request.

CHRIS SMITH
178 Green Street
Carson City, NV 89703
(702) 555-5555
csmith@e-mail.com

PROFESSIONAL OBJECTIVE

A challenging, growth-oriented position in the fast-food industry in which academic training, work experience, and a commitment to excellence will have valuable application.

EMPLOYMENT

2005–Present THE PIZZA PLACE, Carson City, NV

Server

- Participate in opening of new store outlets.
- Assist with public relations, food service, and register control.
- Resolve conflicts in high-pressure environment.

2003–2005 NEVADA TELEPHONE, Las Vegas, NV

Data Input/Repetitive Debts Collection/Commercial

- Responsible for commercial account installation and verification of records and old accounts for new service.
- Maintained computer for bill revisions through referrals.
- Executed customer services, fielded inquiries, and consumer services.

Summers 2000–2002 BLACKTHORN DAY CAMP, Plaistow, NH

Recreation Director

- Planned, programmed, and supervised camp activities for summer outdoor education and camping services for juvenile coeds.
- Supervised cabin group, counseled, and instructed in aquatics, sports, and special events.

1997–1999 SISYPHUS GROCERY, Manchester, NH

Cashier/Produce Section

- Maintained produce inventory, cash control, public relations, and in-house advertising for special sales and events.
- Strong communications and interpersonal skills required.

EDUCATIONAL BACKGROUND

MANCHESTER HIGH SCHOOL, Manchester, NH
Diploma, College Preparatory, 2004
Varsity Sports (four years), Blue Key Club.

CHRIS SMITH
178 Green Street
Peoria, IL 61603
(309) 555-5555
csmith@e-mail.com

PROFILE
Certified flight attendant with over four years experience working overseas/domestic flights. Specialized training in CPR and emergency evacuation/crisis procedures. Fluent in Russian and English; knowledgeable in German language.

SKILLS
Communication
- Bachelor of Arts degree in Communications.
- Developed interpersonal skills, having dealt with a diversity of professionals, clients, and associates.
- Fluent in Russian and English; knowledgeable in German language.

Customer Service
- Over five years experience in retail and sales, dealing with a wide variety of clients.
- Adept at handling customer complaints and problem-solving.

Specialized Training
- Certified flight attendant.
- CPR certified.
- Participated in three-day intensive training seminar: "Reacting in an Emergency."

PROFESSIONAL EXPERIENCE
9/06–Present WANDER IN WONDER WORLD AIRWAYS, O'Hare Airport, Chicago, IL
Flight Attendant, overseas/domestic flights
- Assist in customer boarding.
- Supervise equipment/supply loading.
- Ensure passenger safety and comfort.
- Maintain passenger manifest and seating allocations.
- Handle bilingual safety instructions and travel problems (emergency landings, etc.).

OTHER EXPERIENCE
2006 THE CRAFTY BOUTIQUE, Orlando, FL, **Salesperson/Manager's Assistant**

2005–2006 BEST BET BUSINESS TEMPS, Chicago, IL, **Account Representative**

2004–2006 THE TAX TASKMASTER, Normal, IL, **Sales Assistant**

2002–2004 THE CHASIN BANK, Joliet, IL, **Teller/Customer Service Representative**

EDUCATION
FANTASTIC FLIGHTS TRAINING CENTER, Orlando, FL
Received Flight Attendant Certificate, 2006
ILLINOIS COLLEGE, Jackson, IL
B.A. in Communications, August, 2004

PERSONAL
Extensive travel including Europe, Asia, and the United States. Willing to relocate.

CHRIS SMITH
178 Green Street
Charleston, WV 25314
(304) 555-5555
csmith@e-mail.com

OBJECTIVE

To contribute developed customer relations, managerial, and accounting skills to a challenging position in hotel management.

SUMMARY

- Capable manager and motivator of staff.
- Function well in high-stress atmosphere.
- Detail- and goal-oriented.
- Highly developed interpersonal skills.
- Developed innovative and efficient system of reconciliation.
- Skilled in utilization of various computer systems.

EXPERIENCE

2005–Present DONNELY HOTEL, Charleston, WV
Assistant Manager, Housekeeping

- Manage 100 employees.
- Ensure standards of guest rooms.
- Prepare biweekly and monthly housekeeping inventory.
- Develop budget worksheets utilizing FileMaker.
- Assist in weekly labor forecasting and scheduling.
- Certified in Interaction Management.

2003–2005 NEWPORT HEIGHTS HOTEL, Montgomery, WV
Chief Night Auditor/Manager On Duty

- Managed technically proficient and hospitality-oriented staff.
- Supervised reconciliation of all Front Desk and Food and Beverage transactions.
- Maintained hotel computer system. Required weekly reorganizations and various other functions.
- Compiled and distributed Daily Business Summary, using Excel.
- Administered overnight operations of Front Desk, Security, and Food and Beverage outlets.
- Nominated Manager of the Year, 2004.

2000–2002 **Night Auditor**

- Coordinated check-in and check-out of all guests.
- Assisted in reconciliation of all transactions.
- Cooperated in implementation of Food and Beverage cashiering system.
- Developed and implemented efficient system to reconcile Food and Beverage transactions.
- Dealt with preparation of Daily Business Summary.

EDUCATION WEST VIRGINIA STATE COLLEGE, Institute, WV
Course: Principles of Accounting I & II, 2000.

CHRIS SMITH
178 Green Street
East Troy, WI
(414) 555-5555
csmith@e-mail.com

PROFESSIONAL EXPERIENCE

2005–Present **Case Worker/Legal Advocate, The Women's Safe Place** East Troy, WI

Night manager of shelter for abused women and their children. Monitor 24-hour hotline and authorize admitting residents on an emergency basis. Organize, prepare, and present seminars to high school students on domestic violence and lead discussions to raise awareness. Assist Associate Director in planning public relations and fundraising events. Assist women in completing Temporary Restraining Orders. Provide support and access to legal resources to women in crisis situations. Advocate for women before judges in family court proceedings. Act as Coalition observer during domestic violence legal cases and report outcomes to staff.

2003–2005 **Associate Editor/Program Coordinator**
Baby's Breath Press Madison, WI

Developed, wrote, and edited articles for monthly business management newsletter. Writing involved combining multiple sources of information and organizing pertinent facts for a business-oriented audience. Developed and wrote articles with outside authors involving case studies on management-development within their organizations. Assisted editorial department in planning content of newsletter by selecting topics for publication. All work performed in a strict deadline-oriented environment. Worked with the fifty people who presented at the annual conference by assisting them with their presentations.

2002–2005 **Writer, *The Republic*** Madison, WI

Researched a variety of sources incorporating various philosophies and wrote articles on women's issues for a quarterly literary magazine in Madison.

EDUCATION

2003 Beloit College Beloit, WI

Bachelor of Arts in Sociology, Concentration in Economic Stratification and Social Hierarchies. Courses include Poverty and Crisis, Gerontology, and Women in Society. Independent study topic: "The Feminization of Poverty in the United States." Member of the Phi Beta Kappa honor society. Member of student-run Volunteers for a Better World program. Codirected campus food drive. Contributing writer for the Vanguard Press.

CHRIS SMITH
178 Green Street
Washington, DC 20008
(202) 555-5555
csmith@e-mail.com

OBJECTIVE

A challenging and progressively responsible position in COUNSELING.

EDUCATION

American University, Washington, D.C.
Bachelor of Science in Psychology and Sociology, 1995

Coursework included the following:

Drugs and Society	Death and Mourning
Sociology of Medicine	Psychology of Women
Speech Pathology	Experimental Psychology

STRENGTHS

Fluent in German; mature, sound decision-making skills; ability to establish trusting relationships with individuals; keep accurate records; relate positively with people from diverse backgrounds; strong communication skills; enthusiastic; genuine desire to be of service to people.

EMPLOYMENT HIGHLIGHTS

American University, Washington, D.C.
Record Coordinator Create, maintain, and update academic records. Assess student charges. Instruct and assist students in registration procedures. Act as liaison with academic and administrative offices. Supervise activities of part-time personnel.
(1996–Present)

Natack & Company, Washington, D.C.
Assistant Controller/Full Charge Bookkeeper Directed activities of all bookkeeping personnel, including training and orientation. Prepared quarterly reports and financial statements.
(1986–1994)

REFERENCES

Furnished upon request.

CHRIS SMITH
178 Green Street
Fort Lauderdale, FL 38314
(305) 555-5555
csmith@e-mail.com

PROFESSIONAL OBJECTIVE

A counseling position in which my education and bicultural experience will have valuable application.

PROFESSIONAL EXPERIENCE

1999 to Present — AMERICAN SCHOOL OF RECIFE, Recife, Brazil
Counselor, International Primary School

- Administer psychological and educational testing for students ranging from pre-kindergarten to fifth grade.
- Counsel students, families, and teachers.
- Design remedial and therapeutic plans.
- Lead group activities for self-image enhancement and behavior modification.
- Work with teachers in preventive strategies for social and disciplinary problems.

1998 to 2000 — INSTITUTE OF AMERICA, Sao Paulo, Brazil
Guidance Counselor

- Counsel individuals and families for students ranging from pre-kindergarten to twelfth grade.
- Designed complete record-keeping system for all students.
- Performed valuable clarification exercises with students.
- Implemented behavior modification programs.
- Administered achievement, vocational, and college-prep tests.
- Made policy on admissions and discipline.
- Worked with teachers on individual educational programs.

1998 to Present — PRIVATE COUNSELING PRACTICES, Miami, Recife, and Sao Paulo
Counselor

- Bilingual English and Spanish counseling.

EDUCATION

Master of Arts in Counseling Psychology, Nova University
Fort Lauderdale, Florida, 1998
Concentration: Community Clinical; GPA: 3.7
Bachelor of Arts in Developmental Psychology, Barry University
Miami Shores, Florida, 1996
Associate of Arts in Human Development, Barry University
Miami Shores, Florida, 1995
Cum Laude Graduate

References available upon request.

CHRIS SMITH
178 Green Street
Elmhurst, IL 60126
(312) 555-5555
csmith@e-mail.com

OBJECTIVE

To contribute comprehensive experience and educational background to a challenging position as a Human Services Worker.

SUMMARY OF QUALIFICATIONS

- Thorough knowledge and management of cases for juveniles and families, which required assessment, development of clinical treatment plans, facilitation of crisis intervention procedures, and informal family therapy.
- Developed exceptional counseling skills, motivating several individuals to enter programs for substance abuse treatment.
- Extensive experience and familiarity with child abuse and neglect cases.
- Excellent rapport with children; superior communication abilities.

EXPERIENCE

2003 to Present — **Investigator/Ongoing Case Manager**
SOCIETY FOR THE PREVENTION OF CRUELTY TO CHILDREN — Chicago, IL

- Conduct assessments and develop treatment plans for family caseload.
- Maintain ongoing written documentation of contracts.
- Provide crisis intervention and informal family therapy.
- Serve as advocate for clients in court and with community agencies.

2001 to 2002 — **Intern**
FARMINGTON JUVENILE COURT — Farmington, IL

- Established monitor contacts and composed monitor reports.
- Tracked abuse and neglect cases to ensure that status reports and petitions were filed accurately and on time.
- Observed court hearings and trials and established court expectations.

2000 to 2001 — **Intern**
PEORIA JUVENILE COURT — Peoria, IL

- Provided individual and group counseling for juvenile offenders in detention.
- Reviewed case files and incident reports.

1999 — **Intern**
DEPARTMENT OF MENTAL HEALTH — Gardena, IL

- Assisted mentally challenged adults in the enhancement of motor skills and encouraged the development of self-esteem and self-sufficiency.

EDUCATION

BRADLEY UNIVERSITY — Peoria, IL
Bachelor of Science degree: Human Services, 2002

REFERENCES FURNISHED UPON REQUEST.

CHRIS SMITH
178 Green Street
Chalmette, LA 70043
(504) 555-5555
csmith@e-mail.com

EDUCATION

TULANE UNIVERSITY New Orleans, LA
Master's in Social Work May, 2002

LOYOLA UNIVERSITY New Orleans, LA
Bachelor of Arts, Psychology May, 2000
Research assistant to Dr. Sophie Dillon. Project involved studying intrinsic and extrinsic motivation in children.
Dean's List.

PROFESSIONAL EXPERIENCE

CHALMETTE CHILDREN'S HOSPITAL
Early Intervention Program Chalmette, LA
Social Worker/Case Manager August 2002–Present
Member of interdisciplinary team serving children who are at environmental and/or biological risk. Responsibilities include: clinical, concrete, and supportive services, education for families, and developmental stimulation for children. Services provided via home visits and participation in classroom team for children.

NEW ORLEANS TEEN CLINIC New Orleans, LA
Intern September 2001–May 2002
Provided individual social work to children and adolescents, including pregnant teens and foster parents. Cooperated with Department of Social Services regarding treatment and placement of children in foster care.

VETERAN'S ADMINISTRATION HOSPITAL OF NEW ORLEANS New Orleans, LA
Intern September 2000–May 2001
Medical and psychiatric social work involving direct patient care with both individuals and groups at outpatient clinic. Cooperative experience with nationally recognized pain team at New Orleans Outpatient Clinic.

PROFESSIONAL INTERESTS

Adolescent behavior, Gifted Children, Neuropsychology

REFERENCES

Available upon request.

CHRIS SMITH
178 Green Street
Houma, LA 70363
(504) 555-5555
csmith@e-mail.com

EXPERIENCE

THERAPIST 2006–Present
Private Practice Houma, LA

Render quality counseling services to private clientele with varied psychological disorders. Develop rapport and relationships of trust; facilitate clear communication. Assess symptoms and personal information to diagnose problems and devise effective treatment strategies.

- Assess client progress and effectiveness of treatment plans.
- Involve guardians and family members in supporting therapeutic activities.
- Make referrals to specialists or social service organizations as appropriate.
- Maintain knowledge of new developments in the field and applications to personal practice.

COORDINATOR OF PROGRAM SERVICES
COUNSELOR/ADVOCATE 2003–2006
Domestic Violence Services, Inc. Orono, ME

Provided leadership and management expertise for efficient daily operations of this nonprofit organization specializing in counseling and services for victims of domestic violence. Assessed needs and coordinated delivery of information, referrals, advocacy, and counseling.

- Responded appropriately to hotline calls and emergency situations.
- Provided one-on-one counseling to battered women and children.
- Conducted play groups for children living in the shelter, as volunteer in 2003.
- Served as Intern Advocate for victims before the Orono Superior court.

EDUCATION

MASTER OF ARTS IN PSYCHOLOGY, 2006
Teacher's College, University of Maine, Orono, ME
Master's Thesis: Impact of Classroom Learning on Students' Behavior

BACHELOR OF ARTS IN PSYCHOLOGY, 2003
Colby College, Waterville, ME

Additional courses, workshops, and seminars:
Identification and Treatment of Trauma and Abuse • Rational Emotive Therapy
CareerPro Leadership Seminar • Group Facilitation • Cultural Diversity
AIDS • Drugs and Alcohol Abuse • Supervision and Management Training
Family Therapy • Battered Women Syndrome • Women Portrayed in Media

CHRIS SMITH
178 Green Street
Seattle, WA 98102
(206) 555-5555
csmith@e-mail.com

EDUCATION

EVERGREEN STATE COLLEGE — Olympia, WA
M.S., Criminal Justice; G.P.A., 3.5, 2006
WHITMAN COLLGE — Walla Walla, WA
B.A., Psychology; G.P.A., 3.3/4.0, 2005

Honors:
Psi Chi National Honor Society in Psychology
Dean's List six consecutive semesters
Who's Who in American College Students

EXPERIENCE

OFFICE OF THE COMMISSIONER OF PROBATION, Seattle, WA — 2006
INTERNSHIP
- Assisted with the integration of probation violators into the Seattle Boot Camp; researched and prepared results for the Commissioner on recidivism rate; attended meetings with judges.

BAY HOUSE HOTEL, Seattle, WA — 2005
INTERNSHIP—SECURITY DEPARTMENT
- Worked closely with Director of Security in developing a fire safety and security manual for evacuations with floor plans and procedures to facilitate emergency situations.

UNIVERSITY OF WASHINGTON, Seattle, WA — 2004
RESEARCH ASSISTANT—DEPARTMENT OF PSYCHOLOGY
- Assisted Dr. Rocky Clapper, Professor of Research Methods and Psychology in coding and data entry for experiments on drug use in juvenile delinquents.
- Trained in research methods and interpretation of collected data.

EMPLOYMENT

BINNACLE FASHIONS, Seattle, WA — 2003–Present
COUNTER ASSOCIATE—JUNIOR MANAGEMENT
- Responsible for customer returns/service; nightly financial transactions.
- Oversee employees; vigilant regarding shrinkage problems and loss prevention.

COMPUTERS

PCs and Macs, Microsoft Word, Excel.

CHRIS SMITH
178 Green Street
Plymouth, NH 03264
(603) 555-5555
csmith@e-mail.com

EDUCATION

Plymouth State University, Plymouth, NH
M.A. in Marketing, Dec. 2005
Courses include International Marketing, Marketing Research, Business Communications, and Statistics.
Member, National Honor Society
Pratt University, Brooklyn, NY
B.A. in Accounting, 2003

EMPLOYMENT

THE PLYMOUTH PLAYER, Plymouth, NH
6/06–Present New Hampshire's largest daily newspaper (circ. 30,000)
Marketing Assistant (part-time)

- Design and manage market research to determine the satisfaction of former subscribers with editorial content. Supplement data with focus group research.
- Develop strategic marketing plans. Propose new marketing management strategies and systems; study online news distribution and creation of new print publications.
- Initiate telemarketing campaign to sell ads for a special section. Targeted advertisers outside usual geographic territory. Although 1/10 of salesforce, sold 1/3 of total ads (sold 6k of total sales of 20k).
- Selling display advertising space. Meet with advertisers, negotiate prices and design ads.

PILGRIM TRAVEL, Plymouth, NH
1/04–6/04 Discount travel company specializing in trans-Atlantic cruises
Marketing Intern

- Managed nationwide client base. Monitored sales, marketing, research, analysis, reports, and presentations.
- Developed and executed marketing plan. Coordinated marketing communications; published monthly client newsletter; created, marketed, and conducted seminars; and managed direct mail campaigns.
- Analyzed finances of client organizations. Performed analysis of multivariate revenue, insurance revenue, and accounts receivable.

COMPUTERS

Microsoft Word, Excel; Macintosh and PC.

REFERENCES

Available upon request.

Chris Smith
178 Green Street
Gaffney, SC 29341
(803) 555-5555
csmith@e-mail.com

OBJECTIVE

An entry-level position in the public relations and/or media field.

EDUCATION

GAFFNEY PUBLIC HIGH SCHOOL
Graduated with academic degree, 2006

SKILLS

Typing, data entry, PC computer system, Microsoft Word, editing, filing, and clerical skills. Has worked with Video, Video Production, and Editing. Has a pleasant and professional phone manner. Work well with little supervision; energetic, responsible, well-organized, and work well under stress. Capable of light bookkeeping, customer service, and inventory. Enjoy working in a busy environment.

EXPERIENCE

LAUREL PARK CINEMAS, Gaffney, SC
10/05–Present Ticket Agent/Concessions Manager
Greet moviegoers, provide tickets, drop nightly deposit at bank, provide food service. Assume responsibilities of manager in event of his absence; open and close facility, call in nightly sales to national entertainment center, schedule employee shifts, etc.

STATE OF SOUTH CAROLINA: DEPARTMENT OF PUBLIC WELFARE
6/05–9/05 Summer Intern
Wrote and edited articles for the newsletter, edited forms, data entry, greeted people, confirmed appointments, answered phones, and filed manuscripts.

BROADWAY VIDEO, Gaffney, SC
1/04–5/05 Sales Assistant
Took inventory of merchandise, greeted/served customers, placed and took orders, answered phones, and performed general office work.

THE BURGER VASSAL, Gaffney, SC
1/03–1/04 Cashier
Provided customer service, performed monetary transactions, took weekly inventory of food/paper supplies.

Chris Smith
178 Green Street
Ogden, UT 84404
(801) 555-5555
csmith@e-mail.com

PROFESSIONAL OBJECTIVE
Seeking a position in the Human Resources/Management field.

EDUCATION

BRIGHAM YOUNG UNIVERSITY, Provo, UT
Master of Business Administration, 2006
GPA: 3.74
Honors: Salutatorian of Graduating Class, Academic Scholarship, Social Service Award for work with disadvantaged teenagers.

UNIVERSITY OF UTAH, Salt Lake City, UT
Bachelor of Public Administration Degree, 2005
Concentration: Financial Management
GPA: 3.50

PROFESSIONAL EXPERIENCE

SUNRIDGE LABORATORIES, Ogden, UT
Supervisor 2005–Present
- Provided personnel with secretarial, transcription, computer equipment operations, and general clerical services.
- Interview, select, and manage support services staff; developed training and facilitating programs for various levels and created a secretarial floater pool.

Technical Employment Representative/Affirmative Action Counselor 2004–2005
- Acted as initial contact for prospective employees; evaluated resumes, conducted preliminary interviews, calculated salaries, etc.
- Participated in job/career fairs.
- Served as Loden Valley Summer Program Administrator.
- Active member of the Loden Valley Affirmative Action Committee.
- Community Relations duties included representing company on various boards ranging from Chambers of Commerce to Social Service agencies.

OFFICE OF MANAGEMENT SERVICES/DEPARTMENT OF PUBLIC WORKS, Salt Lake City, UT
Intern 2004
- Coordinated complete automation of the Office of Management Services by establishing an "Engagement Plan" outlining the time frame to complete all phases of the system; generated a final report, incorporating the system's effects on user personnel and corresponding recommendations, evaluation of supporting software, and related matters.

CHRIS SMITH
178 Green Street
Mitchell, SD 57301
(605) 555-5555
csmith@e-mail.com

OBJECTIVE

To secure an administrative position where supervisory and training expertise will be fully utilized.

QUALIFICATIONS

- Seven years administrative experience.
- Five years experience in the Health Care field.
- Supervised and trained up to ten on staff in Medical Records.
- Organized and revamped medical records filing system as well as Navy personnel filing system.
- Computer Skills: Mac, Windows, and UNIX

STRENGTHS

- Accurate
- Dependable
- Organized
- Enthusiastic
- Calm under pressure
- Strong written communication skills

EXPERIENCE

2006–Present MILITARY/HEALTH CARE
U.S. NAVY / E-4 Specialist **Switching Systems Operator**

- Performed extensive administrative tasks, including the maintenance of records of Navy personnel. Composed and typed correspondence.
- Set up equipment, antennae, security codes, and ensured communications were established.
- Honorably Discharged.

2002–2004 HUMAN NUTRITION RESEARCH CENTER, Rapid City, SD **Nurse's Aide**

- Took patients' vital signs, specimens; stock supplies.

1998–2002 S. DAKOTA GENERAL HOSPITAL, Shadehill, SD **Medical Records Controller**

- Trained and supervised staff.
- Provided record maintenance in File Room.

EDUCATION

NATIONAL COLLEGE, Rapid City, SD 2002–2003
HURON COLLEGE, Huron, SD 2003–2004
Courses in Marketing, Business Administration, Statistics, Computer Science, and Liberal Arts. Volunteer for Student Legal Aid.

Chris Smith
178 Green Street
Walcott, IA 52773
(319) 555-5555
csmith@e-mail.com

OBJECTIVE

To secure a full-time management position.

EXPERIENCE

10/04–Present KLINE AND COMPANY, Moline, IA
Supervisor, Mailroom Services
Coordinate incoming mail; disperse inter-building correspondence. Manage courier services and shipping/receiving. Administer employee evaluations/appraisals; schedule hours. Research and account for certified, registered, and express mail. Responsible for office supply procurement. Obtain/maintain lease agreements for electronic machinery and equipment.

3/04–9/04 EXPRESS MAIL, Blue Grass, IA
Courier
Delivered time sensitive packages throughout area. Sorted incoming/outgoing express packages.

1/01–2/03 GASTON, ROSE & BROOKS, Milan, IA
Supervisor, Mailroom Services
Supervise shipment of weekly overseas pouches and biweekly payroll to thirty domestic offices. Sorted/distributed in-house payroll for 500 employees. Coordinated in-house and U.S. office stock distribution. Acted as building management contact and Chief Fire Warden for 75,000 square feet of office space. Assisted in office relocations throughout U.S.

12/97–12/00 P. GEDELLO FINANCIAL GROUP, Bettendorf, IA
Supervisor, Incoming Mail/Messengers and Stock Distribution
Manage computer facility forms and negotiable forms stored in house vault.

EDUCATION

9/95–11/97 SAINT AMBROSE COLLEGE, Davenport, IA
Course work concentrated in Personnel and Human Resources Management. Participant in SAFE Escort Program for Students.

9/94–5/95 LOVAS COLLEGE, Dubuque, IA
Two courses in Communications.

REFERENCES

Furnished upon request.

Chris Smith
178 Green Street
Cavendish, VT 05142
(802) 555-5555
csmith@e-mail.com

OBJECTIVE
To contribute acquired culinary skills to a restaurant position.

SUMMARY OF QUALIFICATIONS

- More than four years of progressively responsible food-related experience.
- Bachelor's degree in Culinary Arts.
- Dependable, detail-oriented team worker; capable of following directions precisely.

EDUCATION

CULINARY INSTITUTE OF AMERICA, New Haven, CT
Bachelor's degree in Culinary Arts
Culinary Arts Diploma (2006)

UNIVERSITY OF WASHINGTON, Department of Correspondence Study Nutrition Course—three semester hours credit (2005)

EXPERIENCE

AUTUMN OAKS INN, Cavendish, VT — 2006–Present
Cook
Assist chefs in meal preparation. Responsibilities include cutting meat, making sauces, rotating food, cooking, and serving at special faculty functions of more than 300 patrons.

SHADE HILL INN, Branford, CT — 2005–2006
Cook
Prepare breakfast for over 200 patrons daily.

REDWING FOOD SUPPLY, Hartford, CT — 2004–2005
Stock Person
Dated and rotated products. Supplied food to homeless shelter cafeterias.

THE WOLFSONG TAVERN, Butte, MT — Summer 2004
Prep Cook
General responsibilities as above.

Assistant Prep Cook — Summer 2003
Busperson — Summer 2002

Chris Smith
csmith@e-mail.com

School Address	**Permanent Address**
178 Green Street	23 Blue Street
Dayton, OH 45469	Oakwood, OH 45873
(513) 555-5555	(419) 555-4444

EDUCATION

University of Dayton — **Dayton, OH**
Bachelor of Arts degree, Summa Cum Laude, May 2006
G.P.A.: 3.6/4.0 Dean's List, First Honors
Majors: Secondary Education, English

HONORS

Selected to speak at Commencement ceremonies
National Education Award, 2006
National Dean's List, 2005–2006, 2006–2007
Who's Who Among Students, 2006, 2007

ACTIVITIES

Student Admissions Program
Peer Advisement Program
Freshman Assistance Program
School of Education Senate
Student Representative to Educational Policy Committee

EXPERIENCE

Spring 2006 **Substitute Teaching** — **Oakwood High School, Oakwood, OH**
Work as substitute teacher in various disciplines for students in grades 7–12.

Fall 2005 **Student Teaching Full-Time Practicum** — **Kerrigan High, Kerrigan, OH**
Travel to site daily and assume full teaching responsibility for two eleventh-grade accelerated American Literature classes and one ninth-grade fundamental English class. Prepare, lecture, discuss, and evaluate units in literature and writing. Design and present lessons on Puritan writers, focusing on Nathaniel Hawthorne's *Scarlet Letter.* Provide writing instruction for paragraphs and essays.

Fall 2005 **Student Teaching Field Pre-Practicum** — **Central High School, Dayton, OH**

Spring 2005 **Kerrigan High School** — **Kerrigan, OH**
Visit site weekly to observe classes and gain practical teaching experience.

REFERENCES

Available upon request.

Chris Smith
csmith@e-mail.com

School Address	**Permanent Address**
178 Green Street	23 Blue Street
Ripon, WI 54971	Charlotte, NC 28277
(414) 555-5555	(704) 555-4444

EDUCATION

RIPON COLLEGE
B.S. in International Relations: GPA. 3.20, Major 3.33
Minor: Marketing
Courses: Marketing Research, Sales and Distribution, Management, Promotional Management, Consumer Behavior, Global Communications, and Social Change in Developing Nations.

OXFORD UNIVERSITY Oxford, England
Spring 2005
Related Courses: International Marketing and Advertising, and International Economics and World Trade.

*Financed 50% of college tuition as well as all personal expenses through part-time college and full-time summer employment.

WORK EXPERIENCE

JACKSON ELECTRIC COMPANY Ladysmith, WI
Customer Service Representative Summer 2005
Worked in the Marketing Department for the Power Integrated Circuits Division of Jackson answering both domestic and international customer inquiries regarding product and pricing. Processed product sample requests, packaged and shipped samples. Developed reports on sample requests and manufacturing orders received for District Managers worldwide. Assisted other marketing personnel in various tasks as required.

THE INTERNATIONAL CONNECTION Ripon, WI
Evaluation Intern Spring 2004
Composed, edited, and dispersed to management summaries of project reports for IESC, a nonprofit organization which sends retired corporate executives into third world countries to advise and assist them in efficient production methods.

THE WOODTIP CORPORATION Ripon, WI
Student Manager 2003–2004
Organized blueprint files, order entering, and materials inventory; handled accounts payable and accounts receivable; worked with materials purchasing; and replaced receptionist for plant which manufactures aircraft engine parts.

ADDITIONAL EXPERIENCE

Ripon College Marketing Club (2003–2005), College Marketing Association (2004–2005), International Relations Club (2005–2006), Circle K Club (2005–2006).

Studied in London, England (2005), and traveled through Western Europe and the United Kingdom. Working knowledge of French.

Chris Smith
csmith@e-mail.com

Current Address
178 Green Street
Bloomington, IN 47405
(812) 555-5555

Permanent Address
23 Blue Street
Evansville, IN 47712
(812) 555-4444

OBJECTIVE

To utilize acquired skills in biotechnology research toward project responsibility in nutrition/health industry.

EDUCATION

Bachelor of Science in Nutrition
INDIANA UNIVERSITY
Degree Anticipated: 2007
Courses include Organic Chemistry, Anatomy and Physiology, and Food Service Administration.
Thesis topic: "Advances in Refrigeration Techniques and Their Application to the Fresh Meats Industry."

EXPERIENCE

2006 to Present **Intern**
Nutrition Evaluation Laboratory, Human Nutrition Research
CENTER ON AGING AT INDIANA UNIVERSITY

- Assist seven researchers in routine and esoteric biochemical analysis. Implement ten different non-clinical assays of vitamins, amino acids, and other biomolecules in support of human and animal tissue culture studies. Develop and implement new types of assays and improve existing analytical techniques.
- Interact with investigators and assist in organization and implementation of analysis. Provide literature search and publication of developed methodologies in scientific journals.
- Provide maintenance for a wide variety of laboratory and analytical equipment.
- Train on microprocessor and personal computer driven analytical instruments and robots: Waters hardware and software, analytical, and chromatography software.
- Initiated independent research project concerning detection of non-enzymatically glycated amino acid residues in proteins.

2005 to 2006 **Teaching Assistant**
Department of Biochemistry and Biophysics
INDIANA UNIVERSITY
Bloomington, IN

- Led group of seven students in weekly laboratory experiments.
- Administered quizzes and evaluated lab results.

PERSONAL

Willing to travel.

Chris Smith
csmith@e-mail.com

School Address
178 Green Street
Charlotte, NC 28277
(704) 555-5555

Home Address
23 Blue Street
Banner Elk, NC 28604
(704) 555-4444

EDUCATION:

University of North Carolina at Charlotte
Bachelor of Arts, Projected May, 2007
Major: Philosophy
GPA: 3.8/4.0
Dean's List seven consecutive semesters.
One of five candidates chosen to assist in teaching Freshman Seminar orientation class.
Self-financed 50% of education.

EXPERIENCE:

9/05–Present **Cake Decorator**
HARPER LEE SUPERMARKETS, Charlotte, NC
Fill custom cake orders and maintain cake shelf on sales floor. Associate of the Month award in August, 2006. Received corporate-wide recognition for cake production idea which increased company cake sales 10%. Represented Bakery in Associate Task Force. Time commitment of thirty hours per week.

9/06–Present **Learning Center Tutor**
UNIVERSITY OF NORTH CAROLINA AT CHARLOTTE
Tutor students on an individual basis in all aspects of writing and literature and the concepts of molecular, genetic, and evolutionary biology. Average of three hours per week.

Summers 2004–05 **Store Manager**
JERRY K. PANTS, INC., Charlotte, NC
Full profit and loss responsibility for high volume package store employing twenty-five people. Managed purchasing, inventory control, cash handling, financial reporting, merchandising, advertising, special promotions, and personnel hiring, training, and supervision.

- Implemented purchase control system, thus reducing inventory levels by $75,000.
- Achieved average annual sales growth of 20%.

2003–05 **Assistant Store Manager**
ANCIENT OAK FOOD MARKET, Wilmington, NC
Scheduled and supervised fifteen to twenty staff members and managed daily operations and inventory. Involved in extensive customer service and cash handling during full- and part-time employment. High volume store with up to $300,000/weekly.

Chris Smith
178 Green Street
Newark, NJ 07102
(201) 555-5555
csmith@e-mail.com

Education:

Rutgers University, Newark, NJ
Bachelor of Arts in Women's Studies, 2006. Thesis topic: *The Political Economy of Our Domestic Health Care System.* 3.63 Grade Point Average.
Member of Varsity Crew Team. Designed and painted university-sponsored mural with the theme of cultural diversity.

Work Experience:

12/05–6/06 Summer Orientation Leader
Rutgers University, Newark, NJ
- Aided over 400 students in registration process.
- Led groups through rigid itinerary in strict time schedule.
- Provided initial contact to services and advisors for freshman and transfer students.
- Facilitated dialogue on issues following group diversity exercise.
- Presented campus-wide tours to incoming students and their families for university Open House.

9/05–5/06 Editor-in-Chief, Layout and Design Editor, Activities Editor
The Amber Store, Rutgers University
- Successfully worked within a $30,000 budget to create a 400-page publication from scratch.
- Served as accountable leader of student-run organization.
- Interviewed and selected personnel.
- Acted as teacher, advisor, and supervisor to team of eight.
- Established deadlines for book completion and staff contracts based on academic calendar and publisher expectations.

Summer/Winter Breaks:

2005–2006 Teller
Alpine Savings Bank, New Brunswick, NJ
- Achieved excellent balancing record with daily cash flow.
- Processed large and numerous transactions responsibly.
- Promoted bank services and benefits.
- Mastered the Unisys computer terminal.

2003–2004 Snack Bar Staff
Clover Fields, Camden, NJ
- Organized inventory, storage, and daily tasks for new snack bar.
- Assisted in managing front line customer transactions and behind the scenes operations while training new applicants.

Interests:

Enjoy photography, yoga, and collecting nineteenth-century Russian novels.

CHRIS SMITH
178 Green Street
Northfield, MN 55057
(507) 555-5555
csmith@e-mail.com

OBJECTIVE

A challenging position in AIRCRAFT MAINTENANCE which allows for broadening professional experience and room for growth toward management.

EDUCATION

NORTHFIELD COMMUNITY COLLEGE, Northfield, Minnesota
Currently attending Applied Science Degree Program in Aeronautics

UNITED STATES AIR FORCE AIRCRAFT MAINTENANCE SCHOOL
Grissom Air Force Base, Indiana
Graduated 170-hour program—KC/RC/EC-135, Periodic
December 2006
Graduated 110-hour program—KC/RC/EC-135, Able Chief
May 2006

UNITED STATES AIR FORCE AIRCRAFT MAINTENANCE SCHOOL
Sheppard Air Force Base, Texas
Graduated 150-hour program in Tactical/Airlift Bombardment
December 2006

AIRCRAFT MAINTENANCE COURSE
Lackland Air Force Base, Texas
Graduated 120-hour program
September 2005

PRACTICAL EXPERIENCE

Trained in maintenance, servicing, and troubleshooting on all areas of KC/RC/EC-135 aircraft from wing tips to landing gear, nose to tail, interior and exterior, including removals and replacements of component parts, repairs, lubrications, refueling, and flight-line launching and recoveries.

Perform inspections of J57-59 Turbo Jet Engines, plus troubleshooting of component parts. Certified in aircraft towing, aircraft power and battery connections and disconnections, and engine cowl removal and installation.

RELATED INFORMATION

Received honorable discharge.

Available immediately . . . Willing to relocate . . . References on request.

CHRIS SMITH
178 Green Street
Burlington, VT 05405
(802) 555-5555
csmith@e-mail.com

OBJECTIVE:

To pursue a technical career in television or video with opportunities for training and merited enhancement.

EDUCATION:

Trinity College, Burlington, VT
Associate's degree in Radio-Television-Film Technology, Dec. 2006
Cumulative GPA: 3.4; GPA in major: 3.7
Selected Radio, Television, and Film Courses: Newswriting and Production, Film Production, Television Production, Community Video and Industrial Production, Writing for Radio-Television-Film, and Station Organization and Operation (FCC Laws).

Film Direction Workshop. Sponsored by the American Film Institute. Covered the essential narrative, visual, and organizational elements of the director's craft. Examined all phases of film production from the special point of view of the director.

Scriptwriting: An informal discussion. Sponsored by the Burlington Film Festival. Workshop explained how a studio system works, and how scripts are submitted and evaluated.

EXPERIENCE:

December 2006–Present — Master Control Room Technician, **KSTG** Channel 68, TTP Affiliate
Responsible for "on-air" switching of various program sources, commercials, promos, and public service announcements. Recorded satellite feeds. Dubbed commercials and movies. Maintained proper transmitter, program, and operational discrepancy logs. Required the ability to perform with accuracy during periods of high stress.

Fall 2006 — Internship, **KARR-TV** Channel 3, NLS Affiliate
Operated studio camera and television prompter. Lighted commercials and public service announcements. Operated dimmer board.

Spring 2005 — Film Production Class
Wrote, produced, and directed for short films. Acted as camera person for two short films.

Fall 2004 — Community Video and Industrial Production Class
Operated a portable camera. Directed two exercise videos.

CHRIS SMITH
178 Green Street
Alpha, NJ 08865
csmith@e-mail.com

CAREER OBJECTIVE:
Develop training programs in a corporate or academic environment and present the material in a clear and interesting manner.

BACKGROUND SUMMARY:
Fifteen years of experience in the microcomputer industry with skills ranging from system design to project management. Special expertise in creating and presenting training programs covering a wide variety of topics.

EMPLOYMENT:
THE RACE BANNEN COMPANY, Rockaway, ME
Program Management Training Specialist/Network Administrator 2004–Present
Prepare and teach classes in program management techniques and the use of program management software. Manage and maintain the computer network for the department of Program Management. Reconfigure the computer network resulting in 60% increase in the efficiency of the electronic mail system. Developed the course material for seven different classes and presented them to over 300 employees.

Program Manager Computers 2002–2004
Coordinated all efforts going into the successful development of computer products from their inception through their discontinuance. The activities managed included electrical and mechanical engineering, publications, purchasing, and regulatory. Successfully managed seven different computer models to market.

Marketing Support Engineer 1999–2002
Possessed working knowledge of computer products. Represented the company at computer trade shows. Answered technical questions from dealers, distributors, and prospective customers. Field tested computer products and performed other "continuing engineering" functions.

Software Documentation Writer 1996–1998
Authored documentation for computer products including a complete revision of the original operating system manual.

SINEAD KIERNEY CORPORATION 1994–1996
Technical Staff
Codesigned a disk interface for word processor to photo-typesetting equipment. Wrote all of the machine language firmware for the design.

EDUCATION:
Ramapo College of New Jersey, Mahwah, NJ
Master's degree in Physics

COMPUTERS:
Programming: FORTRAN, Basic, Assembly
Applications: MS Word, QuarkXPress, Illustrator

Chris Smith
178 Green Street
Bristol, RI 02809
(401) 555-5555
csmith@e-mail.com

OBJECTIVE:
Freelance or full-time gallery employment as Art Director in an established advertising agency.

EMPLOYMENT:

CURTIS ASSOCIATES/CHERRY HILL, Boston, MA
Art Director, 2006–Present
Major responsibilities included:

- The design, art direction, illustration, and concept-development of black-and-white and full-color promotional samples for black-and-white, color-copying, and ink-jet printing divisions.
- Art direction on photography sessions for direct mail marketing pieces.
- Quality control management on press runs for promotional pieces printed in and out of house.
- Design in-house company morale promotional pieces such as anti-drug abuse posters, company picnic and Christmas dinner/dance posters and tickets, as well as completing most of the paste-up on all projects.

WOLFSONG, INC., Northampton, MA
Assistant Art Director, 2003–2006
Designed and/or rendered full page cooperative free standing insert ads for regional and national name brand pet food companies.

- Designed and/or rendered FSI's accompanying point-of-sales materials (header cards, tear-off pads, soft sheets, and shelf talkers), trade promotions (ad reprints, dealer sell sheets, and marketing lists), and bounce-back coupons.
- Utilized illustrative talents to complete black-and-white product illustrations for bounce-back coupons and ad slicks.

EDUCATION:

RHODE ISLAND SCHOOL OF DESIGN, Providence, RI
Associate's Degree in Specialized Technology (2003)

MONTSERRAT COLLEGE OF ART, Beverly, MA
Completed three-year program in Commercial Art (2001)

SKILLS:

Mac and PC applications; QuarkXPress and InDesign; inkjet printers, color photo copiers, and retouching and page layout software.

Chris Smith
178 Green Street
New York, NY 10019
(212) 555-5555
csmith@e-mail.com

SUMMARY OF QUALIFICATIONS

- More than six years orchestral experience as violinist/violist.
- Ability to comprehend administrative needs from the perspective of a performer.
- Acquired skills as orchestra librarian/personnel manager.
- Organizational abilities; detail-oriented.

RELEVANT EXPERIENCE

Orchestra—2nd Violin

- *La Musique, C'est Magnifique!*
  Play, Paris, France
- *White Willows in Glasgow*
  Opera and Ballet, Scotland
- Sun Symphony Orchestra of L.A.
  Los Angeles, California
- The Lighthouse Orchestra
  Bar Harbor, ME
- *Bang a Ceramic Gong: The Tale of a Chinese Emperor*
  Play, Boston, MA

MIDAS TOUCH CHAMBER ORCHESTRA, New York, NY 2005-2006
Personnel Manager. Recruited players. Arranged for substitutes. Assisted Conductor/Music Director. Scheduled recitals, announcements, and member contact regarding changes, problem resolution, etc. Required ability to deal with personality conflicts and musical problems as well as fielding suggestions from members. Instituted rotating string sections. Handled membership payment. Acted as liaison between musicians and union.

EDUCATION

O'BURN INSTITUTE, New York, NY 2006
Teacher Workshop Courses

THE JUILLIARD SCHOOL, New York, NY 2004
Bachelor of Arts, Music

References and MP3s Available on Request

Chris Smith
178 Green Street
Winterthur, DE 19735
(302) 555-5555
csmith@e-mail.com

OBJECTIVE

To become an artist and repertoire representative for a major field.

EXPERIENCE

Ricochet Management Inc., Wilmington, DE
Personal Manager (2005 to Present)

- Selected six local bands and brought them to national recognition: Top of the Charts, Sights, New York Talk, and Spunk Awards 2006.
- Advised artists on performance and repertoire, resulting in three major-label signings.
- Oversaw and coordinated the production, promotion, and marketing of four major label projects.
- Initiated and devised extraordinary prerelease promotions for a debut album, resulting in immediate college chart movement on release (Kieley and Briody).
- Tour managed three album tours, one regional and the others national, all 20–25% under budget.

Moonchild Records, New York, NY
Label Manager (2003–2005)

- Achieved three regionally Top Ten selling and charting records, and a top selling single in Europe.
- Devised and oversaw promotion and marketing on limited budgets of $10,000 to $15,000.
- Oversaw production, mastering, manufacturing, artwork, and distribution.
- Coordinated career development with artists and their management.

Aural Erosion Records, Los Angeles, CA
Product Manager (2002–2003)

- Created a showcase club for up-and-coming alternative acts: Crudeness, Drink the Foam, Your Mangy Mother, Corporate Mind Wipe, Clubbed Knee, and Four Evil Extraterrestrials and Their Dad.
- Conceived entirely new club concept: music format, design, and marketing strategy. Increased revenues from an average $10,000 to over $2 million, and profit on live shows from 52% to 99%.

EDUCATION

Stanford University, Stanford, CA
Major: Public Relations
Master's degree, May 2000

CHRIS SMITH
178 Green Street
Chicago, IL 60622
(312) 555-5555
csmith@e-mail.com

OBJECTIVE

A career continuation as a Director of legitimate theatre on or off Broadway.

SKILLS AND QUALIFICATIONS

- Over thirteen years experience stage directing with clear understanding of playwrights' texts and creative analysis.
- Provide theatrical direction to actors attuned to both the Stanislavsky and Method styles of acting.
- Focused on the physical requirements and restrictions of stages ranging from in-the-round, proscenium arch, mechanical stages, and special effects.
- Communicate well with actors in relation to lighting and sound technicians.
- Involved in all aspects of costuming and makeup to enhance actors' performances and facilitate their taking direction accurately and precisely while maintaining their own "voice" and force on stage.
- Able to deal with producers and financial backers in structural, aesthetic, and artistic feasibility of a play.
- Work closely with producers and board of directors on time, focus, budget, creative, and practical expectations among director, actors, and powers-that-be.

SELECTED DIRECTORIAL EFFORTS

- *THE IMPORTANCE OF BEING EARNEST*
- *SUNSET STRIP*
- *FENCES*
- *THE FANTASTIKS*
- *PEARLIE*
- *GREASE*
- *THE WIZ*
- *THE REAL INSPECTOR HOUND*
- *SHADOWLANDS*
- *AGATHA CHRISTIE'S THE MOUSETRAP*
- *EVITA*
- *OLIVER!*
- *BARNUM*
- *THE LITTLE FOXES*
- *WAITING FOR GODOT*

EDUCATION

EMERSON COLLEGE, Boston, MA	M.A., Directing	1995
EMERSON COLLEGE, Boston, MA	B.A., Theatre	1993

References and Portfolio Available on Request

CHAPTER 13

Write Your Cover Letter

WRITING RIGHT MEANS doing research, identifying what it is you want to say, writing a first draft, polishing it, and sending it off. This chapter will give you something else—more specific information about appropriate cover-letter format, wording, and issues related to electronic communication.

Putting Your Best Foot Forward

Your cover letter is the first writing assignment you will complete for a prospective employer. It's a preview of your work. To demonstrate your future performance, it only makes sense for you to stay on task and focused, presenting relevant information in an easy-to-read format. In your cover letter, you should be specific, focusing on the job you're applying for or a function you're interested in. You have to impress the readers in a subtle way, by presenting the information they need and suggesting what you think the next step should be. A cover letter must be independently strong yet complementary to your resume. Together, these two documents motivate readers to invite you to interview.

Which Comes First, the Resume or Cover Letter?

You present the cover letter to an employer as an introduction to your resume—remember, it "covers" the resume. But when it comes to writing, you should complete the resume first.

Cover-Letter Formats

There are three types of cover letters: letters of application, letters of introduction, and networking notes. Each is written with a particular purpose and to target specific readers, yet all three types share common content and format. As you review samples in this book, you will see obvious differences in some cases and more subtle ones in others.

Letters of application and letters of introduction should be written in either traditional or memo style. Networking notes, on the other hand, can use an informal tone and style. A traditional business letter begins with your name, address, phone number, and e-mail address appearing letterhead-style across the top of the page. Underneath and in left-justified block form goes the date (for example, June 1, 200–), followed by extra line breaks, and the name, title, and address of the letter's recipient. Following a few more line breaks, include the salutation, such as "Dear Ms. Cummings:".

You can also choose to use memo style for your letter. Memos present DATE:, FROM: [*your name*], and SUBJECT: or RE: after capitalized headers on the left of the page. You will also in most cases want to include a TO: line to address the letter to the attention of a particular person or department. The memo style is a good choice if you do not know the name of a contact person at an organization, and you need to send a letter to a department ("Human Resources Department") or unspecified person ("Hiring Manager").

You don't include a salutation ("Dear . . .") in a memo-style letter; instead, the body of the letter begins directly (after one blank line) below the RE: or SUBJECT: line. This lack of a salutation enables you to avoid writing such dated and impersonal constructions as "Dear Sir/Madam" or "To Whom It May Concern."

You may choose to use the memo style even when you do in fact know the name of the person you are writing to. For one thing, this format can help to give your letter a serious, businesslike tone. Also, if you are unable to determine whether the person you are writing to is a man or woman, using the memo style is an effective (if slightly sneaky) way of avoiding the entire problem of choosing "Dear Mr." or "Dear Ms." In other circumstances, you might actually know the person you are writing to, but only slightly, leaving you unsure whether "Dear Pat" or "Dear Ms. Cummings" is more appropriate. The memo style can help you to sidestep that choice as well.

One more word on formats: When you send an e-mail, your e-mail program will likely automatically include "Date:", "From:", "To:", and "Subject:" lines in a box at the top of the e-mail. This leaves you the choice of beginning the body of the e-mail cover letter directly with a salutation ("Dear Ms. Cummings:" or "Dear Pat:") or with several lines of text in the memo style. One important difference between regular letters and e-mails is that in e-mails your contact information (street address, phone number, and e-mail address) will usually be placed at the end of the e-mail after your name, and not in a header at the beginning.

Letters of Application

The most common cover letter is a letter of application, used to respond to postings. Letters of application should contain job-specific phrasing and match qualifications with those listed in the posting. This type of letter is the easiest to write because you have the job ad to help you figure out what you need to say. An effective letter of application should focus on two or three key requirements and corresponding resume entries. The goal of this letter is to show the employer that you have the skills and qualifications they are looking for in filling their job opening.

The following situations call for a letter of application:

- ***Employer postings***—These postings include the company name and may or may not provide a contact name. In this case, make sure you do some research on the company and incorporate it into your cover letter. If you don't have a contact name, use the memo format to write the letter.
- ***Confidential postings***—These postings don't identify the employer. A letter in response to a confidential posting must focus on the job description and on your analysis of the skills required to succeed, which you should demonstrate that you possess.
- ***Employment agencies***—When you are contacting a headhunter or other professional who specializes in job placement, you may use phrases such as "should you judge my candidacy worthy of an interview for this position with your client firm . . . ."
- ***Executive search firms***—These firms deal with filling senior and executive positions. Again, focus your letter on motivating the reader to support your candidacy and to forward your information to the client (the hiring organization) with a recommendation to interview.

Most cover letters are about 200 to 400 words long, and networking notes are fewer than 200 words. Communication done via e-mail should be shorter, but you can attach additional files like your resume and a more official cover letter. In any case, it's not really the length that's most important. It's the content used to support your candidacy that is crucial and that has the most impact on your being offered an interview.

Letters of Introduction

These are proactive letters that introduce your candidacy to potential employers or allies. The challenge is to be strategically focused, even though you'll be tempted to be general and cast as wide a net as possible. Even though this letter isn't written in application for a specific job, you must communicate functions you are most interested in and qualified for. You may want to write a letter of introduction in the following situations:

- ***Contacting a targeted employer***—If you're interested in a specific company, you can send a letter of introduction to a particular person (if you can get a contact name) or at least to human resources.
- ***Before an on-campus interview***—Employers will be impressed if you send a letter of introduction after being selected to meet.
- ***Before a career fair***—This is a way to better your chances of being granted an interview for post-baccalaureate jobs or internships.
- ***Broadcast letters***—This popular method is ineffective if a generic, unfocused letter is sent to hundreds of employers. Not to worry! You can make it work as long as you stay focused, identifying functional areas of interest and addressing the employer directly.
- ***Initial contact***—You can use letters of introduction to make contact for the first time. You might, for example, send letters to people listed in directories for professional associations or specialized fields. Whatever the case, don't be shy about contacting someone and introducing yourself and your goals.

Networking Notes

These are brief, informal statements, usually e-mailed. They concisely request consideration, advice, or referrals from advocates and potential network members. Because e-mail has become the medium of choice for these messages, brevity and clarity are crucial. Also be sure to attach your resume and mention that you will send a cover letter later.

Content Is Crucial

You probably already know that a cover letter and a resume should each be one page in length. But how are you supposed to fill that page? Choose the information about you and your skills and achievements that is pertinent to the particular job or field. This information goes in a certain order.

Introductory Focus Paragraph

The initial paragraph cites the job title or functional area you are interested in and requests an interview. This first section can identify the foundations upon which you will rest your candidacy. Is it education? Is it work experience in general, or can you claim one or two specific accomplishments? Is it a specific project that matches stated requirements? Remember what you once learned about the five-paragraph essay? Begin your essay with a clear thesis statement that is supported by three paragraphs and then end with a conclusion. Cover letters are pretty similar—think of each letter as having an introduction, supporting paragraphs, and a conclusion.

Qualification and Motivation Paragraphs

These two paragraphs, which may be presented as a series of bullet-point lists, discuss your qualifications and motivation. They identify examples from your past that project abilities to perform in the future. This is where you review cover-letter samples and job ads, and identify resume "keys." What key resume points will you present here? How can you connect previous achievements to the listed job requirements? Be specific! The more you use the language of the field you wish to enter (special phrases and key words), the better. Use appropriate language to ensure that you will soon walk into an interview with confidence.

Closing Paragraph

Restate your desire for a interview, perhaps suggesting a phone interview as a convenient next communication. State that you will follow up to confirm the contact's receipt of the letter and accompanying resume. If you wish, you can close with the most critical point you wish to cover during the interview. Of course, also say thank-you. While you must sign any cover letter you fax or mail, when using e-mail (more and more the case), you can use a script font to represent your signature, if you like.

Special Circumstance Statements

These can be added in the last paragraph or as postscripts. You may want to note that you anticipate being in a particular city at a particular date, that you have an offer in hand and limited time to conduct interviews, or that you also have enclosed supporting documents like writing samples, letters of recommendation, or other materials. Basically, cover letters have three components—an introductory paragraph, qualification and motivation summaries, and a closing paragraph. Effective letters focus on particular titles or functions, and they present specific traits and abilities that match those required to do the job.

Myths and Realities

It's likely that you'll start getting all kinds of advice from those around you. Unfortunately, there seem to be a lot of misconceptions about the most effective and ineffective ways of looking for a job. Let's identify some cover letter myths in order to prevent misguided action and achieve positive outcomes faster.

Myth #1: No One Reads Cover Letters

Some employers who screen candidates prefer resumes. Others read both resume and cover letter. A lot depends upon the job and the field, but it's safe to say that in many cases cover letters are very carefully reviewed. If writing talents are critical to job performance, this document will be scrutinized with particular attention. Also, electronic key-word search capabilities include cover letters. So someone almost always reads your correspondence.

Myth #2: Getting Attention by Being "Different"

If creative talents are associated with job requirements, you can be as creative as you wish in formatting your cover letter. However, direct, concise, and skill-focused cover letters will still get more attention. Matching desired capabilities and achievements is more important than being different. Cover letters stand out when they express qualifications effectively and when letters and resumes together project interview-worthiness.

Myth #3: You Can't Upload a Cover Letter

When using online job sites, you can post your cover letter along with the resume. Some posting and resume submission sites seem to allow you to upload only resumes, but in most cases you can transmit your cover letter as well. Just create and upload a two-page document, with the first being the cover letter and the second the resume.

Myth #4: Individualized Cover Letters Are Impossible

On the contrary, individualized cover letters are easy (and a must). Always refer to the name of the company and, when possible, use the actual job title in the first and last paragraphs. Ideally, also reveal to readers that you have reviewed the job posting and the mission statement of the firm. You are a unique individual and candidate. Your letter should be, too.

GETTING A NAME FOR THE ADDRESS

Try to get a name by calling or exploring a company's website. If you can't find a name, don't fret. Use memo format and focus on the content of the letter, not on the recipient. The most important person is you—the writer, the candidate.

Common Mistakes

While it is always best to see the metaphorical glass as half full, remaining optimistic and positive, sometimes we can learn from common mistakes. In all cases, it's okay to fill strategic plans with good ideas and best steps to success. Here are some of the more common mistakes job applicants are prone to:

Mistake #1: Too Much Creativity

Unless the job you are applying for involves copywriting, scriptwriting, or artistic and graphic creativity, it's best to avoid too much creativity. Instead, just be direct, enthusiastic, and clear. Stories about someone sending a cover letter and resume in a shoebox, and stating, "Let me put my best foot forward with your organization" are urban myths. Effective job-seekers don't deliver resumes in shoeboxes, nor do they print cover letters and resumes on T-shirts or huge posters. You can be effective with a traditional approach, allowing your skill-focused writing style and follow-up techniques to support your request for an interview.

Mistake #2: No Job Stated

This sin of omission can be costly. If readers have no clue about the job you want, serious consideration is impossible. Be sure you state the job when writing letters of application and your functional areas of interest when writing letters of introduction. Your networking notes should also clearly identify your chosen positions. Always make your goal clear, and you'll be more likely to get a positive response.

Mistake #3: No Reference to Employer

Include the name of the organization you are applying to somewhere in your cover letter. Broad requests that do not state your desire to interview with and work for a particular firm are less effective. First and last paragraphs are best for stating the name of the firm, while all paragraphs are appropriate for citing job titles and functions.

Mistake #4: Lack of Focus

Those who fear focus are most prone to send open letters, stating an eclectic mix of talents and a wish for the reader to identify a best fit. It's ironic that trying to be open ends up getting the door closed on you for serious consideration. Your cover letter is there for you to project goals and qualifications. It is not the responsibility of readers to analyze your candidacy and determine what jobs are right for you. You are the one who must state what you want and what you are qualified to perform.

New Issues for the E-Generation

Only a decade or so ago, job-seekers were limited to mailing resumes and cover letters. Then came express mail, which speeded the process and magnified the importance of messages delivered by a next-day carrier. Next, faxing introduced immediate communication and allowed for follow-ups minutes after resumes and cover letters were faxed. Now, almost all job-seekers must become "e-fficient": able to effectively use the Internet and electronic communications in their job search.

Access to the world wide web is essential for job-seekers today. You must use the web to identify and respond to postings, to explore potential employer websites, and to e-mail your resume and cover letter (plus other supporting documents) as attachments. If you don't have your own computer and a way to connect to the web, use the free resources at your local public library.

E-mail Etiquette

E-mail is an acceptable way of sending cover letters and resumes, but follow proper strategies when doing so. When e-mailing, include the name of the job in the subject heading whenever possible. Keep your e-mail text concise, or adapt what would be the initial paragraph and refer to the "attached cover letter and resume." Spell-check your e-mail—typos characterize you as someone who does not pay attention to detail. A good feature of most e-mail programs is the ability to send yourself a secret copy of your messages. Another option is to save all the messages you send. This will allow you to review those messages at a later date, just like saving a paper copy.

Voice Mail

Voice mail is also appropriate for transmitting messages to potential employers and advocates, but try to stick with brief statements and don't expect responses immediately. Keep messages brief and to the point, always ending with a question, like "Should I call again or will you e-mail me your response?" If possible, alternate between e-mail and voice mail, so you won't appear to be a nuisance. And be patient regarding responses. A day or two may seem like forever, but it's perfectly normal.

Resume Uploading Systems and Sites

Unrealistic expectations associated with online job-search services are endless. On sites like *www.monster.com* and *www.hotjobs.com*, you have the option of uploading your resume so that potential employers may browse through it. Although this is a passive approach to searching for a job, it does occasionally work and is probably worth your while. Plus, when you do find good postings, you may be able to simply forward your uploaded resume in application for those positions.

You can upload cover letters into web-based systems, even if they appear to only allow resumes. Create and then upload a multiple-page document. Make the first page the cover letter and subsequent pages the resume. Always supplement resumes with cover letters, even when using Internet resources.

Key Words

Often, before any actual person reviews your cover letter and resume, the documents are electronically scanned by key word. Potential employers identify and read only those documents that contain predetermined words and phrases. Knowing this will surely make you appreciate the importance of using key words appropriate to your chosen field and, if applicable, in the job description.

E-mail Won't Fail

Some postings offer the option of e-mailing, faxing, or mailing cover letters and resumes. Whenever you can, e-mail first, but if you want to be sure, follow up with a mailing. Your e-mail message will be the "cover note," and your resume and lengthier "cover letter" will probably be attached as Microsoft Word files. The first line of the e-mail message should state your purpose: "I would like to interview for the Account Executive position." Subsequent lines state qualifications concisely and clearly. E-mails should be quick, direct, and informal. Lengthy and overly formal e-mails are hard to read. The attached letter can be more business-like.

E-mail is the transmission method of choice for most initial contacts and follow-up communications. Of course, you may have to use the phone to identify the e-mail address of your desired contact person. A quick search of an organization's online directory (if one is available) might give you this information as well.

Microsoft Word is used by more than half of all business professionals. To ensure your documents will be accessible when you attach them to e-mails, use Word when drafting and editing cover letters and resumes. Here's a word of warning, though: Do not use the templates provided. They limit your ability to personalize documents and to present the most important content first.

Crucial Challenges to Overcome

As you read this book, you will realize that cover-letter writing can be simple. Too many job-seekers find reasons for putting off this critical job-search task. Now that you know about letters of application, letters of introduction, and networking notes, and you are ready to communicate via electronic and traditional means, nothing should stop you from taking all steps required of job-search success. To motivate the best attitude and actions during trying times, President Franklin Roosevelt said: "The only thing we have to fear is fear itself." To motivate your efforts, you must overcome psychological and logistical concerns.

Fear of Focus

Some job-seekers mistakenly fear that stating goals in a cover letter limits the scope of consideration. These candidates send off broad and ineffective letters, hoping that employers will find something of interest—or they don't act at all. They wait for inspiration to strike, when they should be conducting active research into fields of interest, functional areas that match their qualifications, and firms that they may be interested in contacting. Remember, being "open to anything" often leads to nothing. Get focused and stay focused.

Follow-Up Phobia

Use the phone, fax machine, and e-mail to follow up. Don't be afraid of being too pushy. If you treat others the way you would like to be treated, you will be following the golden rule of follow-up. Follow-ups can always be politely posed as a query, like so:

- "Did you receive the resume and cover letter?"
- "Would it be appropriate to arrange an interview?"
- "Am I among the candidates receiving continued consideration?"
- "Should I send additional documentation?"
- "When should I call back?"

All of these are proper questions to ask. Don't be afraid of following up, hoping to avoid rejection. As you will see later in this chapter, you can and should also follow up rejections.

Over-Analysis Paralysis

Too often, too much thinking delays action. Don't overanalyze what your cover letter should contain or fret over every word, comma, or period. Have confidence in your abilities. Be optimistic that your candidacy will be granted appropriate consideration. As long as you start with a first draft and then edit it to the final version, you've done enough. Don't try to overthink the format or content, delaying transmission. If your well-crafted documents lead to interviews, wonderful. If not, following up can rekindle consideration or yield referrals to other persons, places, or postings. Also, you can send revised documents, getting second and third chances to make good impressions.

If you find a posting that is close to but not exactly what you are looking for, send a letter of introduction rather than a letter of application. Tell the employer, "I was inspired to contact you regarding similar opportunities when I reviewed a posting that appeared on your website," then state your goals and refocus the reader on the job you want and on the attached resume.

Follow Up on Your Letter

You may have finished your final draft and mailed it off, but this doesn't mean you're done. An important but often forgotten part of writing cover letters is following up on them. Waiting passively for employer responses is not strategically sound. You are not done after you have been granted an interview and extended an offer. You are done after you accept a position. Once you have transmitted a formal acceptance letter, all job-search efforts must stop. While you could (and should) send updates to all on your networking hit list, thanking them for help and informing them of your decision, no direct requests for consideration should be made.

Strategies and Subtleties

Everyone knows you should send a thank-you note after an interview, but other ways of following up may be less obvious. You can respond to a confirmation of resume receipt. Send a very positive, job-focused thank-you letter with a renewed request for an interview. Even if you don't receive confirmation, follow up a week or two after your first contact. Via voice mail, e-mail, or fax, state, "My interest in this position remains sincere and my desire to interview strong," and attach another resume "to remind you of my background and for your files." Don't assume they remember your name or have easy access to the documents submitted earlier.

Also try to get your advocates involved in the follow-up. Ask them to send brief e-mails to specific employers, stating, "I strongly encourage you to grant this candidate an interview." And, advocates can also send post-interview recommendations to further enhance your chances of receiving an offer.

Remember, advocates can be professional peers, faculty, or other individuals who can attest to your abilities to do a great job. Passively, they are "references," but actively and strategically, they are advocates.

Follow-Up Faux Pas

Even those who try to be polite and persistent—not pesky—sometimes make mistakes. While these errors of judgment may be avoidable, they will not cost you a chance for an interview. Trust prospective employers to understand how enthusiasm may lead to less-than-perfect communication.

Don't fear follow-up, but do try to avoid making any faux pas by following these simple do's and don'ts:

- Don't follow up every day for a week or more.
- Do leave voice-mail messages whenever you call, briefly stating why you called and leaving a phone number or e-mail where you can be reached.

- Don't overuse voice mail, calling more than once a day or, frankly, more than twice a week, unless you have been told to do so. (Phone tag should only be played by mutually agreed-upon contestants.)
- Do vary your mode of communication, including phone, e-mail, and fax.
- Don't pressure the employer by appearing impatient.
- Do use someone within the company as an advocate, especially if they are in a position of power, and let them communicate on your behalf with decision-makers.
- Don't ask for feedback regarding how to improve your cover letter, resume, or interview skills.
- Do ask for reconsideration or referrals to other departments or organizations after receiving "We'll keep you on file" or "Sorry, we've selected another candidate" messages.
- Don't use deceptive techniques to bypass "gatekeepers," such as using "information conversations" as ruses to gain interviews.
- Do be assertive, confident, and communicative when stating and restating sincere requests.

Responding to Rejection

It's human nature to ignore those who reject you, so this is the most underused follow-up technique. But you are definitely encouraged to follow up rejection messages or communicate anew with an employer after you are told you won't get an interview. If you do get a "No thank-you" note from an employer, or if several weeks have passed, follow up by seeking reconsideration or referrals to other departments or organizations.

CHAPTER 14

Sample Cover Letters
and Notes for Every Occasion

178 Green Street
Stoughton, MA 02072
(617) 555-5555

July 27, 20--

Pat Cummings
Administrator
Any Corporation
1140 Main Street
Chicago, IL 60605

RE: Assistant Hospital Supervisor position

Dear Ms. Cummings:

I am writing in response to your advertisement in this past week's *Boston Phoenix*.

I recently took a sabbatical and finished my Bachelor of Arts degree in May at Emerson College. I am currently seeking full-time employment.

My employment background consists of twelve years at the Deaconess Hospital, where I provided a wide range of administrative, financial, and research support to the Chief Executive Officer. I have a strong aptitude for working with numbers and extensive experience with computer software applications.

I would be interested in speaking with you further regarding this position. I am hopeful that you will consider my background in administrative support, as well as my word processing, database, and spreadsheet skills, an asset to Any Corporation.

Thank you in advance for your consideration.

Sincerely,

Chris Smith

Enc. Resume

178 Green Street
Marietta, GA 30060

August 20, 20--

Pat Cummings, R.N.
Head Nurse
Any Hospital
1140 Main Street
Savannah, GA 31404

Dear Ms. Cummings:

I believe I have the combined clinical nursing and research skills that would qualify me as an ideal candidate for the Clinical Research Nurse opening you advertised in *Nursing Today*.

I am a dedicated professional capable of working with physicians and nursing, laboratory, and professional specialty groups, and can offer more than fourteen years of responsible experience ranging from Staff Nurse and Charge Nurse to Clinical Research Nurse with a major teaching hospital.

I hold a Bachelor of Science in Nursing, and my graduate studies have focused on epidemiology and international health. My experience encompasses sound knowledge of nursing quality assurance programs and in-service education programs. Throughout my career, I have worked both independently and as part of a team on studies involving psoriasis, cardiology, AIDS, sickle-cell anemia, amyloidosis, diabetes, and oncology.

Please contact me at the above address, or call (404) 555-5555 to arrange a mutually convenient time for a meeting. I am very interested in joining the nursing staff at Any Hospital and hope to speak with you soon.

Thank you for your consideration.

Sincerely,

Chris Smith, R.N., B.S.N.

Enc. Professional profile

178 Green Street
St. Paul, MN 55105

July 10, 20--

Pat Cummings
Principal
Any High School
1140 Main Street
Minneapolis, MN 55404

RE: Preschool Director Position

Dear Mr. Cummings:

As a Speech/Language Clinician with extensive experience in the management and administration of programs dealing with special needs in education, I feel I have the qualifications necessary to succeed in the position of Preschool Director as advertised in the *Star Tribune*.

During the past eleven years, my experience with a professional, private agency has been concentrated in the area of special needs programs for multiple school districts. Prior to that, my work as a Speech Language Clinician involved the development and implementation of programs directed toward special education for preschoolers through twelfth grade in a public school system.

Although my positions were diverse and my achievements provided professional satisfaction, I am interested in making a new association with a large, highly recognized institution such as Any High School. As Part-Time Preschool Director, I hope to utilize my broad-based experience in special education to make a meaningful contribution to your professional management staff.

The enclosed resume summarizes my background and experience. I would appreciate the opportunity to meet with you to further discuss my qualifications and how I can best contribute to your needs. Please contact me at the above address or by phone at (612) 555-5555.

I look forward to hearing from you.

Yours sincerely,

Chris Smith

Enc. Resume

To: *patcummings@anyfitnessclub.com*
From: *chrissmith@jobsearch.com*
Subj: Job #ABC004687

Dear Mr. Cummings:

I am pleased to submit my application for the position of Administrative Assistant with Any Fitness Club. I believe my positive attitude and exceptional people skills, combined with my willingness to work both independently and as part of a team, make me an ideal candidate for this job. As my attached resume indicates, I have more than six years of experience providing administrative and support services to the professional staff of a golf and tennis club in suburban San Diego, where my responsibilities included word processing and data entry, purchasing, inventory control, office equipment maintenance, and assistance with special events and promotions as needed. In addition, I hold an Associate's degree in recreation management and, as a volunteer for the local chapter of the American Cancer Society, have served on the steering committee for the 20-- and 20-- "Run for the Cure" mini-marathon run/walk events, which drew more than 10,000 participants each.

I would appreciate the opportunity to meet with you to further discuss my qualifications and how I might utilize them to the benefit of your facility and club members. I look forward to hearing from you.

Yours sincerely,

Chris Smith

178 Green Street
La Jolla, CA 92037
(619) 555-5555
chrissmith@jobsearch.com

To: *patcummings@anyfirm.com*
From: *chrissmith@jobsearch.com*
Subj: Job #999888ZYWX

Dear Mr. Cummings:

I believe I am ideally suited to the position of Business Operations Manager which you posted recently on Careerbuilder.com. I am a seasoned professional with more than eighteen years of business and corporate experience in the areas of cost accounting and financial analysis, procurement and contract administration, negotiations and contract procurement, budget oversight and forecasting, and business impact analysis. Supported by a Master in Business Administration degree in Finance and a Bachelor of Arts degree in Economics, my strengths include the ability to manage multiple projects of a diverse nature and a proven ability to analyze operational units in order to arrive at alternative methods of service delivery. I am equally adept at working with supervisors, colleagues, and subordinates, and have "hands-on" knowledge of computer programs for rigorous analysis, financial reporting, and high-quality presentations.

My goal is to join a firm that requires immediate use of these skills to either increase a rate of established growth, or to effect a turnaround situation. The attached resume describes my qualifications in greater detail. I will call you within the week to determine when your calendar might permit time for a personal interview. Thank you for your consideration.

Sincerely,

Chris Smith

178 Green Street
St. Louis, MO 63110
(314) 555-4444
chrissmith@jobsearch.com

To: *patcummings@anyhotel.com*
From: *chrissmith@jobsearch.com*
Subj: Job #XYZ007800

Dear Ms. Cummings:

I was delighted to read your advertisement on truecareers.com for the position of Concierge for two reasons: 1) I share your philosophy concerning the role of a concierge in maximizing the overall guest experience, and 2) I believe I am the ideal candidate to fulfill this role at your hotel. My dedication to providing exemplary customer service is evidenced by more than six years of progressively responsible positions in upscale retail establishments and luxury hotel properties. My professional demeanor, organizational abilities, and exceptional attention to detail and follow-through, have garnered accolades from clients and employers alike. I know my way around the Internet and I am especially adept at securing whatever arrangements are necessary to ensure that every guest feels welcomed and well cared for during their stay, and that each one leaves, looking forward to his or her next return.

I would greatly appreciate the opportunity to learn more about this position and to discuss in greater detail how we might work together for the benefit of your guests. I hope we can get together soon, as I am anxious to share my ideas. In the interim, I attach my resume for your additional information about my qualifications. Thank you for your consideration.

Sincerely,

Chris Smith

178 Green Street
Charlottesville, VA 22906
(804) 555-5555
chrissmith@jobsearch.com

178 Green Street
Vienna, VA 22211

June 1, 20--

Human Resources Director
P.O. Box 7777
Arlington, VA 22203

Dear Human Resources Director:

I am writing to express my interest in the Assistant Personnel Officer position as advertised in the May 30 edition of the *Washington Post*.

As the enclosed resume indicates, I offer extensive experience, including my most recent position as Assistant Staff Manager at Virginia General Hospital. In this capacity I have recruited and trained administrative and clerical staffs, ancillary and works department staffs, and professional and technical staffs. I have also evaluated personnel, conducted disciplinary and grievance interviews, signed employees to contracts, and advised staff on conditions of employment, entitlements, and maternity leave.

Should my qualifications be of interest to you, please contact me at the above address or by phone at (703) 555-5555. I look forward to hearing from you.

Sincerely,

Chris Smith

Enc. Resume

178 Green Street
Mobile, AL 36608

October 13, 20--

P.O. Box 7777
Gainesville, GA 30503

RE: Catering Manager

Dear Sir/Madam:

I write in response to your recent advertisement for a Catering Manager in the *Southern States Service Weekly*. Currently, I am seeking a new position with a firm than can benefit from my ten years of professional experience in the food service industry. Allow me to elaborate.

I have held positions of responsibility in banquet/special event catering, functions management, and restaurant food service operations. I have additional experience in front desk operations, and I possess good organizational, leadership, training, and supervisory skills. I can also provide quality service and performance in a high-volume setting, and manage food, beverage, and kitchen staff with ease.

The enclosed resume summarizes my experience. I would like the chance to expand on my qualifications in a personal interview. I am anxious to learn more about your firm and the available position, and to show you how I can meet your requirements.

Please contact me at the above address or at (205) 555-5555 so that we may schedule a meeting time. I thank you for your time.

Sincerely,

Chris Smith

Enc. Resume

178 Green Street
Quincy, MA 02171

July 22, 20--

Personnel Director
P.O. Box 7777
Amherst, MA 01003

RE: Librarian

Dear Personnel Director:

In response to the July 21 advertisement in the *Boston Sunday Globe*, I have enclosed my resume for your review.

In addition to an M.L.S. degree and ALA accreditation, I have twelve years' experience as a Bibliographer and Acquisitions, Special Collections, and Reference Librarian with concentration in history and additional experience in philosophy and religion. In these positions, I provide general and specialized reference services, develop and manage collections, perform faculty liaison work, and conduct bibliographic instruction sessions at undergraduate and graduate levels. I am also experienced in assisting and training others in the use of electronic resources including CD-ROM, the World Wide Web, and other networked information resources for research.

Although my present position provides a challenging and rewarding atmosphere, I am interested in making a change where I can contribute my knowledge and experience in an academic setting. I have the ability to undertake a broad scope of responsibility and work effectively with a diverse population of students, faculty, and staff.

I am anxious to learn more about this position. Should you require additional information, please contact me at the above address or by phone at (617) 555-5555. I look forward to your response.

Sincerely,

Chris Smith

Enc. Resume

178 Green Street
Lawton, OK 73505

February 10, 20--

P.O. Box 7777
Platteville, WI 53818

RE: Medical Assistant

Dear Sir or Madam:

My interest in the position of Medical Assistant that you advertised in *Health Support Monthly* has prompted me to forward my resume for your review and consideration.

In addition to ten years of experience as a Home Health Aide, In-patient Claims Representative, and, since 20--, Medical Assistant with Smith Rehabilitation Hospital, I have good knowledge of medical terminology, procedure codes, and medical office systems including related computerized applications. I have an Associate's degree in Sociology, was graduated as a medical assistant, and am currently a candidate for an Associate's degree in Nursing.

My career objective is to develop further my medical and support skills in areas that will give me the opportunity to participate in the administration of quality health care. I would welcome the opportunity to discuss whether my abilities and goals suit your requirements and expectations. Please contact me at the above address or at (405) 555-5555 during the daytime to schedule an interview.

Thank you.

Yours sincerely,

Chris Smith

Enc. Resume

RESPONSE TO A "BLIND" ADVERTISEMENT

178 Green Street
Tyler, TX 75799

July 20, 20--

Department of Human Resources
P.O. Box 7777
San Antonio, TX 78297

RE: Staff Photographer

To whom it may concern:

I am responding to your July 18 advertisement in the *San Antonio Express* for a staff photographer.

As you will be able to see from my resume, I hold a Bachelor of Fine Arts degree in photography from the University of Texas. My extensive photography experience includes several years of printing and processing with a variety of black-and-white materials, and custom and production printing of color negatives. In addition, I am familiar with traditional 35 mm, 2-¼, and 4 × 5 equipment, as well as digital formats. I also have experience teaching photography in a bachelor's degree program.

I would very much like to arrange an opportunity to meet with you and review my portfolio. I am confident that I can convince you of my skills as a photographer, as well as my dedication to producing a product of the highest quality.

I can be reached at the above address or by phone during the evening at (903) 555-5555. Thank you for your consideration of my application.

Sincerely,

Chris Smith

Enc. Resume

178 Green Street
Hunt Valley, MD 21031
(712) 555-5555

January 20, 20--

Pat Cummings
Senior Operations Manager
Any Airline
1140 Main Street
Baltimore, MD 21226

Dear Mr. Cummings:

I am very interested in securing a challenging position in an aviation-related operation, and have admired the fast-growing quality reputation Any Airline has built in the national arena.

I possess nine years of diverse full-time and part-time experience within the airline industry, ranging from Ground Crew and Operations Agent to my current position as Senior Operations Dispatcher for a highly personalized, worldwide courier service. This experience is supplemented by a Bachelor of Science degree in Aviation Science/Aviation Management, and comprehensive advanced training courses in these areas.

My enclosed resume provides a summary of the experience and training I feel can be put to effective use for your company. After you have had an opportunity to review my credentials, I would like to arrange a personal meeting so that I can more fully expand on my immediate and long-term potential. I am happy to make myself available at your convenience.

I look forward to hearing from you.

Sincerely,

Chris Smith

Enc. Resume

178 Green Street
Pueblo, CO 81001

November 7, 20--

Pat Cummings
Product Development Supervisor
Any Corporation
1140 Main Street
Gunnison, CO 81231

Dear Mr. Cummings:

I am interested in a challenging position requiring product management, product development, and clinical research/nursing skills. Any Corporation's research facility has earned a reputation as the most technologically advanced in the field and, for this reason, I am eager to join your staff.

My expertise includes the management of product development from clinical research for FDA approval to commercial marketability. I offer thirteen years of professional clinical experience with major teaching and trauma hospitals as a Staff R.N. and Therapeutic Apheresis Nurse Specialist. My most recent three years have been spent as Project Manager of Clinical Services and Product Manager with a firm specializing in clinical research and product development, concentrating in applications for autolymphocyte therapy (ALT).

I have excellent communication, computer, and writing skills and am well qualified to assume responsibility for clinical, regulatory, and related functions.

I am anxious to discuss how I might contribute to your organization. Please contact me at the above address, or call (719) 555-5555 to arrange a mutually convenient time for a meeting. Thank you for your consideration.

Sincerely,

Chris Smith, R.N.

Enc. Resume

178 Green Street
Bunkie, LA 71322
(318) 555-5555

December 5, 20--

Pat Cummings
Hiring Director
Any Corporation
1140 Main Street
Chicago, IL 60605

Dear Mr. Cummings:

I am an experienced Computer Programmer and I am ready, willing, and able to join Any Corporation.

I offer extensive knowledge of five computer languages and strong management, sales, and sales support experience. As a Computer Specialist, I was responsible for the management of a center handling the complete line of IBM computers and peripherals for home and commercial use. In addition to a Bachelor of Science degree in Business Administration, I will receive a certificate in Programming in May 20--.

I feel confident that, given the opportunity, I can make an immediate contribution to Any Corporation. I would appreciate the opportunity to meet with you to discuss your requirements. I will call your office on Tuesday, December 12, to schedule an appointment. Thank you for your consideration.

Sincerely,

Chris Smith

Enc. Resume

178 Green Street
Washington, DC 20024

November 6, 20--

Pat Cummings
Director
Any Agency
1140 Main Street
Washington DC 20005

Dear Mr. Cummings:

During the past ten years, my experience has been concentrated as an Area Office Manager and Child Advocate Coordinator in the coordination and management of human services information and resources for multicultural, multilingual populations in the Washington, D.C., area.

Currently, I am seeking a new association with an agency, in the public or private sector, which has a need for a qualified professional. I can offer broad experience working with and coordinating the efforts of public, private, and charitable resources, educational systems, and providers of human services to community residents or company employees.

I am especially interested in the field of human services as I am dedicated to improving the quality of life and learning for the less fortunate. I possess strong organizational, communication, and teaching skills, as well as the ability to work well under stressful or crisis situations.

I would be glad to make myself available for an interview at your convenience to discuss how I might put my knowledge and experience to work for Any Agency. Should you require additional information prior to our meeting, please contact me at the above address or by phone at (202) 555-5555. I plan to make a follow-up call within a few days.

I look forward to speaking with you.

Yours sincerely,

Chris Smith

Enc. Resume

178 Green Street
Neptune, NJ 07754
(415) 555-5555

July 18, 20--

Pat Cummings
General Manager
Any Store
1140 Main Street
Cherry Hill, NJ 08002

Dear Ms. Cummings:

I am a recent graduate of the Gemological Institute of America with a year of successful experience in the purchase and sale of precious metals, gems, and antique jewelry.

Currently, I am looking for a new position with a major jewelry store where I can apply my sales and customer relations skills to continue my proven track record of increasing profit and market share. During my year at Monahan Jewelers, I was responsible for increasing company sales by 10 percent while creating a substantially larger customer base.

The enclosed resume summarizes my experience. I am very much interested in Any Store because of your top-notch reputation in the field. I am confident of my ability to represent you in an ethical and professional manner, and look forward to hearing from you soon.

Yours sincerely,

Chris Smith

Enc. Resume

"COLD" LETTER TO A POTENTIAL EMPLOYER

178 Green Street
Glendale Heights, IL 60139
(708) 555-5555

February 26, 20--

Pat Cummings
Hiring Coordinator
Any Law Firm
1140 Main Street
Chicago, IL 60606

Dear Ms. Cummings:

I am a 20-- graduate of Chicago-Kent College of Law interested in a position as an Associate with Any Law Firm. I am particularly interested in the firm's real estate, corporate, finance, and litigation departments.

As my enclosed resume indicates, upon graduation I accepted a job with the Chicago-based law firm Glavin and Joyce. As a first-year associate, I worked in the firm's litigation, real estate, finance, and corporate departments. In May of 20--, I accepted a position with the Brussels-based international consulting firm Brunkhorst and Associates. On their behalf, I act as a consultant and advisor on American law as it relates to the offshore funding of U.S. commercial real estate.

Although I enjoy my present position, I would very much like to become associated with an up-and-coming firm such as yours so that I can continue my development as a lawyer. My association with a well-established, full-service law firm would also enable me to better service Brunkhorst and Associates and its clients.

If my qualifications are of interest to you, I would like to visit your offices for an interview. I will contact you Monday, March 4, to discuss available opportunities. Thank you for your attention and I look forward to speaking with you.

Sincerely,

Chris Smith

Enc. Resume

178 Green Street
Kingsport, TN 37660

January 11, 20--

Pat Cummings
Director of Human Resources
Any Corporation
1140 Main Street
Yukon, MO 65589

Dear Mr. Cummings:

My interest in associating with an established firm such as Any Corporation has prompted me to forward my resume, which briefly summarizes my experience in office and departmental management.

As Office/Department Manager at Kimco, I was responsible for directing and coordinating the activities of accounting and support personnel in a $10 million manufacturing operation. I concurrently managed the cutting room and handled the purchasing of approximately $5 million in raw materials, supplies, and capital equipment used in manufacturing, sales, and distribution of branded and private label products through mass merchandisers.

This position required entrepreneurial skills and the capability to "wear many hats" in a small, active manufacturing operation. During my six years at Kimco, the company nearly doubled its profits and was able to expand its staff by 15 percent.

I would appreciate the opportunity to discuss, on a one-on-one basis, openings within your company. I can be reached at the above address or by phone at (615) 555-5555. If I do not receive a response, I will call within a few days to arrange a mutually convenient meeting time.

Sincerely,

Chris Smith

Enc. Resume

178 Green Street
Santa Clara, CA 95053

June 22, 20--

Pat Cummings
Director, Health Care Services
Any Corporation
1140 Main Street
Colorado Springs, CO 80903

Dear Ms. Cummings:

As Assistant Director of Pharmacy with a high-volume, forty-store chain, I have the management and sales expertise necessary to deal with multidisciplinary health care professionals as a member of your management team.

In addition to holding a Bachelor of Science degree in Pharmacy, I am a Registered Pharmacist with eight years of progressively responsible experience encompassing general management and in-house and field sales experience in a rapid growth environment.

I am well versed in regulations controlling therapeutic drug treatment, have sound knowledge of medical terminology, work well in either an independent setting or team effort, and enjoy both the clinical and nonclinical aspects of working with health care products and/or services. Based on my experience and professional credentials, I consider myself well qualified to handle the responsibilities of a management position at your company.

I hope to hear from you to schedule a personal interview at your convenience. I can be reached at the above address or at (408) 555-5555 from 9 A.M. to 5 P.M. weekdays or at (408) 555-4444 on weekends. I am willing to relocate for the right professional challenge and compensation package.

Sincerely,

Chris Smith

Enc. Resume

178 Green Street
Topeka, KS 66612

April 18, 20--

Pat Cummings
Director
Any Employment Agency
1140 Main Street
St. Paul, MN 55401

Dear Ms. Cummings:

I am writing with the hope that one of your clients in the field of Advertising/Graphic Design is in need of an entry-level assistant.

I possess strong verbal and written communication skills and pay close attention to detail, while maintaining a flair for creativity. I feel that I am a well-disciplined, highly motivated person with a strong desire to succeed in Advertising/Graphic Design. To support my enthusiasm, I possess excellent PC and Macintosh computer skills and a typing speed of 55 wpm.

Thank you in advance for reviewing the enclosed resume. I would be happy to further discuss my experience and qualifications with you in person. Please feel free to contact me at (913) 555-5555 if I can be of further assistance. Once again, thank you for your consideration.

Sincerely,

Chris Smith

Enc. Resume

178 Green Street
Sioux Falls, SD 57117
(605) 555-5555

April 5, 20--

Pat Cummings
Director
Any Employment Agency
1140 Main Street
Dayton, OH 45402

Dear Mr. Cummings:

I will be moving to the Dayton area next month, and would like to submit my qualifications for any suitable opportunities available through your agency.

I am an accomplished cook with experience in a wide variety of food service institutions, including restaurants, catering services, and banquet functions. My areas of expertise include all aspects of food preparation, from ordering ingredients to presentation.

As you can see from my enclosed resume, I most recently worked as a Rounds Cook at the McGuiness Inn. In addition to cooking to order, I performed several supervisory duties, such as scheduling shifts, overseeing inventory control, and troubleshooting problems.

I will be visiting Dayton to secure housing arrangements during the week of April 17–23. I would be available to meet with you or a client within this time frame. In the interim, I will call your office next week to see if I can provide you with any additional information.

Thank you in advance for your consideration.

Sincerely,

Chris Smith

Enc. Resume

178 Green Street
Flandreau, SD 57028

March 4, 20--

Pat Cummings
Director
Any Corporation
1140 Main Street
Chicago, IL 60605

Dear Ms. Cummings:

During the past ten years, my experience has been in the liability insurance field in positions ranging from Transcriber to Senior Field Claims Representative. Currently, I am seeking a new association with an underwriter or a corporate liability insurance department in which there is a need for expertise in claims settlement, from fact-finding analysis to negotiation.

I am hoping that among your many clients there may be one or two who are looking for someone who is knowledgeable in the area of corporate liability insurance; if so, I would like to explore the opportunity. I may be reached at (605) 555-5555 during regular business hours or evenings at (605) 555-4444.

I look forward to hearing from you.

Sincerely,

Chris Smith

Enc. Resume

178 Green Street
Salamanca, NY 14779
(716) 555-5555

May 13, 20--

Pat Cummings
Director
Any Corporation
1140 Main Street
Chicago, IL 60605

Dear Mr. Cummings:

In July of this year I will be permanently relocating to the Chicago area. I am forwarding the attached resume for your evaluation because of my desire to contribute my comprehensive experience in real estate/property management to a locally based company.

I have two years of direct experience involving all aspects of the management of 275 apartments and four commercial units in three buildings. My responsibilities include a range of activities, from advertising and promotion of apartments to competitive analysis of rate structures.

My experience also includes contractor negotiations, liaison with government and service agencies, personnel relations, financial management, and other functions basic to the effective management of complex properties.

If you know of any company with a current need for a bright, outgoing property manager with an orientation to sales, please do not hesitate to contact me.

Thank you for your consideration.

Sincerely,

Chris Smith

Enc. Resume

178 Green Street
Redmond, WA 98052
(206) 555-5555

December 24, 20--

Pat Cummings
Executive Recruiter
1140 Main Street
Seattle, WA 98103

Dear Mr. Cummings:

I have enclosed a business profile and request your consideration for any current or anticipated search assignments.

During the past twenty years, I have had the opportunity to apply innovative, leadership, and profit-making skills in positions ranging from President of a successful start-up business developed to $7 million in annual sales, to Vice President, Product Management/Business Development, with a $750 million rapid growth computer resale company.

My skill in undertaking new challenges, ability to implement change, and expertise in developing compatible, professional teams during the transition phases of acquisitions, mergers, and consolidations enables me to provide stability and profitability to growth situations. Presently, I am looking for a position change to a company where I have the responsibility for making meaningful decisions and the authority to implement plans to achieve corporate objectives.

My desire is to find an exciting, growth-oriented position. Thus, I would be willing to relocate to secure a salary in the $100,000 range.

Please contact me should my qualifications be of interest to one of your client firms. Thank you for your consideration.

Sincerely,

Chris Smith

Enc. Business profile

178 Green Street
Kalamazoo, MI 49006

June 15, 20--

Pat Cummings
Executive Recruiter
1140 Main Street
Chicago, IL 60605

Dear Mr. Cummings:

My experience encompasses more than ten years of decision-making responsibility for human resource development, manpower planning, and labor law and relations, affecting hundreds of employees in the public and private sectors. In addition to the training and supervision of sizable staffs, I have been involved in collective bargaining for management, wage and salary administration, employee benefits, safety and training, and making and enforcing labor law considerations.

I am currently interested in a firm that offers stability, growth, and profits. I am willing to relocate if offered a challenging assignment. My salary requirement is $50,000 to $65,000.

I have enclosed my resume for your review. If I may provide you with additional information, please call me at (616) 555-5555. I look forward to discussing my qualifications with you in more detail.

Sincerely,

Chris Smith

Enc. Resume

178 Green Street
Minnetonka, MN 55343
(612) 555-5555

March 23, 20--

Pat Cummings
President
Any Search Firm
1140 Main Street
Minneapolis, MN 55408

Dear Ms. Cummings:

Based on my diverse background and experience with high-end, mid-range, and low-end hardware, software, and network products designed for many industries, I feel confident that I can make a valuable contribution toward new product planning, market development, and expansion at a firm within your client base.

Over the last seventeen years, I have developed and marketed packaged and customized software for many industries in domestic and international markets, but also provided the support products for end-users at all levels. Because of this diversity, I am easily able to transfer my skills to marketing other products.

In addition to a strong marketing and sales background, I have established a record for setting up, staffing, and managing top-producing, profitable district offices.

The enclosed profile is a brief summary of my qualifications. Should you be aware of an advanced marketing and development position within the $70,000 to $80,000 range, please consider my qualifications.

Thank you in advance for your attention to this matter.

Sincerely,

Chris Smith

Enc. Professional profile

178 Green Street
Durango, CO 81301

November 16, 20--

Pat Cummings
Attorney at Law
Any Firm
1140 Main Street
Pueblo, CO 81001

Dear Mr. Cummings:

Recently, Luke Gokey suggested I contact you concerning any assistance you might be able to provide with my job search. I am interested in joining an organization in a position that would utilize my legal, administrative, and managerial knowledge and experience. The enclosed resume will provide you with information concerning my background and abilities.

As indicated, my law-related background is extensive and varied. For twelve years, I have supervised records and staff activities within the Any County Registry of Deeds. Unfortunately, I have reached the plateau of responsibility level within the structure of this position, and am now seeking to continue in my career progression.

I am especially interested in a legal administrative position, preferably with a private firm or corporation. I am willing to relocate and/or travel and am open to negotiation in terms of starting salary.

Should you know of any related openings or contacts to whom I should pass my resume, please do not hesitate to call me at (303) 555-5555. Thank you for your time. I look forward to hearing from you in the near future.

Sincerely,

Chris Smith

Enc. Resume

178 Green Street
Brooklyn, NY 11201
(718) 555-5555

December 5, 20--

Pat Cummings
Regional Manager
Any Corporation
1140 Main Street
Rochester, NY 14623

Dear Ms. Cummings:

During a recent visit to Rochester, my longtime friend Bill Atwood suggested your name as a valuable contact in the field of auto sales. I understand that your corporation has contracted with Bill's agency several times to promote your regional dealerships. I would like to take this opportunity to ask for any assistance you might be able to provide with my job search.

Due to recent downsizing, I am seeking a new, long-term association with an aggressive, fast-paced dealership. During the past eight years, my positions have ranged from Salesperson to Sales Manager with a high-volume dealership. My expertise is in developing, training, motivating, and managing a top-producing sales team in a highly competitive market. I am an effective communicator with presentation skills designed to generate results when dealing with management, personnel, and the general public. I established and continued to maintain a record of achievement as Salesperson of the Month and Salesperson of the Year for generated sales and margin of profit.

Should your schedule permit, I will be visiting the Rochester area next week and would love to meet with you. Your insight into the market and the future of the industry, as well as any specific advice or contact names you could provide, would be very helpful. I will call your office next Monday to see if we can find a convenient time to meet.

Thank you for your consideration, Ms. Cummings, and I hope to speak with you soon.

Sincerely,

Chris Smith

Enc. Resume

178 Green Street
Winchester, VA 22601
(703) 555-5555

August 21, 20--

Pat Cummings
Director, Community Planning
Any Organization
1140 Main Street
Virginia Beach, VA 23456

Dear Ms. Cummings:

I am writing at the suggestion of Barbara Winters, a fellow member of the Community Outreach Organization in Winchester. I am currently in search of a long-term association with an organization in the field of community relations. Barbara mentioned her frequent working relationship with Any Organization, and felt your office may be in need of a skilled professional with my qualifications.

During the past fifteen years, my experience has been concentrated in areas of community relations and government affairs working in public sector, university, and private industry settings. I have extensive experience working with various populations and divergent groups, and have been actively involved and successful in troubleshooting and problem-solving during the planning and decision-making processes pertaining to issues impacting communities.

I possess strong presentation, communication, and interpersonal skills, and I have trained, managed, and molded support staffs into efficient and productive teams. Based on my qualifications, I feel confident of my ability to make a significant contribution to your organization.

Although my resume provides a good summary of my background and experience, I would like to arrange a mutually convenient meeting, during which we can further discuss any availabilities within Any Organization. Please contact me at the above address or phone, or by fax at (703) 555-4444.

Thank you for your time.

Sincerely,

Chris Smith

Enc. Resume

178 Green Street
Canyon, TX 79016
(806) 555-5555

June 4, 20--

Pat Cummings
Vice President
Any Corporation
1140 Main Street
Cedar City, UT 84720

Dear Ms. Cummings:

At the suggestion of Tom Poudrier, I am submitting my resume for the Corporate Treasurer position. I have followed your company's rapid growth during the past two years, and read with much excitement your prediction for further expansion in the trade journal *Real Estates*. I wish to be a part of this exciting atmosphere.

During the past thirteen years, I have compiled a record of success as Vice President/Treasurer of a multicorporate real estate development and management company, and I have ten years of additional experience as Corporate Treasurer and Controller with a nonprofit educational research firm and an electronic manufacturer.

I am pursuing a new opportunity utilizing my financial and management expertise. My interest is in working in a business or nonprofit environment where my associates and I share the common goal of profitable growth and mutual gain.

After reviewing my qualifications, I would appreciate your contacting me for a personal meeting. I can be reached at the above address, by phone, or a message may be left at (806) 555-4444. I appreciate your consideration.

Sincerely,

Chris Smith

Enc. Resume

178 Green Street
Albuquerque, NM 87190
(505) 555-5555

February 14, 20--

Pat Cummings
Director
Any Golf Club
1140 Main Street
Las Cruces, NM 88003

Dear Ms. Cummings:

As a result of a recent referral from Mr. David Stefan regarding an entry-level opening for an instructor at Any Golf Club, I am submitting my resume for your review.

I possess eight years of education, training, coaching, and playing experience. My involvement with the game of golf began in high school and, since then, my skill level and affection for the sport have increased. Currently, I am seeking a career opportunity that will allow me to use my education and experience to make a positive contribution by maintaining high standards and a professional image within a club environment.

I am very interested in this opening. Could I perhaps schedule a personal interview with you at your convenience? I will contact your offices on Monday, February 20, to discuss an appropriate meeting time.

Sincerely,

Chris Smith

Enc. Resume

178 Green Street
Manchester, NH 03105

January 14, 20--

Pat Cummings
Chief Technician
Any Corporation
1140 Main Street
Keene, NH 03431

Dear Ms. Cummings:

In a recent informational interview, Steven Hague of NewMark Industries referred me to your firm. I am interested in joining an organization where I can utilize my strong technical and leadership skills in microwave or related industries.

I have eleven years of experience in the microwave industry working with state-of-the-art microwave communications antennas. My expertise is in test setups for outdoor and indoor test ranges, as well as the design, manufacturing, and repair maintenance of microwave antennas. In addition, I have extensive experience working with customers and inspectors on final tests to FCC regulations. I am well qualified to assume responsibility for managing projects from initial design to final test and operation.

After you have reviewed my background, please contact me so that we may arrange a personal interview to further expand upon your requirements and my ability to meet them. I can be reached at the above address or at (603) 555-5555.

Thank you for your consideration. I await your response.

Sincerely,

Chris Smith

Enc. Resume

178 Green Street
Mesa, AZ 85028
(602) 555-5555

August 22, 20--

Pat Cummings
Systems Designer
Any Corporation
1140 Main Street
Tempe, AZ 85284

Dear Mr. Cummings:

Debbie Swanson of Systems Powerphasing recommended I contact you concerning my interest in securing a position in the field of power systems design. I understand that your corporation leads the field in power-related emerging technologies. Debbie spoke highly of your work and thought you could provide me with some useful information.

My background includes seven years of experience in positions as Technical Sales Representative and Medical Equipment Technician with a medical equipment manufacturer, and Power Systems Engineer with a manufacturer of telecommunications earth stations. My most recent experience involves all phases of power systems design projects from proposal preparation and specification to on-site installations, customer training, and full operation.

I am very interested in continuing my career in power design with a new firm. I know that your expertise in the field and knowledge of the current trends would be very helpful in my search. Would it be possible to meet briefly? I can easily make myself available at your convenience, and will call you on Monday to see when we might get together.

Thank you for your generous consideration, Mr. Cummings.

Sincerely,

Chris Smith

Enc. Resume

178 Green Street
Charleston, SC 29403
(803) 555-5555

April 28, 20--

Pat Cummings
Editor
Any Publishing Company
1140 Main Street
Boston, MA 02210

Dear Ms. Cummings:

I will be graduating from the College of William and Mary in May 20--, and am searching for an avenue that will lead me to a career in publishing.

Lee Jones, an Editorial Assistant at Any Publishing, suggested your company as a possible place to gain experience. I will be living in Massachusetts during June, July, and August and I am hoping that you will consider me for a summer internship. I would welcome the opportunity to work full- or part-time throughout the summer months in order to better understand the workings of a publishing house.

As an intern, I could contribute excellent editing, researching, and writing skills. I am familiar with computers and the general library cataloging systems. Additionally, I am an eager and quick learner, and an observer with a creative eye for detail.

My resume is enclosed; writing samples and references are available upon request. I look forward to hearing from you.

Thank you for your consideration.

Sincerely,

Chris Smith

Enc. Resume

178 Green Street
Glen Burnie, MD 21060

April 26, 20--

Pat Cummings
Regional Manager
Any Restaurant Chain
1140 Main Street
Silver Spring, MD 20901

Dear Ms. Cummings:

I am writing in response to a referral from a colleague of yours, Jim Murray. Jim was the Assistant Manager of your Baltimore location in 20--, when I worked there as a waitress. When I expressed my desire to return to your organization in a managerial position, Jim enthusiastically responded with several contact names, including yours.

I have enclosed my resume as an expressed interest in exploring available management opportunities at Any Restaurants. In addition to an Associate's degree in Hotel/Restaurant Management, I have five years of experience ranging from Roving Manager with a multiunit restaurant operation to General Manager of a full-service restaurant, lounge, and multiple function/banquet facility. My experience encompasses front- and back-of-the-house management, food and beverage preparation, and personnel training and supervision.

I feel confident of my potential to make a significant contribution to your restaurant chain. My previous experience as a waitress not only provided specific insight into your management operations, but also was very rewarding personally.

After you have reviewed my qualifications, please do not hesitate to contact me at the address cited above or call (301) 555-5555. I would like to arrange a mutually convenient time for a meeting to discuss your current or anticipated needs in terms of my qualifications.

I greatly appreciate your consideration.

Sincerely,

Chris Smith

Enc. Resume

178 Green Street
Newberg, OR 97132
(503) 555-5555

February 9, 20--

Pat Cummings
Vice President, Sales
Any Corporation
1140 Main Street
Portland, OR 97201

Dear Ms. Cummings:

For more than ten years, I have been instrumental in opening, selling to, and servicing accounts as well as establishing corporate accounts in a multistate region. Some of my accomplishments include:

- Opening and servicing accounts that resulted in an increase in volume from $50,000 to $500,000.
- Achieving successful sales exceeding 20 percent of entire account inventory.
- Increasing customer accounts by 10 percent in a six-month period.

Currently, I am seeking a new position with a company that can benefit from the efforts of a self-starter who has not only developed new approaches to sales and has experience with customer-controlled computer inventories, but who has also motivated individuals and groups to achieve desired objectives or quotas as both independent contributors and team producers.

I am a dedicated, highly productive, hard-working individual with the kind of persistence that gets results. I work best in a competitive environment and prefer working with an incentive package.

I would be happy to meet in a personal interview to provide you with more detail as to my qualifications and how they can best serve your company.

Thank you for your consideration and early response.

Sincerely,

Chris Smith

Enc. Resume

178 Green Street
Colorado Springs, CO 80903

May 13, 20--

Pat Cummings
Manager
Any Corporation
1140 Main Street
Jacksonville, FL 32231

Dear Mr. Cummings:

I am a veteran of the fashion industry seeking a position with an aggressive, cutting-edge design team. Any Corporation's recent, extensive marketing campaign has confirmed my interest in the company.

I possess three years of diverse experience as an Art Director and Fashion Designer working with a screen-printing company. In this capacity, my principal responsibility has been creating the art and fashion design of clothing lines for national mass markets.

I feel that my creative skills and experience in dealing with sales and buyers can be effectively utilized with a firm such as yours. If you have the need for a highly motivated achiever, then we have good reason to meet.

Please respond at the above address or by phone at (719) 555-5555 to arrange a mutually convenient time for a meeting to discuss my qualifications. A portfolio of my creative work is available for your review.

Thank you for your consideration.

Sincerely,

Chris Smith

Enc. Resume

178 Green Street
Raleigh, NC 27611

September 1, 20--

Pat Cummings
District Supervisor
Any Corporation
1140 Main Street
Fayetteville, NC 28302

Dear Ms. Cummings:

During the past thirteen years, I have been actively involved in positions as Field Manager of Contained Operations and Night Operations Supervisor of freight stations and service centers dealing with domestic and international freight deliveries.

In addition to the supervision of day-to-day operations, my experience encompasses the hiring, training, and supervision of drivers, office and support personnel, and the provision of cost-effective quality service within a multiple service network. I have sound knowledge of computer systems design for freight movement management, and am skilled in both troubleshooting and resolving problems relative to the movement or transfer of materials.

Although my present situation is challenging and diverse, I feel that it is time for me to make a change. I am looking for a new association with a firm that can benefit from my extensive experience with import/export traffic. Depending on the benefits package, salary is negotiable.

I would welcome the opportunity to discuss your requirements and to further outline my qualifications. Should you require additional information, please contact me at the above address or by phone at (919) 555-5555.

Thank you for your consideration.

Sincerely,

Chris Smith

Enc. Resume

178 Green Street
Tulsa, OK 74117
(918) 555-5555

August 12, 20--

Pat Cummings
Director
Any Company
1140 Main Street
Anadarko, OK 73005

Dear Ms. Cummings:

An article in the July issue of *Oklahoma Business Journal* featured Any Company's recent success and growth. As a Program Manager interested in establishing connections with a new, up-and-coming firm, I submit the enclosed resume for your review.

My qualifications include more than twelve years of managing experience with Ricochet Data. In this capacity I developed and coordinated short- and long-range plans for the design and introduction of four new microcomputer products. I also created master charts to track major milestones and critical path activities, directed a management task force to develop a set of work instructions for the introduction of outsourced products, and reduced product time to market by 25 percent.

My work in retail management might also be of interest to you. While employed at Lorenz Company, I generated gross annual sales in excess of $2 million for four consecutive years, managed a sales and service team of twenty people, and provided superior customer service and support.

Should my qualifications match your current or anticipated needs, I can be reached at the telephone number and address above.

Sincerely,

Chris Smith

Enc. Resume

178 Green Street
Payne Gap, KY 41537
(606) 555-5555

April 30, 20--

Pat Cummings
Chief Administrator
Any Hospital
1140 Main Street
Sandy Springs, SC 29677

Dear Ms. Cummings:

I recently read about your need for a Cardiologist in the May edition of the bulletin published by the South Carolina Medical Association. Please accept the following summary of accomplishments as my application for this opportunity.

- Two years as Cardiology Fellow with extensive experience covering the full spectrum of clinical cardiology.
- Experience encompasses: cardiac catheterization and angioplasty, cardiac pacing and electrophysiology, echocardiography, exercise testing and nuclear imaging, in- and out-patient hospital care of cardiac patients.
- Two years of experience as a Clinical Instructor in Medicine at St. Martha's Hospital, teaching interns, residents, and medical students.
- Board certified—Internal Medicine, board eligible in Cardiology.

In my current position as Cardiology Fellow at St. Martha's, I have had the opportunity to utilize state-of-the-art systems, procedures, and techniques covering the full spectrum of clinical cardiology. I am also presently involved in research encompassing clinical evaluation of the Bundeen cross-coronary stent, and have just completed a review article dealing with ventricular arrhythmias. Additionally, I received my Doctor of Medicine degree from the Boston College School of Medicine, and a Bachelor of Science degree in Preprofessional Studies from the University of Pennsylvania.

I am planning to move to South Carolina shortly, and I understand that you need a qualified Cardiologist to fill your vacancy. Would you have a few moments to speak with me next week during a scheduled visit to your area? I am sure I could convince you that I have the capabilities and the motivation to join your staff.

I will call your office on Friday to follow up on this inquiry.

Sincerely yours,
Chris Smith, M.D.

178 Green Street
Clearfield, UT 84016

November 5, 20--

Pat Cummings
Vice President, Operations
Any Corporation
1140 Main Street
Salt Lake City, UT 84104

Dear Mr. Cummings:

I am interested in your advertisement for a Director of Information Services as published in the November edition of the *Salt Lake Tribune*. Several of the qualifications I could bring to this position include:

- Extensive experience in COBOL Programming.
- Proven managerial abilities.
- Self-motivation; able to set effective priorities to achieve immediate and long-term goals and meet operational deadlines.
- Development of interpersonal skills, having dealt with a diversity of professionals, clients, and staff members.
- Ability to function well in fast-paced, high-pressure atmosphere.

For the past eleven years I have had the opportunity to progress in positions of responsibility at my current employer from Programmer to Director of Information Services. In this capacity, I control programming and systems, computer operations, data entry, membership records, and membership promotion and retention departments. I have successfully implemented complete financial reporting systems, inventory, accounts receivable, computerized production of publications, and applications.

In addition to my work experiences, I hold both a Bachelor's and a Master's degree in Business Administration. I am proficient in most computer systems, as well as peripheral equipment and 35 online CRT terminals (COBOL).

I am very interested in learning more about your work at Any Corporation and how I might best apply my skills to your advantage. Please contact me at (801) 555-5555 to schedule a meeting.

Sincerely,

Chris Smith

178 Green Street
Norwalk, CT 06856
(203) 555-555

August 11, 20--

Pat Cummings
Chairperson, Board of Directors
Any Hospital
1140 Main Street
Bridgeport, CT 06605

Dear Mr. Cummings:

Thank you for speaking with me this morning regarding the Hospital Administrator position available at Any Hospital. As per your request, please allow me to present several of my most relevant experiences and accomplishments in health care management/administration.

For the past year, I have been working as Acting Director of the Norwalk Medical Center. In this capacity, I am responsible for the supervision/coordination of all administrative services for the city's public health care program. This includes the health care and hospitalization for indigent, low-income, and welfare patients, consistent with care-afforded insurance and fee-for-service patients. In addition, I troubleshoot staff and general administration conflicts and resolve policy issues, as well as develop reports for budgeting proposals and expenditure control.

Previous to my current position, I spent six years as Central Administrator of Emergency Services for the same institution. I coordinated all administrative details of the department, prepared the department budget, and monitored expenditures. As Administrator, I also supervised ward secretaries, interpreters, and ancillary personnel. This same duty was performed in the position of Unit Manager, which I held from 20-- to 20--. This position gave me exposure to several aspects of administrative support, vendor relations, and inventory control.

My work experience is supported by a Master of Science degree in Health Service Administration, a certificate in Management Development from the Connecticut Hospital Association, and a Bachelor of Arts degree in English.

I am very eager to apply my acquired knowledge of health care administration to the position at Any Hospital. I hope my qualifications match your requirements, and that I will have the opportunity to speak with you again in a personal interview.

Thank you for your consideration.

Sincerely,

Chris Smith

178 Green Street
Fort Worth, TX 76111
(817) 555-5555

April 11, 20--

Pat Cummings
Vice President
Any Corporation
1140 Main Street
Fort Worth, TX 76101

Dear Mr. Cummings:

Is your corporation in need of a motivated professional with comprehensive product management experience? If so, I would like to present my qualifications for your consideration.

In my vast experience, I have gained valuable insight into all aspects of product/protocol development and management to obtain FDA product approval. As Product Manager for Estrade, Inc., I provided extensive coordination of all product development activities for a large medical supply corporation. This acquired knowledge of clinical research would be especially beneficial to your development team.

I have consistently maintained a strong motivation for developing innovative product design and management, as well as a flexibility toward new approaches and marketing techniques. I am thoroughly proficient in most major computer applications, including Microsoft Word and Excel; I can navigate the Internet with ease. Much of my work has necessitated collaboration with systems consultants on the design and implementation of data management systems, including remote access.

I would be happy to further outline my skills during the course of a personal interview. After you have reviewed my qualifications, please contact me to schedule a time that is convenient for you to meet.

I appreciate your consideration and look forward to speaking with you.

Sincerely,

Chris Smith

Enc. Resume

178 Green Street
Mountain View, CA 92715
(415) 555-5555

July 23, 20--

Pat Cummings
Director
Any Advertising Agency
1140 Main Street
Sausalito, CA 94966

Dear Mr. Cummings:

I am very interested in a freelance or part-time position in graphic design or advertising production. I forward the attached resume for your evaluation.

Please note that in addition to a Bachelor of Arts degree and current enrollment in the Massachusetts College of Art's Graphic Design Certificate Program, I offer more than seven years of valuable experience in the production and traffic areas of print and graphic design, and in related fields including fundraising and direct and mass mailings.

As you can see from my resume, I left the field three years ago with excellent references to raise a family and manage a household. Now, with my family well established, I am highly motivated to return to the work force and contribute the valuable experience gained before and during my hiatus.

I would like the opportunity to make a significant contribution to the success of Any Advertising Agency. I am available at the above address and phone number should you have any further questions.

I look forward to hearing from you.

Sincerely,

Chris Smith

Enc. Resume

178 Green Street
Palm Harbor, FL 34683
(727) 555-5555

April 24, 20--

Pat Cummings, M.D.
Any Pediatric Clinic
1140 Main Street
Tampa, FL 33614

Dear Dr. Cummings:

In response to your ad in Sunday's *Tampa Tribune* for a medical receptionist, I am pleased to enclose my resume for your consideration. A graduate of Plant High School, I have completed courses in medical terminology, billing, and transcription at Hillsborough Community College. For the last two years, I have worked as a receptionist and clerk typist in the Admitting Department at Tampa General Hospital. I am knowledgeable in a variety of software programs, including Microsoft Office, Word, and Excel. My typing speed is 60 wpm.

While I am sure that, like me, most of the applicants for this position can offer a pleasing telephone voice, professional demeanor, and exceptional organizational skills, I bring one competency that few of them probably have—I am fluent in both English and Spanish. A visit to the doctor is stressful enough for children and their parents, but for those who do not speak the language, it is doubly so. I will be able to immediately put them at ease and to help them complete the necessary paperwork as well as assist you and your staff with your translation needs during examinations and treatment.

I believe I could make a positive contribution to your practice and I would welcome the opportunity for an interview. Thank you for your consideration and I look forward to hearing from you.

Sincerely,

Chris Smith

Enc. Resume

178 Green Street
Daytona Beach, FL 32115
(904) 555-5555

August 18, 20--

Pat Cummings
Hiring Manager
Any Advertising Agency
1140 Main Street
Orlando, FL 32816

Dear Mr. Cummings:

I am very interested in pursuing my career in the advertising industry at Any Advertising Agency. While researching area firms, I read an exciting piece in *Ad World* about your recent campaign for Homeloving soups. Congratulations on receiving a Clio Award for your efforts.

I would love to join your winning team in an entry-level, administrative position. I can offer more than eight years of administration, promotion, and communication experience. The following achievements would be especially beneficial to your firm:

Administration: Record keeping and file maintenance. Data processing and computer operations, accounts receivable, accounts payable, and accounting research and reports. Order fulfillment, inventory control, and customer relations. Scheduling, office management, and telephone reception.

Promotion: Composing, editing, and proofreading correspondence and PR materials for my own house-cleaning service.

Communication: Instruction, curriculum and lesson planning, student evaluation, parent-teacher conferences, and development of educational materials. Training and supervising clerks.

Computer Skills: Proficient in Microsoft Word, Lotus 1-2-3, Excel, FileMaker Pro, and ADDS Accounting System.

I would like to request a personal interview to further outline my skills, and how they could be immediately applicable to an administrative position at Any Advertising Agency. I will call your office on August 23 to schedule a convenient meeting time.

Thank you, Mr. Cummings. I look forward to our conversation.

Sincerely,

Chris Smith
Enc. Resume

178 Green Street
Norfolk, VA 23529
(804) 555-5555

July 20, 20--

Pat Cummings
Director of Real Estate Development
Any Corporation
1140 Main Street
Alexandria, VA 22312

Dear Mr. Cummings:

After several years of diverse and successful experience as a Municipal Bond Broker, I decided to pursue a career encompassing a broader scope of real estate development. To achieve this objective and establish myself as a professional in the field of real estate development, I have spent the past year completing a comprehensive graduate program and earned a Master's degree in Real Estate Development from the University of Virginia.

Presently, I am investigating career opportunities with a progressive developer emphasizing the financial and field aspects of project management. My experience, prior to entering said graduate program, required extensive involvement in the purchase and sale of bonds for financing public and private developments. These included private and public construction developments and business ventures that required the ability to work with decision makers and financial/investment professionals in the field of real estate development.

I am a dedicated, energetic self-starter who can recognize opportunities and has always been willing to devote the time necessary to complete any task thoroughly. With this attitude, I feel confident that I can readily become a valuable asset as a member of your management team.

I am presently available for an interview, and will be glad to meet with you at a mutually convenient time. My resume is enclosed for your review.

I appreciate your consideration.

Yours sincerely,

Chris Smith

Enc. Resume

178 Green Street
Provo, UT 84603
(801) 555-5555

November 19, 20--

Pat Cummings
Chief Executive Officer
Any Corporation
1140 Main Street
Salt Lake City, UT 84110

Dear Mr. Cummings:

Todd Duncan, of your operations department, suggested I contact you concerning employment opportunities. Todd mentioned that you were considering expanding your sales staff, and thought you might benefit from a professional with my qualifications.

I offer more than twenty years of progressively responsible experience in sales, culminating in my most recent position as Director of Sales and Pricing with a $750 million, 120-store chain. As a senior-level manager, I have been responsible for all aspects of store operations, including merchandising management, buying, strategic planning, marketing, and staff development and management.

Although I have thoroughly enjoyed my present position, corporate downsizing has prompted me to search for a new position. I feel that my years of successful management experience can be more advantageously utilized by a growing and diversifying firm such as Any Corporation.

If you are looking for a well-organized, innovative individual with the ability to garner results, please contact me. I would be happy to meet with you at your convenience.

Sincerely,

Chris Smith

Enc. Resume

178 Green Street
El Segundo, CA 90245
(213) 555-5555

December 14, 20--

Pat Cummings
Director of Marketing
Any Corporation
1140 Main Street
Los Angeles, CA 90089

Dear Mr. Cummings:

I am currently seeking an entry-level opportunity in a successful marketing department, and have learned about Any Corporation through the *L.A. Top Sellers Guide*. Congratulations on such an outstanding year.

As you can see from the enclosed resume, since completion of my Bachelor of Science degree, my professional associations have been extensive and diverse. Throughout my experiences, I have developed several important skills that I believe could benefit your marketing department. I possess solid communication skills, both in person and by phone. I am proficient with Macintosh, PC, and spreadsheet applications, and I can effectively manage all aspects of daily business operations, including inventory management and account maintenance. Above all, I possess a strong work ethic and enthusiasm to learn.

Last month I took an intensive seminar entitled "Marketing for Success!" This investment conclusively confirmed my desire to pursue marketing as a career. I know that, if given the chance, I could quickly prove my worth as a member of your staff. Would you permit me that chance?

I look forward to your response.

Sincerely,

Chris Smith

Enc. Resume

178 Green Street
Eagan, MN 55122
(612) 555-5555

September 12, 20--

Pat Cummings
Senior Accountant
Any Corporation
1140 Main Street
Bloomington, MN 55438

Dear Ms. Cummings:

I am currently searching for an accounting position in which I may contribute my financial expertise as well as my ability to interface effectively with the business community on an international scale.

I offer more than twelve years of comprehensive accounting experience, in both public and private firms. My skills include audits, Chapter 11 filings and bank reconciliation, preparation of financial reports, and accounts payable/receivable. In my most recent position as Senior Accountant, I was solely responsible for the setup and modification of a new computer system, and for leading a steering committee to select the general ledger package, which is currently in use.

As you will note from my resume, the majority of my work experience has been focused in Madrid, Spain. Last year, I made the decision to permanently move to the United States with my family, and am very interested in securing a long-term association with a firm such as Any Corporation. Please be assured that although English is my second language, I have been speaking it fluently for more than twenty years. As a Staff Accountant at your firm, I could provide translation services to your international department if needed, and an extensive knowledge of European financial dealings.

I would very much like to meet with you for further discussion. I will call your office next week to confirm a meeting time that fits your schedule. In the interim, please contact me if I can provide you with any additional information.

Sincerely,

Chris Smith

Enc. Resume

178 Green Street
Mukilteo, WA 98275
(206) 555-5555

October 3, 20--

Pat Cummings
Director of Human Resources
Any Corporation
1140 Main Street
St. Charles, MO 63302

Dear Mr. Cummings:

I recently learned from your Vice President of Operations, Marsha Ponnif, that you might be in need of a Meeting Planner to join your management structure. I am submitting the enclosed business profile for your review.

During the past sixteen years, I have successfully demonstrated solid troubleshooting and problem resolution skills in management, marketing, and sales. My progressively responsible experience includes:

- Corporate/institutional meeting planning.
- Hospitality service coordination.
- Destination management/program coordination.
- Employee/client incentive programs.
- Sales/customer service.

Although my positions have been fast-paced and broad in scope, I would like to make a change and am very impressed by the products and services offered by Any Corporation. Could we meet for an interview? I will contact you next week to schedule a convenient time for further discussion.

Thank you, Mr. Cummings. I look forward to our next conversation.

Sincerely,

Chris Smith

Enc. Business profile

178 Green Street
Vermillion, SD 57069

June 26, 20--

Pat Cummings
Museum Director
Any Museum
1140 Main Street
Rapid City, SD 57701

Dear Ms. Cummings:

I am a recent graduate of the University of South Dakota with a well-rounded art history background. I would like to put my skills and knowledge to use in an entry-level position at your prestigious museum, perhaps as an Assistant Director to the Curator.

As my resume indicates, I participated in an exclusive summer program for art history majors at the Louvre in Paris. There, I studied some of the most significant works of European art and attended a very interesting seminar about the workings of the Louvre itself. I also worked for two summers at the Metropolitan Museum of Art in New York City, where I served as a Museum Assistant at the information booth. My coursework in African-American art, modern art, and museum science has also prepared me well for an entry-level position in a fine arts museum.

I have long been a lover of art and art museums. I have been visiting your museum since I was a small child and would be thrilled at the opportunity to become a part of your excellent staff.

Enclosed is my resume for your consideration. I may be reached at (605) 555-5555 after 3 P.M. on weekdays and anytime on weekends. I hope to hear from you soon.

Sincerely,

Chris Smith

Enc. Resume

178 Green Street
Bartow, FL 33830
(813) 555-5555

August 2, 20--

Pat Cummings
Principal
Any Junior High School
1140 Main Street
St. Petersburg, FL 33716

Dear Mr. Cummings:

Recently I bumped into long-time friend and colleague, Harry Nestor, Superintendent of St. Petersburg Schools. Harry tells me that Any High School is currently searching for a part-time Math Instructor for the upcoming school year. I would like to express my interest in assuming such a position.

As my enclosed professional profile reflects, I possess more than thirty-three years of experience in junior high and high school education. Before assuming my most recent position as Principal of Sacred Heart Junior High School in St. Petersburg, I taught math and science courses to middle school children for thirteen years. My expertise ranges from remedial math to precalculus for advanced students. In addition to my Master's degree in Education, I hold a Florida State Teacher Certification.

Although retired for more than two years, I feel I still have much to offer in the field of education, and would once again like to apply my skills to the personal and intellectual advancement of all students.

I look forward to hearing from you further regarding this position.

Sincerely yours,

Chris Smith

Enc. Professional profile

To: *patcummings@anybooks.com*
From: *chrissmith@bluepencil.com*
Subj: Assistant Editor position

Dear Ms. Cummings:

I am pleased to attach my resume in response to your recent advertisement in the *Boston Globe* for an Assistant Editor. I believe that my strong written and verbal communication skills, as well as my proficiency in both Microsoft Word and WordPerfect and several desktop publishing programs, including InDesign, make me the ideal candidate for this position. For the last two years, I have worked as a reporter and copyeditor for a weekly newspaper; previously, I was features editor, graphic artist, and reporter for various college publications.

I would welcome the opportunity to meet with you to further discuss my abilities as they relate to your specific needs. May we schedule an appointment soon? I look forward to hearing from you.

Sincerely,

Chris Smith

178 Green Street
Worcester, MA 01610
(508) 555-5555
chrissmith@bluepencil.com

To: *patcummings@anyfirm.com*
From: *chrissmith@digsdirt.com*
Subj: Civil Engineering opportunities

Dear Ms. Cummings:

I have more than ten years of progressively responsible experience acquired during roadway, civil, site, hazardous waste, and waterfront projects, as well as Certification in Surveying Technology and a Bachelor of Science degree in Forest Resource Management. At present, I am investigating new and broader career opportunities that would allow me to put my extensive technical and supervisory skills to work for a progressive firm such as yours.

The attached resume describes my qualifications and accomplishments in greater detail. I am confident of my ability to make a positive and immediate contribution to Any Firm and would welcome the opportunity to personally discuss your current or anticipated staffing requirements face-to-face. I can be reached by e-mail at the address above or by phone at (401) 555-5555. I await your reply.

Sincerely,

Chris Smith

178 Green Street
Providence, RI 02903
(401) 555-5555
chrissmith@digsdirt.com

To: *patcummings@anyzoologyassociation.com*
From: *chrissmith@infosearch.com*
Subj: Membership directory

Dear Mr. Cummings:

I am currently conducting a search for job availabilities in the field of zoology within the Midwest and would appreciate any assistance you may be able to provide with regard to the members of your association. Do you publish a membership directory that I might use in my job-search efforts, and if so, how may I go about obtaining a copy?

Thank you for your time. I look forward to your return response.

Sincerely,

Chris Smith

178 Green Street
Tempe, AZ 85285
(602) 555-555
chrissmith@infosearch.com

178 Green Street
Tulsa, OK 74103
(918) 555-5555

January 24, 20--

Pat Cummings
Human Resources Director
Any Publishing Company
1140 Main Street
Philadelphia, PA 19130

Dear Ms. Cummings:

Thank you for taking the time to talk with me on Friday, January 20, about your firm's opening for a Production Assistant. I am very interested in this position and believe it would be an appropriate place to learn more about the publishing field.

I enjoyed our conversation and look forward to hearing more about this opportunity. Thank you for your time and consideration.

Sincerely,

Chris Smith

Enc. Resume

178 Green Street
Geismar, LA 70734
(504) 555-5555

January 18, 20--

Ms. Pat Cummings
Vice President
Any Corporation
1140 Main Street
Lafayette, LA 70504

Dear Ms. Cummings:

It was a sincere pleasure making your acquaintance on Tuesday regarding the position of Engineering Consultant. The personal dynamics that you exude, the predicted corporate growth, and the position's promised personal fulfillment, have left me very enthused.

Thank you for your consideration. I look forward to meeting with you again in the near future.

Sincerely,

Chris Smith

178 Green Street
Nashua, NH 03060
(603) 555-5555

July 14, 20--

Pat Cummings
President
Any Corporation
1140 Main Street
Manchester, NH 03103

Dear Ms. Cummings:

I found our interview this morning to be most refreshing. Your staff was hospitable, your facilities impressive, and our discussion informative. I am very interested in becoming your Personal Secretary.

You mentioned during our meeting that you are looking for an assistant with extensive knowledge of computer systems and applications. My computer literacy includes proficiency in Microsoft Word, Excel, Access, Windows, and desktop publishing. I also have experience with spreadsheets inventory management.

I believe I have much to offer your company, and I hope I will receive the opportunity to prove my worth to you. Thank you for extending me your time, Ms. Cummings.

Sincerely,

Chris Smith

178 Green Street
Gary, IN 46402
(219) 555-5555

February 1, 20--

Pat Cummings
Retail Sales Manager
Any Store
1140 Main Street
South Bend, IN 46626

Dear Mr. Cummings:

I want to thank you for meeting with me on January 27 regarding the position of Sales Associate. I enjoyed the opportunity to learn more about the responsibilities and opportunities available at Any Store.

I also want to reiterate my interest in the position. I feel confident that my seven years of acquired sales experience, combined with well-seasoned communication and interpersonal skills, would make me an ideal candidate for this position.

Thank you again. I look forward to hearing your final decision.

Sincerely,

Chris Smith

178 Green Street
Washington, DC 20071
(202) 555-5555

March 25, 20--

Pat Cummings
Publisher's Assistant
Any Publisher
1140 Main Street
New York, NY 10108

Dear Ms. Cummings:

I am writing to inquire about Any Publisher. Please send me information regarding your company size and target markets, as well as a catalog of your most recent publications.

I have enclosed a self-addressed stamped envelope for your convenience. Thank you for your attention.

Sincerely,

Chris Smith

178 Green Street
Tampa, FL 33681
(813) 555-5555

April 6, 20--

Pat Cummings
Human Resources Manager
Any Hospital
1140 Main Street
Ocala, FL 32674

Dear Ms. Cummings:

Last month, I sent my resume in response to your advertisement in the Monday, March 13, edition of the *Tampa Tribune* for Staff Nutritionist. I am still very interested in this or similar openings at Any Hospital.

For this reason, I would like to make you aware of an address change from my previous inquiry. I have since moved from Jacksonville to the address listed above. I have enclosed an updated resume for your convenience.

Thank you. I look forward to hearing from you in the future.

Sincerely,

Chris Smith

Enc. Resume

178 Green Street
Albany, GA 31701
(912) 555-5555

November 29, 20--

Pat Cummings
Assistant to the President
Any University
1140 Main Street
Doraville, GA 30340

Dear Ms. Cummings:

I am writing to express my thanks for your kind reference regarding my summer internship application. The selection committee at the State House informs me that you were contacted, and that you spoke highly of my work in the President's office.

I will contact you in early January when my application is processed and I hear of the outcome. Once again, I am very grateful for your help.

Best wishes,

Chris Smith

178 Green Street
Washington, DC 20007
(202) 555-5555

September 6, 20--

Pat Cummings
Professor of Art History
Any College
1140 Main Street
Worcester, MA 01610

Dear Dr. Cummings:

Knowing how busy you are with different projects, I really appreciate the time you took to write a recommendation for my graduate school applications. I have since received three letters of acceptance and I am confident that your letter contributed to my success.

Again, thank you for your continued support. I will be sure to keep in touch as I pursue my degree.

Sincerely,

Chris Smith

178 Green Street
Richardson, TX 75083
(214) 555-5555

September 19, 20--

Pat Cummings, M.D.
Ophthalmologist
Any Hospital
1140 Main Street
Irving, TX 75038

Dear Dr. Cummings:

Although I regret that you did not have the need for an Assistant, I would like to thank you for referring me to Dr. Wilson in Richardson. In my meeting with him on Tuesday, I received several other contact names.

Should you become aware of any opportunities for a Medical Assistant, please let me know. I am still very interested in gaining hands-on experience before I begin graduate study in the field.

I hope to speak with you in the future.

Sincerely,

Chris Smith

178 Green Street
Newark, DE 19713
(302) 555-5555

September 18, 20--

Pat Cummings
General Manager
Any Inn
1140 Main Street
Wilmington, DE 19801

Dear Ms. Cummings:

Thank you for being so gracious with your time on Friday. I found your description of current trends in hospitality very enlightening.

I appreciate the suggestions you made regarding my resume. I think the new version is much improved. I have enclosed a copy in the hope that you will feel free to make any further comments or to share it with anyone in the industry you feel might be interested in someone with my qualifications.

As per your suggestion, I will contact James Moller with Daylight Hotels this week. Again, thank you for all of your assistance.

Sincerely,

Chris Smith

Enc. Revised resume

178 Green Street
Elko, NV 89801

July 27, 20--

Pat Cummings
Billings Supervisor
Any Corporation
1140 Main Street
St. Louis, MO 63121

Dear Mr. Cummings:

Thank you for considering my resume. Your time is greatly appreciated.

I wanted to inform you that I will be relocating to Missouri in the near future. My plans are to further my career in the accounting and finance industry in the St. Louis area. As an added note, I am taking a computer spreadsheet course, which should enhance my skills in the field.

I am still very interested in furthering my career at Any Corporation and would ask for your consideration regarding any future availabilities. Until my move to St. Louis on August 28, I can be reached by phone at (702) 555-5555. I will call again in six weeks' time.

Thank you again. I look forward to speaking with you.

Sincerely,

Chris Smith
Enc. Resume

178 Green Street
Shawnee, OK 74801

November 21, 20--

Pat Cummings
Vice President, Editorial
Any Publishing Company
1140 Main Street
Oklahoma City, OK 73125

Dear Ms. Cummings:

Please allow me to update my previous letter to Any Publishing Company with regard to your search for a Freelance Copyeditor. You will notice my resume has been revised to include more relevant experience.

My most recent assignment for Southwestern Publications involved copyediting material intended for educational television and geared for a high school audience. Many of my line corrections, as well as my editorial suggestions for improvements, were used in final versions. My work was found to be thorough, precise, and consistent.

I also edited a Master's thesis in Business Administration for a Langston University student. The text needed many corrections in spelling, grammar, usage, and style. I offered suggestions for improving content as well. The feedback on my work was quite good.

You may also recall that I am proficient in desktop publishing. I print high-quality resumes, essays, and formal letters for clients who contract for my services. I apply strict standards to all of my work and operate in a thoroughly professional manner.

Thank you again, Ms. Cummings, for considering me as a potential freelancer for Any Publishing Company. I will be following up this letter with a phone call in the next few weeks. Should you wish to contact me sooner, my phone number is (405) 555-5555. I look forward to communicating with you in the near future.

Sincerely,

Chris Smith

Enc. Resume

178 Green Street
New Rochelle, NY 10801

January 4, 20--

Pat Cummings
Production Manager
Any Radio Station
1140 Main Street
Garden City, NY 11530

Dear Mr. Cummings:

Last week, I spoke with your assistant, Linda McMillian, regarding the initial resume and demo CD I sent as application for the On-Air Announcer position you have available. Although Ms. McMillian could not confirm whether you had had the chance to review my materials, she did inform me that the position is still available.

I would like to take this opportunity to express my continued interest in becoming an Announcer at Any Radio Station. Since I moved to New York three years ago, I have listened to and admired your station's broadcasts. I would love to contribute to the success of what Radio NY considers to be "Westchester's Best News Station."

As your newest Announcer, I would bring almost thirteen years of experience in diverse areas of AM and FM announcing, newscasting, and audio production, including current responsibility for a regular on-air shift with WJBF AM (1170), New Rochelle, New York.

I have enclosed another copy of my resume and CD. After you have reviewed these materials, I would like to arrange a meeting to further discuss the position. I can be reached at (914) 555-5555.

I look forward to speaking with you.

Sincerely,

Chris Smith

Enc. Resume, Demo CD

178 Green Street
Wadesboro, NC 28170
(704) 555-5555

September 5, 20--

Pat Cummings
Head Counselor
Any Center
1140 Main Street
Charlotte, NC 27706

Dear Ms. Cummings:

Thank you for meeting with me last Friday regarding your current vacancy. Although I regret not being chosen for the Counselor position, I found the interview process very informative.

Please note that I have applied for a Master's degree in Social Work program to begin in January of 20--. I would be very interested in pursuing the field work required for my M.S.W. degree in a counseling capacity at Any Center.

I will contact you again in the future to inquire about suitable opportunities.

Thank you again for your consideration.

Sincerely,

Chris Smith

178 Green Street
Decatur, IL
(217) 555-5555

December 12, 20--

Pat Cummings
Captain
Any Fire Department
1140 Main Street
Palos Heights, IL 60455

Dear Mr. Cummings:

Last week I met with you to discuss your opening for a Firefighter. I was very impressed by the team of people working at Any Fire Department and the facility itself was one of the most technologically advanced I have seen.

Although I am convinced I would have enjoyed the position, I must withdraw my candidacy. My family and I have decided to relocate and the move will take us out of state.

Thank you again and best wishes.

Sincerely,

Chris Smith

178 Green Street
Woodbridge, NJ 07095
(908) 555-5555

March 4, 20--

Pat Cummings
Hiring Manager
Any Law Firm
1140 Main Street
Cherry Hill, NJ 08034

Dear Ms. Cummings:

Thank you very much for offering me the chance to work as a full-time Paralegal at Any Law Firm next fall. I realize what a challenging and gainful experience this opportunity represents.

As I explained in our interview on February 28, I had also submitted law school applications for the upcoming year. Early this week, I received notification of my acceptance at Fordham University.

After weighing my choices, I realized that the best decision would be to begin law school without delay. However, I sincerely wish to thank you for your trust in my skills.

Should you need a summer intern or part-time Law Clerk within the next three years, I would welcome the opportunity to work for your firm.

Sincerely,

Chris Smith

REJECTION OF OFFER

178 Green Street
London, NWI 4SA UK
(44) 71 555 55 55

October 20, 20--

Pat Cummings
Vice President, International Division
Any Corporation
1140 Main Street
Los Angeles, CA 90071

Dear Ms. Cummings:

I am writing to inform you that I have decided to return to the United States or Canada to establish a more permanent base for my family as of November 10.

I regret leaving Any Corporation, but as you know, I have asked several times, without success, for relocation to a position in the North American division. I had enjoyed working for Any Corporation and would have liked to continue. However, I have established an excellent reputation and the credentials for quality and profitability in both food and beverage and general hotel operations over the years, and I am confident these will assist me in securing a new position within the industry.

Once again, I regret having to resign from my position. I wish you much success in the future.

Sincerely,

Chris Smith

178 Green Street
Pittsburgh, PA 15222
(412) 555-5555

August 4, 20--

Pat Cummings
Internship Coordinator
Any Television Station
1140 Main Street
Allentown, PA 18101

Dear Mr. Cummings:

With this letter, I would like to offer notice of the termination of my production assistantship. As I am preparing to return to school, August 18 will be my last day of employment.

My experience at Any Television Station has been both educational and enjoyable. I know that the production work I have been involved in will continue to benefit me in the future.

Thank you for affording me this experience. I am grateful to have contributed to Any Television Station in return for the skills and knowledge I have gained.

Yours truly,

Chris Smith

178 Green Street
Mayville, WI 53050
(414) 555-5555

May 1, 20--

Pat Cummings
Principal Architect
Any Corporation
1140 Main Street
Columbia, SC 29208

Dear Mr. Cummings:

I am pleased to accept the offer to assist you on the Glendale Shopping Complex project. The proposal you gave me sounds very exciting, and I am excited about being given the chance to add my expertise to such a challenging endeavor.

As you know, I am in the process of securing housing to facilitate my move to Columbia. I expect to be settled in your area by the end of the month, in plenty of time to start work in mid-June. Should this arrangement present a conflict, please let me know.

I will keep in touch as my start date nears. Thank you again for your kind offer.

Sincerely,

Chris Smith

PART III

Acing the Interview

With these interview preparation skills under your belt, you're all set to get out there and make a great impression.

CHAPTER 15

Get Ready for the Interview

YOU'VE GOT A SPIFFY new resume, a perfectly written cover letter, and a list of industry contacts more than a mile long. Recruiters are looking for employees who not only have the skills and experience to do the job well but can also easily fit into the company culture. They are checking to see how well your personality and ideas will complement those you will be working alongside. There are plenty of ways that you can convince an interviewer that you are that person.

Interview Research

Preparing for an interview requires a lot of time and patience. It is not something that can be crammed into the ten minutes you have before leaving to meet with the recruiter. Luckily, it is also something that becomes easier with time. You begin to know which questions to expect and decide which answers work best. The more interviews you participate in, the closer you are to winning that perfect job.

While you should be prepared to field calls from recruiters after sending out your resume, don't waste time waiting by the phone. In preparation for screenings, however, keep pens and paper by the phone with a list of companies you've sent your resume to, the positions they were hiring for, and some company background.

One of the most time-consuming parts of the entire job interview process is researching a prospective employer. However, it is also the most important part of the process. The easiest way to set yourself apart from the rest of the candidates is to leave the interviewer with a positive impression. And the easiest way to do that is to know the company inside and out. Remember, this is not something you should do early in the job search game. Wait till you've been offered an interview before researching the company in-depth.

How to Find the Information You Need

There are a number of ways and tools you can use to find the information you need. The first is obvious: Do you know someone at the company? If you don't know someone, you may be able to develop a contact. Perhaps a friend or relative of yours knows someone who works at the company and can put you in touch with that person. Take advantage of this to gain an inside perspective on the company.

You will need to find information on the company's competitors. There's a wealth of information at the library in journals, newspapers, and magazines. Focus on the stats; zero in on companies in the same ballpark as the one you're interviewing with, but also take a close look at the leaders in the field. A fact or two about them can come in handy in an interview.

One enterprising job seeker was able to develop a contact at the company she was researching simply by hanging out at a restaurant and pub that company employees frequented. She was able to gather useful information about the company's current employment needs and what it was like to work there.

Look for everything! Pretend that a professor or a supervisor has asked you to make a ten-minute presentation on the company, and learn as many facts as you can that would allow you to speak intelligently about the company for that amount of time. You need to know the types of products and/or services the company offers, the types of customers it most often deals with, the name and business of the parent company, and the names and businesses of any subsidiaries. You should try to learn about the company's rank in its industry, sales and profit trends, type of ownership, size, and anything else you deem important. You should make yourself familiar with the company's biggest competitors and the direction in which the industry, as a whole, is headed. If you don't know much of the industry jargon already, learn it. If you know the name of the person who is interviewing you, you can even get a little background information on him (not to the degree that you invade his privacy, but enough info to keep you talking).

Pick up a trade paper, join online discussion groups, visit industry organization meetings, and peruse websites. Research time is time well spent. Don't overlook the smaller companies. You may think that the number of opportunities for advancement will be greater at a large corporation, but if you choose an up-and-coming small company, advancement may come quicker than at a major organization.

Discover every resource you can that relates to the specific company you are applying to and its business in general. Read the company's website. Familiarize yourself with its catalog. Look into additional job openings it has posted to get an even better idea of the types of employees it is seeking. If you're not sure who their competitors are, try searching, "related: [website address]" in Google. Bizjournals.com is also a good tool to use. Make use of Internet search engines and read any article that comes up with that company name in it. Some people who have done this have uncovered information about a company that they did not like—information such as lawsuits or customer complaints. The more time you spend researching, the better off you will be in the interview.

You can usually find a company's website by simply typing its name into a search engine like Google. You can find a company's address and phone number or a list of companies in a specific industry and location at *www.superpages.com* or *www.switchboard.com*.

Even if you get a call one day and are asked to interview the following day, don't think you can sneak through the interviewer's door and do well without having taken at least an hour or so to acquaint yourself with the company and its business. One caveat: Though it may seem like a good idea to try to get a lot of this research work out of the way early on in the game, intensive company research should not be performed until you have secured a date and time for an interview. Otherwise, you may waste countless hours of your time researching companies that may never call you.

Internet Research

There are plenty of places online where you can get the needed information quickly and effectively. The best place to start is with a company's website. In addition to basic company information, you can often obtain annual reports, lists of company executives, the company's mission statement, and its history. If there is a section for press releases, read the latest ones. You can learn about pending mergers and other key developments within a company. This is a great way to show the interviewer that you know the most current happenings in the company. There are also a number of sites that will arm you with the facts you'll need to know about an industry and/or a specific occupation that you are interested in. A few of these sites are profiled here:

Monster

www.monster.com

Monster advertises itself as the "World's Leading Career Network." Use its resources to create resumes, search for jobs, and prepare for interviews to help launch the career you want.

Careerbuilder

www.careerbuilder.com

In addition to providing tons of job postings—1.5 million jobs, according to its website—Careerbuilder.com will even e-mail job postings to your mailbox. Browse the latest job listings and fill out job applications on this well-organized site.

Yahoo! Hotjobs

www.hotjobs.yahoo.com

Here's another all-in-one site that can help you find a job, prepare for the interview, and research a company all with one visit! This site is an invaluable source for job search information. You can post your resume for potential employers to come to you, or you can peruse listings and apply to the jobs that interest you.

Career Voyages

www.careervoyages.gov

The result of a collaboration between the U.S. Department of Labor and the U.S. Department of Education, Career Voyages is targeted at students and adults who have been out of the work force for a while and also those adults who have never worked before. The site is designed to provide information on high-growth, in-demand occupations along with the skills and education needed to attain those jobs. Don't forget online resources like ValueLine and LexisNexis and the major business publications: *Forbes*, *Money*, *Kiplinger's*, *The Wall St. Journal*, and *Investors Business Daily*.

Practice Makes Perfect

If it's your first time out in the real world or if it's been a while since your last job interview, don't be surprised if your first interview turns out to be somewhat disastrous. Though your first interview won't necessarily flop because you are out of practice, you'd be wise to try to schedule your first interview with a company you don't have all that much interest in. Interviewing with your dream company for that ideal job the first time out may not be your best move. If you don't know what to expect from an interviewer, you could blow your chances of employment.

No job-hunting experience is a bad one if you can learn from it. Even if you have a horrible interview, at least you can analyze what went wrong to improve your chances in the next one. Consider each job-hunting activity as an additional step in enriching your abilities, and take criticism as an opportunity to improve yourself.

Don't despair if that first interview is less than perfect. Certainly you've heard the saying "Practice makes perfect." It's true. The more you interview—or even practice for an interview—the more likely you are to master the art of it. Refer to the later chapters in this book to learn some of the most commonly asked interview questions, and practice your answers to them. Figure out the kinds of answers that an interviewer would be looking for, and then think of a way to answer these questions as they relate to you and your own experience.

That said, try to get one or two interviews under your belt before you decide to meet with the hiring manager of the company of your dreams. If that's not possible, make sure you practice until you've got it nearly perfect, as you've only got one shot at making a good impression.

Mock Interview

If you think about the answers carefully enough and practice through a mock interview with a friend or family member, you are more likely to breeze through that first interview in a confident manner. Sit down with your best friend and have her fire some questions at you. Ask for her feedback. Do you sound assured and confident or are your answers rambling and off-the-mark? Would she hire the person answering the questions? If not, you have some work to do.

Have your friend tape you with a video camera. You'll get a look at yourself through the interviewer's eyes. Make sure to keep an eye on your body language, as it can tell a great deal about you. Do you slouch in your chair, or do you sit up straight and attentively? Are you able to maintain eye contact without staring? Your body language should show the interviewer that you're alert and focused—no folded arms, no crossed legs. Your hands can work against you in an interview—if you're used to talking with them, don't. Your hands belong on your lap; let your mouth do the talking. Analyze the way your answers sound on your tape. You'll be able to hear little mistakes you didn't notice when you were in the midst of the mock interview. You may talk too quickly or start every answer with "um . . . ." On your next run-through make a conscious effort to make yourself sound more professional.

If there's no one available to help you test out your interviewing skills, enlist the help of a tape recorder and a mirror. Look and listen carefully.

When you answer a question, do you look straight ahead in a confident manner? Is the pitch of your voice and the tone pleasant? Do you slur your words, or do you speak clearly and distinctly? All these things will give you plenty to work on before that eventful day when you have your first interview.

Dress for Success

As superficial as it sounds, employers will judge you on the way you are dressed. This does not mean that if you wear anything less than Prada, the job will go to someone else. It simply means that the interviewer looks at your exterior as a representation of your interior. If it is obvious that you took the time to choose the right clothes for this interview, it is likely that you will put the same amount of thought into your work. Arriving for an interview too casually dressed tells the interviewer that you don't care enough about the job or the company to put your best self forward. Dress up a little bit more for your interview than you would if you were actually going to work at the company. The rules of dress laid out here for both men and women are very specific and should be strictly followed. Though the lines between what men and women can and do wear to work on a regular basis are becoming more and more blurred—khakis and a button-down shirt can work well on either of the sexes—there are two definite sets of rules during the job interview process.

For Men

If you are a man interviewing for a professional position, you should always wear a suit. A shirt and tie might be sufficient to make you the best dressed guy at your current job, but it won't cut it in an interview. More conservative colors—colors like black, navy blue, or charcoal gray—are the best colors to choose. Bright and flashy colors will only serve to distract the interviewer from what you are saying.

For men, the tie has become one of the few creative outlets when it comes to dressing professionally. A bad choice in the neckwear department can spell almost certain doom. A solid dark color with tiny geometric patterns is the safest bet. Also remember: A cheap tie is one of the easiest things in the world to spot. Don't become a fashion victim.

You can change the look of a conservative colored suit dramatically by changing the tie, the shirt, or both. If you only have one suit, these changes can help you out tremendously when you're interviewing with companies that require two or more meetings on separate occasions. Avoid shiny shirts; they are a major no-no and should be reserved for the nightclub scene. Socks should blend in well with the shoes and pants. Steer clear of any kind of a cutesy pattern, and stick with a color that won't stand out.

For Women

The rules of proper workplace attire for women have been changing over the past several decades. The power suit that once ruled the scene has been replaced with the traditional pantsuit that doesn't differ much from the men's version. Still, the rules of job interview dress have not caught up with general workplace appropriateness. Professionalism still dictates that women wear a skirt to an interview. The length of the skirt, obviously, should be tasteful and professional. Knee length is always appropriate. Again, regardless of the company's particular dress code, women too are expected to wear a suit to the interview.

One detail not to overlook: your shoes. Interviewers often gauge a candidate by his or her shoes—are they worn, polished, fashionable? While it is something a candidate might neglect, it's a very telling detail for the interviewer and one that might cost the candidate a job.

Colors should be conservative. A black or navy blue skirt and jacket is the best choice. Avoid colors like pink and powder blue. They won't help you assert your professionalism. Don't wear anything that dangles. That goes for earrings, bracelets, and necklaces. Avoid clothes that are too tight; you'll be less comfortable and you won't be taken as seriously.

Grooming

Personal grooming is another matter each candidate must attend to before heading out the door to an interview. Careful grooming indicates both thoroughness and self-confidence. There are advantages to scheduling a few interviews in one day. For one, you'll already be decked out in your interviewing gear, and your briefcase or bag will be stocked with the essential spare resume, work samples, and reference sheets. Some people find they get into a mental zone after one interview that lets them gear up for additional interviews.

Women should not wear excessive makeup or jewelry. If you have painted nails, make sure they are of a conservative color. Ladies should consider a clean look, such as a French manicure. Men should be sure to check that any facial hair is neat and trim. If you have a beard or a mustache, make sure it is well groomed. Otherwise, men should make sure that they are clean-shaven when they arrive for an interview. If your five o'clock shadow comes at three o'clock and your interview is at four, make sure you have time to run home quickly and shave.

All candidates should wear very little—if any—perfume or cologne. Cigarette-scented clothing may also offend an interviewer with a sensitive nose. Remove any nose rings, cover your tattoos with long sleeves, and tuck your water bottle in your briefcase, not a knapsack.

Pre-Interview Preparations

Chances are good that the person who invites you in for an interview will also offer to give you directions to the building. Take these directions! Even if you have a good idea of the location of the company, you'll want to know exactly where you are going. If you are unfamiliar with the area, it might be a good idea to drive to the company before you actually have to meet for the interview. Map out the directions and time how long it will take for you to get there.

Before you go out the door, make sure you have the following items:

- Resume
- Cover letter
- Writing implement
- Spare tie or pair of pantyhose
- List of professional references
- Driver's license and social security card

Add a few extra minutes for traffic or any other unforeseen delays. Plan to arrive for the interview at least ten to fifteen minutes early. When scheduling your interview, be sure you know the name of the person you will be meeting with. The person who calls to screen you over the phone is not always the same person you'll be interviewing with. Find out the person's name, title, and phone number. That way, if a problem arises, you can contact this person directly.

Ten Ways to Ace an Interview

You can make a conscious effort to impress an interviewer to make sure that she remembers you, even after you've shaken hands and said goodbye.

1. ***Be prepared.*** Being prepared for a job interview entails more than just knowing what questions you are likely to be asked. Preparedness calls for bringing along an extra copy of your resume and carrying some reading materials in the event that you have to wait a little while before meeting with someone.

2. ***Dress appropriately.*** You don't want the interviewer to see you as "the guy in the T-shirt." Interviewers notice these things and are not likely to hire anyone who arrives on the scene in less than conservative business attire. Unless you're donning your old prom dress, you can never be too overdressed for a job interview.
3. ***Be confident.*** Getting a call to come in and interview for a company is like a getting a nod of approval from an interviewer. Even if you think you may be completely underqualified for a position, evidently the interviewer sees something different in your resume. Always remember that the company that calls you believes you are capable of performing the job at hand; it's important for you to believe the same thing. Projecting an air of confidence—without sounding cocky or conceited—is one of the easiest ways to get an interviewer to remember you. Talk about your skills and experience with pride and—above all—let the interviewer know that you think you could do a good job.
4. ***Make eye contact.*** One of the easiest ways to project confidence is to be attentive and maintain direct eye contact with an interviewer throughout your meeting. Always look this person directly in the eye to assure him that you are both on the same page. If you are interviewing with more than one person, make eye contact with the person asking you the question. When answering a question in front of two or more people, move from person to person, but make sure to establish eye contact with each person long enough so that you don't seem shifty.
5. ***Show your enthusiasm.*** Even more frustrating to an interviewer than a candidate who lacks confidence is a candidate who lacks enthusiasm. When the interviewer discusses the different aspects of the job you'd be taking on, show how willing and excited you are to take on these new tasks. Even if the interviewer discusses your having to perform a skill that you are not familiar with, show her how eager you are to learn. As when showing confidence, there is a line you have to walk when showing enthusiasm. Be sure to seem excited but not obsequious or insincere.
6. ***Know the position.*** Whatever the position you're applying for, you should know something about it. Reread the job description a few times to get an idea of the type of person the company is looking for. Research similar opportunities and learn more about the kind of person who makes a perfect match for this type of job. Talk to friends or people you know in the same job—or in the industry—to learn about the tasks involved. Know what you are getting yourself into before you go into the job interview; prepare

answers to the questions you are likely to be asked relating to this job. Don't go to an interview until you can rattle off a few of the tasks you think you'll be asked to perform.

7. ***Know the industry.*** You should also know about the industry to which you're applying, as well as whether the position can be found in many industries. For example, human resources professionals can jump from industry to industry throughout their career, as they are a needed department in almost every organization. Find out as much as you can about the industry and show the interviewer that you are well equipped to deal with the day-to-day duties of the job at hand and that you have a strong knowledge of the industry as a whole.
8. ***Know the company.*** More important than knowing the industry, and just as important (if not more so) as knowing the job, is knowing a little something about the company to which you are applying. If the interviewer does not come out directly with a statement such as "Tell me everything you know about this company," he is likely to ask a few questions that will test your knowledge of the company. He may hint at company issues to see whether you pick up on these allusions. More impressive than a candidate who has the skills to do the job well is a candidate who has the skills to do the job well and has a strong knowledge of the company.
9. ***Practice.*** The only way to gauge your readiness for an interview is to practice. Whether you sit in front of a mirror or role-play with a friend, practicing your answers to likely questions is the key to projecting a calm and confident exterior during the interview.
10. ***Follow up.*** You've shown an interest in the company before, so why stop once the interview ends? After the interview, be sure to follow up with a quick note or a short but friendly phone call to the person with whom you spoke. A follow-up will help keep your name at the forefront of the interviewer's mind. It is permissible to send a thank-you note by e-mail, and you can also follow up with more formal mailed correspondence.

Ready, Set, Go!

With these interview preparation skills under your belt, you're all set to get out there and make a great impression. It's time to learn the best and most effective ways to prepare for a job interview. Think of your role in the job interview as that of a salesperson. You're trying to sell yourself to the interviewer.

Just as a salesperson would, you should take the time to get to know the company and think about why you and your skills would fit in well here. You should make a list of your most marketable skills and develop a sort of pitch for yourself. Why should this company decide to "buy" your skills? What can you offer them? Get your suit pressed, put on your greatest smile, and go out there and ace that interview!

CHAPTER 16

Revealing Your Personality

YOU'VE MET THE INTERVIEWER, shaken his hand, and now you're settling into your seat. Okay, bring it on. You're ready for anything he's going to ask. You can talk about each job you've had, your skills, and your accomplishments. Suddenly you find yourself fielding a barrage of personal questions. The interviewer is asking about things that seem to have nothing to do with work. Why does he need to know so much about you?

Why the Personal Questions?

Why would an employer want to know what you like doing for fun, your strengths and weaknesses, and even how many siblings you grew up with? Then along comes the most dreaded request: "So, tell me about yourself." Your heart begins to pound so loudly you're sure the interviewer can hear it. "Tell you about myself? Have you got a few hours?"

Be assured the interviewer usually doesn't want to know all the private details of your life. As a matter of fact, he doesn't have the right to ask for that kind of information. What a prospective employer is interested in learning about are your personal qualities, or your character traits. This information will help him decide whether to hire you.

Basically, the prospective employer wants to know if you have what it takes to work at his company. Yes, you may have the skills and experience, but do you have the personality? Aspects of your personality are a strong indicator of whether you will be a good employee. The interviewer wants to know whether or not you procrastinate, are discreet, and are a team player. He wants to know if you work well on your own and how you make decisions, handle stress, and solve problems.

Before beginning the interviewing process, a hiring manager may have gone through hundreds of resumes looking for candidates who have the skills and experience required for the job in question. The interviewer's job now is to be a detective. He wants to know what makes you a better choice than another candidate who has the same experience and skills.

An interviewer will try to learn about your personality by asking you either direct questions, e.g., "Do you tend to begin a project as soon as it is assigned or do you begin working as you get close to the deadline?" or by asking you questions that get you to reveal this information, e.g., "Tell me how you approach a new project." Give careful consideration to every question the interviewer asks. He has a reason for asking every one of them. Figuring out the reason for each question can help you give the best answer.

TOO MUCH INFORMATION! **Don't reveal more about yourself than is necessary during a job interview. While you should be honest with the interviewer, don't tell her more than she needs to know. Revealing too much information can get you into trouble.**

Now, let's get back to the dreaded question: "Tell me about yourself." The interviewer doesn't want your memoirs. The rule of thumb is to keep it simple. The interviewer is interested only in knowing whether you have the skills and qualities necessary to fulfill the requirements of the position for which you are interviewing. Interviewees sometimes make the mistake of revealing too much when what the prospective employer really wants to know is "Can you do the job?" and "Will you fit in here?"

Questions and Answers

Tell me about yourself.

Answer ▶ I attended Ace Business College, where I earned my associate's degree in office technology five years ago. I started working as a library clerk right after I graduated, and I was promoted to assistant circulation manager after a year. I helped the library switch over to a new circulation system about two years ago. I was part of the team that selected the new system and I helped train our department in its use. In addition to my technical skills, I am adept at troubleshooting. I also work well with customers, helping to solve any problems that arise. I'm now ready to take on a job with more responsibility and I know I will make a great circulation manager.

This candidate tells the interviewer about his skills and experience and shows why he is qualified for the job. He doesn't wander off course or reveal information that is irrelevant. Although this answer is a bit long, it is to the point and tells the interviewer only what she needs to know.

Never Say: "I was born in Wisconsin, one of three children. I did well in school. I was on the football team and editor of my high school newspaper. I moved to Chicago to go to college and . . . . " The interviewer doesn't want your life story. Keep your answer limited to the parts that will affect your suitability for the job.

Do you work well on your own?

Answer ▶ Yes, I do. I'm very focused and efficient.

This is a very simple and honest answer. Most jobs will require you to work on your own sometimes, if not all the time.

Never Say: "I would much rather work on my own." In addition to sometimes working on your own, many jobs also require you to be part of a team at times. Don't volunteer information that makes you seem difficult to work with; just answer the question.

What do you consider to be your biggest weakness?

Answer ▶ I am very dedicated to my job and I expect the same level of dedication from other people. Not everyone feels the same way about work and sometimes my expectations are too high.

Wouldn't every boss love such a dedicated employee? This interviewee knew he had to find a weakness that his prospective employer would see as a strength. Another option is to pick a weakness that is somewhat innocuous, such as your love of chocolate.

Never Say: "I don't have any weaknesses." Oh, come on. Who's going to believe that?

What would your friends say is your biggest weakness?

Answer ▶ Whenever my friends and I travel together, I do a lot of advanced planning. Most of my travel companions appreciate it, but some find it annoying. We just went to the Southwest, and three months before we were going I had already put together a list of all the things we had to see. I kept everyone going all day long, every single day. In the end we all had a great time.

This candidate chooses to talk about something that could be perceived as a weakness but that also demonstrates her skills. By giving this answer she demonstrates three skills—planning, research, and strong leadership qualities. Some of her friends may not appreciate her advanced planning, which is why she considers this a weakness, but she also shows that everything worked out in the end.

Never Say: "I never see my friends because I'm always working."You know what they say about all work and no play. A little time away from the office is good for everyone.

How do you handle success?

Answer ▶ I give myself a quick pat on the back and move on to the next project. Of course, I take the time to figure out what helped me succeed and use that experience to help me the next time.

This prospective employee takes appropriate pride in his success but also believes in the old adage "Don't rest on your laurels." He also learns from his experience.

Never Say: "I make sure everyone knows about it. If I don't brag about my own success, then who will?" That's true, but there are more subtle ways of getting the word out. Besides, if he's so busy bragging, who's doing all his work?

How do you handle failure?

Answer ▶ I give myself a short time to feel sad, but I don't dwell on it. Who has time for that? I don't spend too much energy on my failures, but I always try to figure out where things went wrong. If I don't do that, I won't know what I need to do to succeed next time.

This isn't someone who wastes any time feeling sorry for herself. She's also smart enough to learn from her mistakes.

Never Say: "I never fail, so I don't have to handle it." Everyone has failures, so the interviewer can only assume this candidate is lying or joking. Either way, she may be able to count this interview among her failures.

What are your long-term goals?

Answer ▶ I want to move into a supervisory position eventually. I know that will take time and hard work, but it is something I expect to achieve.

That's a good answer as long as the applicant isn't implying that he wants the interviewer's job. Making the interviewer feel threatened will not win him any points. It's important to emphasize not only that you have goals, but that you are willing to do the work to reach them.

Never Say: "I want to run this place." Wait. Doesn't the interviewer already run this place?

What are your short-term goals?

Answer ▶ I want to work for a growing company in a position that allows me to use my skills to help that growth. I know your company is trying to expand into the teen market. My experience selling to that market will help your company reach its goals.

This interviewee's goals are aligned with those of the company. By giving an example of how she will help the company meet its goals, she has forced the employer to visualize her as an employee. This answer also shows that the interviewee took the time to research the company.

Never Say: "I plan to begin working on my MBA as soon as possible." While this interviewee is clearly ambitious, she hasn't shown how her goals have anything to do with the job for which she's interviewing.

Do you prefer to work alone or as part of a team?

Answer ▶ Each situation is different. When I'm working on some projects, I prefer to be part of a team, while I'd rather work alone on other projects. I enjoy being part of a team, but I can work independently, too.

This interviewer shows that he's flexible and can adapt to working in either situation.

Never Say: "Teams are clearly a better use of resources. I'm a team player all the way." It's important to show flexibility because most jobs require you to be able to work independently at least some of the time, as well as on a team.

What do you consider to be your greatest strength?

Answer ▶ My greatest strength is my ability to see a project through from its inception to its completion. Each project I am assigned is important to me and I always make sure it gets the appropriate amount of attention.

Notice the interviewee said each project gets the "appropriate amount of attention" and not "all my attention." She clearly knows some projects need more attention than others and indicates that she knows how to prioritize.

Never Say: "I'm a hard worker and I always get to work on time." Getting to work on time is expected of all workers, as is being a hard worker. These are requirements of most jobs, not strengths.

How many siblings did you grow up with and how did that influence who you are today?

Answer ▶ *Answer 1:* I grew up as one of five children. When you grow up in such a large family, you must function as a team. Everyone takes on different responsibilities. Because my parents were so busy all the time, I also learned to be very independent.

Answer ▶ *Answer 2:* I grew up as an only child. I was very independent. When I got to school I had to learn how to share my toys with other kids. It was a difficult lesson, but it helped me become a better team player.

The interviewee, regardless of the size family in which he grew up, shows that he can work alone or as part of a team.

Never Say: *Answer 1:* "I grew up with five brothers and sisters. It was always really noisy. I think that's why I love being alone now."

Never Say: *Answer 2:* "I was an only child. I got so used to being alone that I really like it better that way." Uh-oh. Neither answer shows that the interviewee is flexible enough to be a team player when he needs to be.

Do you like to take risks or are you cautious?

Answer ▶ I'll take risks but I always proceed with caution, so I guess I fall somewhere in between. I like to see what my odds are before I take a risk. I also want to know what I stand to gain or what I stand to lose.

This candidate is a careful decision-maker who isn't afraid to take risks if there is a high probability of success. She also wants to make sure the risk is worth taking. She's not a gambler, but she's not afraid to take chances when it's appropriate to do so.

Never Say: "I'm a risk-taker" or "I'm cautious." Most employers want someone with a combination of these traits.

Do others think of you as a leader?

Answer ▶ I believe those who have seen me in action are confident in my ability to lead them. Whenever we had to work in committees in my marketing class, my fellow committee members always chose me to be chairperson.

This answer is honest and to the point. Although he is interviewing for his first job, he is able to draw on his college experience to come up with an example.

Never Say: "I lead and others follow." Confidence is good, but cockiness is not.

Do you consider yourself a leader?

Answer ▶ I am willing to take on responsibility, I am persuasive, and I can delegate. All these qualities make me a good leader. If a situation calls for someone to take charge, I will certainly step forward.

This interviewer states the qualities that make her a good leader but knows to tread lightly here. She wants to show she can evaluate the needs of each situation and step forward if necessary, while making it clear she's a team player.

Never Say: "Yes. I like being in charge." This candidate doesn't tell the interviewer why she is qualified to lead, but sounds determined to take a leadership position no matter who she steps on.

ANSWER THE QUESTION

Make sure to fully answer the question. Explain yourself clearly and don't give answers that are too short, but also avoid ones that are too lengthy. Try to figure out why the interviewer has asked a particular question and prepare your answer with that in mind.

How do you handle pressure?

Answer ▶ I take a deep breath and figure out what needs to be done. Then I take care of it. One afternoon at 4 P.M., my boss came to me with a big research project that needed to be completed by the following morning. I rounded up my team and divided the project among us. We got it done with enough time to get home to sleep for a few hours before returning to work in the morning.

This interviewee has a strategy in place for dealing with pressure. He demonstrates how he dealt with one difficult situation using some valuable skills, including the abilities to delegate and work as part of a team.

Never Say: "I work best under pressure." That may be true, but this interviewee needs to elaborate.

Are you a procrastinator or do you like to get things done right away?

Answer ▶ Though I've been known to procrastinate on occasion, I don't make a habit of it. When someone hands me a project that needs to be done in a timely fashion, I will get it done.

Who hasn't procrastinated on occasion? What matters is that this candidate knows the difference between a project that can wait and one that needs to be done right away, and can finish the pressing ones in time to meet deadlines.

Never Say: "I never procrastinate." Really? This doesn't sound like an honest answer since everyone procrastinates at least some of the time. Everyone has flaws. Your goal on a job interview is to make yours not look so bad.

What pet peeves do you have about coworkers?

Answer ▶ Too much negativity has always bothered me. I think if you're going to complain you should be able to offer some solutions to fix the things you think are wrong.

By giving this answer, this candidate is saying, "I'm not a negative person. If I see a problem, I figure out how to fix it."

Never Say: "I say live and let live. They can do what they want; it doesn't bother me." It's virtually impossible to spend forty hours a week with a group of people and get along perfectly with them all the time. This candidate seems to be too easygoing. She'd rather let things slide than deal with them.

We're not a company that does things the same way year after year. How do you react to change?

Answer ▶ When it's appropriate, change is important. For example, when I heard about a new payroll system at a conference last year, I did a little investigating, found out it was better than what we were using, and recommended my employer move over to it.

This interviewee has shown that he doesn't shy away from change and even provides a good example of how he initiated it at his current job. He has also shown that he doesn't jump into change just for the sake of doing something different; instead, he does his homework first.

Never Say: "Change is great. Without it I get bored." The interviewer might wonder if the candidate's love of change includes finding a new job every other year.

What is the best money you ever spent?

Answer ▶ I really wanted to go to a school out of state, but my parents couldn't afford to send me to one, so I took a year off after high school and worked two jobs to earn enough money to cover the difference between the local school they could afford and the one I wanted to go to. It was a great experience. I got a great education and living away from home taught me to be independent.

This man knows how to reach her goals and she's not afraid of working hard.

Never Say: "I got this awesome new sports car. It's so sharp and guys love it." Not only does this answer sound immature, it may make the interviewer question the applicant's priorities. Does she really want to hire someone who will be chasing after all the men in the office, possibly opening up the company to sexual harassment suits?

What was your worst purchase?

Answer ▶ I'm almost embarrassed to admit this. There were these boots that were popular a few years ago. They literally cost everything I earned working during the summer. I bought them, they lasted one season, and then they were out of style.

So you spent all your earnings on a pair of boots? That's pretty innocuous as far as frivolous purchases go. The interviewee makes sure to point out that it happened a few years ago when he didn't know any better, and that he has learned from the mistake.

Never Say: "I bought my girlfriend this really expensive engagement ring and then we broke up because she was seeing my best friend behind my back." This answer reveals way too much personal information.

What is the last thing you read?

Answer ▶ I just finished the latest book on management techniques by Jane Brown. I'm always trying to keep up with the latest literature in the field.

Reading is a great way to keep up with changes in one's field and this interviewee knows it. She proves that her interest in the field goes beyond the nine-to-five job.

Never Say: "My job keeps me so busy I really don't have time to read." Even if you don't have time to read for pleasure, you should have time to keep up with your professional literature if you want to be seen as a dedicated applicant.

LIKES AND DISLIKES

Discuss your likes and dislikes on a job interview only if you can relate them to your career or to the job for which you are interviewing. For example if a prospective employer asks what you like to read, stick to talking about professional literature.

Do you have any hobbies?

Answer ▶ I love woodworking. I've made tables, chairs, and a bookshelf. I love the satisfaction I get from taking a few pieces of wood and turning them into something I can use.

The applicant takes this opportunity to emphasize one of his strengths. This answer shows that he can see a project through from beginning to end.

Never Say: "Who has time for hobbies?" A successful job candidate must show that he is well rounded.

How do you make decisions?

Answer ▶ I evaluate the situation before I decide what I need to do. If there is someone who has had experience with similar situations, I'm not afraid to ask for advice.

This interviewee isn't going to make a decision without considering it carefully. She is also very resourceful; seeking advice from people with more experience is always a good idea.

Never Say: "I usually go with my first instinct." This interviewee clearly doesn't put a lot of thought into things, including how to best answer this question.

What do you as an employee owe your boss and what does your boss owe you?

Answer ▶ I owe my boss hard work, respect, and honesty. My boss owes me respect, honesty, and recognition for my hard work.

In a world where honesty isn't always easy to find, this prospective employee is promising a rare commodity. The same can be said for respect. Hard work is a must, of course, but some employees only do the minimum. He is also clear about what he expects from his prospective employer.

Never Say: "I owe my employer everything. I'm at my boss's disposal. What do I expect in return? My salary." This may be every employer's dream employee . . . if it were true, which interviewer knows it probably isn't.

BE POSITIVE

Interviewers are generally quite perceptive, and therefore they will know when a job candidate is giving answers that are too good to be true. It is important to frame your answers so they are as positive as possible, but don't go over the top. Keep your answers realistic.

I see that you worked full-time while attending graduate school. How did you manage to balance everything?

Answer ▶ It was difficult, but I managed not to fall behind at work or school. I worked five full days a week and took classes two evenings a week. I studied on the other three nights and on the weekends.

This candidate shows that she was determined to complete her degree, but not at the expense of her job.

Never Say: "I walked around exhausted all the time." This doesn't answer the interviewer's question or tell him anything about the candidate other than that she doesn't handle stress well.

LISTEN!

Always pay attention and listen carefully during the interview. If you don't understand a question completely, it's okay to ask for clarification. It's better than answering incorrectly. You won't be able to answer a question properly unless you understand what the interviewer is asking you.

How do you feel about lying?

Answer ▶ I think lying has the potential to get you into trouble. It's much better to be honest and up front. If you are caught in a lie, the person you lied to will not have a reason to trust you in the future.

This interviewee doesn't just say lying is bad, but he also backs up his opinion by giving a negative result of lying.

Never Say: "I never lie." That wasn't the question.

Did you enjoy school as a child?

Answer ▶ Not really. I always got good grades but I think I was bored. Most teachers just talked at us. My favorite classes were the ones where group discussions happened frequently.

Someone who didn't like school won't necessarily be a bad employee. This interviewee is honest, and he gives a reason for the way he feels.

Never Say: "I hated school. I couldn't wait to get out of there. All those teachers telling me what to do drove me crazy." Even though this interviewee had the same experience as the previous one, he is a little too vehement about his feelings without giving an explanation.

Can you describe your ideal work environment?

Answer ▶ I want to work in an environment where I can use my presentation skills to help the company increase its client roster. It's important that I work in a fast-paced environment because I like being busy. I want to work somewhere where employees are recognized for their contributions.

Based on some research, this candidate is able to describe both the job that she's interviewing for and her potential employer. By showing that her ideal fits with what the job requires, she shows that she is the perfect fit for the position.

Never Say: "I want to work in a clean office with good lighting. I prefer to be on a lower floor. I really don't like cubicles." Even if this candidate had done her homework, and this was an accurate description of her potential employer's offices, this answer doesn't say anything about the job or her qualifications for it.

If you won a million dollars, what would you do?

Answer ▶ I know some people would say they'd quit their jobs and go off to some island, but they haven't considered the fact that a million dollars won't take you very far. Besides, I find this type of work fulfilling. I'd probably take a nice vacation and buy a new car. Then I'd go back to work and invest the rest of the money.

This interviewee is practical, a trait a prospective employer should find valuable.

Never Say: "I would quit my job and move to the south of France." Aside from the fact that this applicant is saying he'd leave his job if something better came along, he isn't very practical.

Why did you choose this career?

Answer ▶ When I started college, I wasn't sure what I wanted to do. I visited the career office and they gave me some self-assessment tests. Based on the results, they gave me a list of careers that might be suitable and told me how to research them. I did, and this is what I thought I'd like best.

This is a great answer that demonstrates this candidate's ability to go about making life-altering decisions in a methodical fashion.

Never Say: "My parents had a friend in the field and she thought I'd be good at this." That is the wrong way to make a career choice. It may make the interviewer wonder how this person will make other decisions.

CHAPTER 17

Discussing Your Skills and Abilities

YOUR SKILLS—that's what they pay you the big bucks for. Well, maybe not the big bucks, but it is why they pay you anything at all. Who you are as a person will help an employer decide if you have the characteristics that make you a good fit for his company. To fit into a particular job, you'll also need a certain set of skills. Your skills represent your ability to do the job at hand.

Hard Skills Versus Soft Skills

Skills can be divided into two categories: hard skills and soft skills. Hard skills are the technical skills that define your job. Soft skills are less tangible. They begin with how you present yourself in your first encounter with your prospective employer, whether it is a phone call or a sit-down interview. Your prospective employer will want to know that you will fit into the work environment at her company and that you are able to handle the demands that will be placed upon you.

Hard Skills

Simply put, a baker must know how to bake, an accountant must know how to balance the books, a nurse must know how to care for patients, and a teacher must know how to teach. Of course, these basic skills can be broken down into more specific hard skills. For example, an accountant might be skilled in particular areas—specifically, accounts receivable, accounts payable, auditing, taxation, and payroll.

What you do at work can vary greatly from your formal job description. In addition to your regular job duties, you may be required to write, make presentations, use a computer, or do research. These are also hard skills, but they are not necessarily part of your "official" job description. Nevertheless, you will be required to be proficient in these skills and your prospective employer will want you to prove this to him in the job interview by drawing on specific examples of how you have used your skills.

LEARNING HARD SKILLS

Hard skills are usually skills you learned in school or through some other formal training or prior work experience. You will typically choose a job based on the hard skills you possess, but some employers are willing to let you pick them up on the job.

Soft Skills

Soft skills are the skills you must have in order to excel at work in general. These skills vary greatly. They aren't specific to any occupation, but instead are the things that enhance your performance regardless of what your actual job is. Examples of these soft skills include decision-making, time management, delegating, multitasking, and problem solving.

LIST YOUR SKILLS

When you prepare for a job interview, make a list of all your soft skills and all your hard skills. Think of specific examples of when you've had to use each of them, especially those that are most relevant to the job for which you are interviewing.

Remember, when the job interviewer asks whether you have a particular skill, she doesn't want a simple yes or no answer. She wants to know how you obtained the skill, how you've used the skill, and how you plan to use it to benefit her company.

Skills You Haven't Used Professionally

You may be concerned if you have a particular skill, but you haven't actually used it on the job. You may have learned the skill in school and never used it at work. If this is the case, can you think of a time you used that skill for an extracurricular activity or in another situation? Perhaps you used your fundraising skills to raise money for an organization for which you volunteer or your organizational skills to plan an event.

When discussing skills you've picked up through volunteer work or some other unpaid experience, talk about the skill as if you used it on a job. Highlight how your skills benefited the organization with which you were involved. For example, if you raised funds for an organization, give dollar amounts; if you organized an event, state how many people attended it. If you haven't actually used a skill in a real-life situation, you can still lay claim to it. Come up with an example of how you would use that skill to benefit your prospective employer.

LEARN FROM EVERYTHING

People develop skills in a variety of ways that are unrelated to paid employment. You may have learned a new skill when you participated in a school club or organization. You may use certain skills in running your household or in your volunteer work.

Questions and Answers

How well do you think you perform as a manager?

Answer ▶ I've never officially had the title "manager," but I've often had to act as manager when my boss is out of the office. He's always been very pleased with the job I've done.

This candidate doesn't let the fact that she's never actually had the title of manager stop her from explaining why she can do the job. She found some managerial experience from which she was able to draw. Even supervising a small project would have sufficed.

Never Say: "Well, since I've never been a manager, I don't know." If you've had some managerial experience, even if it was just supervising a single project, you should talk about that. If you've had no managerial experience, then you can talk about it hypothetically.

How are your presentation skills? How do you prepare for presentations?

Answer ▶ I didn't always like making presentations, but since I had to make a lot of them in my last two jobs, I've gotten very good at it. I do a lot of research before any presentation. I try to find out as much as possible about the client, the market they are trying to reach, their competitors, and the industry. Sometimes, if the budget allows for it, I hire an expert to help me with the research.

This client answered honestly. He knows it's not that unusual to dislike presentations, so he's not afraid to admit that. It also gives him the opportunity to show off his experience and how it has gotten him over his fear. In addition, he knows the importance of having good information and knows what resources he needs to use to get it.

Never Say: "I love making presentations. I only have one real problem; if I'm too prepared, my presentation sounds scripted." This is not a well-thought-out answer. This candidate would have benefited from a little preparation to get him through the interview.

You haven't worked in this field before. What makes you think you'd be good?

Answer ▶ I am very organized, I work well on a team, and I have very good communication skills. Although I haven't worked in this particular field before, I know these skills will make me a valuable employee.

This applicant doesn't let the fact that she's new to this field stop her from showing the interviewer why he should hire her. She has some very desirable skills for this and any field, which she makes a point of letting the interviewer know.

Never Say: "I haven't worked in this field before, but I'm a fast learner." This candidate makes the mistake of dwelling on lack of experience instead of her strengths.

Have you ever been in a situation where the majority disagrees with you? What did you do?

Answer ▶ I haven't been in that situation, but here's what I would do if I were: first I would listen to why the majority felt the way they did. Then I'd have to decide whether I needed to reconsider my position. If I still felt strongly about it after hearing their side, I would try to persuade them to come over to mine.

This candidate knew better than to dismiss the question just because he couldn't draw on his experience to answer it. Rather than make something up, he tells the interviewer what he would do if he were in that situation. His answer shows that he is flexible enough to try to see things differently, but strong enough in his convictions to not automatically go with the crowd.

Never Say: "We were designing our new brochure and I thought yellow and purple would look great. Everyone else wanted to go with burgundy and blue. Since I had the most seniority, they had to do it my way." Flexible? No. A bully? Maybe.

Please describe your work in the military.

Answer ▶ As an Army finance specialist, I audited financial records, disbursed cash and checks, and recorded details of financial transactions using standard forms.

This job candidate, an Army veteran, clearly states what her military work involved. Since military job descriptions are often different than civilian job descriptions, it was not only important for her to state what her title was, but to also describe her duties.

Never Say: "I was a finance specialist." This isn't descriptive enough, particularly since the title may differ from the actual job description.

How are you at delegating?

Answer ▶ I have such a high level of trust in my staff members that delegating to them is easy. I know each person's strengths and weaknesses, so I can easily decide who can handle certain jobs and duties. I try to give people projects that challenge them but won't defeat them.

This candidate is obviously a good manager. He puts a lot of thought into how to delegate responsibilities and makes a point of knowing his staff very well.

Never Say: "I'm good at delegating. I don't want to do all the work myself." This guy just sounds lazy.

Tell me about a crisis you encountered at work and how you handled it.

Answer ▶ Last year a virus was causing our computers to send out thousands of e-mail messages to our clients. We were being inundated with angry phone calls before we knew what was going on. Our technical support person was on vacation, so I made a few phone calls and found someone to fix the problem. Then, once she removed the virus from our system, I drafted an apology that was sent out by e-mail to our clients.

This answer is good because the candidate clearly describes the problem and gives specifics on how he solved it. In addition, the crisis is one that could have caused his company to lose clients, something that would strike fear into the hearts of most employers, including the one interviewing him.

Never Say: "My assistant called in sick right before I was leaving on vacation. I was counting on her to run some errands for me. Since she wasn't there I had to get one of the interns to do it." This candidate is resourceful, but he shouldn't have had anyone running his errands on company time.

How do you manage your time?

Answer ▶ I prioritize my work. I figure out what needs to get done first, next, and so on. Then I calculate how much time I will need to spend on each activity or project. I set a schedule for myself and get going.

This applicant has a plan. He knows how to prioritize and apportion the proper amount of time to each activity.

Never Say: "I get to work early and stay late to get everything done." This answer doesn't show that the applicant can manage his time well. Rather, he can get everything done as long as he works long hours, which could cost the employer in overtime.

How do you solve problems?

Answer ▶ First I assess the problem. Then I figure out what I need to do to solve it. For example, last month we were hosting a conference. Our receptionist, who was supposed to greet attendees, called in sick. With the conference scheduled to start in an hour we had to do something fast. I quickly went through a list of employees who might be able to handle hosting duties but found that each was involved in some other aspect of the conference. I got my boss's approval to call my contact at a local temp agency, and we had a replacement host shortly.

Not only does this applicant discuss how she solves problems, she gives a real-life example.

Never Say: "If you do your job well, you shouldn't have any problems to solve." This candidate is in a state of denial. Problems always pop up and she has shown that she will have no idea how to deal with them when they do.

We use PQR Write to lay out our brochures. Do you know how to use it?

Answer ▶ I use a program that is similar to that. I also have a friend who uses PQR and I'm sure she'd be happy to give me a crash course. I know I can learn it by the time I start.

There are so many software programs out there, it would be impossible to know how to use all of them. This candidate knew better than to lie about his experience and instead told his prospective employer how he would get the skills he needs. Notice how he says he'll know the program by the time "I start work," not "if I get this job."

Never Say: "No, I only feel comfortable with Super Page. Couldn't I just keep using that?"

Are you computer literate?

Answer ▶ I'm proficient in several programs, including Microsoft Word, Excel, and Quick Pages.

Instead of just saying she is computer literate, this candidate goes beyond that and discusses which software programs she knows how to use. The programs she chooses to highlight are those that are relevant to the job for which she's applying.

Never Say: "I know how to go online and I can use a word processor." This candidate should be more specific, making a point of mentioning programs that are specific to his field.

We handle a large volume of tax returns here. How has your experience prepared you for this?

Answer ▶ During college, I participated in the IRS's Volunteer Income Tax Assistance program. For two nights a week from February through April, I spent a few hours preparing individual tax returns in a public library near my college. I prepared about five returns each evening.

This job candidate, although he doesn't have professional experience, is able to demonstrate his skills through his volunteer experience. He speaks about the number of tax returns he processed, demonstrating that he can work efficiently.

Never Say: "I do a few returns each year but I'm sure I'll be able to handle the volume." Even if this candidate can't demonstrate that he has practical experience preparing a large volume of tax returns, he should find some past experience that proves to the interviewer he can handle a large volume of work.

Have you ever had to juggle two or more projects at the same time?

Answer ▶ That happened all the time on my last job. Several months ago, I was in the midst of working on one huge project for one of my bosses, when my other boss came to me with another project that needed to be completed in two days. After evaluating the second project, I realized I could complete it in one day. Since I still had about a week before the deadline for the first project, I decided to get started on the second one. I completed it by the end of the next day and went back to my first project.

The interviewer asked for an example and this candidate gave one. She demonstrates how her ability to prioritize helped her.

Never Say: "I can't think of any right now. Can I get back to you on that one?" The interviewee should have prepared for this in advance.

What does your desk look like?

Answer ▶ I try to keep it organized, which is not always an easy feat with the volume of work that comes across it. I find that if I know where everything is I can work much more efficiently.

This is a vague question, but this interviewee has quickly figured out that the interviewer wants to know how well-organized he is. He gives a realistic answer. He knows the importance of having an organized work area, but he also knows that it's sometimes difficult to keep it that way, especially when you're very busy.

Never Say: "It's brown and made of wood." This isn't what the interviewer wanted to know.

We need someone with very strong auditing skills. Do you qualify?

Answer ▶ Yes, I do. As a staff accountant at Crabgrass and Weed, I regularly performed audits of our clients' financial records. I examined financial source documents to make sure procedures were followed correctly and generated adjusting journal entries as needed. I also prepared final reports for our clients.

The interviewee specifically states how her experience has prepared her for this position.

Never Say: "Yes, I do. I had some auditing responsibilities on my last job." This applicant has the necessary skills, but she needs to elaborate on them.

How do you take direction?

Answer ▶ I think the ability to listen is one of the most important skills anyone should have. I always make sure to pay attention to what my supervisor is saying and then ask any questions I have. I find out when the project must be completed and if there are any special issues I must be attentive to.

This candidate demonstrates that he has no problem taking direction from his superiors, or for that matter, following those directions.

Never Say: "Why should that matter? Won't I be in charge?" Even if this person is applying for a high-level position, he will still have to answer to someone, unless he plans to buy the company.

As assistant to the director of human resources, employees will come to you if they feel their supervisor has discriminated against them in some way. How will you handle these complaints?

Answer ▶ As an HR professional I know the importance of being well versed in the laws that affect the workplace. First, I will interview the employee, asking for an explanation of exactly what happened. Then, I'll interview the supervisor and get her side it.

This candidate will take a balanced look at the situation. He will evaluate it using his knowledge of employment law and then try to solve the problem.

Never Say: "I'd refer it to our company's legal counsel." This applicant needs to show he knows how to deal with issues that regularly occur before dumping them in someone else's lap.

What skills can you bring to our school?

Answer ▶ As you can see from my resume, I've been a teacher at the Parkside School for five years. I've taught second and third grades. I form strong relationships with my students. They trust me, as do their parents. Many view me as a strict teacher, and in fact, I am an excellent classroom manager. My students know what I expect of them and are generally very cooperative. I am a skilled communicator. I structure my lessons so that I reach all my students. My classes always perform well on statewide exams.

This applicant knows what skills make a successful teacher and she has shown that she possesses them all.

Never Say: "I love kids and I'm a good teacher."This candidate needs to do more than state the obvious.

As principal, the most frequent complaint I hear from parents is about teachers who don't maintain good communications with them. What have you done as a teacher to help maintain communication with parents of your students?

Answer ▶ First of all, parents can reach me by e-mail, by sending in a note, or by telephone. If I am not able to respond immediately, I always get back to them before the end of the day. I encourage parents to come to the classroom to read to the children. I send home a "Dear Parents" letter every two weeks explaining what we've covered in the classroom during the prior two weeks and what we will be covering during the upcoming weeks.

This job candidate talks about what he is currently doing to maintain good communications with parents. Not only does he communicate with parents when he has an issue to discuss, he also keeps the lines of communication open.

Never Say: "When there's a problem, I contact the parents immediately." The principal wants to know how this teacher communicates regularly, not only if there's something that needs to be discussed.

Have you ever done therapy with a group before?

Answer ▶ Yes, I have. When I worked at the University, I organized a support group for students coping with panic attacks. I met with them once a week. I also took over a support group for families of cancer patients when I worked at Old Hills Hospital.

This job candidate has given two examples that demonstrate her skills, even highlighting a time that she not only worked with a group but organized one.

Never Say: "Yes, I have." Remember, you need to back this up with an example.

You have many of the skills we're looking for. However, we also need someone with very strong sales skills. I don't see anything on your resume that indicates you have that kind of experience.

Answer ▶ Yes, it's true that I don't have any formal experience in sales. I do have some informal experience, however. I ran the book fair at my son's school for the past few years and raised $3,000. I also sold jewelry that a friend made. We rented tables at craft fairs all over the region and sold about twenty pieces at each one. Even after covering the price of the table and supplies and paying me, she made a decent profit.

While a candidate can't make up experience, he should draw on unpaid or volunteer experience that demonstrates his skills. He gives very specific examples.

Never Say: "No, I don't have any sales experience, but I can learn." This candidate should try to find some past experience that demonstrates his skills. If he truly has no sales experience, he might consider the qualities that make a good salesperson and find a way to demonstrate that he has those qualities.

We expect the executive director to handle a lot of fundraising. Do you have any experience with that?

Answer ▶ Yes, I do. I spearheaded a campaign that raised more than $10,000 for a small library for our members. I also run an annual campaign to raise money for our after-school center. Over the last five years, we've increased donations by about 6 percent each year.

This candidate quantifies her accomplishments. It's one way of saying here's what I did for my current employer and this is what I can do for you.

Never Say: "I've done some fundraising on my job." This candidate needs to be more specific.

Why should we hire you to be senior manager of our technical support department? You don't have any experience in technical support.

Answer ▶ While I don't have any experience in technical support, I do have six years of experience in customer service and management. I know how important it is to provide a good experience for customers. It builds loyalty, which will keep them coming back. I've managed customer service departments with staffs that ranged from fifteen to 100 employees.

Although this candidate's experience is not in technical support, he has managed departments that deal with consumer issues. He explains how that experience qualifies him for this position.

Never Say: "I use computers all the time, so I know how to answer the questions we would get." Computer skills do not qualify this applicant for a managerial position.

What is your management style?

Answer ▶ I'm a hands-on manager. I dive right in and work alongside my employees. This not only sets a good example for them, but also helps keep me aware of everyone's strengths and weaknesses.

This interviewee knows how to keep people motivated. She provides a reason for having chosen that style.

Never Say: "I'm very strict. I say how and when things get done." Ruling with an iron fist does not lead to a satisfied staff.

Are you good at doing research?

Answer ▶ I haven't done a great deal of research at work, but I do a lot of it on my own. Before I make any major purchases, take any medication, or go on vacation, I do a lot of research. I'm very good at it. The librarians at my local library are a great resource, so I make sure to go to them when I need help.

It would have been nice if this job candidate could have drawn on work experience to highlight his research skills, but since he couldn't, he did the next best thing. He gave examples of what kind of research he has done and explains how he does it.

Never Say: "I guess so. I like using the Net." An avid Internet user does not necessarily make a good researcher.

As you know, this is a new programming director position. We're thinking about having the person in this position also handle promoting our programs. Is that something you can handle?

Answer ▶ My primary responsibility as program director at the Art Council was program development. However, we had a very small staff, so I was usually responsible for promotion as well. I wrote press releases, designed print ads, and compiled mailing lists. This would be a great way to utilize my skills.

While highlighting her primary skill, program development, this applicant also draws upon some of her secondary responsibilities to explain why this job is a good fit.

Never Say: "I would be thrilled to be doing publicity. That was my favorite part of my last job." The interviewer said that publicity *might* be part of this job. If it turned out not to be, would this candidate be disappointed and quit?

How do you think others rate you as a supervisor?

Answer ▶ Turnover since I was promoted to supervisor five years ago has decreased from 30 percent to 10 percent. The reason, I believe, is that I treat those who work under me fairly. When a big deadline is coming up, I'm right there working late with them and not heading out the door at 5 P.M. I've had employees tell me they appreciate that.

This candidate knows that saying he's highly regarded as a supervisor isn't enough. He needs to back up his claim, which he does by telling his prospective employer how much turnover in his department decreased since he's been there. He goes on to tell the interviewer why he believes this is so.

Never Say: "They think I'm a good supervisor. They never complain and they do what I tell them to do." There's more to being a good supervisor than this.

What skills can you bring to the pediatric unit at St. Ernestine?

Answer ▶ I worked with children for about eight years as an assistant nursery school teacher before going back to school to become a nurse. When I began nursing school, I knew I wanted to specialize in pediatrics. I relate well to children and they relate well to me. I am a compassionate nurse as well as a skilled one. I offer patients the comfort they need when they are terrified of being in the hospital.

This answer demonstrates the candidate's experience working with children as well as his nursing skills.

Never Say: "I've spent four years training to be a nurse." This isn't enough information.

I see from your resume this isn't your first job working in a medical office. What skills did you pick up on your two previous jobs that you think would help you on this job?

Answer ▶ When you described the job to me, you said you needed someone who was good with patients. You also said you wanted someone who knows a lot about the different insurance plans. My primary responsibility at both these jobs was billing. I had to deal with insurance companies every day. I found that if I learned how each one worked, it was a lot easier for the doctors in my practice to get paid and for patients to get reimbursed. I also worked at the reception desk at these jobs. Many patients who came in were clearly anxious. I was happy to be able to calm them down and hopefully offer some reassurance.

This candidate listened to what the employer said and was able to clearly state how her skills would fill this medical practice's needs.

Never Say: "You wanted someone who is good with patients and insurance. That would be me." This candidate needs to elaborate.

Please discuss a project you supervised.

Answer ▶ I managed the expansion project at the shopping mall in Greenhaven. It involved increasing the size of the mall by 20 percent. I supervised a staff of fifty-five project team professionals. We completed the project within our budget.

By giving details about this project, including specific numbers, this interviewer demonstrates the type of work of which he's capable.

Never Say: "I supervised a mall expansion right outside the city. It went well." This answer is too vague.

What traits will a person need in order to become successful? Do you have these traits?

Answer ▶ To be successful, a person needs excellent organization and time management skills. She has to get along well with her boss, coworkers, and clients. She must always be willing to learn new skills. Yes, I have all these traits.

This interviewee has chosen to discuss some very valuable skills—organization, time management, willingness to learn, and getting along with others.

Never Say: "A person must be good at office politics. I've had lots of experience with that, and I'm very good at it." Knowing how to play the game may help you be successful, but your success may not be based on any real skills.

CHAPTER 18

Highlighting Your Accomplishments

WHEN YOU GO IN for a job interview, the prospective employer will be very interested in learning about your accomplishments as well as your personality and skills. Your accomplishments give him insight into what you are capable of doing for him and his company. An accomplishment, also known as an achievement, can be defined as something that you successfully completed as a direct result of your efforts.

Listing Your Accomplishments

Prepare a list of your accomplishments prior to your job interview. The accomplishments you choose to highlight should demonstrate your skills and abilities. Remember to use examples of things that came about as a direct result of your efforts. They shouldn't be things that happened to you, like raises or promotions, but rather things you made happen. That's not to say you shouldn't mention that your employer promoted you or rewarded you in some other way because of something you accomplished—you should talk about that. Before you do, however, discuss the accomplishment that led to your reward and the role you played in making your accomplishment come about.

The accomplishments you include on your list should be realistic and verifiable. Never stretch the truth—not even a little bit—on a job interview. The interviewer might be suspicious of something that sounds too good to be true and decide to check up on it. If she tries to verify something you told her and cannot, it will certainly reflect poorly on you. Telling a lie is much worse than not having a long list of accomplishments.

When possible, quantify your accomplishments. Use actual numbers or percentages when you are discussing anything that can be expressed in quantifiable terms, such as increases in profits or decreases in costs. Being able to say you increased sales by 20 percent or cut your department's costs by 35 percent is much better than saying "I increased sales a lot" or "I cut costs greatly."

KEEP A CAREER JOURNAL

Consider keeping a career journal to record all of your achievements and the steps you took to achieve your goals. This will help you be specific on future job interviews. Listing accomplishments as they occur is easier than trying to think back and recall them.

When deciding which achievements to discuss on an interview, always remember to choose the ones that best demonstrate your ability to do the job for which you are interviewing. Highlight skills you think the prospective employer is looking for in a new employee.

Discussing Your Accomplishments

You will have many opportunities to talk about your accomplishments throughout a job interview. The prospective employer will, of course, ask you direct questions about your accomplishments. You can also impress the interviewer with additional accomplishments if you answer his questions about your skills by discussing how a particular skill helped you achieve something.

A prospective employer is likely to ask you questions about your goals, both work-related and personal. Your goals are merely accomplishments waiting to happen. Discuss goals you have already reached and those you are moving toward reaching. Talk about the steps you took, or are taking, to do so.

This is your time to brag about what you have done and what you can do. People are often quite hesitant to speak highly of themselves. They are under the impression that being boastful is obnoxious. This may, in fact, be true in our private lives. But the job interview is not the time for modesty. You must sell yourself, and to do so you have to show off.

DISCUSSING PERSONAL GOALS

You may be asked about your personal goals as well as your professional ones. Even when discussing personal goals and achievements, make sure they highlight an ability related to work; for example, perseverance or organizational skills.

Questions and Answers

Can you tell me about your greatest accomplishment at work?

Answer ▶ I'm particularly proud of the mentoring program I started about five years ago. I noticed that new employees were having trouble getting acclimated to the company, causing a very high turnover rate during the first year of employment. I developed a program that allowed us to assign each new employee to an employee who had been with the company for at least three years. This allowed new hires to make a smoother transition. Now, 90 percent of new employees are still with us after their one-year anniversaries, up from 50 percent before we started the mentorship program.

The interviewee provides a specific example in response to this question. She also highlights the fact that she took initiative in developing it—she saw a problem and found a solution. Notice that she uses actual numbers to illustrate the result of her efforts.

Never Say: "I was promoted to assistant director of human resources." While it is important to share this information, this interviewee doesn't indicate what led to that promotion.

How did you progress at your last job?

Answer ▶ I was hired as a sales associate by K. R. Nickel Stores seven years ago. I became assistant manager of the girls' clothing department two years later. My boss said she never saw a young associate work as hard as I did. After two more years I was promoted to manager of that department.

This candidate simply describes his ascent up the corporate ladder, giving details, as he was asked to do.

Never Say: "I started as a sales associate and seven years later I'm manager of girls' clothing." This interviewee must talk about how he got from point A to point C.

How do you feel about the way your career has progressed so far?

Answer ▶ I'm pleased with how my career has progressed. When I graduated from college, I was hired to work as a trainee at Rogers, Inc., a small advertising agency. Being a trainee meant I answered the phones and made coffee. I took the initiative and asked for additional work. That gave me the opportunity to prove myself, and I was promoted to assistant account executive after eight months. After two years in that position, during which I worked on several successful ad campaigns, I was promoted to account executive. I'm proud of my work there, but it's time for a position with more responsibility.

This candidate takes the time to explain how her career has progressed since her graduation from college. She also makes sure to point out how she contributed to her firm's success.

Never Say: "I am very happy with it. I started off answering phones and now look where I am." Don't assume the interviewer knows where you are right now or how you got there.

Why do you think you've been successful in your career so far?

Answer ▶ I've been successful so far because I've always worked hard and I've been willing to accept any challenges that are offered to me. Actually, I usually seek them out. I have excellent time management skills that have allowed me to complete projects on time.

This interviewee hasn't relied on luck to achieve success. He has used his skills and motivation to get where he wants to be.

Never Say: "I've always been in the right place at the right time." This candidate doesn't seem to think he had anything to do with his own success. If he doesn't believe it, who will?

WHAT IF I'M A RECENT GRADUATE?

If you don't have much work experience, draw upon your experiences as a student. Look at what you achieved while you were in college, either in your classes or through extracurricular activities.

Which of your accomplishments has given you the most satisfaction?

Answer ▶ Last year I initiated a program that sent our executives into schools to work with the Young Entrepreneur Program. We sent teams into two area high schools to help the students learn how to run their own businesses. Our executives taught them how to write a business plan, design an ad campaign, make sales calls, and deal with clients. We ended up hiring some of the kids as interns, which worked out really well.

The accomplishment this job candidate has chosen to highlight involves giving back to the community, which is certainly admirable. While it doesn't directly benefit the company in terms of sales or earnings, participation in a program such as the one she describes is good for a company's public image.

Never Say: "My boss made me Senior Community Liaison. Finally having a title has been great." This candidate needs to focus on what she did to deserve that title.

Do you consider your progress on your current job indicative of your ability?

Answer ▶ Yes, I do. I was promoted twice on my current job. I was hired as a marketing trainee. After about a year I was promoted to associate account executive, and then after two years I was promoted to account executive. My promotions came about because I proved that I could successfully meet deadlines, win the confidence of clients, and solve problems.

This candidate discusses how and why he was promoted on her job.

Never Say: "Yes." This answer lacks specifics.

Describe how you accomplished a work-related goal.

Answer ▶ When I started working for Daylight Publications, I discovered that I had inherited a huge file cabinet full of photographs. We used photographs in our magazine but usually wound up purchasing stock photos, because our own collection was so disorganized it was impossible to find anything. I designed a filing system and set about putting things in order. I set aside fifteen minutes each day and was able to work my way through the whole collection in about seven months.

This answer demonstrates how the interviewee took the initiative to set a goal in order to save her employer money. She then talks about how she went about reaching that goal by using her organization and time management skills.

Never Say: "I wanted to make $50,000 per year by the time I was twenty-six. I switched jobs a few times and was able to do it." This in no way demonstrates any job-related skills the interviewee has.

Can you describe how you accomplished a personal goal?

Answer ▶ I wrote a short story and my goal was to get it published. I went to the library and researched which magazines accepted short-story submissions. Then I sent my story to those publications that published stories in the same genre as mine. My story was accepted by one of them and was published a little over a year ago.

This candidate talks about the steps he took to reach his personal goal. While the goal isn't related to the job for which he is applying, he talks about his ability to do research, a skill he knows this prospective employer will value.

Never Say: "I won a hot dog-eating contest. I trained for about six months." This answer does not demonstrate any skills that are needed in the workplace.

Tell me how you were of value to your previous employer.

Answer ▶ My previous employer valued my ability to deal with difficult clients. Whenever we had a client who was very demanding, my boss would ask me to be the one to work with her. He said he knew I was so levelheaded that I would always stay calm, even when a client was really trying my patience.

By giving this answer the candidate not only says why she thinks her boss values her, she talks about it from her boss's perspective. She presents a skill that this employer will appreciate as well.

Never Say: "I always showed up on time." Showing up on time is expected and doesn't set this candidate apart from any other.

Have you ever had to take over an assignment at the last minute?

Answer ▶ I've had to do that more than once—actually several times. The most recent time was when a colleague was scheduled to attend a meeting out of town and came down with the flu two days before he was supposed to leave. My boss asked me if I could attend the meeting and make the presentation my colleague was supposed to make. I had two days to learn everything about the project. I went over pages and pages of notes and put together a presentation of my own, incorporating input from my colleague, who I spoke to on the phone several times a day.

Not only does this interviewee say she has taken over an assignment at the last minute, she talks about a specific case. She shows how she stepped in and learned what she needed to learn in order to make a successful presentation.

Never Say: "Yes, it has happened." She should give an example.

Have you ever received formal recognition for something you accomplished?

Answer ▶ Yes. I won Salesperson of the Month four times when I was working for Ace Stereo. Those with the largest increase in sales over the previous month were rewarded in this way. I believe I had increased my sales by 15 to 20 percent each time.

This candidate chose to discuss being rewarded for something that would be valued by any company—high sales volume. He gives actual numbers to quantify his answer.

Never Say: "I won best dressed at the annual holiday party." Unless this is a candidate for a fashion consulting position, this answer doesn't highlight any skills that will impress the employer.

What has been your greatest accomplishment as part of a team?

Answer ▶ I worked on a team that developed a program for children who were going home to an empty house after school because their parents worked. We had volunteers who would help the kids with their homework and give them time to just burn off energy after sitting in a classroom all day. By the time we actually opened the center, we had seventy-five children enrolled. That told us we were providing a service that was clearly needed.

This candidate describes in detail the project she considers the greatest accomplishment she achieved as part of a team. She talks about what was needed, what they did to fill that need, and what the end result was.

Never Say: "I never feel like I accomplish that much on a team." This candidate just admitted she's not a team player. It was a bad idea to do that. The interviewer probably asked the question because working on a team is probably typical of the position for which he is hiring.

Name the two work-related accomplishments of which you are proudest.

Answer ▶ I converted a manual payroll system to a computerized system, which cut down the amount of time we spend on payroll each week. I wrote a manual that explained all bookkeeping department procedures in our company. New employees receive a copy of this manual, which helps them learn their job faster.

Each of the accomplishments this candidate discusses has had a positive result on the company and highlights his many skills.

Never Say: "I received a good performance review every year. I was promoted to a supervisory position after just two years." While these are definitely positive things and a reflection of this candidate's ability to do a good job, they really don't address how his accomplishments affected the company. They also don't explain how he earned his good reviews and promotion.

Tell me about the personal accomplishment that you are the proudest of.

Answer ▶ Last year I ran a marathon for the first time. I've been a runner for years, but I never ran more than four miles at a time. I began training four months before the big day. It was hard, but I kept going and I ended up finishing in just over four hours, which I've heard is pretty good for a first-time marathoner.

By discussing running a marathon, this candidate demonstrates that she will work hard to reach her goals. She is not afraid of a challenge, something her prospective employer should appreciate.

Never Say: "I bought my first house." Without an explanation of how she reached this goal, this candidate doesn't show off any strengths when she gives this example.

If I asked your current employer to tell us about your accomplishments, what do you think he would say?

Answer ▶ He would probably talk about the time he asked me to present a new marketing campaign to one of our more difficult clients. I spent over a week preparing for that presentation. Since I knew this client was hard to please, I had to make sure I anticipated every objection she might have. She actually loved the presentation and the campaign increased her company's sales by 50 percent.

This question gives the candidate a chance to talk about an accomplishment he is proud of. He talks about anticipating possible difficulties, as well as the end result, an increase in sales.

Never Say: "I doubt my boss recognized any of my accomplishments. If he did, he certainly didn't tell me." This candidate breaks one of the cardinal rules of job interviewing—never speak negatively about a former boss.

If I asked a college professor about one of your accomplishments, what would he or she say?

Answer ▶ I worked on a major research project under the supervision of my psychology professor. We collected data over the course of a year, and we analyzed it and wrote up the results as an article that we submitted to the *Journal of Kangaroo Psychology*. It was accepted and it was published a month before I graduated.

This candidate chose to talk about something that had a tangible result—publication of an article in a professional journal.

Never Say: "I got an A in a class that was very difficult." Even though this may have been a great personal achievement for this interviewee, it is probably not something a professor would recognize as a great achievement.

What does success mean to you?

Answer ▶ I feel I am successful when I do the best job I can possibly do, such as complete a project on time and under budget, and meet or go beyond my own expectations or those of my boss or my client. I also want to achieve the desired result, whether it is to make a profit or reduce a loss for my employer.

This candidate defines success by what he can accomplish for his employer rather than what he can accomplish for himself.

Never Say: "Success to me is making a six-figure salary."

Have you ever had to overcome a major obstacle? How did you do it?

Answer ▶ Yes, I did. My family couldn't afford to pay for college. I applied for as much financial aid as possible, but I still had to work to pay for whatever that didn't cover. In the end, in addition to a college degree, I also had valuable work experience under my belt.

The story this candidate tells demonstrates that she can set a goal—getting a college degree—and reach it through hard work. She even points out that, because of her need to overcome this obstacle, she now has valuable work experience.

Never Say: "I've been very lucky. I really haven't had any obstacles to overcome." Luck isn't what is going to get this candidate hired. She needs to demonstrate perseverance and therefore should try to find some obstacle to speak about.

What accomplishments have you made so far in reaching your long-range goals?

Answer ▶ My long-range goal is to be a school principal. I've been teaching for ten years, first at PS 118 and then at PS 114. After five years of teaching second grade at PS 114, I was asked to be grade leader. My experience working with other faculty members and developing new programs for students has prepared me for the position of assistant principal. I look forward to using my skills to work on some of the projects we discussed earlier.

This candidate has demonstrated how he has taken steps to reach his goal and plans to continue to do so. He also makes a point of talking about the contributions he plans to make in the job for which he's interviewing.

Never Say: "I want to be an assistant principal." Since this is the job that he's interviewing for, this answer doesn't show motivation to reach any goals beyond that.

What motivates you to go above and beyond the call of duty?

Answer ▶ Honestly, I don't have a sense of what is above and beyond the call of duty. It's not like I can just do enough to get by and then stop. When I work on a project, I do my very best, always.

This statement shows that this job candidate is truly a hard worker who cares about her work. It's more than just a job to her. She can't justify giving less than her best effort to any project entrusted to her.

Never Say: "Hopefully, if I go above and beyond the call of duty, I'll get recognition for my work." This candidate doesn't seem to be self-motivated since her rewards come from the outside.

What one thing do you think you've done very well on your last job?

Answer ▶ I think I was very successful in all aspects of my last job. I'm particularly proud of my work with new hires. I developed programs that helped integrate them into the company and this in turn helped our ability to retain them as employees.

Because the interviewer has asked for one thing this person has done well, he is forced to only talk about one thing. He explains why he is particularly proud of that one accomplishment and explains how his success benefited his employer. He also makes a point of saying that this isn't his only success.

Never Say: "I can't think of just one thing." If you are asked for one thing, you should be able to come up with something. If not, it appears that you can't think of *anything* you did well at your last job.

How has your employer rewarded your accomplishments?

Answer ▶ My employer initially rewarded me by trusting me enough to give me additional responsibility. This gave me a chance to really prove myself and I was ultimately rewarded with a big promotion.

This candidate discusses how at first her reward was simply being asked to do more. Did she object to that? No. It only gave her the opportunity to further prove herself so that she received the reward of a promotion.

Never Say: "Rewarded? He didn't reward anyone for anything. I guess he thought our paycheck was good enough." This interviewee shouldn't speak with such animosity about his employer.

You seem to have accomplished a lot in your current job. Do you know why you weren't promoted?

Answer ▶ I wasn't promoted because unfortunately there wasn't a position to promote me to. JFR was a very small family-owned firm. The boss's two sons held the top positions, which were right above my position.

The candidate explains why he couldn't move beyond his current position in spite of his accomplishments. He doesn't seem resentful, but rather accepts this fact.

Never Say: "Sure I do. One word—nepotism. The boss's sons hold all the good positions. It doesn't matter how hard you work. You aren't moving up." This candidate is clearly resentful of the way things are at his current job and makes the mistake of letting the interviewer know that.

Have you ever come up with new ways to solve a problem?

Answer ▶ Yes, I have. We had a problem with dismissal from our after-school program. Too many children were leaving at once, causing chaos in our parking lot. I developed a system for releasing children alphabetically so that parents could pick up siblings in different grades at the same time. If we had released children by grade, parents would have had to wait around for children who were in different grade levels. That would have added to the chaos.

The candidate states a specific problem and then discusses the steps she took to solve it. She even mentions how she anticipated and then prevented a potential problem.

Never Say: "I'm lucky. I haven't had to solve any problems." If this candidate hasn't had to solve any problems, how can she be expected to do so in the future?

Have you ever "saved the day" for your employer?

Answer ▶ Yes, I have. It was the afternoon before our company was hosting a big luncheon. We called the caterer to confirm the details, but his number had been disconnected. We found out he had gone out of business and didn't let us know. I called friends at other companies and got a list of caterers together, called them, and got someone to do the job. My boss couldn't believe I managed to hire someone on such short notice.

The interviewee, by giving this example, shows how her resourcefulness helped her solve her employer's problem.

Never Say: "I've saved many days for them. I always have to fix everyone else's mistakes." This answer, even if it is true, makes the interviewee seem arrogant.

Have you ever been asked to take on a project because of your unique skill or ability?

Answer ▶ Our senior developer regularly asks me to troubleshoot new programs. I've been very successful at figuring out why programs aren't working properly and I can usually do it pretty quickly, allowing the team to move forward.

This candidate chose to talk about a skill that will be as valuable to his prospective employer as it is to his current one.

Never Say: "I'm very good at planning parties, so when my boss's secretary was retiring she asked me to plan the party." This skill probably won't be very important to the prospective employer.

Have you ever done something that directly helped your employer either increase profits or decrease costs?

Answer ▶ I recently found a way to help my employer save money on office supplies. For years, they bought office supplies from the same place. It was several blocks away, so it was pretty convenient. I have found that shopping online is almost always less expensive than shopping in a store, so I did a little comparison shopping and I found an online source for our office supplies at a savings of 40 percent from what we were paying for the same items. Plus, the order is delivered to the office, which is even more convenient. As long as we order several items at once, delivery is free.

This interviewee's answer illustrates how he looks out for his employer's best interests.

Never Say: "I just go about doing my job. I guess that increases their profits, doesn't it?" This candidate needs to remember he's trying to sell himself to this employer. Instead of saying he'll "just do the job," he needs to show why he'd be great at it.

Have you ever been assigned a project you didn't think you'd be able to get through? If so, what happened?

Answer ▶ I've been assigned many projects that seemed difficult at first, but I refuse to think of any project as impossible. Before I begin any project, I think about how I'm going to tackle it. I come up with a plan and take it step by step. If I think I need help with a project, I ask for advice from those with more experience.

This candidate demonstrates that she will not be defeated by any project, yet she is not averse to asking for help when she needs it. She explains how she approaches all projects in a systematic fashion.

Never Say: "There isn't a project I can't get through." There's a difference between self-assurance and cockiness. Without explaining what she does in order to get through difficult projects, this candidate just sounds cocky.

It seems like you've accomplished a lot. I know everyone fails, at least occasionally. Tell me about something you failed at.

Answer ▶ When I was a freshman in college I decided to run for president of the management club. My opponent was in his junior year. I came up with what I thought and still think was a great platform. I campaigned vigorously. Unfortunately I lost the election. I'm pretty sure it was due to my lack of experience. I ran too early in my school career. Two years later I ran again and I won.

The applicant chooses to discuss a failure that isn't work-related and attributes it to her lack of experience rather than something she had control over.

Never Say: "I ran for president of the management club and lost." The applicant must give a more detailed answer. This one leaves the interviewer to wonder why the applicant lost the election.

Is there anything I've missed?

Answer ▶ Well, I did want to mention that I was honored by my organization's board of directors for developing a program that reached out to a large number of senior citizens in need of financial assistance. We now help just over 650 seniors each year.

The candidate uses this opportunity to bring to the interviewer's attention an accomplishment he didn't discuss previously.

Never Say: "No. I think you just about covered it all. Are we done?" This candidate sounds like he's in a hurry for the interview to be over. Since it is unlikely that everything has been covered, he may be missing a chance to discuss something that can work in his favor.

CHAPTER 19

Questions about Your Education

WHEN PROSPECTIVE EMPLOYERS interview recent graduates without much experience, they can learn a lot about them by asking questions about their school experience. Therefore, if you're interviewing for jobs straight out of school, you should be prepared to answer a lot of questions about your education. Even if you've been working for a few years, you may still be asked about your education, so it's important to have your answers ready.

How You Spent Your College Years

The interviewer will want to know about your performance as a student. As you know, the grades on a college transcript don't always tell the whole story. A failing grade may mean more than an inability in a particular subject and a high grade may mean more than great achievement.

The interviewer will want to know how you felt about particular subjects, which ones you found challenging, and which ones you thought were a piece of cake. She may ask which instructors you liked and why. All of this information lets her get a better look at who you are.

In addition to simple questions like "Where did you go to school?" and "What was your major?" the interviewer will likely ask you about activities you participated in outside the classroom. She will want to know about your involvement in extracurricular activities such as participation in on-campus clubs and organizations, work on student-run publications, and community service. All these activities contributed to your education and make up who you are today—and what you will bring to an employer. Think about your activities in terms of the skills they helped you develop.

When you can't prove your worth by talking about your work experience, you must prove it by discussing what you did during your time in school.

LISTING YOUR INTERESTS

When asked about extracurricular activities, you should think of each one as a job. What contributions did you make to a particular club? Can you quantify them? Did you help raise money for a charity? How much? Did you work for your school newspaper? How many hours a week did that involve? What were your successes and what were your failures?

Many students gain valuable work experience by doing an internship. If you did one, be prepared to discuss it in great detail. Even if you didn't get paid, you should consider it equivalent to a job. The interviewer will want to know what you did there, what you learned, and what contributions you made to the company or organization.

The prospective employer has something else on her agenda, too. She is interested in knowing why and how you made your choices over the last several years. For example, she wants to know how you chose what college to attend. She wants to find out how you decided on your major. Seeing how you made these very important choices offers her the opportunity to learn what your decision making process is generally like.

Questions and Answers

I see you majored in English. Are you prepared for a job in marketing and sales?

Answer ▶ As an English major I had to do a large amount of reading and needed to retain all of the information. Reading and absorbing the literature on the products I'll be selling will be a snap. I believe college also prepared me to manage my time well. I do have hands-on experience in this field as well; I worked in various sales positions in order to put myself through school.

Notice that the interviewee doesn't make any excuses for wanting to work in a field outside his major. Instead, he talks about how his major qualifies him for this job. He also talks about the fact that he has sales experience.

Never Say: "I guess I could teach at a college with my English degree but then I'd have to get a PhD. I definitely don't want to do that." The interviewer knows what this applicant doesn't want to do, but she still doesn't know how the interviewee can transfer his skills to this field.

Why did you choose Adams University?

Answer ▶ Adams University has an accredited business school. It is ranked third in the nation. The university also has a great cross-country team and I wanted to try out for it.

This candidate put a lot of thought into choosing a college, implying that's how she makes all her decisions. She also uses this opportunity to brag about the quality of her education.

Never Say: "My best friend was going there." This applicant doesn't demonstrate that she puts a lot of thought into making important decisions.

MY MAJOR AND MY CAREER CHOICE

If you did not major in a subject that traditionally prepares people to work in the career field you are pursuing, you are going to have some explaining to do. Be ready to discuss how your major prepared you for this occupation even though they are seemingly unrelated to one another.

I see you majored in marketing. What courses did you take outside your major?

Answer ▶ I took a few psych classes because I felt that knowing how people think would be to my advantage in marketing. I took some art classes because I really enjoy them. I also took writing courses, because I thought that was an important skill to have.

Instead of just giving a list of courses, this candidate talks about why she took them. She even explains how two of the subjects will help in her career.

Never Say: "I decided just to take extra courses in my major." While this candidate may think she's showing how much she knows about her field by having taken extra courses in it, she is actually showing that she's not well rounded.

Did you have any teachers who influenced you?

Answer ▶ Yes, I did. Mr. Danzer was my earth science teacher in junior high school. He loved the subject and he loved teaching. I think both these things came across in his ability to teach. It showed me that if a person loves what he does, he's more likely to excel at it. That was good to know when it came time to choose a career.

This candidate answers the question with just enough information to satisfy the interviewer.

Never Say: "No." If you can't think of one single teacher, perhaps you can mention the qualities of several who had some sort of impact on you.

Why did you choose to major in philosophy?

Answer ▶ From a very early age I wanted to be a lawyer. When I started to do my research, I found out that undergraduates who want to go to law school should take a lot of liberal arts classes. During my freshman year, I took different courses in the school of liberal arts and sciences and I liked philosophy the best, so I decided to make it my concentration.

This applicant shows that she made an informed choice when choosing her major.

Never Say: "It looked interesting." While you should choose a major you think is interesting, that shouldn't be your only criteria.

What did you gain from attending college?

Answer ▶ I gained knowledge about this field. I was able to use what I learned in class on the internship I did last summer at the *Tallahassee Tribune.* College is where I learned to be independent. There wasn't anyone pushing me to complete assignments on time, so I had to learn how to manage my time well and stay organized.

This candidate talks about things he learned both in and out of the classroom. He includes technical skills as well as soft skills—time management and organization.

Never Say: "I got my degree." Isn't that on the resume? The candidate needs to come up with a more detailed answer than this one.

What was your favorite subject in high school? What was your favorite subject in college?

Answer ▶ English was my favorite subject in high school. I did a lot of writing in English. I liked working hard to put together a paper and then getting feedback in the form of a grade. My favorite classes in college were those in my major. I actually took only one marketing class before I declared marketing as my major. I found the subject matter so interesting that I started looking into it as a career choice.

This candidate explains why English was her favorite subject and in the process demonstrates her skill as a writer, which she knows will be an important part of her job. By stating that her major was her favorite subject in college, she shows her dedication to the field.

Never Say: "In high school I liked social studies. My favorite subject in college was sociology." This candidate needs to explain why these two subjects were her favorites.

YOUR LEAST FAVORITE CLASS

If the interviewer asks what your least favorite class was, pick one that is as unrelated as possible to your career field. If your least favorite class is one in which you received a failing grade, pick another one. Don't bring up a failing grade unless you are asked a direct question about it.

What were your least favorite subjects in high school and college?

Answer ▶ My least favorite subject in high school was home economics. I helped with the housekeeping at home, and I didn't want to have to deal with it at school, too. I liked most of the classes I took in college. If I had to pick my least favorite I guess it would have to be biology. We had to dissect a fetal pig, and I had a problem doing that.

The candidate picked classes unrelated to the job for which he's applying. Also notice that he didn't say he disliked the classes because he found them difficult. Never imply that you don't like challenges.

Never Say: "My least favorite classes were geometry and matrix algebra. I couldn't get it. I guess math isn't my strong suit." This candidate makes the mistake of volunteering information about his weaknesses. While they may not be related to this job, they are challenges that defeated him.

What extracurricular activities did you participate in?

Answer ▶ During my junior year of college, I was president of the psychology club. Then in my senior year I was editor of the yearbook. I wrote for both my high school and college newspapers, too.

This candidate highlights her leadership experience and writing skills, two very valuable attributes.

Never Say: "Academics took up all my time. I didn't have much time for anything else." This candidate may think she's showing what a dedicated student she was, but extracurricular activities enhance one's college experience. She should try to think of some valuable experience she had outside the classroom.

I see it took you four and a half years to graduate. Can you explain that?

Answer ▶ I had a difficult time adjusting during my freshman year. I wasn't quite ready for all the demands of college. I had to take a few classes over. During the summer between my freshman and sophomore years, I went to a few workshops to help me improve my study skills and my time management skills. By the time I was a sophomore, I was a much more serious student.

This candidate doesn't make excuses for his failings, but rather speaks about how he overcame them and how he succeeded in the end.

Never Say: "I had these really tough professors my freshman year. They wouldn't cut me any slack. When you're a freshman, you get stuck with teachers no one else wants." This candidate tries to blame everyone else for his failure.

Aside from coursework, what was the most enriching part of your college education?

Answer ▶ I was very involved on the programming committee. As a matter of fact, I was chair during my senior year. We were responsible for planning on-campus events for the student body. The goal was to hold events that were well attended and safe. That meant hiring entertainment that appealed to the majority of students and making sure campus security was present to enforce the rules. Our events were attended by between 60 and 70 percent of dormitory residents.

This applicant talks about her work on this committee as if it were a job. She highlights her leadership skills as well as other skills she drew upon in order to organize these events. This candidate also explains her goals and how she met them, giving actual numbers.

Never Say: "I was in some campus clubs and that was fun." This applicant needs to do a better job of explaining what those clubs were and how she participated in them.

I see you had an internship in this field. What did you learn from it?

Answer ▶ My internship at Carlson Corporate allowed me to get some hands-on experience in this field that I wouldn't have gotten in classes alone. I learned that jobs in this field are often stressful and long hours are usually required. On the other hand, I got to find out how wonderful it is when you're on a team that helps land a big account as a result of hard work.

This applicant speaks about what he gained from the internship and what he learned about the positive and negative aspects of working in the field.

Never Say: "Not a heck of a lot. I was just a glorified gopher." Even if all he did was deliver mail and make copies, this candidate should be able to come up with something he learned just from being exposed to the work environment of this particular field.

Why haven't you done any internships?

Answer ▶ I would have loved to have done an internship, but unfortunately I had to work my way through college. Most internships don't pay that well. However, as you can see from my resume, I made a point of finding work within this industry. Even though I was in the mailroom, I was still exposed to the field.

While internships are important, sometimes extenuating circumstances get in the way. This candidate has no choice but to be honest about that. However, she explains how she tried to make up for not being able to do an internship.

Never Say: "I won't work for free." This candidate sounds like she's only concerned with money and experience is worth nothing to her.

How did you spend your summers during college?

Answer ▶ I worked every summer to earn money for books and part of my tuition. I had this great job at a day camp. I started off as a counselor the summer before my senior year of high school, moved up to group leader the summer after I graduated, and then became assistant director.

This applicant takes the opportunity to show off a little. He stayed at the same job for several years and was promoted to a supervisory position.

Never Say: "I rested. School's hard." If he thinks school is hard, wait until he tries working—and he probably won't get two months off each year.

HOW I SPENT MY SUMMER

How you spent your summers while in school says a lot about you. Your experience may not be career-related, but it may give you the opportunity to highlight some positive qualities about yourself. If you were asked back to the same job summer after summer, your prospective employer can assume you earned that because of your job performance.

What grade did you receive in your favorite class?

Answer ▶ My favorite class was Intro to Journalism. It was actually pretty tough at first. Everything I handed in came back marked up in red ink. There were a few times that my professor commented that I had found just the right words to describe an event, though, and I loved that feeling. I plugged away and kept trying harder. Fortunately, my professor gave us the opportunity to redo our work for a higher grade, and although it took a lot of extra work, ultimately I got an A in the class.

It's easy to like a class if you don't have to work hard for a good grade. This applicant explains why journalism was her favorite class despite it being difficult. Perseverance and the ability to meet a challenge are attributes all bosses value in their employees.

Never Say: "Intro to Journalism. I got an A." Without saying more than that, the interviewer is left to wonder whether the candidate liked that class simply because she got an A in it.

What grade did you receive in your least favorite class?

Answer ▶ My least favorite class was Art History. I know students who took the class with other professors, got a C, and loved it. I hated the class and got an A. I didn't learn anything. I just had to show up for every class and do little else.

Clearly this candidate doesn't mind working hard as long as he learns something. He isn't impressed with getting rewarded for "just showing up."

Never Say: "I got a D in it. It was Organic Chemistry, the hardest class I ever took. I can't believe how much I studied and all I ended up with was a D." Other than getting a bad grade, this candidate doesn't explain why this was his least favorite class. He just sounds like a sore loser.

Why did you decide to major in elementary education?

Answer ▶ When I was in high school, I took an assessment test to help me figure out what career I should go into. When I got my results, teaching was one of the occupations on the list, along with several others like psychology, social work, and nursing. When I started researching the occupations in more detail, I discovered that teaching was the one that appealed to me most.

This candidate put a lot of thought into choosing an occupation. This answer not only shows her dedication to teaching but also indicates that she makes decisions carefully.

Never Say: "I like children." While it's important to like children if you want to teach them, liking children doesn't necessarily mean you'll be good at teaching.

I see you transferred to Hamford University from Sannau County Community College. Why did you start you college education at a two-year school?

Answer ▶ I knew I wanted to earn a bachelor's degree. I also wanted to go to Hamford, but the cost of a four-year education there was extremely high. I decided to take my core classes at a community college to save money. I first checked to make sure Hamford would take my credits. Since Sannau is a very well-respected community college, I knew I would get a decent education there.

By giving this answer, the interviewee demonstrates that he is a very practical person. He spends money wisely but doesn't compromise his goals. He also doesn't do something without first investigating it.

Never Say: "I thought Sannau would be a good place to start my education." This doesn't explain what led to the transfer.

What would your professors say about you?

Answer ▶ My professors would say I always turned in high-quality work. They would say I contributed to classroom discussions by offering interesting comments and asking good questions. They would also say I was willing to help other students.

This candidate takes the opportunity to highlight some positive attributes.

Never Say: "They liked me." This interviewee doesn't take the opportunity acknowledge her attributes. She should explain why her professors liked her.

What courses best prepared you for a job in this library?

Answer ▶ I took a course in research and bibliographic methods that provided me with the technical skills to do this job. The most important thing I learned in that class was that there is a resource available to answer almost all questions. I also took several classes in children's and young adult literature. I saw from the job description that the person who takes this position will also have to spend several hours a week in the children's department. Those courses have certainly helped prepare me for that.

This candidate not only lists some courses he took, but also explains how they will help him do the job should he be hired.

Never Say: "I took research and bibliographic methods and some children's lit classes. I think they'll be helpful." This candidate tells what classes he took but isn't specific about how they will enable him to do his job.

Are you planning to get your MBA?

Answer ▶ I would like to do that. I'm looking for a program with a schedule that won't interfere with work.

This interviewee knows that an MBA is highly valued in her field, but she anticipates that her potential employer might be concerned that her work schedule would be compromised if she pursues one. She heads off those fears.

Never Say: "I've already been accepted at NJU. The classes start at 5:45, so I'm hoping it will be okay if I cut out of here early three days a week." If the employer had a choice between this candidate and one who wouldn't need her schedule adjusted, who do you think he would choose? In addition, any discussion of that sort should wait until a job offer is received.

What elective accounting courses did you take?

Answer ▶ I took three auditing classes because I knew I wanted to work in public accounting. I also took an international accounting class. In this global economy I knew that would come in handy at some point in my career.

This candidate explains how she chose courses she would be able to use professionally.

Never Say: "I took a taxation class, an auditing class, and a corporate accounting class that all fit nicely into my schedule." This answer doesn't show that the candidate selected classes that would benefit her in her career.

Have you ever had a disagreement with a professor? How did you handle it?

Answer ▶ I disagreed about a grade I received once. I spent a lot of time researching and writing a paper for a history class. When I got the paper back with a B, I was very disappointed. After thinking about it for a day, I decided to talk to the professor. He asked me what grade I thought I deserved. I said I thought I had earned an A on the paper and explained why. He said he would read the paper over and re-grade it if he found my arguments were valid. The next day he told me he changed my grade to an A.

This applicant proves that she knows how to stand up for herself when there is something she feels strongly about. She demonstrates how she persuaded her teacher to change her grade by presenting her arguments in a calm manner after waiting a day to collect her thoughts.

Never Say: "I was very unhappy about a grade a professor gave me, but I didn't bother saying anything about it."

What was the most difficult assignment you had while in school?

Answer ▶ I took a creative writing class. It was one of several electives I could choose from outside my major. I had to write a poem. I discovered I'm not really good at that sort of thing.

This interviewee chose to discuss an assignment that was entirely unrelated to his major and to anything he would be expected to do at this job.

Never Say: "I hated writing papers, so any assignment that involved doing that was difficult." Since some writing is generally required at all jobs, this candidate should have answered differently.

Your GPA wasn't very high. Can you please explain that?

Answer ▶ During my first two years of college, I was kind of immature and didn't work hard enough. I worked really hard my junior and senior years, but unfortunately those first two years really brought down my GPA. It was hard to recover from that.

This candidate acknowledges that she was responsible for her low GPA but also talks about how she worked hard to raise it.

Never Say: "Just bad luck, I guess."

HOW SHOULD I EXPLAIN POOR GRADES?

With few exceptions, you earned your grades, whether they were good or bad, so you should take full responsibility for them. Explain what happened without appearing to beat yourself up, e.g., don't say "I was such an idiot." If you can, discuss the measures you took to improve your GPA. You can also talk about what you could have done differently.

What was your favorite thing about high school?

Answer ▶ My favorite thing about high school was working on the school newspaper. I was the managing editor during my senior year. I learned how to stick to deadlines and I helped our editors organize projects on which they were working.

The interviewee picked something that allowed him to show two of his skills—time management and organization. He knows that employers in his field value these skills.

Never Say: "I loved everything about high school." While the interviewer may appreciate the candidate's positive attitude, this answer doesn't tell her anything about him.

What did you like most about college?

Answer ▶ I really enjoyed playing on the volleyball team. During my freshman and sophomore years the team wasn't as strong as it could have been. We pulled together and worked very hard, and by my junior year we were ranked number two in our division. By my senior year we were in first place.

This candidate's mention of his participation on an athletic team draws attention to his ability to work on a team. From his research, he learned that this company's employees often work on teams, so he decided this was a good opportunity to show off this attribute.

Never Say: "I loved my classes." While that is admirable, this candidate doesn't say why this is so. If his classes were truly his favorite part of college, he needs to explain how his own actions contributed to his feeling that way.

Why did you choose to go away to college rather than going to a school closer to your home?

Answer ▶ I wanted to be responsible for myself, and I knew that wouldn't happen at home. By living in the dorms, I had no choice but to manage my own time, budget my money, and set my own limits.

This candidate saw going away to college as a learning experience, both in and out of the classroom, and presents it that way to the interviewer.

Never Say: "My parents didn't like the boy I was dating, so they sent me away to school." Have you ever heard of giving too much information?

Why didn't you go to college?

Answer ▶ I didn't know what I wanted to do at the time and I didn't want to waste my parents' money. I thought I would gain more from working than I would from school. Now that I have work experience and I know I want to stay in this field, I plan to get my degree. The city university has a program that accommodates working adults.

The interviewee's decision to postpone college, as he explains it, was a clearly thought-out one. While he indicates his intention to continue his education, he is also quick to point out that it won't affect his work schedule.

Never Say: "I don't know. I didn't really give it much thought." Not giving a lot of thought to such an important decision doesn't say much about this applicant, or maybe it says too much.

Why didn't you finish college?

Answer ▶ I left school because of financial reasons. My parents couldn't afford my tuition, so I decided to work for a few years. The experience was actually a great one for me. I learned a lot from it. I'm planning to take some classes next semester. I just heard about a great program that offers classes online. I even checked the program out with the state education department and it's legitimate.

Dropping out of school for financial reasons is certainly legitimate. This candidate speaks positively of her work experience, claiming she gained something from it. She goes on to explain how her plan to take some classes won't affect her work schedule, something the employer would probably appreciate.

Never Say: "I didn't really like school that much." This interviewee gives the impression that she doesn't make well-informed decisions.

CHAPTER 20

Discussing Your Work History

WHILE EXPERIENCE ISN'T EVERYTHING, it does count for a lot when a prospective employer must decide between you and other qualified candidates. What you have done in your past jobs is significant and an interviewer will spend a lot of time learning about your work history so he can discover how it will affect your future performance. That is why it is so important that you take great care to present your past well.

How to Present Your Past

What does it mean to present your past well? After years of spending many of your waking hours working, here's a chance to let your past jobs work for you. Answering questions about your work history gives you the opportunity to highlight things you want to call to a prospective employer's attention. At the same time, you want to downplay things on which you would rather not have her focus. You want to tell your side of the story in your own words and in greater depth than you could ever do on a resume.

When prospective employers ask questions about your work history, they want to know more than where you worked, how long you worked there, and what your job duties were. They can learn that from your resume. They would love to hear about the skills you gained at each of your previous jobs, but that information is probably on your resume as well. Now it's time to get beyond the resume and learn more about you than they ever could from a one- or two-page document. Employers want to know not only what skills you picked up on your prior jobs, but how you used those skills. They want to know what you liked about each job, and what you didn't like. They want to find out if you got along with your boss. Employers want to know why you left each of your jobs, or why you stayed. They want to know what motivates you. They want to know how your career has progressed and how you expect it to progress in the future. Most importantly, employers want to know what you can bring to them as an employee.

USE YOUR RESUME

As you prepare to answer questions about your work history, use your resume to guide you. Look at each job and try to recall specific details about every one. Write down those facts and commit them to memory. Preparing in advance can help save you from awkward moments of silence as you try to answer a prospective employer's questions.

When you give answers to questions about your work history, make every one count. Each response should tell the interviewer how your experience qualifies you for this particular job. You should give specific examples drawn from your experiences. When an interviewer asks if you've ever performed a particular activity on a past job she generally expects more than a yes or no answer. As with every type of question so far, you must give detailed answers.

Questions and Answers

What was your first job?

Answer ▶ My very first job was in a deli. I worked there every summer from ninth grade until I graduated from college. At first I was hired to do odd jobs, but once I was old enough, I worked behind the counter serving customers. I was the youngest employee there, but my boss always said I was the hardest-working one.

By discussing his longevity on this job, as well as his former boss's favorable opinion of him, this candidate lets the interviewer know he was a valued employee. He doesn't dwell on the fact that the job was not in his current career field.

Never Say: "It was just in a deli." This candidate needs to give more details about his job and use it to show off his attributes.

Out of the jobs you've had, which was your favorite?

Answer ▶ My favorite job was teaching at the Wee Ones Preschool. I like my current job at Parkside Elementary, but I realize now that I prefer to work with preschoolers. That's why I want to work here.

This candidate has chosen to discuss a job that is related to the one for which she is being interviewed.

Never Say: "I loved working at Sam's Steakhouse in college. The other waitresses and I had so much fun together." Not only does this candidate choose a job unrelated to her chosen field, she doesn't sound very serious about working at all.

Tell me about your current job.

Answer ▶ I am a junior architect at James, Jones, and Johnson. I work in the commercial building division. As part of a team of five architects, I help design shopping centers and office complexes.

The interviewee describes his current job as he is asked to do. He discusses his work as part of a team because he knows that this prospective employer also utilizes a team structure.

Never Say: "I work at James, Jones, and Johnson. It's right there on my resume." The interviewer wants the candidate to give a detailed description of his current job. Since it is probable that he has already read the resume, it does the candidate no good to simply reiterate what is there.

Tell me about a typical day at work.

Answer ▶ Every day is different. The one constant is that I spend from two to three hours working at the reference desk each day, assisting patrons. That leaves either four or five hours to tend to what I refer to as "behind the scenes" work. I'm in charge of library publicity, so I might have to write and send out press releases or update our mailing list. If it's the middle of the month, I'll be working on the monthly newsletter. When I'm not working on publicity, I'm selecting books to order or weeding outdated material from our collection.

The candidate takes this opportunity to discuss her many responsibilities.

Never Say: "Every day is different. I do so many things, it's hard to say what a typical day is." This person indicates she's busy, but she needs to talk about what her responsibilities are.

What do you like about your job?

Answer ▶ I like it when I can successfully resolve a customer's problem. If the customer walks away satisfied, I'm happy.

By giving this answer, the candidate shows that keeping customers happy motivates him. This is surely something this employer will see as a positive trait, since happy customers are repeat customers.

Never Say: "My boss is nice." While speaking well of your boss is good, this candidate should have chosen something about his job that gives him satisfaction.

What kinds of jobs did you have during college?

Answer ▶ I had a variety of jobs while I was going to college, and since I was paying my own way I sometimes had more than one job. I worked as a waiter, a door-to-door salesman, and a data entry clerk. I learned a lot about interacting tactfully with different people, and I also developed my office and computer skills.

In addition to demonstrating how industrious she is (working her way through school), this candidate shows how she developed skills in different areas through her experience.

Never Say: "I just had menial jobs." No matter how menial she thought those jobs were, she should have taken time to figure out what skills they helped her develop.

FOCUS ON WORK

When you are asked to discuss something you like about your job, choose something that is related to your work. Talk about job duties, specifically ones that are related to those you will have if you are hired by the company with which you are interviewing. Try to demonstrate how you have benefited your employer by performing these tasks well.

Describe your favorite boss.

Answer ▶ That would have to be my boss at Triangle Optical. Paul was the most demanding boss I've ever had. He expected so much from our department. What set him apart from other supervisors was that he worked tirelessly alongside us and he was just as demanding of himself. He always gave everyone the credit they deserved.

This applicant values having a demanding boss. In addition, by telling her prospective employer what traits she valued in a former boss, this applicant is letting him know what she will be like as a supervisor if she is hired for this job.

Never Say: "I like a boss who is flexible and fair." While the candidate doesn't reveal anything negative by giving this answer, she should be more specific.

Describe your least favorite boss.

Answer ▶ I'd rather not mention names since this industry is so small. I had a boss who never planned anything in advance. We were always racing to meet deadlines, running out of supplies, or finding ourselves short staffed because she couldn't say no to anyone who asked for a day off.

While it's generally best not to say something negative about a former employer, the interviewee must answer the question. In saying he won't reveal the name of his least favorite boss, he demonstrates tact and discretion. He is also somewhat restrained in his criticism. All this candidate says is that he prefers someone who is more structured. Rejecting his former boss's management style implies that this is not what he'd be like as a manager.

Never Say: "Her name was Josephine Josephson and she was my boss at BRK Audio. She was too demanding." This applicant doesn't hesitate to reveal his boss's name and doesn't give enough of a reason for choosing her as his worst boss. The interviewer may be left wondering why he considered this person too demanding.

You seem to be climbing the corporate ladder in your current job. Why leave now?

Answer ▶ I'm choosing to leave now because my goals have changed. I feel I can better use my public relations skills at a nonprofit organization such as this one.

This applicant is making a change to another industry, but shows how she can still utilize her skills to meet her new goals.

Never Say: "My bosses are crazy. I can't stay there anymore." Remember that making negative comments about any employer is a bad idea.

I see three jobs listed on your resume. Can you tell me what you learned from each of them?

Answer ▶ I learned a lot on each of my jobs, so it's hard to pick one thing from each, but I'll try. When I worked in customer support at CSV, I learned how to help our software users troubleshoot problems. When I worked as a software trainer at Circle Tech, I learned that I needed to find a common ground when teaching a large group of people, because not everyone has the same level of skills. I learned to manage employees at my job as assistant to the head of training at APCO.

Knowing about the job that he's applying for helped the applicant answer this question. He has picked one skill from each of his previous jobs that will be required for the position with this employer.

Never Say: "I learned to be at work on time from my first job. Then from my second job, I learned to keep my mouth shut." While it's good that the applicant has learned these things, they don't demonstrate why he will be a valuable employee.

Do you find your job rewarding?

Answer ▶ I found my job very rewarding for a long time, but lately it hasn't been as rewarding. While I love my new responsibilities, I miss working with clients. That is what attracted me to this position—the combination of supervisory responsibilities and client contact.

It's okay for the interviewee to say she doesn't find her current job rewarding. She explains why she feels this way without placing blame anywhere. With this answer, she also shows she knows about the position for which she's interviewing and explains why she is better suited for it.

Never Say: "No, I don't. When the new manager came in he took away everything I liked about my job." This candidate sounds very angry.

What about your current job isn't very rewarding?

Answer ▶ I think every job has something about it that isn't rewarding. There is a lot of paperwork and I don't find that particularly rewarding, but I know it needs to be done.

This candidate understands the reality of work. Some job duties are rewarding, while others are not. She chose something that many people don't find particularly rewarding—paperwork.

Never Say: "Everything about it is rewarding." The interviewer, who knows every job has things about it that are not rewarding, will question this applicant's sincerity. Furthermore, he will wonder why the applicant is leaving her current job if she finds everything about it rewarding.

How have your other jobs prepared you for the one at this company?

Answer ▶ I've worked on the retail end of the office supplies industry for the past ten years. I know what customers want and what the retail outlets want. I know the industry and I know the products. That is what qualifies me to be a sales rep for Roxy Staple Company.

This candidate shows confidence in her abilities as a salesperson and in her knowledge of the industry of which the prospective employer is a part.

Never Say: "I learned a lot on my previous jobs. My skills qualify me for a job with your company." By giving such a brief answer, the interviewer will have to follow up with the question, "Which skills would those be?"

Your last job was very different than the ones you had before it and very different than this one. Why did you take that job?

Answer ▶ I was thinking of going back to school to be a veterinarian. I mentioned this to my neighbor, a vet, and he offered me a job in his office. I love animals, but before I made the commitment to go to veterinary school, I wanted to make sure I'd be happy working with them and especially dealing with sick ones. It turned out that wasn't right for me after all.

This candidate has a good explanation for why she took a job that deviated from her career path. In providing it, she also shows off her decision-making skills—she didn't jump into a new career without careful consideration.

Never Say: "The job was available and they wanted to hire me." This candidate had no particular reason for taking a job outside her field, leading the potential employer to question her goals.

How do you feel about the way your department was managed on your last job?

Answer ▶ I think it was managed effectively.

This isn't a glowing review, but the candidate didn't say anything negative, either. Even if he thinks his manager was a bumbling fool, he avoids saying so. Badmouthing his boss would make the applicant look bad.

Never Say: "The manager was awful." Making a negative statement like this one is generally not a good idea, but if he has to do it, he should give more of an explanation that would back up his claims.

You've never worked in widget manufacturing before. How have your jobs in the publishing industry prepared you for this?

Answer ▶ Taking a product, whether it's a widget or a book, from its inception to the hands of the consumer takes a lot of planning. You have to put together a budget and set deadlines. You need to make sure your current staff can handle the work and hire consultants if necessary. You may even have to handle crises, should problems arise. I dealt with such things on a daily basis while working in publishing, and I would be able to use the same planning and management skills to help your company.

By focusing on her job responsibilities and talking about them in general terms, this candidate is able to show how she can transfer her skills from one industry to another.

Never Say: "I had to work long hours in publishing and I know people in your industry work long hours, too." This doesn't tell the interviewer much about the candidate or what skills she has.

How would your current supervisor describe you?

Answer ▶ Mr. Roberts respects me. He would describe me as a diligent worker who takes great care to do an excellent job on every project he assigns to me. I complete all work on time. He appreciates the fact that I am very friendly and usually asks me to be our department's "welcome wagon" when a new employee starts.

A little bit of bragging on a job interview is a good thing. This applicant knows that to answer with anything less than this amount of confidence might lead the interviewer to think she's unsure of himself.

Never Say: "I've worked there for three years and he's never complained." Saying your boss never complained about you doesn't exactly shout "great employee!"

What decisions have you had to make on your current job?

Answer ▶ When I planned career workshops for students, I had to decide what topics to feature, when to hold the workshops, and who would speak at them. I had to decide what software to purchase for our public computers within the constraints of our budget. I also made decisions about hiring and firing student aides.

By giving specific examples, this candidate highlights his skills in planning events, making purchasing decisions, working within a budget, and making personnel decisions.

Never Say: "I didn't really get to make too many decisions." This applicant should realize the interviewer is asking this question because decision-making is required on this job. He should take a moment to think of one or two decisions he has made. Even if they don't seem significant, it is better than not giving an answer.

What were the reasons you went to work for your two prior employers?

Answer ▶ I went to work for Pear Computers right out of college. They had an excellent one-year training program, and I knew I would learn a lot there. After I completed the training program, I stayed there for three years. I went to work for my next employer, Bell Technology, because they offered me a position with greater responsibilities than Pear Computers could.

This candidate takes advantage of the opportunity to mention her participation in a training program where she was able to enhance what she learned in school. When she says she stayed at the company for a while after taking part in the training program, she demonstrates her loyalty—she didn't just take the training and run. Her next job was clearly a step up from her first one, which shows how her career has progressed so far.

Never Say: "Each of my last two employers offered a good salary and benefits." This applicant should better demonstrate how she makes decisions. More thought should go into choosing to go to work for someone.

Why did you leave your last job?

Answer ▶ I left my last job because I knew the industry was facing an uncertain future. I researched this industry, saw the growth potential, and knew I could make a significant contribution.

This job candidate shows that he knows how to plan for the future. He doesn't make decisions without doing his homework first.

Never Say: "I was bored." Without giving further explanation, this isn't a good enough reason to leave your job.

You've been at your job for several years. What makes you want to leave?

Answer ▶ I've completed what I set out to do. When I first started working there, the company was just getting started. They needed someone who had the skills to help them grow. They are very successful now and I feel like I've completed my mission. I know I could better use my skills in a growing company such as yours.

Not only does this applicant show off her accomplishments at her current job, she tells her potential employer what she can do for his company.

Never Say: "I want to make more money." This may be this candidate's reason for leaving her job, but it isn't a good enough one to give to a prospective employer.

How is your present job different from the ones you had before it?

Answer ▶ As a senior accounting clerk, I supervise three payroll clerks and a bookkeeper. This is the first time I've had to supervise people.

By discussing her increased responsibilities, this applicant shows how she has moved up in her career.

Never Say: "I have to use a computer now and I also have to work late." Neither of these things illustrates the candidate's growth.

What duties of your last job did you find difficult?

Answer ▶ I found it difficult to fire people. Even though I always put a lot of thought into deciding whether or not to terminate someone, I knew I was affecting someone's livelihood.

No one could fault someone for disliking this unpleasant duty.

Never Say: "Dealing with my boss every day." Oops.

Describe how your career progressed over the last five years. Was it aligned with the goals you set for yourself?

Answer ▶ When I graduated from the community college, I knew I wanted to be a store manager. I also knew I would have to work my way up, so I took a job as a sales associate at Dress Corral. After two years, and a lot of hard work, I was promoted to assistant department manager. After being in that job for a year, P. J. Coopers hired me to be manager of the ladies' accessories department. I've been there for the last two years. With my experience, I'm ready for the next step—store manager.

This job candidate shows exactly how his career has progressed and how he is now ready for a job with this employer.

Never Say: "I really didn't set any goals. I took the sales associate job because it was the only place that wanted someone with my skills. It's been nice to be able to move up." It's okay if this candidate didn't have a plan to start with, but he should have made one along the way. It seems he's let others set goals for him. If he doesn't have a plan, this prospective employer can't predict what he'll do next.

How would those who worked under you describe you as a supervisor?

Answer ▶ My staff at AQA Associates knew I was someone who worked hard and expected the same of them. They also felt I was fair, never asking them to do something I wasn't willing to do myself. My office door was always open and they felt they could come to me to discuss any problem they might have.

This applicant describes the qualities of a good supervisor. Not only does she tell the interviewer how her staff felt about her, she tells them why they felt that way. Notice how sure she is of her answer, never saying, "I think they felt this way." She knows exactly how she is regarded as a supervisor.

Never Say: "I think they thought I did a good job." The applicant doesn't provide enough information.

This job carries with it much more responsibility than you've had before. Are you ready?

Answer ▶ I am definitely ready. I've been working as assistant registrar for five years. I have learned a lot at Burberry College. I've worked very closely with my boss and I know what his job entails. He is also confident in my ability to move on.

This candidate restates her experience and shares with the interviewer the vote of confidence her boss gave her.

Never Say: "Sure. Why not? I've paid my dues."

Have you had to do any traveling for work?

Answer ▶ I've had to do some traveling for my job. I went to Asia several times. I enjoy traveling and hope to do more of it on this job. I find it helpful to have face-to-face meetings with clients periodically rather than doing everything through conference calls.

This applicant knows that his potential employer requires extensive traveling. Although he hasn't done a lot of it, he makes sure to point out that it's something he wants to do more.

Never Say: "They had me traveling all over the place." This candidate doesn't sound very enthusiastic.

What do you think this job offers that your last job did not?

Answer ▶ This job offers me the opportunity to use my research skills. I have mostly administrative duties on my current job, with some research duties. I look forward to a job that is primarily research oriented with some administrative duties.

This applicant has both administrative and research skills, as she points out to the interviewer. She wants to use them in a different way than she does on her current job. She knows, based on what she has learned about this position, that research is a big part of the job.

Never Say: "This job offers me the opportunity to do research. I've always wanted to do that." There's nothing to indicate that this person has any research skills. If there are many candidates from which to choose, the employer may not be willing to hire someone who still requires training.

What kind of person do you find it difficult to work with? What kind of person do you find it easy to work with?

Answer ▶ I find it difficult to work with someone who does sloppy work, takes credit when he hasn't earned it, or tries to get away with doing as little as possible. I find it easy to work with someone who is ambitious, takes the time to do the best job possible, and does more than is asked of her.

"That's not me" is what the interviewee is really saying when he reveals which traits he doesn't like in a coworker. Ambitious, does the best job possible—"now, that's me," the job candidate is saying.

Never Say: "I don't like working with someone who isn't friendly. I prefer someone who wants to hang out after work." These traits have little to do with work.

How do you think your boss will react when you tell her you're leaving?

Answer ▶ I've already discussed it with her, so she won't be surprised. She doesn't want to lose me, but she knows I'm ready for more responsibility, and she can't offer that to me. The only job with more responsibility than I currently have is hers.

By giving this answer the job candidate clearly demonstrates that he has a good relationship with his boss.

Never Say: "I think she's going to be very upset. I don't know how she's going to replace me." While it's appropriate to be very confident on a job interview, this candidate is being very unrealistic if he thinks he's irreplaceable.

What was your salary when you started your current job and what is it now?

Answer ▶ I earned $40,000 per year when I started and now, after five years, I'm up to $50,000.

As long as this information is accurate, this is a good answer.

Never Say: "I'm not sure what I made when I started, but I'm making $50,000 per year now." The candidate should be ready to provide this information; if she truly doesn't know the answer, she can offer to provide it later.

CHAPTER 21

Your Interpersonal Skills

WOULDN'T IT BE NICE if everyone got along with one another? Unfortunately, a world in which everyone gets along is only a dream. There will always be personality conflicts and differences of opinions, whether they are within families, on the playground, or at work. They cannot be avoided. What is important is how we deal with conflicts and differences of opinion when they occur. If handled well, they can lead to new ideas and growth.

An Employee Balancing Act

Each time an employer introduces a new member to his company or department, he disturbs a delicate balance. Depending on how well the new employee gets along with her new coworkers, this addition may completely tip the scales in one direction or another, or they may move only slightly.

Any change could cause a drop in productivity. An existing employee may find it difficult to concentrate on work when he is worried about what the new coworker meant when she gave him "that look" a few minutes ago. Serious drops in productivity occur when coworkers are too busy arguing to get any work done.

Chapter 16 discussed the personal questions you may be asked on an interview. Employers ask personal questions so they can learn about your personality or character traits. One reason they want to know about this is so they can determine whether you will fit in with the other company employees. These character traits are only a piece of the puzzle, however. A potential employee may have skills and experience that make her the most qualified candidate, but her character traits may differ greatly from those of other employees. This probably won't matter to the employer as long as the candidate knows how to make the most of those differences instead of getting sidetracked by them and causing productivity to suffer.

DO YOU PLAY NICELY WITH OTHERS?

A potential employer will try to find out if you are someone who either causes conflicts or doesn't know how to resolve them when they occur. If you indicate that you have a tendency to have difficulties getting along with others, a red flag will go up and he will be less likely to hire you.

How Do You Resolve Conflicts?

When an employer is trying to find out how you interact with others, she may ask questions about hypothetical situations. For example, you may be asked how you would resolve a problem with a coworker. Alternatively, the interviewer may ask you to discuss times you actually did experience conflict with another individual. You should always present a balanced look at those situations. Everyone knows there are three sides to every story—your side, the other person's side, and the truth. Instead of taking sides, try to offer a look at the situation from everyone's point of view and talk about how you effectively dealt with the problem and solved it. Just as you should avoid placing all the blame on someone else, you should also avoid taking all the blame yourself.

An employer may be interested in knowing how you resolve serious conflicts before they escalate. Too often we hear about an angry employee losing control and doing something to physically harm his employer or coworkers. Your prospective employer will want to know you are a calm and reasonable person who doesn't let her anger get out of hand. If you are interviewing for a supervisory position, the interviewer will want to know whether you have the ability to defuse other people's anger.

MAKING A SAFER WORKPLACE

Workplace violence is an issue in modern American society. The U.S. Occupational Safety and Health Administration estimated that there were 2 million victims of workplace violence in 2002. OSHA has suggestions for making the workplace a safer place on its website, *www.osha.gov*.

Questions and Answers

Unfortunately every office has personality conflicts. What do you do when you work with someone you don't particularly like?

Answer ▶ While I know you don't have to be buddies with all your colleagues, workplaces are more productive if everyone gets along. I would try to resolve my differences with that person. If that wasn't possible, I'd find something about that person I could admire and respect and I'd focus on that instead of the things I didn't like.

This applicant shows he's proactive when he says he would try to work out his differences with his coworker but realistic when he says that if he can't, he will find something to respect about his coworker.

Never Say: "I get along with everyone, so this won't be a problem." Is this person too good to be true? Probably.

Describe the relationship that should exist between a supervisor and a subordinate.

Answer ▶ The relationship between a supervisor and a subordinate should be professional, yet friendly. At one of my earlier jobs I had a supervisor who set a perfect example for what this relationship should be like. She always acted professionally but also seemed interested in her workers as people. For example, she made a point of asking us if we had a nice weekend and how things were going, but she never pried into our personal lives. She was friendly without trying to be our friend.

This interviewee not only correctly states what the relationship between a supervisor and subordinate should be, but he also talks about his role model for such a relationship.

Never Say: "Strictly professional." This applicant should elaborate on his answer.

What would you do if you disagreed with your boss?

Answer ▶ It would depend on the situation. If I disagreed with her about whether the office is warm or cold I might not say anything. However, if I disagreed with my boss about whether the new marketing campaign was going to work, I'd share my thoughts with her.

This applicant knows he has to choose his battles wisely. There's a difference between being disagreeable and disagreeing.

Never Say: "I would never tell my boss I disagreed with her." This applicant is too passive.

ASSERTIVE VERSUS AGGRESSIVE

Being assertive and being aggressive aren't the same thing. Those who are assertive are self-assured, aren't afraid to express their opinions and are adept at the art of gentle persuasion. People who are aggressive are more likely to force their opinion on others, which often causes problems in a work environment. Most employers value workers who are assertive but not aggressive.

What do you expect someone you supervise to do if she disagrees with you?

Answer ▶ I would expect that person to let me know what she's thinking. It could influence my decision. If she doesn't share her thoughts with me, I won't have the opportunity to hear her take on things.

This job candidate respects his coworkers' opinions. He knows it wouldn't be wise to make decisions without taking their comments into consideration.

Never Say: "Disagreeing with your supervisor? Isn't that a little disrespectful?" This candidate's answer implies that he is more interested in his own image and power than in his company's success.

What would you do if your supervisor handed you an assignment but you didn't quite understand it?

Answer ▶ I would first make sure I didn't just need to take a closer look at the project to better understand it. Once I did that, I would ask questions if I needed to. I'd rather ask questions before I begin than have to correct mistakes later on.

This candidate tries to work independently when possible, but knows that clarification is sometimes necessary and is not afraid to ask for it.

Never Say: "I would try to figure it out on my own." This interviewee is trying to show that she is independent but her answer may send up red flags. The employer will wonder if this independence will cause the candidate to make mistakes.

What would you do if your boss asks you do something that is clearly not part of your job description?

Answer ▶ It would depend on what it was I was asked to do. I wouldn't expect to run personal errands for my boss, but if I were asked to do something to help the company that wasn't normally part of my job, I wouldn't have a problem with it.

The applicant shows his flexibility. However, this extends only to situations where the request is appropriate. If the boss is looking for someone to run her personal errands and that is something the candidate refuses to do, it's better to set things straight from the start.

Never Say: "I would do anything I was asked to do." While flexibility is important, no one should be a pushover.

How did you get along with your last supervisor?

Answer ▶ We had a great relationship. I really respected him and I know he respected me, too. My supervisor knew he could trust me with any project, so he always assigned me those that were very challenging.

This candidate describes her relationship with her boss on a professional level, yet manages to say something very positive about herself.

Never Say: "We got along so well. We had lunch together all the time." It sounds more like this interviewee is describing a buddy than a supervisor.

How do you evaluate the work of others?

Answer ▶ Giving a critical opinion of someone's work is very tricky. Some people are more receptive than others, so I try to be careful while still getting my point across. I always make sure to talk about what someone has done right before mentioning what he has done wrong. I offer guidance to help my subordinates make the changes they need to, yet I give them room to make their own decisions.

This candidate shows that she knows how to handle a potentially sticky situation. She respects her subordinates and wants to maintain a good relationship with them. That, however, doesn't stop her from offering criticism when it is necessary.

Never Say: "I'm always straightforward. If someone doesn't want to be criticized, he should do a good job in the first place." A supervisor should know how to be diplomatic. This candidate shows that diplomacy isn't her strong suit.

What would you do if a member of your staff seemed upset about something but you didn't know what the problem was?

Answer ▶ I would ask if he wanted to talk about what's bothering him and make sure he knew I was available. If he didn't want to talk, I wouldn't push because it might be something personal. However, if it were work-related, I would hope he'd be able to be honest about it so we'd be able to solve the problem together.

This candidate demonstrates both sensitivity and professionalism with this answer. She is sensitive to the needs of her staff and indicates that she is approachable, especially when it comes to work-related issues.

Never Say: "I feel like I have to maintain a distance between myself and my staff. If there's something I need to know, my employee should come to me. If it's a personal problem, he can just leave it at home where it belongs." This candidate shows that she hasn't yet developed an understanding of what it means to be a good manager.

MANAGERIAL SKILLS

Employers want managers who can strike a balance between compassion and professionalism when dealing with their subordinates. They prefer managers who don't become so personally involved with their staff members that it clouds their judgment, but, at the same time, are approachable and understanding.

Have you ever had a boss you didn't like?

Answer ▶ Of course I've worked for some bosses I've liked more than others, but I try to stay professional and always make an effort to get along with everyone.

"Never complain about a former boss" is the line that keeps running through this candidate's head. Rather than do that, he keeps his answer as positive as possible.

Never Say: "Have I ever! Let me tell you about my last boss." This candidate seems eager to talk about his employer behind her back. Is that the kind of person the interviewer wants around his office?

What would you do if your company implemented a policy you disagreed with?

Answer ▶ Before taking any action I would need to evaluate the situation. I would have to determine whether I just needed time to get used to the new policy or if the policy had serious flaws that would affect the well-being of the company. If I determined that the latter was true, I would express my disapproval as soon as possible. It's difficult to be the one to make waves, but I would have to look out for the company. I wouldn't just criticize the new policy; I would suggest ways to make useful changes.

This interviewee demonstrates that she stops to think before taking action. However, if she determines she needs to take action, she does so in a constructive way. She looks out for her employer's welfare and puts the interests of the company first.

Never Say: "I don't like making waves. I'd probably just keep my mouth shut." This candidate's answer tells the interviewer she isn't proactive.

What would you do if you received what you felt was an unfair evaluation?

Answer ▶ I would wait a little while before I approached my supervisor—probably until the next morning. I wouldn't want to talk to my supervisor while I was angry because I might say the wrong thing. I would write down point-by-point why I thought the evaluation was inaccurate. Then I would present my thoughts to my supervisor calmly.

This candidate shows that he does not act on emotion. He takes the time to evaluate a situation before making a move. After doing that he makes an effort to calmly present his case.

Never Say: "I'd march right into her office and tell her how wrong she is." The last thing an employer wants is an employee who acts only on his emotions. A job candidate should come across as someone who thinks carefully before he acts or speaks.

What would you do if someone you supervised came to you because he felt your evaluation of him was unfair?

Answer ▶ I would ask him to explain to me why he thought the evaluation was unfair. If he had a valid argument to back up his claim, I would reconsider the evaluation. If not, I would sit down with him to discuss what improvements could be made so that his next evaluation would be better.

This interviewee illustrates how she takes the time to listen to her subordinates. She shows she is willing to make changes to the evaluation if she realizes she needs to, but if not, will help the employee improve.

Never Say: "I'm really careful when I write evaluations, so they are always accurate." This job candidate doesn't realize that everyone makes mistakes, even those who are really careful.

Describe the ideal coworker.

Answer ▶ The ideal coworker is one who respects those around him. He doesn't engage in behavior that would be offensive to others. He offers constructive criticism and accepts it as well. He contributes to the department and company and doesn't try to compete with his coworkers. He shares responsibility for victories as well as defeats.

This applicant lists a number of desirable qualities and shows that he understands what makes a good employee. Hopefully this candidate is also describing traits he possesses.

Never Say: "I prefer someone who keeps to himself. I really don't want to make friends at work." If this is what this candidate believes, he will have trouble being part of a congenial environment.

Describe the ideal manager.

Answer ▶ The ideal manager expects a lot of her employees. She respects them. She knows their individual abilities and makes sure they utilize them to the fullest. She continually challenges them to do more and recognizes their accomplishments.

This answer can mean one of two things. The candidate may be describing her own abilities as a manager. In that case, this is a manager who will retain a productive staff. Alternatively, she could be describing the type of manager she'd like to work under. If that is the case, an employee who likes to work under a supervisor who expects a lot is someone who is willing to live up to those expectations.

Never Say: "The ideal manager is one who doesn't interfere too much with her employees. I like someone who just lets everyone do their jobs." If this candidate is describing herself as a manager, she shows that she lacks managerial skills. If she is describing a manager she'd like to work for, she has shown herself as a worker who, for some reason, doesn't want anyone to know what she is doing.

Describe the ideal employee.

Answer ▶ The ideal employee is one who always does more than he is asked to do. He is open to challenges and is always willing to learn more and take on more responsibilities. He is also receptive to constructive criticism.

Hopefully this candidate has described himself, and any employer would be happy to have an employee like this.

Never Say: "The ideal employee is one who does what is asked of him. He doesn't ask a lot of questions." This candidate, if describing himself, sounds weak.

YOU MUST FIT IN

Every work environment is different, and the interviewer wants to know if you will succeed in this. Employers put a lot of effort into making sure they hire the most suitable candidates possible. The candidate must be able to carry out the necessary job duties, and she must fit in well with the other employees.

What would you do if someone came to you to complain about his supervisor?

Answer ▶ First, I would ask him if he had talked to his supervisor yet. If not, I would ask him to do that first. I would make sure he knew how to approach the supervisor and offer him tips if he didn't. If he had already talked to his supervisor but hadn't gotten anywhere with her, I would have him tell me his side of the story. Next, I would talk to his supervisor to get her side of the story. After considering what both people had told me, I would decide how to resolve the problem.

This job candidate shows he knows how to follow protocol when he says he would ask the employee to speak to his supervisor first. He demonstrates that he won't take sides and must hear both sides of a story before deciding what to do.

Never Say: "I'd listen to what he had to say and then call his supervisor down to my office so I could deal with the problem immediately." This interviewee indicates that he wastes no time, but this is not the best way to deal with a serious problem.

What would your current coworkers say about you?

Answer ▶ My coworkers would say I'm very committed to my job. I work hard to contribute to each project's success and I always share credit with everyone else who contributes to that success.

This interviewee portrays herself as someone who is a team player. She sticks to talking about work-related matters.

Never Say: "They would say they like me." That's nice, but the applicant should try to think up something a little more concrete to show why she is a good employee.

What would you do about a long-term employee whose work has been slipping lately?

Answer ▶ I would talk to my employee to find out what was going on. Obviously if this person always did a good job, something must have happened to change that. As a supervisor, it is my job to find out what that is and help the employee fix the problem; it is also preferable to firing someone. It is generally more cost effective to retain a worker who already knows the job than to train someone new. It also is better for the morale of that person's coworkers, who don't want to see a coworker lose his job.

This answer shows that the candidate has good managerial skills. While dismissing an unproductive employee may seem like a quick and easy solution in the short term, it can have a detrimental affect on the company in the end.

Never Say: "Whoever doesn't pull his weight has to go. I would just fire the employee." This candidate may know how to solve a problem quickly, but she doesn't account for the repercussions.

What would you do if an important client asked you out on a date?

Answer ▶ I would politely decline, explaining to the client that I make a point of never mixing business with pleasure. I would then thank him and end the conversation as quickly as possible.

Good answer. This candidate won't compromise her integrity.

Never Say: "How important is this client?"

Have you ever had to persuade someone to accept your point of view? How did you do it and were you successful?

Answer ▶ I have had to do that several times. A few months ago, for example, we were in the process of planning a new publication. We were deciding whether to hire a permanent employee or a freelancer to edit it. My manager felt we should go with a permanent employee. After analyzing the options, I felt strongly that hiring a freelancer would work best. I presented him with my reasons for wanting to hire a freelancer, including a cost analysis. I convinced my manager to try it my way, and so far it has worked out very well.

This interviewee gives an example that explains how she gathered information to help her make a decision and then presented the information to her manager to persuade him that this was the best choice.

Never Say: "I've had to do that several times. I can always get people to come around to my point of view." It is unclear how this candidate persuades others to come around to her point of view. Is she assertive or aggressive?

How do you handle an angry employee?

Answer ▶ Way too often you hear about an employee whose anger turns to violence. As a supervisor it would be my job to recognize potentially volatile situations. Once I recognized a problem, I would help the employee remove herself from the situation long enough to cool down. I would tell her where she could go for help.

This applicant knows anger can be serious and what to do before it escalates.

Never Say: "I'd fire her." This applicant shows that he knows how to further escalate a potentially violent situation.

What do you do when you have a very unhappy customer?

Answer ▶ My first step is to let the customer know I will listen to what she has to say. If the company has a strict policy regarding customer complaints, I will follow it. However, if I must use my own judgment, I would strike a balance between keeping the customer happy and not costing my employer too much. If I see that the customer's complaint is legitimate, I will do what it takes to remedy the situation.

This applicant plays by the rules. He knows a satisfied customer will return, but he also realizes that a company is always concerned about its bottom line.

Never Say: "The customer is always right. I will just give a customer what they want." If every customer is right, it will cost the company a lot of money.

THE CUSTOMER COMES FIRST

Employers want to know that those they hire won't drive customers away. They want employees who know how to keep customers satisfied but will be attentive to the company's bottom line and not just hand out free stuff left and right.

A customer is extremely angry because, according to store policy, you can't accept an item she wants to return. How do you handle it?

Answer ▶ Sometimes these situations get out of hand. If it looks like a situation may turn violent, I will do what is necessary to rectify it. If it costs the company a little money, well, the company's bottom line is important, but not as important as people's lives.

This job candidate shows he is practical. He has his priorities in order—lives before money.

Never Say: "Don't you worry. A customer's anger doesn't scare me. I'll always defend the company's policies." This candidate may be loyal, but his judgment is faulty.

As a supervisor, what do you do when employees working under you don't get along?

Answer ▶ I actually encountered this situation a few months ago. There were two employees in my department who were both very nice people, but they got off on the wrong foot when one of them transferred into the department. I called a meeting with them and asked them to try to resolve their differences for the good of the department. I can't actually say they like each other now, but there is a level of respect between them.

Nothing is better than a real-life experience. This job candidate was lucky enough to have one she could draw upon. She solved this problem in a very logical way and was very honest about the outcome.

Never Say: "It's really none of my business if my employees don't get along." Wrong answer. The interviewer has asked this question for a reason—a supervisor should be very concerned if two of her employees don't get along. She must deal with it.

If you were unhappy with your job, how would you discuss this with your boss?

Answer ▶ I've always had good relationships with everyone I've worked for, so I think it would be to everyone's benefit for me to be direct with my boss. First, I would make a list of the things I'm unhappy with, as well as suggestions for improving each situation. I would then ask for a meeting with my boss to go over the list point by point, being careful not to place any blame.

This interviewee smartly points out that he maintains a good relationship with his boss that can withstand this type of discussion. He explains how he would be proactive in helping to find a solution for the problems he is dealing with at work.

Never Say: "I don't think I'd bother discussing it. I would just look for another job." This answer may indicate that this candidate makes rash decisions and may not be loyal to this job if he gets it.

How do you handle criticism?

Answer ▶ I think criticism can be a valuable tool. It forces me to take a look at my own work to see how I can improve on it.

This candidate shows that she doesn't get all bent out of shape if someone has an unkind word for her.

Never Say: "If someone can't say something nice, maybe they shouldn't say anything at all."

Suppose one of the people you supervise complains that his officemate is slacking off at work. How would you handle it?

Answer ▶ This happened to me at my last job. I already knew that the supposed slacker actually had higher productivity than the employee who complained. It's important to take such a complaint with a grain of salt. If this happened again I would politely tell the employee that I would handle the situation if necessary. Then I would keep an eye on the complainer, who apparently has too much time on her hands.

This manager portrays himself as someone who is very observant and is aware of what his staff is doing. He also handles the situation well by politely putting his employee in her place.

Never Say: "I would tell her to mind her own business." An effective supervisor needs to have a little more tact than that.

What would you do with an employee who seems to do her work slowly? She gets her work done on time, but it's always very close to the deadline.

Answer ▶ Some people work more slowly than others. If her work is accurate and it's being completed before the deadline, I don't think there's anything to worry about.

The interviewee is very practical. He knows that everyone has different work styles and working quickly doesn't necessarily mean better performance.

Never Say: "I'd ask her to speed up and start asking for progress reports." This candidate sounds like someone who will cause unnecessary tension among the people he supervises.

FIX PROBLEMS FIRST

Show that you can resolve problems on your own before you bring someone else into it. A candidate who indicates that she will go running to her supervisor to report difficulties with a coworker will be viewed by the interviewer as too high maintenance.

The person in the next cubicle spends endless hours on the phone talking to his girlfriend. Not only is he not getting his work done but his chatter is keeping you from doing yours. What do you do?

Answer ▶ I would talk to him before I did anything else. He may not realize how loud his phone conversations are. I would politely let him know that I can hear what he's saying and hopefully that would be enough to get him to lower his volume. I might also consider getting a noise machine—something that plays soothing sounds—to block out his voice. If nothing else helped, I would try to move to another cubicle.

This job candidate shows that she's determined to solve problems on her own before involving her supervisor.

Never Say: "I would tell my supervisor. Who does this guy think he is, talking on the phone instead of working?" The prospective employer will see this interviewee as someone who will make waves. He has better things to do than worry about helping his employees solve petty disputes.

CHAPTER 22

Did You Do Your Homework?

RESEARCHING A PROSPECTIVE EMPLOYER is one of the most important things you can do to prepare for a job interview. Keep up with the latest news about a company and find out about its line of business, financial condition, customers and clients, and the industry in which it operates. Arriving at the interview armed with this information shows the prospective employer how serious you are about the interview and about the job.

Proving Your Knowledge

During the course of a job interview, the person conducting it will ask you to discuss what you know about her company and the particular job for which she is hiring. Obviously, the interviewer is not asking you for this information because she wants or needs it herself. She wants to know you made an effort to do the research needed to get this information.

A job candidate who walks into an interview armed with knowledge about the employer demonstrates several things to the interviewer. He demonstrates that he isn't just looking for a job with *any* employer. He wants to work for this particular company because of what he knows about it. He also shows that he was ambitious enough to do the necessary research to learn what he could about the employer.

The interviewer may ask you direct questions regarding what you know about the company. If you haven't done your research, you won't be able to answer these questions. She will ask you about the company's services and its products. She may also ask you to talk about the industry of which the company is a part.

The interviewer may also ask you questions that aren't as straightforward. You may not even realize at first that she is testing your knowledge about the company.

For example, the interviewer may ask you what you can contribute to the company and what changes you would make if you were hired. She may ask you why you want to work for the company and how this opportunity fits into your career plans. Base your answers to these questions on the information you gathered through your research.

START WITH THE SITE

To find basic information about a prospective employer, start by looking at the company's website. You can learn about a company's product line and key personnel. Public companies often make their annual reports available on their websites. Some also provide a list of clients.

Highlight Skills That Fit the Company

Throughout a job interview you will be asked many questions about your skills, work history, and accomplishments. The interviewer will ask you these questions because he wants to find out what you can bring to his company. The more you know about this employer, the better you can demonstrate that you have the particular attributes he values. Use what you have learned through your research to frame your answers. For example, if you learned that the company is in the process of expanding its web presence, talk about your skills, work history, and accomplishments in that area. Your goal is to not merely talk about your attributes in general terms. You will instead discuss them as they relate to this job in particular.

INDUSTRY RESOURCES

In order to become knowledgeable about a particular industry, you must learn as much as you can about it. The United States Bureau of Labor Statistics publishes industry information online. Industry at a Glance (*www.bls.gov/iag/iaghome.htm*), for example, provides information on more than 100 industries.

Questions and Answers

Now that you've told me about yourself, can you tell me what you know about us?

Answer ▶ Costello Laboratories is a pharmaceutical company with annual sales of over $15 billion. The company recently introduced a new medication to treat bipolar disorder, and I read that it is working on a new cardiac medication.

This answer shows that this candidate has done her homework. She knows what the company does and has even kept up with the latest news.

Never Say: "I haven't been able to find out anything about it." Unless you've been called for an interview an hour before it is to take place, there is no excuse for not doing your homework.

What do you think it takes to be successful here?

Answer ▶ I understand that Q & H Corporation introduced five new products to the market in the last year alone. In order to be a successful employee of such an innovative company, one would have to be very creative. In a competitive industry such as soaps and toiletries you need employees who can keep up with what consumers want.

This person has obviously done his homework. He not only knows about the company, but he seems to know about the industry as well.

Never Say: "In order to be successful, employees must work hard and do a good job." This can be said of employees of any company. If this candidate had done his homework, he would know more about this particular company.

Based on what you know about this company, how will you contribute to it?

Answer ▶ I see that most of your company's clients are in the food industry. Since I spent ten years working for AMJ Bean Company, I am very familiar with that industry. I know my experience in the industry is something your clients will appreciate.

This candidate has researched her prospective employer and knows that her experience in the food industry will help her should she be hired. She is able to make a point of mentioning that on the job interview.

Never Say: "I have great organizational skills and I can manage my time well." While most employers value these skills, the candidate does not explain why they will benefit this particular company.

There are a lot of companies that can use someone with your skills. Why do you want to work at this company?

Answer ▶ Home Warehouse has been more successful than any other company in the hardware industry. The company has seen steady profit growth over many years and it appears it will continue to do so. However, critics of the company are quick to point out that customer service is seriously lacking. As the director of customer service I will implement new procedures that will turn that negative image around.

This answer shows the interviewee's knowledge of the company, including its weaknesses. He already has a plan in mind to fix that weakness, as he shares with the interviewer.

Never Say: "I heard you pay really well." This candidate shows that he doesn't really know a lot about the company and how he will fit in as an employee.

What do you know about this industry?

Answer ▶ The retail industry is tremendous. It is the second largest industry in the United States, in terms of the numbers of both establishments and employees. There has been a decline in sales over recent years, but industry analysts think that will turn around when the economy improves.

This job candidate has done enough research to be able to intelligently discuss what she knows about the industry.

Never Say: "I don't know a lot about the retail industry. I've only worked in the financial industry, so this is all new to me." Knowledge about an industry does not have to come from experience. There are many resources this interviewee could have accessed to gather information.

Why do you want to work in this industry?

Answer ▶ I'm ready for a new challenge, and since more commercial banks have begun to offer investment services over the last few years, I know I can use the skills I learned as an investment banker to work in the commercial banking industry.

By giving this answer, the interviewee is able to demonstrate that he knows about this industry and what he can bring to it.

Never Say: "The hours are much better than they are in the investment banking industry." This answer doesn't show that the interviewee knows more about the industry than the number of hours one must work, and it certainly doesn't show what he can bring to it.

How much do you know about our company's recent growth?

Answer ▶ I know that XYZ Brands is a multinational company. I was particularly intrigued by your acquisition of ABC Corporation last March. It seems like it's going to open up a whole new market for this company.

Not only does the interviewee show that she took the time to learn about the company, she also shows she's kept up with the latest news about it. Notice that the interviewee said "it's going to open up a whole new market for this company" not "your company," so as not to create distance between herself and the employer.

Never Say: "I see your commercials on TV all the time, so you must be a pretty big company."

What interests you about our products and services?

Answer ▶ Turning Corporation provides products and services that help so many people. Just the other day I was reading about the new motorized scooter Turning developed. Those in health care and advocates for the disabled are very excited about it, according to everything I've read.

This candidate has obviously made a point of learning about his prospective employer, including keeping up with news about the latest products.

Never Say: "I don't know much about your products, but by the looks of your offices, they must sell really well."

Is there anything you've heard about our company that you don't like?

Answer ▶ It's really nothing specific to your company. I know the industry is a little shaky now, so of course I have some concerns about that. Based on what I've been reading, though, it looks like things are improving some.

This candidate shows that she did her homework, yet avoids bringing up anything that may cause awkward feelings. However, if there was something splashed across the front page of newspapers, the candidate would look ignorant if she didn't talk about it.

Never Say: "I heard you fire people who don't agree with you. Is that true?" That is something that might only be a rumor. Bringing it up during the interview could cause a lot of embarrassment.

Is there anything you find troubling about this industry?

Answer ▶ Actually, no. I've been reading about this industry and everything I've seen so far is positive. This industry has made a great recovery after the decline about a decade ago. Since then it has been growing steadily and actually saw record growth last year.

Although he doesn't have anything negative to say, this candidate takes this opportunity to show that he did his homework.

Never Say: "No. It's nice to be in an industry like this, isn't it?" This interviewee may have done his homework, but he needs to elaborate on his answer to prove that.

Where do you think this company is going to be in five years?

Answer ▶ Based on what I've been reading it seems this company will be fully expanded into the international market by then. Parker Corporation opened offices in Japan and

Switzerland last year, and I read that they are looking into opening Canadian offices next year.

This candidate is aware of what her prospective employer has in store for the future because she did her homework.

Never Say: "The future is always so fuzzy. Who can ever predict what is going to happen?" This interviewer didn't ask this candidate to look into a crystal ball. He wants her to make a prediction based on her current knowledge.

Do you know what your job duties will be if we hire you?

Answer ▶ As eligibility clerk, I will use my interviewing skills to help determine whether individuals are eligible to receive assistance from various government programs. I will interview people and write reports that will be sent to the appropriate agencies.

Because she looked into it, this candidate knows what the general duties are for the job.

Never Say: "I didn't get a chance to look into that." The interviewer will wonder how this candidate can interview for a job she knows nothing about.

How does this job fit in with your career goals?

Answer ▶ As I mentioned earlier, my long-range goal is to be an elementary school principal. Reaching that is several years off, of course. I have a lot to learn about school administration. I've attended several workshops you've run and I am always impressed by your knowledge, and I know I can learn a lot from you. From what I've heard through the grapevine, you always place a lot of trust in everyone you hire and give employees a chance to grow. I know I can gain valuable knowledge and experience here at Oakwood, in addition to what I can contribute as an assistant principal.

This candidate demonstrates his knowledge about his prospective employer. He has personally learned from her in the past. He has also talked to other people who know her and how the school is run. Mentioning his aspiration to move beyond this job is a little bit risky, but since it will be quite a while before he can do that, he takes a chance.

Never Say: "It's an assistant principal job and clearly it's the next step I need to take in order to become a principal." In other words, this interviewee doesn't care where he gets his experience as long as he gets it.

If we hire you, what aspect of this job do you think you'll like best? What aspect of the job will you like least?

Answer ▶ I will enjoy working with clients one-on-one best, as I have in my previous position. The part I will like least is completing the massive quantity of paperwork that is required by all government agencies. However, I know it's a necessary part of this job and I've learned that if you keep up with it, it is much easier to deal with.

Demonstrating what she knows about the job, this candidate is able to discuss what she likes and doesn't like about it. She picks the major part of her job, working with clients, as the thing she likes best. When saying what she doesn't enjoy, she is upbeat and quick to point out that she knows it is necessary.

Never Say: "I love working with clients but I hate doing all the paperwork." It would have been better for this candidate not to be so vehement about her dislike of paperwork.

What would you like to accomplish here if we hire you?

Answer ▶ I read that this company is expanding into the children's clothing market. With my background in that area, I know I can help make that clothing line successful.

The interviewee bases his answer on what he has learned about this employer. He explains how his experience will help the company reach its goals.

Never Say: "I hope to move up to the executive suite." The candidate may have researched the layout of the office to determine that this suite exists, but that's not exactly the type of research that will impress a prospective employer.

Since all your experience has been in another industry, you must be a little concerned about making this change. What do you think working in this industry will be like?

Answer ▶ Everything in this industry seems to go at a very fast pace. I think the transition will be an easy one for me because in the magazine industry, I also worked at a fast pace. There were tight deadlines and sudden changes that needed to be dealt with on a moment's notice. From what I can tell, this industry involves the same things. I think I will be able to make a seamless transition to this industry.

This candidate's answer conveys that she has some knowledge of the magazine industry and she feels she can adapt to working in it.

Never Say: "I think it will be fine." This candidate needs to explain why she feels that way.

What do you know about some of our major clients?

Answer ▶ I know your major clients are all in the canned food industry. BBR represents Heller Foods, Green Products, and Acorn Corp. I read in *Advertising Digest* just last week that Heans hired you to run their new broadcast campaign.

This candidate has done his homework, even keeping up with the latest industry news.

Never Say: "I haven't had a chance to find out who they are." There is never an excuse for not attempting to learn what you can about a prospective employer.

Describe your ideal job.

Answer ▶ Ideally, I'd like to work as a senior project manager overseeing the development of housing complexes.

Through her research this candidate has learned the job for which she is interviewing will eventually lead to the one she is describing. She demonstrates that she will be loyal to the company if it hires her.

Never Say: "I'd love to teach one day." It's nice to have career aspirations, but they should at least be related to the job you are applying for.

YOUR DREAM JOB

When a prospective employer asks you to describe your dream job, choose one on your career path. You don't want to describe a job that is unrelated to the one for which you are applying. The job you describe should also be several rungs above your current one on the career ladder. Show how you want your career to progress.

Describe your ideal company to work for.

Answer ▶ I'd like to work for a software company where I will have the opportunity to contribute to the business by utilizing my programming skills as well as my teaching abilities.

When describing his ideal company, this applicant speaks in terms of what he can bring to it. Any company is ideal to him if he can use his skills to benefit it, he seems to be saying. Having done his homework, he knows he is describing the company at which he is interviewing.

Never Say: "I'd really like to work for a big company but none of them are hiring right now." Honesty isn't always the best policy.

Our latest venture has been all over the news. What would you do to make the transition go more smoothly for our employees?

Answer ▶ I would make sure employees know how the merger between this company and Pacific Pencil Company will affect them. I would hold meetings to discuss how procedures will change and schedule workshops to help employees adapt to these changes. When my former employer merged with RQR International, I assisted the vice president who was responsible for handling the transition, so I have experience in this area.

By referring to the venture by name, this candidate shows she knows what the interviewer is talking about. She has clearly given some thought to how this merger will affect the company and knows how to deal with it, and she draws upon her experience with a similar situation.

Never Say: "What venture is that? I haven't had time to pay attention to the news."

Can you define this position as you understand it?

Answer ▶ This position involves supervising a staff of about fifty-five data entry clerks. I would be responsible for scheduling employees, delegating work assignments, and quality control.

This candidate understands the job for which he is interviewing. He has read the job announcement and has listened carefully during the interview.

Never Say: "Data entry supervisor." It's good that the candidate at least knows the title of the job he is interviewing for. However, it's not good enough. He needs to elaborate if possible.

I DON'T KNOW MUCH ABOUT THIS JOB

Sometimes employers release little information about open positions. If the interviewer asks you what you know about the job but you haven't managed to find many details, say so. You can tell her what you know so far and use this opportunity to ask for a better description.

Are you available during the hours we're open?

Answer ▶ Yes, I am. I took a look at your website and saw that the library provides service Monday through Saturday from 9 A.M. to 9 P.M. I'm available during all those times.

This interviewee knows what the hours are and can commit to working when he is needed.

Never Say: "What hours are you open?" The candidate should have been able to find this information.

RELIGIOUS OBSERVANCES

An employer should not ask if you are unable to work on a particular day due to religious observance. The Civil Rights Act of 1964 prohibits employment discrimination on the basis of religion. If you can't work on a particular day, hold off on having this discussion until you have received a job offer.

You are aware you will have to relocate to this city if we hire you. Do you think you will like living here?

Answer ▶ I've done some research about this city and I think it would be a great place to live. The crime rate is pretty low and the climate is just about perfect. There are so many museums and theaters here, it won't be hard to find something to do on my time off.

This answer proves that this candidate has done her research about this city. She is prepared to make a well-informed decision if the employer offers her the job.

Never Say: "I can be happy anywhere." This interviewee may show that she is flexible, but since she didn't do any research into moving to a new location, this prospective employer may not see her as someone who is committed to making a permanent move.

I see from your resume that you were a member of Students Against Teen Smoking. Since a large tobacco company is our major client, will your antismoking stance pose a problem for you when dealing with this company?

Answer ▶ When I first discovered that Wyatt and Smokey Incorporated was one of Krull Media's clients, I hesitated to apply. I decided to do some research to learn more about W & S and found out that the company has never marketed its product to teens or tried to make it appealing to them in any way. Actually, I saw the company ran a campaign last year that addressed the issue of underage smoking. I understand your agency worked on that campaign.

This candidate did research in order to learn about his prospective employer. In doing so, he learned that he might have philosophical differences with one of the employer's clients. Not wanting to compromise his principles or take himself out of the running for the job, he did further research to help him learn more about the client in question.

Never Say: "I had no idea one of this company's clients was a tobacco company." Had this candidate known that, he would have been able to make an educated decision about whether to even interview for the job. He might be wasting the interviewer's time.

Do you know who our major competitors are?

Answer ▶ Yes, I do. There are four big names in the communications industry. There's BCD, DRG, Parrot, and of course, this company, Chime.

This candidate couldn't have answered this question had she not done her homework.

Never Say: "Nope."

Would you rather be a big fish in a small pond or a small fish in a big pond?

Answer ▶ I would much rather be a big fish in a small pond. Working for a small company provides me with the opportunity to use more of my skills. I like it when my job duties are diversified. Most of my experience has been with small companies, so I understand the unique challenges that can come up. For example, I know how to be careful when scheduling out-of-town business meetings so there are always enough people in the office to deal with emergencies that come up.

This candidate is interviewing for a job in a small company. He explains why this is a better fit for him.

Never Say: "Whichever." This candidate should use this opportunity to explain why he is a good fit for this employer.

What do you think will be different about working for this company than working for your current employer?

Answer ▶ My current employer sells home furnishings, while this company sells office furnishings. This means I will work with a different group of clients and new products; however, I can utilize my skills as a decorator and as a salesperson here as I do with my current employer.

This candidate knows enough about her prospective employer to answer this question. She makes a point of discussing how her skills can be used to work with a different product and different clientele.

Never Say: "It's a much shorter commute." This may be true, but it doesn't really have much to do with what this candidate can bring to her prospective employer.

How well do you understand our mission?

Answer ▶ From my research, I understand your mission is to develop high-quality toys that enhance learning and provide entertainment for children between preschool and ten years of age.

This candidate states the company's mission as he understands it, which is exactly what the interviewer asked him to do.

Never Say: "Well . . . I know you sell toys." While you may not always be able to find out what a company's mission is, you should at least try to do the research.

If you were interviewing potential employees for a job here, how would you describe this organization to them?

Answer ▶ XRT, Inc. manufacturers windows and sells them directly to the consumer. The company has a sales force of about twenty people who respond to customer inquiries by visiting their homes or places of business.

This answer shows that this interviewee has a firm grasp of what this business is all about.

Never Say: "It's a window company in Chicago." This answer doesn't prove this candidate knows much about this company.

If you had the opportunity to develop a new product to add to our line, what would it be?

Answer ▶ Since Perfect Posies currently sells flowers and other gift items, I think a line of chocolate would be a good choice. I recently saw a survey that said that consumers spend $150 billion on chocolate gifts each year, so this would be a great market to enter. And since this company already has a great reputation in the mail-order gift industry and the systems in place to handle the addition of this product, this would be a natural expansion of Perfect Posies' product line.

This is an extremely well-thought-out answer based on this candidate's knowledge of the company and the gift industry in general.

Never Say: "I don't know much about your current line. Do you offer anything besides flowers yet?"

CHAPTER 23

What Would You Do If You Were Hired?

WHEN A PROSPECTIVE EMPLOYER looks at you, she sees you in three ways—past, present, and future. Your work history and your education make up your past. Your personality, strengths and weaknesses, and skills make up your present, or who you are today. Finally, a prospective employer wants to know the future—that is, what you would do if she hires you. Without a crystal ball, she must ask a lot of questions in order to get a clearer picture of who you are.

What You Can Bring to the Company

The interviewer's primary concern is to find out if you will be able to carry out the duties of the job. In most situations, you will have had the opportunity to read a job description in advance of your interview. If not, try your best to determine what the typical job duties are for the position you are applying for. You should be ready to explain why you are qualified to carry out each duty.

A prospective employer might talk about some specific projects he has in store for his new hire. He will want you to discuss how you will approach those projects. This would be a good time for you to talk about how you approached similar projects in the past. The interviewer may also present a number of hypothetical situations and ask you to explain how you will handle them. Whenever possible, draw on your past experiences to illustrate how your skills will enable you to deal with each situation.

USE SPECIFIC EXAMPLES

Arm yourself with a cache of examples that best illustrate that you are the most qualified candidate for the job. These examples will come from your work experience and, in lieu of that, from your experience as a student, whether in class or through your participation in extracurricular activities.

What the Company Expects of You

Every employer has different expectations for her employees. While one might require you to work long hours on a regular basis, another might expect you to work late occasionally, perhaps during a particular busy season. Some jobs involve frequent travel. For other jobs you must be on call during weekends. The interviewer will try to determine whether you can meet a particular job requirement by asking you direct and indirect questions about it.

It is in your best interests to be honest about what you are willing to do regarding traveling and working late. If you know you must pay your dues and will be amenable to doing whatever your boss asks of you, then by all means indicate that during the interview. However, if you are not, you should let the employer know right away. It is always best to be up front and not create false expectations.

WILL YOU TRAVEL?

If an interviewer asks you about your willingness or ability to travel or to work late, saying you can't do it will probably take you out of the running for the job. With that in mind, speak up only if you are positive that you are not able or willing to do something. However, if you don't speak up during the interview, you must do so before accepting a job offer.

A job interview is about more than the employer deciding whether he should hire you. You can use the information you gather to decide whether the company is a good fit for you. You will be able to learn about the demands of the job from some of the interviewer's questions. You may uncover a deal-breaker that was not mentioned in the job description. For example, when an interviewer asks if working late is a problem for you, that indicates the employer will probably expect you to do that. If you can't or don't want to, this is probably not a good place for you to work. You should consider yourself lucky to have learned this now rather than further along in the hiring process, or even worse, once you have accepted a job offer. If extenuating circumstances prevent you from fulfilling a certain job requirement, for example, if you can't work late because of another obligation but you can come in early and are willing to do so, let the interviewer know. Your prospective employer may be able to work within the parameters of your schedule.

In addition to trying to learn what you will bring to the company, a prospective employer may also want to find out what you expect to get from it, particularly your salary requirements. If possible, avoid discussing salary during a job interview, or at least during a first interview. That topic is best put off until you are closer to receiving an offer. If the interviewer asks what salary you are looking for, attempt to turn the question around on him by asking what salary they are offering. If that doesn't work, talk about the typical salary range in your field, leaving an extensive discussion of specifics for later.

Questions and Answers

The department you would be in charge of hasn't had a supervisor in months. This is going to be a big transition for the staff. How will you handle it?

Answer ▶ I wouldn't want to make any big changes for at least the first two weeks. I find it's better to just observe how things are done before trying to make any improvements. I want to gain the staff's trust first and listen to their concerns.

This candidate has a plan in place and she lays it out step by step. She knows that employees who have been unsupervised for a long time need to get used to having someone overseeing their work.

Never Say: "Well, the first thing I would do is make some changes around here. If there hasn't been a supervisor running things for a while, things are sure to be messed up." This is not a well-thought-out answer and could indicate that the applicant might make impulsive decisions.

The person who fills this position will have to work on his own most of the time. Can you handle that?

Answer ▶ I am used to working independently. On my last job, I edited the company newsletter. I was responsible for compiling the material, writing the articles, and preparing the newsletter for publication each quarter. I had to set my own deadlines for each step along the way.

This candidate explains how a project he was responsible for prepared him to work independently.

Never Say: "I love working on my own. It's less distracting." This answer shows that this candidate may be able to work on his own, but he's inflexible. If he had to work with others, could he?

How do you feel about working long hours?

Answer ▶ Can you explain what you mean by long hours? Does that mean working late or getting to work early?

The applicant knows she already has a commitment two nights a week. She doesn't mind getting to work early, though. She decides it's better to find out what her prospective employer's expectations are before she rules anything out or commits to something with which she won't be able to follow through.

Never Say: "I love working long hours. It means I don't have to go home and deal with my family." Even if the applicant is trying to be funny, this is not the place to bring up personal issues.

I DON'T UNDERSTAND THE QUESTION

If you don't understand what the interviewer is asking you or you just need something clarified, it's okay to ask questions during the interview. It is preferable to giving a response that doesn't answer the question.

We're kind of casual here. I see you've worn a suit today. How would you dress for work if I hire you?

Answer ▶ I would adhere to the culture of this company and dress in slacks and a nice shirt.

This candidate knows it's important to fit in with the culture of the workplace. Only after a quick assessment of the interviewer's attire does he go on with the second part of his answer.

Never Say: "I feel more comfortable in a suit." Perhaps he would feel more comfortable elsewhere.

Senior citizens represent a huge market now and we want to convince them to buy our product. If we hired you, how would you help with that?

Answer ▶ In addition to being a big market, the senior market is also a growing market. They are a group with an active lifestyle. Many have expendable income and they choose to use their savings on travel, so it's clear we have a product they will want and we need to reach them. I would do research to find out what publications seniors read and what television shows they watch. Only then can we embark on an advertising campaign.

This candidate demonstrates the methodical approach she would take. She shows her understanding of the market.

Never Say: "Seniors don't have a lot of money to spend, so why would we target them?" This interviewee doesn't know the market and contradicts the interviewer.

We're about to change over to a new software program for our shipping and receiving department. We'd like the person we hire for this position to do the training. Are you the right person for that job?

Answer ▶ I am definitely the right person for this job. As you can see on my resume, my last job was with a software distributor. One of my responsibilities was to travel to our clients' offices to provide software training.

This is one confident candidate who clearly illustrates he has the skills the company is seeking.

Never Say: "Um, I kind of did some training." This applicant doesn't sound very confident.

In about a year we want to open a new branch on the other side of town. We plan to train the person who takes this position to run that office. Is that something you'd be interested in?

Answer ▶ I would welcome that opportunity if it arises.

Notice the applicant says, "If it arises." She wants to express her eagerness to take on more responsibility with this employer without sounding like she'd leave if that opportunity doesn't come up or if such an opportunity comes up sooner with another company.

Never Say: "That's exactly what I'm looking for." Since the candidate only just learned of these plans, how can a job running a new but currently nonexistent office be exactly what she's looking for? What about the job for which she's currently interviewing?

If we hire you, will you be willing to get your certification? You have all the skills we're looking for, but we really need someone who is certified.

Answer ▶ I was planning to take my certification exam in June. That's the next time it's being given.

While it would have been okay for this candidate to say he would get his certification because the prospective employer has asked him to, it's even better that he said he was planning to do it anyway.

Never Say: "I don't understand why certification matters so much, but if you need me to do it I will." Show some enthusiasm, please.

The person who last held this position took ill and has only been able to work off and on for the last three months. Last month he resigned. Things are a huge mess, which the person we hire will need to sort out. Are you up for the challenge?

Answer ▶ I love a good challenge. First I'll sort through the mess to organize it. Then I'll see which things require immediate attention and which things I can work on later.

The interviewee, by giving this answer, shows that she knows how to both organize and prioritize. These are two skills that are extremely important for someone taking over a job that has been neglected.

Never Say: "I'm sure once I see the mess I can figure out what to do with it." Even though this candidate shows confidence, she doesn't present a plan.

The person we hire will have to respond to customer complaints occasionally. Will you be able to do that?

Answer ▶ Years ago I worked in customer service. I'll put that experience to good use.

The interviewee finds some past experience that will help him with this aspect of the job.

Never Say: "I'm sure it won't be too big a deal." If the interviewer bothered to ask this question, it may, in fact, be a big deal.

We often work on teams. Would you rather work on a team or on your own?

Answer ▶ I work well both independently and on a team. In my previous jobs I had to do both. We often worked on teams to complete larger projects. I like how working on a team allows you to draw on the strength of each of its members.

This interviewee shows she is flexible enough to work on either a team or independently but addresses the focus of the question by emphasizing her teamwork skills.

Never Say: "On a team, of course." This candidate just says what she thinks the interviewer wants to hear without giving any proof to back up her answer.

We have several clients with outstanding bills. If we hire you, how will you handle this situation?

Answer ▶ First, I would want to go through the paperwork to make sure these clients were properly notified their accounts are delinquent. If I find out they were notified, I'll call each one personally to discuss this. There might be extenuating circumstances. It's important not to be too heavy-handed in dealing with these types of situations. After all, these are our clients. We don't want to lose them entirely.

This candidate gives a clearly thought-out answer illustrating that he knows how important it is to be diplomatic when dealing with clients.

Never Say: "My first priority would be getting on the phone and getting payment from them quickly." While this might work, it would also alienate clients.

Our clients expect a very quick turnaround on the projects we do for them. Can you handle that?

Answer ▶ Yes, I can. While I was in graduate school, I had several professors who assigned projects that were due only a few days later. I became an expert at scheduling my time around completing these assignments.

Since this interviewee doesn't have work experience to draw upon, she talks about her experience as a student. In the process she highlights a valuable skill—time management.

Never Say: "I'm sure I can." This interviewee needs to give a specific example or, in the absence of one, talk about any skills she possesses that will help her.

If you are hired for this position, you will go from managing your current staff of ten to managing fifty people. Will you be able to oversee a substantially larger staff?

Answer ▶ Yes, I will. Although I've never managed a staff of that size before, I know I have the skills necessary to do it. I am a strong leader. I am good at communicating with my staff so that each member knows what he or she needs to accomplish. I am also adept at delegating responsibilities, which will be even more important with such a large staff.

This candidate lets the interviewer know that he has all the skills that a good manager should have, even though he doesn't have experience with the exact situation he will face.

Never Say: "Since I've never managed such a big staff, I might find it overwhelming. I'm sure I'll be able to handle it, though." This interviewee focuses on the negative rather than on why he can handle the job despite his lack of experience. He should never mention feeling overwhelmed.

We're implementing a new computer system in this department. If we hire you for this position, you'll need to spend a month in Seattle learning how to use it. Are you okay with that?

Answer ▶ That would be fine.

This is a yes or no question. The interviewee doesn't need to say any more than this. However, if the answer is "no" she will need to provide an explanation.

Never Say: "That sounds great, but do you know when that would be? It rains a lot in Seattle and I hate the rain. Don't you?" This candidate has said way too much.

When we are in the process of developing a new product, it's essential that information about it doesn't leak out. How are you at keeping secrets?

Answer ▶ After working in the technology field for the last three years, I know how important it is to keep information confidential until a product is released.

This candidate demonstrates that confidentiality has not been a problem for him in the past.

Never Say: "Wouldn't I have to sign a confidentiality agreement or something?" Is threat of being sued for breach of contract the only thing that would keep this applicant quiet?

CAN YOU KEEP A SECRET?

Companies are always racing to release new products before the competition. They expect their employees to keep any information they learn about the new product behind company doors. You may be asked questions about your ability to adhere to such a requirement.

We currently have several employees who have problems with things like tardiness and excessive personal phone calls. How would you deal with this if we hired you as supervisor?

Answer ▶ First, I would need to find out what is happening. Then, prior to singling out any one employee, I would circulate a memo to the entire department that reiterated the rules. If the behavior continued, I would have a private meeting with each employee who isn't following the rules. I would stress the importance of following the rules and try to find out if there are extenuating circumstances that could be remedied. If the employee continues to break the rules, there would be repercussions.

This interviewee is clearly not one to leap without looking. She knows how important it is to evaluate a situation before taking action. However, she will take action in an expedient manner.

Never Say: "You won't have to worry about anyone breaking the rules once I take over." This candidate must put forth a series of steps she will take to remedy the situation.

Four times a year we work around the clock for about a week. Will that be a problem?

Answer ▶ That's fine with me. I understand the beginning of each season is a very busy time.

Not only is this job candidate willing to work late, he knows enough about the industry to know what times of year this would be expected of him.

Never Say: "Do you let people take vacation during those times?" He hasn't even started and he sounds like he's trying to wiggle out of responsibility.

As my assistant, would I be able to trust you to take over for me whenever I'm out of the office?

Answer ▶ Absolutely. I would follow whatever rules you set forth. I also have excellent judgment, so I can handle whatever comes up.

The applicant uses this opportunity to highlight her skills.

Never Say: "Does that happen a lot?" This answer makes the applicant seem unsure of whether she can handle this responsibility.

Whoever fills this position will need to write next year's budget, which needs to be 10 percent lower than the current one. Could you do this?

Answer ▶ I had to do something similar when my department went through funding cuts last year and I was in charge of writing the new budget. First I reviewed the current year's budget and removed amounts that had been budgeted for one-time events. Then I found a few areas where our actual expenditures were lower than we had budgeted for, and I was able to bring the amount down to more realistic levels, of course accounting for possible price increases. Finally, I went through it to see what cuts would have a minimal effect on services. I cut a program that traditionally had very low attendance. This eliminated the need to hire a part-time instructor. I was able to submit a budget that was 12 percent lower than the one for the previous year.

This candidate demonstrates how he takes a practical approach to trimming a budget. He shows how he is able to get the job done with a minimal effect on service.

Never Say: "Some of the budget cuts I make may be unpopular, but saving the agency money is my priority." It's true that saving money is important. However, there are consequences of making radical cuts that will affect service.

This job requires some travel. Is that a problem?

Answer ▶ I understand that traveling is common in this industry and that's fine with me. I look forward to representing this company around the country.

This candidate has done her homework and wisely speaks of herself as if she has the job.

Never Say: "I love traveling. There are so many places I want to visit." This candidate's mistake is talking about how she will benefit from traveling rather than talking about how her trips will benefit her prospective employer.

The students in this school can be very challenging to manage. As a teacher here, will you be able to handle them?

Answer ▶ I worked with special needs children when I was an assistant teacher at Ardsley School. I learned it is important to look at each child as an individual. Each one has different strengths and weaknesses. If you look at it that way, you can figure out what strategy you need to use to work with each child. Children will trust you when they know you see them as individuals and will usually respond by doing what you need them to do.

Although this candidate is applying for his first professional job, he is still able to draw on past experience. He explains what he learned from his previous experience as an assistant teacher.

Never Say: "I'm a strict disciplinarian, so this won't be a problem." This answer doesn't demonstrate that this interviewee has a strategy for dealing with difficult children.

Anyone who takes this position will need to handle stress well. Are you good at handling stress?

Answer ▶ Yes, I am. My last job was very stressful, but I found that practicing some relaxation techniques like deep breathing helped me combat the stress. I also made sure to take a lunch break every day, since that gives me time to regroup and start the rest of my day with a positive attitude.

This candidate demonstrates that she has strategies in place to help her deal with stress.

Never Say: "If you love your job, you don't find it stressful." That is unrealistic. Even if you love your job, it can be stressful at times. Those who have a coping mechanism will be better able to deal with stressful situations.

In this fast-paced environment we need someone who can think on his feet. Are you that person?

Answer ▶ Yes, I am. I have experience making thoughtful decisions under pressure. I worked at a daily newspaper for five years. Every day we had to make last-minute decisions about what to include in the next day's edition. There was no time to waste when the paper had to go to press within the next half-hour.

This candidate shows how his experience has taught him how to be decisive.

Never Say: "Uhm . . . well, let me think about this. . . . Let's see . . . hmm . . . ." This candidate's hesitation says more than any answer could.

Each employee in this department is on call one weekend a month. How do you feel about that?

Answer ▶ That is fine with me.

The candidate gives a succinct answer, which is all that is needed here.

Never Say: "Would I get paid for being on call?" That question can wait until a job offer is made and salary is negotiated.

Are you willing to work late occasionally?

Answer ▶ I know what it's like when a deadline is coming up. In my last job I was asked to work late from time to time. It was never a problem for me. When a deadline is quickly approaching, I'll be able to make sure we meet it.

By giving this answer, the interviewee not only uses language that lets the interviewer visualize her in the position for which she's interviewing, but also tells her prospective boss that she's worked late in the past.

Never Say: "I'll work late every night if you want me to." Is this interviewee just saying what she thinks the interviewer wants to hear?

WHAT ABOUT RELIGIOUS HOLIDAYS?

If you can't work on a particular day because of your religious beliefs, tell your prospective employer you'd be happy to make up the time on another day. Remember, an employer must reasonably accommodate employees' sincerely held religious beliefs and cannot base a hiring decision on this.

As a contact person for our clients, part of your job is keeping them calm. That means not sharing inconsequential details with them. For example, we never would want a client to know about a small mishap that occurred with a project we were working on for them as long as it was resolved and didn't cause any real problems. Would you be comfortable with that?

Answer ▶ I'm always inclined to be honest but I would always do my best to preserve our relationships with our clients. As long as there was no long-term damage that would reveal itself at a later date, I'm well aware that our clients don't need to know everything that goes on when we are working on their project. No need to worry anyone unnecessarily. Of course, I will work to make sure the problem is resolved as quickly as possible.

Knowing what common practice is in his field helps this candidate answer this question. He know that withholding some information—as long as it isn't damaging in the long run—is okay.

Never Say: "I never ever tell lies, so I can't not tell our clients everything. It's wrong." This candidate may not know the field well enough to give the correct answer. While it may sound virtuous to never tell lies, he doesn't realize that some things shouldn't be shared outside the company for which he works.

It's getting too expensive to operate a business in this city. Would you be willing to relocate?

Answer ▶ I'd be willing to relocate anywhere within the United States.

This candidate gives an honest answer.

Never Say: "I love to move around, so that's really good news." This applicant's answer alludes to the fact that stability isn't his strong suit.

What salary are you looking for?

Answer ▶ From my research, I know the salary range for those with my experience working in this industry here in New York is $51,000 to $55,000 per year. I'm confident we can agree on a salary that is acceptable.

This applicant has done her homework. She gives a range rather than an absolute number, showing her flexibility.

Never Say: "I have to make $52,000 per year." One should always avoid giving an absolute number when discussing salary on a job interview.

I see from the salary history you sent that you were earning $45,000 on your last job. We've taken some losses over the last year and won't be able to pay you that. Will that be a problem?

Answer ▶ I'm sure we can agree on a reasonable salary.

This applicant knows it's better to discuss salary after the employer makes an offer.

Never Say: "How much less than that will it be?" Don't make the employer think you're only in it for the money. The salary discussion should wait until later.

CHAPTER 24

Difficult or Embarrassing Questions

DO YOU DREAD going on job interviews because you are afraid the interviewer will ask you about a situation you find embarrassing or difficult to explain? Were you fired from your last job or is there a huge gap in your work history? The interviewer is likely to notice any gaps or inconsistencies on your resume, so you need to be prepared to answer the questions of which you are most afraid. Here are strategies for coping with that aspect of job interviewing.

I Hope They Don't Ask Me That

When a prospective employer reviews your resume, he will look for things like lengthy gaps between jobs or jobs that don't fit in with the rest of your experience. He will also notice if you hopped around from job to job or if you had a series of jobs that didn't move in an upward direction. An employer will probably question why you were at a job for a short period of time; or he may question why you have been with one employer for your entire career.

An interviewer may ask questions about your lack of experience if he feels you haven't been in the field for long. If you appear to be overqualified, the interviewer will question you about that as well. If you don't have the formal education that is called for, you will be asked to explain why. If your education is in one area and the job you are interviewing for is in another, the interviewer will inquire about that, too.

WHAT A RESUME DOESN'T REVEAL

An interviewer will ask you to discuss things he can't ascertain from reading your resume. While your resume gives the period of time you worked at every job, it doesn't show why you left each one. A prospective employer will want to know about that. He may also ask you to discuss your relationships with supervisors and coworkers.

How to Answer Difficult Questions

When you answer difficult questions, be honest. Don't make excuses for things, and do not lie. For example, if you got fired from a job, don't tell the interviewer you quit. She can learn the truth from a simple call to your former employer or through a background check, so you are better off being up front no matter how embarrassed you feel. The interviewer will appreciate your candor. If you lie, you will have two strikes against you. Not only will a prospective employer know you got fired, but you will have shown her you are dishonest. Don't place blame on your former employer or speak negatively about him. When possible, highlight the positive and talk about what you have done to overcome whatever it is that put a blemish on your past.

If an employer asks about a gap in employment, be honest about why it's there. Discuss things you did during that time to enhance your skills. For example, if you took time off to be at home with young children, talk about how you kept up with your career by reading professional literature and taking classes. If you didn't give much thought to your career during that time, or have decided to enter a new field, talk about how you are preparing now for your return to work.

Address concerns about your lack of education or experience by explaining what you've done to compensate for it. If your experience makes up for your lack of a formal degree, say so and explain how this is the case. If you plan to take some courses to enhance your skills, elaborate on that. Remember to be specific when you discuss your plans.

If you were fired from a previous job, you may be concerned that revealing that information will take you out of the running for a job, but don't try to hide it. The prospective employer will probably want to talk to your prior boss before she hires you. When she does, she will learn the truth.

ANOTHER WORD FOR "FIRED"

You don't have to use the word "fired" to say you had to leave a job. It has a negative connotation, as do "terminated" or "dismissed." You can say you had a "parting of the ways" or a "disagreement," which basically means the same thing but doesn't sound as harsh.

If you have been job-hunting for a while, you are probably concerned that a prospective employer will wonder why. You can blame the economy if the current one is bad. Even if the general economy is good, the market for someone with your skills may not be. Make sure the market really is bad; you don't want to infer that you don't understand the industry. State your skills and say that you haven't been able to find a job where those skills are needed.

Questions and Answers

You were at your last job for only six months. Why were you there for such a short time?

Answer ▶ Unfortunately, the job turned out to be much different from what I thought it would be. It's a good thing I discovered this early on before the employer invested more time in me and I invested more time in the company. I know I could put my editing skills to much better use in this position.

Notice the interviewer places no blame on either himself or his employer. He doesn't say the employer didn't tell him the truth about the job or that he misunderstood what he'd be doing. He also shows how he looked out for both his employer and himself by leaving before more time was invested.

Never Say: "My boss blatantly lied to me during the interview. The job turned out to be very different from what she told me." This candidate's mistake was speaking poorly of his boss.

NO NEGATIVITY, PLEASE

Keep your negativity in check when you talk about a former employer. No matter how much you hate him, keep your feelings to yourself. Speak poorly of your former boss and a prospective employer will wonder if someday you will speak poorly of her.

What do your subordinates think of you?

Answer ▶ They think I'm a tough boss. I expect a lot out of them.

This candidate, by giving this succinct answer, provides just enough information to answer the question. He makes no indication of whether his subordinates like him or not.

Never Say: "I'm a tough boss and because of that my subordinates resent me." This interviewee has said more than he needs to.

I see from your resume that you've had five jobs in five years. Why have you moved around so much?

Answer ▶ When I first graduated from college, I wasn't sure what I wanted to do. After trying out several jobs, I have come to the conclusion that this field is the right one for me. I even took some courses to enhance my skills. I know I can do a good job here.

This is an honest answer. The candidate states that she has figured out what she wants to do and is now committed to this field. She then goes on to prove it by talking about how she is enhancing her skills.

Never Say: "I can't stay in one place for too long. . . . I mean, I couldn't stay in one place too long. Now I can." The candidate can't keep her answers straight. Is her need to move around still a problem? This interviewer is sure to be suspicious.

You've been out of the job market for six years. Can you explain that, please?

Answer ▶ I took a hiatus from the workforce to raise my children. I am now ready to come back and use my skills. I have kept up with developments in the field during my absence by reading professional literature and attending seminars.

This candidate doesn't make excuses for his time away from the workforce. He does make a point of letting the employer know he didn't lose track of his career during this time.

Never Say: "I was busy raising my family, but I can't afford to stay home anymore." This doesn't let the employer know that this candidate is ready to return to the workforce and wants to do that, only that he needs to. The interviewer will wonder if this candidate will stop working should his financial situation change.

According to your resume, you were a manager at Crane Computer Store from 1990 through 1995 and then assistant manager at a different branch of the store starting in 1995. Were you demoted?

Answer ▶ This wasn't a demotion. I was originally manager of the paper products department. It was a very small section. When an opening came up for an assistant manager in the home PC department at another store, I jumped at the chance. It was a much better opportunity because it was a much larger department and I knew I would have greater responsibilities.

Although her job title would indicate this candidate had been demoted, she explains why this wasn't actually the case. She was willing to trade the manager title for a job with more responsibility. If she had been demoted, however, she would need to explain why.

Never Say: "I didn't want all the responsibility of being a manager." Should this candidate really say she doesn't want a job with responsibility?

Why did you leave Community Publications Corporation?

Answer ▶ My boss and I had a difference of opinion and we decided it would be best if I left my job.

The interviewee decides to be honest about his reasons for leaving his job. He doesn't blame his boss or berate himself, but simply tells the truth about being fired.

Never Say: "That idiot fired me." Making disparaging comments about your boss is a poor choice.

Tell me how your career progressed at your last job.

Answer ▶ I was hired as assistant to the staff accountant. When she left, I was asked to take her position. After three months, my boss and I decided that I didn't yet have the skills for such a demanding job after all, and I stepped back into the assistant position when they hired someone with more experience. That was three years ago, and I now have the experience I needed back then.

The candidate gives an honest answer. He explains that his "backward" progress from accountant to assistant was due to his lack of experience. He claims that he now has the experience to be a staff accountant.

Never Say: "They promoted me before I was ready and then when they found someone they liked better, they sent me back to my original job." This answer makes the candidate sound very bitter about what happened. He also doesn't say anything about the skills he currently has.

If I asked your previous supervisor for a reference, how would she describe you?

Answer ▶ My supervisor and I often disagreed about many things. One thing we would agree on, I think, is that I did my job well.

This candidate is in a tricky situation. He and his supervisor didn't get along well, but that doesn't mean he wasn't a good employee. He gives this answer hoping his former boss will put their differences aside and be honest about his performance at work if she is called as a reference.

Never Say: "She probably has nothing nice to say. She's always had it in for me." This candidate doesn't give his supervisor a chance to say something bad about him—he does it himself.

Your resume says that you are an administrative assistant, yet you're applying for a job that has much more responsibility. What makes you think you can handle it?

Answer ▶ Even though my job title is administrative assistant, I have many more responsibilities than that title usually implies. I train all new support staff and supervise junior clerks.

This answer explains how this candidate's responsibilities differed from what one might assume from her job title. She chooses to discuss the aspects of her current job that are related to the job for which she is interviewing.

Never Say: "Even though I was technically an administrative assistant, I did a lot of other stuff." The candidate needs to be more specific and explain what that "other stuff" was in order to demonstrate she has experience handling the responsibilities she would have on the job for which she is interviewing.

You seem to be overqualified for this position. Why do you want this job?

Answer ▶ I definitely bring a lot of skills to this job. I look forward to using my experience to help your company grow.

Rather than downplay his skills in response to what the interviewer has said, this candidate chooses to talk about how his experience and skills will benefit the company.

Never Say: "I don't really have that much experience." A job candidate should never make less of his skills, regardless of what the interviewer thinks.

There's a ten-year gap in your employment history. What were you doing during that time?

Answer ▶ I was convicted of theft and was incarcerated at the state penitentiary from 1989 through 1999. During that time I earned a degree in social work that I want to use in working with young people who may be headed in the wrong direction.

A conviction will show up during a background check so it makes no sense for her to lie. She makes a point of discussing why she is qualified for the job for which she has applied.

Never Say: "I took some time off from the work force." The employer may hire the candidate in spite of a prior conviction, especially if she shows that she has turned her life around. However, if she lies about the conviction and the employer finds out the truth, she probably won't get the job.

Have you ever been convicted of a felony?

Answer ▶ Yes, I have. I served three years for a hit and run. I finished my college courses while I was in jail.

This candidate gives an honest answer and hopes it won't affect his chances of being hired. Generally, the interviewer can ask if a job candidate has ever been convicted of a felony.

Never Say: "Why? Are you going to do a background check?" The employer will certainly do a background check after hearing that response or she may simply decide to take this candidate out of consideration for the job.

In your first job out of college you worked as a receptionist. Weren't you a little overqualified?

Answer ▶ My education did overqualify me for that job, but I was determined to work in the advertising industry. I knew if I took that job, it would give me the chance to show off my skills. I volunteered to do some proofreading for the copywriter, and after six months he asked me to be his assistant.

This candidate shows the interviewer that she knew what she had to do to reach her goals. She also tells the interviewer that her plan worked.

Never Say: "It was the only thing available." This applicant did not have a clear goal in mind when she took the job.

On your resume you indicated that you attended Harkin College for a few years, but I don't see a degree listed. Did you graduate?

Answer ▶ No, I didn't graduate. I withdrew from the college during my junior year. I decided that I wasn't getting as much out of college as I should have, so I decided to go to work. I plan to continue my education in the future.

This is an honest answer. The candidate takes responsibility for discontinuing his formal education and expresses his desire to complete his education.

Never Say: "The school was horrible. I didn't want to waste my parents' money." If this was the real reason this job candidate dropped out of school he probably would have finished his education elsewhere.

What were your grades like in college?

Answer ▶ My grades could have been better. If I had it to do over again, I would have studied a lot harder than I did.

The candidate doesn't blame anyone but herself for her poor grades and makes a point of saying she would do things differently now.

Never Say: "They were okay." If the candidate did poorly in school she should admit it. If the employer asks for a copy of her college transcript, which he might, the candidate will be caught in a lie. Furthermore, having described her poor grades as "okay," the interviewer may question why the applicant's expectations are so low she thinks earning bad grades is okay.

If we hire you, the person who will be your supervisor is much younger than you are. Will this be a problem for you?

Answer ▶ If she has the skills necessary to be a supervisor, I will be happy to work for her.

This candidate gives a straightforward answer. He does not know whether the interviewer is concerned about whether he will not be able to take direction from someone younger or if the interviewer is implying the candidate is too old for the job. The applicant chooses to simply address the interviewer's concern about his ability to take direction from a younger supervisor.

Never Say: "Are you implying that I'm old?" The candidate is much too confrontational, which will turn the interviewer off regardless of what her question implies.

A GRAYING WORKFORCE

According to one government estimate, 93 percent of the growth in the U.S. labor force between 2006 and 2016 will be among workers age 55 or older. The 2007–08 recession delayed retirement plans for many older workers.

I see you left your last job about eight months ago. Have you been looking for work since then? Can you explain that?

Answer ▶ Yes, I have been looking for a job for the last several months. I am skilled in technical support, system design and implementation, and training. I haven't been able to find a position for someone with my skills.

This candidate gives an honest answer to the question. He states his skills and then explains that the job market has been tight for someone with those skills. Since he has no control over the job market, he doesn't have to make excuses for it.

Never Say: "I know if I had looked harder for a job, I would have found one. After all, I have great skills." The candidate may think it's better to say he couldn't find a job because he wasn't looking for one, but this answer only shows his lack of motivation.

Why are you applying for a job outside the subject in which you majored?

Answer ▶ I can use the skills I developed as a psychology major to succeed in marketing research. I have taken courses in consumer behavior, statistics, and research design, which I know will be useful in this field.

This candidate shows how her skills are transferable to this field. If she plans to further pursue a career in psychology, she doesn't imply it by giving this answer.

Never Say: "I need to work to save up money for graduate school." The employer has good reason to wonder how long this person will stay if he hires her.

You don't seem to have a great deal of work experience. Why should we hire you?

Answer ▶ I may not have a lot of paid work experience, but I have a lot of volunteer experience. I organized a voter registration drive in my community and registered 300 new voters during the last election. For the past four years I have chaired the committee that runs the book fair at my son's school. We have raised more than $7,000 each year.

While this candidate doesn't have paid work experience, she has been able to hone her skills through her volunteer work. She has persuaded people to register to vote and worked on a committee that successfully ran a major fundraising event. She even gives dollar amounts to back up her claims.

Never Say: "I really want this job, and I know I will be good at it." This candidate needs to tell the interviewer what skills she has and how she will use them to benefit his company.

Aren't you underqualified for this job?

Answer ▶ I don't think I am. While it's true I don't have a lot of experience yet, I do have very good skills, as we discussed earlier. I am willing to learn any additional skills I need to have to do this job.

The candidate doesn't try to explain her lack of experience. Instead she talks about the skills she has (and would have given more details if she hadn't discussed them earlier) and expresses her willingness to learn new ones.

Never Say: "I don't have a lot of experience, but how can I get any if no one will hire me?" Although what she is saying is true, this answer highlights the candidate's inexperience instead of addressing her attributes and willingness to learn.

You've worked at the same company since you graduated from high school fifteen years ago. Why are you looking for a new job now?

Answer ▶ I learned a lot at my current job and I was given the opportunity to take on many different responsibilities. I decided to get some formal training to enhance my skills in bookkeeping and word processing. That training qualifies me for a job that requires greater skills than my current one does.

This candidate wants to use his new skills and therefore must change jobs. This is reasonable and shows he is motivated to do the best he can.

Never Say: "I'm bored." Many people leave their jobs because they are bored. However, that's not a good way to impress a prospective employer. The candidate should name something specific about this new job that he is looking forward to.

You're so young. What makes you think you can do a good job?

Answer ▶ I have a lot of experience in retail. I started working as a retail clerk straight out of high school and over the last three years I worked my way up to assistant manager.

Rather than letting the interviewer lead her into a discussion about her age, this candidate leads him into a discussion about her experience.

Never Say: "What does my age have to do with it?" While it is reasonable to have reservations about the interviewer's motives, her approach is too confrontational.

Your resume doesn't show any formal training in this field. What do you think qualifies you for this job?

Answer ▶ While I don't have formal training in this field, I do have a lot of practical experience. As you can see from my resume, I spent a tremendous amount of time doing research in my last job. I plan to begin taking some courses so I can get my degree in this field.

This interviewee explains how her experience has given her the skills she needs to do this job. She also talks about her intention to get some formal training.

Never Say: "I'm going to get my degree." While this answer shows this candidate plans to develop her skills, it doesn't indicate she currently has the skills necessary for this job.

I see that all of your work experience has been in sales. What qualifies you to work in fundraising?

Answer ▶ Both sales and fundraising involve persuasion. In sales I had to persuade people to buy our products. I was very good at it. I had the highest level of sales of anyone in my division. Now I would like to use those skills to convince people to donate money to this organization.

This candidate discusses how he can transfer his sales skills to a career in fundraising.

Never Say: "I think I will really like this field a lot more." This doesn't adequately explain why he is qualified for the job.

I noticed your three previous jobs were in three different cities. Why did you move around so much?

Answer ▶ My wife was in the Marines, but she is retired now and working as a civilian in this city, so we're finally done moving around.

As a general rule, marital status should not be discussed on a job interview. However, the candidate must explain why he has moved around so much in the past and why he won't be doing that in the future.

Never Say: "I won't be moving around a lot anymore." The interviewee should give a more elaborate answer than this one. If he doesn't want to bring up his marital status, he can say there were reasons he had to move around in the past, but some changes have brought more stability to his life.

I see you were manager at Wanda's Whispers. What type of business is that and what did you do there?

Answer ▶ Wanda's Whispers is a retail store that sells women's lingerie. I was the store manager. I interviewed, hired, and trained the store's sales team.

Although she may be embarrassed to discuss the nature of the business, she proudly discusses her responsibilities there.

Never Say: "The store sells ladies' apparel." The candidate is so flustered when she has to discuss this job that she neglects to discuss what she did there.

AN EMBARRASSING PAST?

You may be embarrassed by the nature of a company you worked for in the past. You don't have to go into details, but remember the employer can do his own research. Focus instead on what your duties were when you worked there and how they relate to the job for which you are applying.

You've been out of the workforce for five years. Why re-enter it now?

Answer ▶ I have a lot to offer. I've developed many skills over the last five years and I want to put them to use. I have excellent organization and time management skills. I am also great at resolving conflicts.

Rather than discuss how re-entering the workforce will benefit her, this candidate instead highlights what she can bring to the job.

Never Say: "I'm in the process of getting divorced, so I have to go back to work." This is more information than the candidate should share.

I see you have a GED. Why did you drop out of high school?

Answer ▶ I guess I was young and foolish then. It was a long time ago. I thought I didn't need school anymore, but I was sadly mistaken. I got my GED three years later and then went on to college. I'm looking forward to applying my training as a registered nurse to this position.

Youthful indiscretions can be forgiven. Although this candidate dropped out of high school, he did continue his education and is planning to move forward with his career.

Never Say: "I don't remember. It was a long time ago." That isn't something one would easily forget. Since the candidate has gone on to complete his education, he shouldn't be ashamed to talk about his past.

You didn't start working until two years after you got your degree. What were you doing?

Answer ▶ I traveled extensively the year after I graduated from college. I backpacked across Europe for three months and then I spent four months in Australia. After that I traveled across the United States.

Had this candidate said that she sat at home watching television for a year after graduating, the interviewer would have assumed she was a little low on motivation. However, she explored the world, which was an admirable use of her time.

Never Say: "I needed to take some time off. College was hard." Even if this candidate didn't have as interesting a story to tell as the previous candidate, she should have explained what she did during that time.

You've been working outside the banking industry for the last year. Can you explain why you want to return now?

Answer ▶ Yes, I can. The job market, as you know, has been bad for the last year and a half. It's been impossible for someone with my qualifications to find a job in the banking industry. In order to support my family, I had to take jobs in retail sales. I was happy to see your ad for a banking job that needs someone with my skills in branch management.

This candidate's only choice is to be honest. He is not to blame for the bad job market, so he makes no excuses for working outside his field for a year.

Never Say: "I wanted to try out a new industry." It's okay to try out a new industry, but this candidate should explain why he wants to return to his old one.

CLEAN YOUR CYBERSPACE

Employers often search the Internet for information about prospective employees. If there's anything inappropriate about you out there in cyberspace, remove it. If you are unsure about what might be considered inappropriate, think of things you wouldn't want your grandmother to see. Make your MySpace or Facebook page private if you have inappropriate content on it.

I did a little web search and found your MySpace page. That's some very interesting stuff you posted. Care to explain?

Answer ▶ Everyone has a work persona and a personal time persona, I think. You should know I take my job very seriously. That means I give it my full attention while I'm working.

This job hunter forgot to make her pages private. Since the interviewer has already found potentially embarrassing material about her online, she knows it's too late for denials. All she can do at this point is stress that her private life won't interfere with her work life.

Never Say: "What page?" or "What I do on my own time is my business." Playing dumb won't work if the evidence of your after-work behavior exists online. As for the second option, while you might feel your private time is yours to do with as you wish, you need to reassure a potential employer that your behavior won't spill over into your work life by, for example, making you late to work or causing you to arrive at work with a hangover.

CHAPTER 25

Dealing with Illegal Questions

EITHER OUT OF ignorance or blatant disregard for antidiscrimination laws, prospective employers sometimes ask questions that are often referred to as "illegal." Whether or not these questions are actually illegal will be discussed in this chapter. The employer usually doesn't have your best interests at heart if he asks them. If you know what your rights are before going into an interview, you will be able to recognize questions that are inappropriate, if not illegal.

Laws That Protect You from Discrimination

There are federal laws that make it illegal for employers to discriminate against employees and job applicants. These laws include Title VII of the Civil Rights Act of 1964, the Age Discrimination in Employment Act of 1967, and Title I of the Americans with Disabilities Act, all of which the Equal Employment Opportunity Commission (EEOC) oversees. The National Labor Relations Act, which is enforced by the National Labor Relations Board, is another law that protects individuals from job discrimination. The Civil Service Reform Act of 1978 prohibits federal agencies from discriminating against their workers and job applicants. Let's look at these laws and how they can protect you in more detail.

Title VII of the Civil Rights Act of 1964

Title VII of the Civil Rights Act of 1964 prohibits employers from discriminating against employees and prospective employees because of their race, color, religion, sex, or national origin.

RACE AND COLOR DISCRIMINATION

An employer cannot reject a job candidate based on the candidate's race or color. If an interviewer requests information that will disclose the candidate's race, the EEOC interprets it to mean the information obtained will be used as a basis for making a hiring decision. The request for that information would likely be used as evidence should the candidate bring charges of discrimination against the employer.

ASKING ABOUT RACE

An employer can ask for information on race if it is needed for affirmative action purposes, in which case it would have to be kept separately from the information that is used to make a hiring decision.

NATIONAL ORIGIN DISCRIMINATION

An employer cannot discriminate against an individual because of her national origin, meaning the country she or her parents are from. Therefore, an interviewer may not ask you where you were born or where your parents were born. He may not ask you if you speak a foreign language unless it pertains to the duties of the job for which you are interviewing.

RELIGIOUS DISCRIMINATION

An employer cannot use an applicant's religious beliefs in deciding whether or not to hire you. An employer cannot ask you what your religion is, if you belong to any religious groups, or if you go to a house of worship. She also cannot ask if your religious beliefs prevent you from working on certain days.

PREGNANCY DISCRIMINATION

The Pregnancy Discrimination Act was passed in 1978 as an Amendment to Title VII of the Civil Rights Act. It states that as long as a woman is able to perform the major functions of her job, she cannot be passed over for employment because of a pregnancy-related condition. An interviewer cannot ask if you are pregnant or if you plan to become pregnant in the future.

The Age Discrimination in Employment Act of 1967

The Age Discrimination in Employment Act makes it illegal for employers to discriminate against employees or job candidates on the basis of age. It protects those who are at least forty years old. An interviewer may not ask you how old you are or when you graduated from high school or college, since providing that information would force you to reveal your age.

Title I of the Americans with Disabilities Act of 1990

Title I of the Americans with Disabilities Act prohibits employers from discriminating against workers or job applicants who have disabilities. This law actually makes asking some questions illegal. The ADA prohibits an employer who has not yet made a job offer to a candidate from asking questions that are likely to reveal a candidate's disability.

For example, an interviewer can't ask questions about health problems, such as a heart condition or asthma, or about mental illness. He cannot ask a candidate if she has a disability that would keep her from performing the job. Even if a candidate has an obvious disability or reveals a hidden one, the employer cannot ask about it. There is one exception. An employer can ask a job candidate to explain how she will perform specific job functions.

IS EVERYONE PROTECTED?

Not all companies must adhere to federal discrimination laws. You can determine whether or not a company is required to follow a particular law by finding out how many workers it employs. This number varies by law but generally falls into a range of between fifteen and twenty employees.

An employer may not require a candidate to take a medical exam prior to receiving a job offer. However, once the employer makes a job offer, he can make it contingent on the employee passing a medical exam, as long as the same is required of all candidates to whom the employer offers jobs in the same category. If the results of that exam reveal a disability, a job offer may be rescinded only if the employer's reason for doing so is "job-related and consistent with business necessity," according to the EEOC.

National Labor Relations Act

The National Labor Relations Act regulates the way in which unions and private-sector employers interact. It gives employees the right to organize unions and to engage in union activities without interference from their employers. According to the National Labor Relations Board, which administers the NLRA, an employer can't discriminate against a job candidate or employee because of her union affiliation.

Civil Service Reform Act

The Civil Service Reform Act of 1978 prohibits federal agencies from discriminating against job applicants and employees on the bases of race, color, national origin, religion, sex, age, disability, marital status, political affiliation and sexual orientation. The U.S. Office of Special Council investigates reports of discrimination against federal job applicants.

STATE LAW VERSUS FEDERAL LAW

State and municipal laws protect against job discrimination. They often take precedence over the federal laws. Some of these laws protect workers and job candidates against discrimination on the bases of sexual orientation, marital status, political affiliation, and parental status. Your local district office of the EEOC can help you determine if a prospective employer has broken a state or local law.

What Questions Are Illegal?

Although we often hear people talk about illegal interview questions, most discrimination laws don't prohibit any questions outright. The exception is the ADA, which actually does say it is illegal to ask a job candidate whether she has a disability.
As far as the other laws are concerned, the asking of the question itself is usually not illegal. It is problematic; it can demonstrate the employer's intent to discriminate. If an employer uses your answer to one of these questions to deny you a job, that can be considered discriminatory.

MAKING A REPORT

If you believe an employer has discriminated against you, you can file a charge of discrimination with the EEOC. Call the EEOC at 1-800-669-4000 or 1-800-669-6820 (TTY) between 8:30 A.M. and 5:30 P.M. Eastern Standard Time to find out how to do this. You can also send an e-mail to *info@eeoc.gov*. In addition, instructions are available on the EEOC website, *www.eeoc.gov*.

If you envision an interviewer being carted off to the police station in handcuffs after asking you an inappropriate question, you will be disappointed to learn that is an unlikely scenario. Even if the questions were illegal or information obtained during an interview was in fact used to discriminate against you, the job candidate would have to report the employer to the EEOC before any action would be taken. The result would be a lawsuit and possible fine, not jail time.

As a job applicant, you may be asked some sensitive questions. The next section deals with the right and wrong ways to handle them.

Questions and Answers

How old are you?

Answer ▶ I prefer to think of myself in terms of experience and not age. I have worked in this industry for quite some time. I have seen it go from a small playing field to what it is today. Fortunately, I have kept up with all the changes by taking classes and constantly updating my skills.

Rather than address the issue of age or the inappropriateness of this question, this candidate has instead decided to address some positive things about himself. He has a lot of experience and he strives to keep himself abreast of changes in the industry by taking classes.

Never Say: "I'm fifty-two, but I look young for my age." This applicant should have avoided revealing his age.

How much do you weigh?

Answer ▶ My weight isn't an issue. I have never had a problem performing my job duties.

This question is not only rude, it may be illegal as well, according to the ADA. This candidate explains how her weight doesn't affect her ability to do her job.

Never Say: "I'm thinking of getting my stomach stapled." Although he has asked a rude and possibly illegal question, the employer has learned that this candidate might need some time off from work, and she hasn't even started yet.

What is your race?

Answer ▶ I'm African American and Asian.

If an employer asks a question about race, her intentions are usually not good, so make a mental note that you were asked. If the employer discriminates against you based on your race, the information you provided in this answer can be used as evidence against her if you file a complaint with the EEOC.

Never Say: "That is an illegal question. You can't ask me that." You are certainly within your rights to take an interviewer to task for asking such an inappropriate question, but the question in itself isn't illegal unless the information garnered from it is used to discriminate against you.

Were you born in the United States?

Answer ▶ I'm not sure why you're asking me that. Can you explain?

This question is inappropriate and the employer probably knows that. The candidate gives him a chance to correct himself. Perhaps the employer needs to know if the candidate is eligible to work in the United States.

Never Say: "I came here from Poland two years ago." The candidate is not required to reveal that information.

Where were your parents born?

Answer ▶ My parents came to this country thirty years ago. They worked very hard to put me through school and are very proud of my successful career. They passed their work ethic down to me.

This candidate chooses not to reveal his national origin and instead manages to talk about her own qualities. There is nothing that says a candidate shouldn't reveal her national origin, only that she doesn't have to.

Never Say: "My parents are from Greece and Portugal." This candidate is giving out more information than is necessary.

Your last name sounds Spanish. Is it?

Answer ▶ Yes, it is.

The applicant has a choice to make. He can refuse to answer or he can just give a simple answer, as he did. If this was the only question of this type, the interviewer may have just been trying to make conversation.

Never Say: "My father was born in Guatemala. My mother was born in Ireland." This candidate reveals more about his national origin than he needs to.

CONFIDENCE WINS YOU POINTS

You should always make a point of sounding confident when answering questions on a job interview. If you sound unsure of yourself, the interviewer will pick up on it. Your confidence—or lack thereof—is also apparent in your body language, so be aware of what your posture and gestures say about you.

What is your sexual orientation?

Answer ▶ I don't think that has anything to do with this job.

Sexual orientation isn't something that should be discussed on a job interview.

Never Say: "I'm gay" or "I'm straight." While employers might, according to some state laws, be prohibited from using the answer to this question to discriminate against a job candidate because of her sexual orientation, this information isn't relevant to the job interview.

SEXUAL ORIENTATION DISCRIMINATION

There currently aren't any federal laws that protect private sector employees and job applicants from discrimination based on one's sexual orientation or gender identity. Some states and local municipalities have such laws, and the Civil Service Reform Act protects federal workers from discrimination based on sexual orientation.

How tall are you?

Answer ▶ I'm five foot seven.

Although an employer shouldn't ask an applicant about any physical characteristics, including height and weight, answering it shouldn't cause a problem.

Never Say: "You can't ask me that." While that is true, that response may unnecessarily cause hard feelings, especially if the interviewer meant no harm in asking it.

What is your religious background?

Answer ▶ I consider religion a very personal thing, so I would rather not discuss it.

The applicant can always choose to politely refuse to answer a question he considers improper.

Never Say: "How dare you ask me that?" While the candidate can refuse to answer the question, there is no reason to be that confrontational. That can certainly hurt your chances of getting hired.

Will your religion keep you from working on Saturday or Sunday?

Answer ▶ Perhaps we can discuss the details of my schedule after we both confirm that I'm the right candidate for this position.

This candidate knows Title VII of the Civil Rights Act requires that an employer reasonably accommodate the religious practices of an employee or applicant as long as doing so doesn't pose a hardship. She also knows that an employer cannot decide to reject a candidate based on the knowledge that this accommodation will be necessary. However, she chooses to wait until she receives an offer before discussing this.

Never Say: "I can't work on Saturday." Although the employer can't make a decision based on this information, it isn't necessary to discuss it at this point.

Do you have any children?

Answer ▶ You may be concerned that having a family might get in the way of someone's career. However, that has never been the case with me. I'm dedicated to my career.

Without giving a direct answer to this question, the candidate has chosen to reassure the employer that having a family, or not having one, will not influence his career.

Never Say: "I don't have children yet." If the employer chooses not to hire this candidate, it may be because this answer indicates he might have children in the future. Whether or not this constitutes discrimination is debatable since he doesn't currently have children.

BALANCING FAMILY AND CAREER

When faced with an improper question about your family or marital status, you can choose to address the issue head-on. You can reassure the interviewer that having a family has not and will not interfere with your career.

Are you planning to have children?

Answer ▶ I am committed to my career. Whether or not I have children will not affect that.

This interviewee tells the employer the only thing she has the right to know—that she is dedicated to her career.

Never Say: "I've always wanted to have children." The candidate did not have to answer this question.

What child care arrangements do you have in place?

Answer ▶ I'm sensing that you may have concerns about scheduling. I have a great attendance record on my current job. I haven't missed a day of work in two years.

This candidate has decided to address the intent of the interviewer's question. Since he believes she is afraid that child care problems will cause him to miss work, he informs her of his perfect attendance record.

Never Say: "My child goes to day care." The employer is out of line in asking this question. However, this candidate's answer only heightens her concern since a child will not be able to go to day care when he is ill. That means Mom or Dad may have to miss work.

Are you married?

Answer ▶ No, I'm not.

Although this question is inappropriate and may even be illegal depending on state or municipal laws, the candidate sees no harm in answering it.

Never Say: "I'm getting married in six months and let's see . . . sixteen days." This answer implies that the interviewee is very immersed in her wedding plans and perhaps may not be able to give the necessary attention to her job.

Do you belong to a union?

Answer ▶ Will I be required to join a union?

The NLRA prohibits employers from questioning applicants about their union sympathies. This candidate chooses to avoid the question by asking his own.

Never Say: "Yes." The employer can't make a decision based on this information and shouldn't have asked it in the first place. The candidate certainly didn't have to answer it.

Are you a Democrat or Republican?

Answer ▶ I've always felt that it's a bad idea to discuss politics with anyone. Therefore, I'm going to refrain from answering that question.

The candidate has given a polite answer but has refused to provide the information the interviewer improperly requested.

Never Say: "I'm a Democrat." Your political affiliation has nothing to do with how well you perform on the job. There is no reason an interviewer needs to know this.

CIVIL SERVICE REFORM ACT

There aren't any federal laws that protect private sector employees or job applicants from discrimination on the basis of political affiliation. The Civil Service Reform Act prohibits federal government agencies from discriminating against employees or job candidates because of their political affiliation. Some state and local laws also make this type of discrimination illegal.

Will your spouse mind the long hours you will have to work here?

Answer ▶ I've always worked very long hours so this won't be a problem.

This candidate chooses to address the question about the long hours she will be required to work rather than address her marital status.

Never Say: "My husband would love me to get a job with fewer hours, but there aren't many like that out there. right now" There is no reason to give this much information. The interviewee's answer will set off some alarms. Since her husband is unhappy with her hours, she would probably take a job with fewer hours if it came along.

IMPROPER QUESTIONS

When an interviewer asks you an improper question, you have three basic options. You can refuse to answer it, you can confront the interviewer, or you can answer it. Information you give voluntarily can be used against the employer if he discriminates.

How do you want to be addressed? Miss or Mrs.?

Answer ▶ You can just call me Robin.

The interviewer is trying to ascertain the candidate's marital status, but she won't play into it. She dodges the issue altogether.

Never Say: "I prefer Mrs. Brown." The candidate could have avoided letting the interviewer know her marital status.

Have you ever been arrested or convicted of a crime?

Answer ▶ No. I have never been convicted of a crime.

According to the law in many states, an employer may not ask you if you have ever been arrested, but, depending on where the employer is located, he may be able to ask you if you've been convicted of a crime. In some states convictions for certain types of crimes can be used when considering whether to hire a job candidate. Notice how this candidate avoids the arrest question. She doesn't want to lie or discuss an arrest that she was not convicted for.

Never Say: "I was arrested once but I wasn't convicted." Again, depending on the law in your state, the employer may only ask about prior convictions. The applicant may not have to talk about her arrest at all.

Have you ever committed a crime?

Answer ▶ If you're asking if I've ever been convicted of a crime, no I haven't been.

If the employer is located in a state that prohibits discrimination based on a candidate's arrest record, but allows hiring decisions to be made based on whether or not someone has been convicted, the applicant is not required to reveal prior arrests or criminal behavior.

Never Say: "Yes, but I was never convicted."

WHAT IF I WAS IN JAIL?

If you were convicted of a felony, this information will be revealed in a background check. You might as well be up front about it. If the prospective employer is located in a state that only allows a conviction to weigh into a hiring decision if it is for a crime directly related to the job description, then the law may protect you from discrimination.

I see you're limping. Did you hurt yourself?

Answer ▶ I'm fine, thank you.

The employer, according to ADA, cannot inquire about an applicant's injury and the candidate is under no obligation to reveal it.

Never Say: "I have cerebral palsy." The candidate is not required to reveal any information regarding his disability.

Do you have a heart condition?

Answer ▶ With all due respect, I don't have to answer that question.

The applicant has a right to refuse to answer this question. The ADA makes it illegal for an employer to ask questions about a job candidate's health.

Never Say: "Yes, I do." The employer is legally prohibited from asking this question and the candidate does not have to answer it.

DISABILITY QUESTIONS

The ADA prohibits an employer from asking about the nature of an applicant's disability. It does allow an employer to inquire about a candidate's ability to perform a job-related task and, in some cases, may even ask the applicant to demonstrate how she will perform that task.

Will you need us to make any accommodations in order for you to do your job?

Answer ▶ I am able to perform all functions of the job as you described it.

ADA prohibits the employer from asking this question, even if he asks it of all applicants.

Never Say: "Yes, I will." The applicant doesn't have to answer this question. If she chooses to, the employer can't decide not to hire her because of her answer, unless the accommodations she needs will cause the employer undue hardship.

Have you ever been treated for mental health problems?

Answer ▶ I have, but everything is under control now. I have always performed well at work and I know I will continue to.

Although he is under no obligation to reveal this information at any time, this candidate doesn't want to lie to his employer and knows that the truth may come out at some point in the future.

Never Say: "No, I haven't" if you have. This candidate just lied to his prospective employer. Although he is within his legal rights to withhold information regarding his mental health, he has to consider whether he plans to reveal this information at a later date and what the consequences may be if he does. Although the employer can't fire an employee because of the employee's mental illness, she may distrust him for lying, which will damage their relationship. He would be better off telling the truth or simply saying he'd rather not discuss it.

Have you ever been treated for drug addiction?

Answer ▶ That was some time ago and I prefer not to discuss it.

This candidate is within his rights not to discuss this. Those who have been treated for drug addiction are covered by the ADA, and a hiring decision cannot be based upon this.

Never Say: "Yes, and I've only slipped up twice since then." The ADA doesn't protect someone who is currently using drugs from discrimination.

DRUGS AND DRUG TESTS

An employer can refuse to hire someone who currently uses illegal drugs. The ADA does not protect the applicant in this case. In addition, tests for illegal drugs are not subject to the ADA's restrictions on medical examinations.

Do you currently take any prescription drugs?

Answer ▶ I've taken medication from time to time, but it has never affected my work.

The candidate doesn't have to answer this question but doesn't want to be dishonest. It's her call to make. This answer does not reveal whether the candidate is currently taking medication, and by law she doesn't have to reveal that.

Never Say: "Yes, I take pain medication." There is no reason the candidate needed to reveal such specific information.

Travel is a big part of this job. Will your family be okay with that?

Answer ▶ I can assure you that traveling will not be a problem. I traveled extensively on my previous job.

This candidate has chosen to let the employer know that his family status will not affect his job. He mentions the fact that his previous job had similar requirements and it wasn't a problem.

Never Say: "Traveling shouldn't be a problem. I just have to make sure my wife and I aren't out of town at the same time." By giving this answer, the candidate acknowledges that traveling could be a problem.

MAKE USE OF YOUR PAST

When discussing what you would do if you were hired, you should draw on your past experience. Talk about how you completed similar projects on your last job or how you made similar decisions.

You're a young single woman living in the city. How do you handle having men chase after you?

Answer ▶ Work has always been my priority.

It is inappropriate for the employer to ask a question regarding the applicant's sex life. The candidate chooses to evade the question by talking about work.

Never Say: "Can you believe I'm dating five different men right now?" This candidate has chosen to answer a question she didn't have to and in doing so may cause the employer to wonder how she will have any time for work.

Whom should we notify in case of an emergency?

Answer ▶ I have to give it some thought. Can I let you know?

The employer does not need this information before the employee begins to work for her. This may be a thinly disguised attempt to learn about the candidate's personal life; for example, his marital status.

Never Say: "You can notify my wife. Her name is . . . ." This answer reveals more than the employer needs to know about the candidate's personal life.

Asked of a candidate applying for a job with the U.S. government: "Are you gay?"

Answer ▶ That isn't relevant to this job.

While a job candidate may or may not choose to answer this question, her answer can't play a role in a federal government agency's decision to hire her. Federal job applicants are protected from discrimination by the Civil Service Reform Act.

Never Say: "None of your business." Being confrontational is never the right way to go, even if you feel a question is inappropriate, rude, or even illegal. If you don't want to share this information, it is always best to be polite.

Do you want to have dinner on Saturday night? We can discuss your job qualifications over a nice bottle of pinot.

Answer ▶ I'll have to say no thank you. I never mix business with pleasure.

If the interviewer is persistent or in any way makes the candidate feel like he will get a job offer only by going out on a date with her, this may be considered sexual harassment, which is illegal under Title VII of the Civil Rights Act of 1964. It can be reported to the EEOC. The candidate makes it clear that the employer's advances are unwelcome, a necessary element to a sexual harassment claim.

Never Say: "What time on Saturday?" The job candidate should never acquiesce to this kind of advance.

CHAPTER 26

Behavioral Interviews

IN CHAPTER 17 YOU learned how to answer questions about your skills and abilities. You were urged to give more than yes and no answers to questions of this sort. It is always wise to provide an example of when you used a particular attribute. Behavioral interviews take this concept of using real-life examples to demonstrate your attributes a few steps further. You will not only have the opportunity to talk about *when* you used a particular attribute, but also explain *how* you used it.

Behavioral Interviews: The Basics

Potential employers use behavioral interviews to help them determine how job candidates will react to certain situations based on how they responded in past experiences.

How Behavioral Interview Techniques Help Employers

When an employer conducts an interview, his main objective is to make sure the person he hires can do the job. The best way to find out whether someone can do a job is to actually watch him do it. Generally, though, a prospective employer has to assess several candidates for an open position, and time is usually of the essence when it comes to making a hiring decision. In most cases, it would be inefficient to evaluate job candidates by actually having them do the job for which they are interviewing. Furthermore, since many people are currently employed while they are engaged in a job search, it would be difficult to schedule these "auditions."

In lieu of actually trying out job candidates to determine which one is best for a particular job, what can an employer do? Many employers use a technique called behavioral interviewing, which relies on the theory that past behavior is a good predictor of future behavior. Specifically, this type of interview attempts to determine how the job candidate drew upon her competencies to handle situations on a previous job or jobs in order to predict how she will handle similar situations if this employer hires her.

What Happens During a Behavioral Interview?

Before an employer begins interviewing candidates, he will determine what knowledge, skills and abilities are required for the job. Together these are referred to as competencies, and they may include the following:

- Decision-making skills
- Time management skills
- Problem solving skills
- Organizational skills
- The ability to multitask
- Interpersonal skills
- Writing and presentation skills
- The ability to work on and build teams
- Flexibility

During a behavioral interview, the interviewer will ask you to demonstrate that you have the competencies needed to do the job. Draw upon real life examples that illustrate how you used a particular competency in a work-related situation.

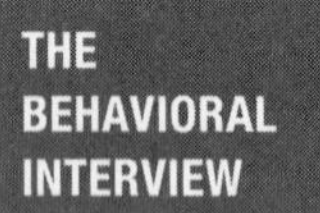

During your job search, you may be faced with a behavioral interview, a standalone entity during which an interviewer asks you only behaviorally oriented questions. Alternately, behavioral questions may be incorporated into your regular interview, in which case only some of the questions an interviewer asks you will be behaviorally oriented.

How to Answer Behavioral Questions

When answering behavioral questions, show the interviewer that you not only have a particular competency, but that you used it to benefit a past employer. Behavioral questions require the most preparation of any you will be asked on a job interview.

If you know what competencies the employer desires, it will be easier for you to prepare for the interview. To find out what competencies an employer requires, first turn to the job description. You may find them listed there; if you don't, you may have to dig a little deeper to learn what competencies an employer requires of a new hire.

START NETWORKING!

Your research will help you figure out how to answer many of the behavioral questions the interviewer might ask you. Use your network to locate people who may have experience with that employer. The more you can find out about a company, the better you will understand the qualities it is looking for in an employee.

Once you know what competencies the employer wants an employee to have, you need to come up with some anecdotes that highlight those competencies. Look to your work history—or your school experiences if you are a recent graduate—to find real-life situations in which you used your knowledge, skills, and abilities to successfully solve a problem or complete a project or task.

When you answer a behavioral question, first present the task or problem you faced. Then explain what steps you took to accomplish the task or solve the problem, making sure to highlight the competencies you used. The interviewer probably won't state what competency she expects you to demonstrate. You will have to quickly analyze the question to figure it out. Give as many details as necessary to best demonstrate each competency you determine she is looking for, but be careful not to go off on a tangent.

Questions and Answers

Tell me about something you've done to motivate your coworkers.

Answer ▶ About a year ago our company went through some tough times and about twenty-five workers were laid off. Morale was lower than I had ever seen it. This happened right around the time we had to start putting together our holiday issue, and no one was really into it. I planned a "winter in July" party to pick up everyone's spirits and to get us ready to work on the magazine. By the time the party was over, we were all in a better mood and we were ready to put together a great issue. I think it was one of the best ones we ever did.

The job candidate has demonstrated that he knows how to motivate others.

What is the toughest group you had to get to cooperate with you?

Answer ▶ I was asked to teach a new procedure to the customer service team. I had heard rumblings to the effect that many people on the team were unhappy with the new procedures, so I knew I wasn't going to have a receptive group to work with. Before I could be effective at teaching them what they needed to know, I had to convince them that the new procedure would benefit them. I set up a presentation that explained how it would save them time. Once the team saw the benefits of the new procedure, they actually looked forward to the training. They learned very quickly and we were able to implement the procedure in less than a week.

The interviewee demonstrates two competencies in her response. She highlights her interpersonal skills when she talks about how she was aware of the customer service team's concerns. Then she highlights her presentation skills.

Describe a situation in which you had a positive influence on someone else's actions.

Answer ▶ One of the new guys in my department was assigned a couple of projects at once and couldn't figure out how he would get both of them done on time. He was really frantic since he had only been there for a short time and was approaching his first performance evaluation. He knew only too well that these projects were crucial to his getting a good evaluation.

When he told me about his concerns, I asked him how he was scheduling his work and whether he was setting deadlines for completing different portions of his project. He had no idea what I was talking about. This was his first real job and it required a different sort of time management than his college courses had. I spent a lunch hour teaching him how to set up work schedules. After we met he set up work schedules for both projects and asked me to look them over. I did and helped him make a couple of changes. He completed both projects by their deadlines and got a pretty good performance evaluation.

In describing how she helped her colleague, this candidate shows that she has good interpersonal skills. She also manages to demonstrate her own time management skills by describing how she taught her coworker to set a schedule for himself.

THE IMPORTANCE OF TEAMWORK

In today's workplace, most people work on teams. A team must function as a single entity whose goal it is to complete a project efficiently and effectively. Members of teams must appreciate one another's differences and be willing to compromise. You must be able to demonstrate that you can work well as part of a team.

We expect the person we hire for this job to be able to take charge of a couple of big projects. Are you ready for that?

Answer ▶ A few months ago the chairperson of my department asked me to assemble a committee, made up of faculty and students, to evaluate the current curriculum. He gave us two semesters to complete the project. The first thing I had to do was decide who to include on the committee. I chose a few members of the faculty who had been with us for a very long time, as well as some who had recently joined the department. The students I picked ranged from freshmen to graduate students. I wanted a wide cross-section of both faculty and students. After that I set up deadlines for certain parts of the project to be completed and I set up a schedule for meetings. Finally, each person was assigned a specific area to look at and then present for discussion at each meeting. Based on the work of this committee, we were able to drop some courses that were not effectively meeting the goals of the department. We were able to add innovative courses that would attract students.

By giving this answer, the candidate demonstrates that she is good at organizing and planning projects.

HOW TO DEMONSTRATE A COMPETENCY

If you can't draw upon real-life experience to answer a question, don't make something up. You can use a hypothetical situation as an example, but let the interviewer know you are doing that.

Have you ever been a member of a group where some of the members did not work well together? Describe what you did.

Answer ▶ Yes, I have. I was a member of a group that was developing a software program for kids. There were three of us on the team. I got along with the two people I was working with, but they didn't get along with each other. They constantly shot down each other's ideas and they expected me to take sides. I refused to do that. Instead I tried to help them see each other's point of view. I explained how they each had good ideas and helped them compromise. In the end we had a successful product.

With this answer, the job candidate demonstrates that he has good interpersonal skills and good team-building skills.

Give an example of a time when you went above and beyond the call of duty.

Answer ▶ I've been teaching algebra for seven years and I know some children really have difficulty understanding it. There's only so much individual attention I can give to each student during class, so any help I give them has to be at another time. I teach five classes a day, which leaves only two free periods. One is a prep period and one is my lunchtime. I decided the kids needed math help more than I needed lunch, so I set aside three times a week when they could come to my room for tutoring. Many students have taken me up on this extra help and their grades have improved significantly. Most of my students do really well on the statewide seventh-grade test as a result of my tutoring them.

This candidate demonstrates how she solved a problem within the time constraints of her job. She shows how her students and the school benefited.

Have you ever been assigned several project at the same time? How did you handle it?

Answer ▶ That happens often, but one time that stands out in my mind is last year during the fall. The managers of three departments—women's outerwear, toys, and women's accessories—asked me to set up their winter holiday displays. They all wanted them up within a week. There was no way I could get that done. Since I know customers are more likely to shop for kids' presents first and kids really enjoy the displays, I decided to decorate the toy department first. I checked with the other two managers to see if they had some flexibility in their scheduling and both did. I scheduled both departments to have their displays up the following week. All three departments were beautifully decorated for the holidays and I completed them all in two weeks.

This interviewee demonstrates knowledge about his industry when he discusses why he chose to decorate the toy department first. He goes on to show how he is good at planning and scheduling.

PRIORITIZE! PRIORITIZE!

The ability to prioritize is highly valued in today's fast-paced workplace. In order to complete projects in a timely fashion, an employee must be able to decide in what order she must complete the required tasks. An employee must also be able to multitask and manage her time well. She must also be highly organized.

Can you give an example of how you adjust to unforeseen circumstances?

Answer ▶ Last summer I was less than a week away from a big presentation. I was in the middle of preparing for it when all of a sudden the power went out. We soon found out the lights were out everywhere on the East Coast and there were no estimates how long that would be the case. Fortunately I was two days ahead of schedule in my preparation, but since I didn't know when power would be restored. I was worried I wouldn't be able to work on my presentation. I knew if I wasn't ready on time, my company would look bad and it could cost us a lot of money. Our battery backup was still working, so I decided to print out the presentation. I wrote a lot of the presentation by hand that day. All I had left to do were my slides, which I did when the power came back on the next afternoon.

The job candidate shows that he knows how to cope with an emergency.

Give an example of a quick decision you made.

Answer ▶ When we were working on our April issue last year, one of the designers we planned to feature backed out just before the photo shoot because she didn't feel her line was ready. We had planned to feature her work on about twenty pages. Now we had to figure out what to do with those pages. We didn't have much time to waste. The photographer was on his way and was going to get paid for a day's work whether we used him or not. It turned out one of my assistant editors knew an up-and-coming designer. I decided to take a chance on the new designer since I trusted my assistant's opinion. The shoot was wonderful and her designs were fantastic. The issue was great and we've featured that designer a few times since then.

This interviewee shows that she knows how to make quick decisions.

This is a busy office and we have a lot of projects going on at once. Everyone who works here must be able to multitask. Can you?

Answer ▶ Since I work for three lawyers, I regularly have to multitask. Just two weeks ago they walked into my office one after another, handed me files, and told me they needed the work in them completed by the end of the week. I looked at the files and I figured out how long each assignment would take. Then I looked to see if there was any overlap between the assignments. I discovered that each required some research, which I was able to do that afternoon. The next morning I began working on the first project. I needed some files to do the other two projects, so I asked one of the file clerks to retrieve those for me while I put the finishing touches on the first assignment. With those files in front of me, I was able to work on the other two assignments.

While explaining his ability to multitask, this candidate also highlights his project-planning skills and his ability to delegate some work to others.

Give me an example of when you showed initiative and took the lead on a project.

Answer ▶ A year ago we noticed that our students' grades on statewide language arts exams were slipping. I had recently attended a seminar that addressed this particular issue and ways to resolve it. I had a program in mind that I thought we could implement at our school. I spoke to my principal about it and she asked me to write a formal proposal. After I did that and she approved it, I put together a committee of teachers and parents who would work with me to implement the program. This year's exam, as you know, won't take place until next month, but I think we'll see big improvements.

By giving this answer, the candidate shows how he recognized a problem and took initiative in resolving it.

Tell me about a report you had to write.

Answer ▶ My boss asked me to develop a plan to improve our quality-control process. She gave me a month to come up with three different ideas and said she would choose the best one based on my report. The first thing I noticed was that we didn't have a written document that described the procedure we were currently using, so I had to put one together. Then I began to research quality-control processes used by other companies. The librarian at our local library was able to tell me what databases I could access to find articles that discussed this issue. Through my research I was able to find which quality-control processes were most successful. I chose the three that I thought would work best for my employer and wrote about them. The report included my recommendation as to which one I thought we should use. My boss was pleased with the report. She agreed with my recommendation and my next project involved implementing the new process, including writing a document that described it completely.

This answer demonstrates this candidate's ability to put together a written report, including using research skills.

VITAL SOFT SKILLS

Certain soft skills are vital to one's performance at work. Without these skills, the employee simply can't do his job. Make a point of demonstrating that you have these valuable skills, even if you aren't specifically asked about them. They include multitasking, organizing, time management, and decision-making.

Give me an example of how you dealt with a conflict between two of your employees.

Answer ▶ A year ago two of my employees started having problems getting along with each other. It came from out of the blue but looked like it had the potential to escalate rapidly. I called separate meetings with each of the employees. They had remarkably similar stories and they didn't blame each other for their hard feelings. They agreed on a joint meeting, where I was able to help them realize that they really were on the same page after all. Things between them are now back to the way they were. They are both productive members of my department, so I'm glad we were able to work things out.

This candidate demonstrates her skill in conflict resolution.

Describe a recent unpopular decision you made and what the result was.

Answer ▶ A few months ago we found that we were having difficulty scheduling people to cover the circulation desk during lunch hours. Almost everyone wanted to go to lunch at 1 P.M., which meant we wouldn't have enough people around to check books in and out for our patrons.

I decided that the only way to deal with this was to schedule lunch hours. We had two lunch hours—noon to 1 P.M. and 1 P.M. to 2 P.M. Staff could go to lunch only at the time they were assigned. No one liked this idea very much because they were used to going to lunch whenever they felt like it. Something had to be done, however, because if we didn't do something service would suffer. Scheduled lunch hours have been in effect for the past three months. The staff have gotten used to it and service has definitely improved.

The interviewer shows he is a good manager who isn't afraid to make decisions that may be unpopular.

Have you ever had to work with someone with whom you had a bad relationship? How did you handle it?

Answer ▶ My boss asked me to work on a project with the one person in my company I don't get along with. I knew we'd be working together for several months and I didn't want those months to be miserable. I decided to swallow my pride and invite my coworker to lunch. We discussed the project and what we would have to do to make it work. We both realized that the company would be the victim if we let our personal differences get in the way of our performance. We divided the project up so that we could each work independently using our individual strengths, but we wound up working together more than we expected, so we learned to appreciate each other's strengths and how to use them in combination to benefit the company. We completed the project and we've worked on several other ones together since then by choice. Even though we still don't always agree on things, we know how to work well together now.

The candidate demonstrates how she used her interpersonal skills to resolve her differences with her coworker.

Tell me about a recent situation in which you had to deal with a very upset customer.

Answer ▶ Just last week one of our customers called and was extremely upset because something we had shipped to him arrived damaged. One of his customers was coming in to pick up the item two days later and he didn't want to disappoint her. I assured him that he would have the item for his customer on time. I brought the merchandise to the shipping department myself and asked that it be sent out by overnight delivery. He called the next day to say his package had arrived. He thanked us for resolving this quickly and placed another order.

The candidate has demonstrated how his good interpersonal skills kept a customer happy and resulted in another sale.

THE RIGHT HIRE

When an employer hires someone, he is investing in that person's future at his company. The more successful that person is and the longer she stays, the bigger the return on the investment. If he makes a poor hiring decision, that investment won't pay off because the person won't succeed and won't stick around. That is one reason employers take job interviewing very seriously.

Tell me about the most difficult person you've ever had to work with.

Answer ▶ That would have to be Jen. Jen was a perfectly nice person but she liked giving her work to others. She didn't have the right to do that. Our supervisor was the one who assigned work to us and he expected each of us to handle that work on our own. One day I decided I had had enough of this. Jen asked me to make some phone calls for her, and I told her we needed to have a talk. We did, and it turned out that Jen was overwhelmed by all the work our boss assigned and she didn't know how to handle it, other than by getting help from her coworkers. I helped her figure out a way to manage her time better and get her work done on her own. Jen is doing a lot better now. She doesn't try to pass off her work to other people anymore.

This candidate shows he has good interpersonal skills and is willing to help others succeed.

Describe a situation in which you were able to effectively "read" another person and guide your actions based on what you understood about her needs and values.

Answer ▶ About eight months ago, a client approached us about a new product they were introducing. There were two people I could have assigned to work on that project. Both would have done a good job; they are equally skilled and had worked with the client before. Knowing what I know about one of those employees, I had a feeling this new product was contrary to some of his personal values. I didn't want to jump to any conclusions, so I spoke to him before I made a decision about this. I was correct. He would have worked on the project, but he wouldn't have been comfortable with it. I decided to assign it to the other person. The client was very happy with the way things went. The product was introduced over the summer and has been very successful. They've had sales of about $1.5 million.

This candidate demonstrates her interpersonal skills by giving this answer.

LOOK BEFORE YOU LEAP

Your impulsive nature may be admired by your friends but it may not be admire by a prospective employer. Your boss expects you to think through all your decisions carefully. Your response to questions on your interview should in no way reveal that you are impulsive.

Have you ever anticipated a problem while working on a project and found a way to avoid it?

Answer ▶ While working on a project in October, I realized the person who had done the budget hadn't included printing costs. It wasn't going to be a huge expense, but it was definitely something that needed to be included in the budget. First I figured out what the cost of printing would be. Then I looked at the rest of the budget to see if the other costs on it were accurate. I found a few places where the costs had been overstated a little bit. I was able to change some numbers around so the money allotted for those expenses could instead be used for printing. We were still a little short, so I had to talk to my boss about increasing the budget. He was able to do that because the amount we needed wasn't very significant.

Not only does this candidate demonstrate that she can anticipate and avoid problems, she also shows that she knows how to budget expenses.

GET YOUR GOALS TO LINE UP

Your goals should always be aligned with those of the employer. If the employer senses that your goals have nothing to do with your prospective job, you probably won't be working for him anytime soon. Goals like cutting costs and increasing productivity are always appreciated. Reaching your own goals will be a byproduct of that.

Have you ever found working on a team disappointing? Did you do anything that helped things improve?

Answer ▶ In a business course I took in college, we were assigned to teams to work on a project that involved running a mock company. At the beginning we had trouble working together. However, we were being graded as a group, so we had to find a way to utilize our differences rather than let them defeat us. I thought the project would be more successful if we drew on every member's strengths and interests. Once I explained this to everyone, we once again divided up the tasks, using our different strengths and interests to put together a successful project. We ended up earning an A.

The interviewee takes this opportunity to demonstrate her team-building skills as well as her leadership skills.

Tell me about a problem you solved.

Answer ▶ I was coordinating a trade show in Washington, D.C. We advertised in all the industry publications and got an unprecedented number of responses from vendors who wanted to display their products. There were 350 companies that wanted to reserve booths. I knew our current venue had insufficient space. We could have turned away some of the vendors, but since they represented a significant amount of revenue, I didn't think this was even an option. I started looking into larger venues. I thought the Washington Convention Center would be perfect. There was plenty of room to accommodate everyone, and with the extra participation we were able to afford the larger site. We went ahead and booked it. The trade show was very successful. Both attendees and vendors were thrilled with the event. Many expressed an interest in attending next year.

The interviewee demonstrates his problem-solving skills.

Tell me about a time when you had to use your presentation skills to influence a client.

Answer ▶ My former employer had one particular client who had to be convinced that our way was the best way to go every time we made a presentation. She always needed a lot of reassurance, which was her right since she was paying good money for our services. There was one particular project I worked on for her where she needed even more convincing than usual. She wanted to redesign the packaging for one of her hair-care products. We put together a package design that was unique; the bottle was oval shaped instead of the usual cylindrical shape. It would really stand out from everything else on the shelves. Since it was an unconventional design and she was pretty conservative, she was hesitant to proceed. I asked our research department to put together some focus groups. Ninety percent of those we surveyed said they liked the new design better than the old one, and 85 percent picked that product from a group of three other similar products. We presented that information to the client and sold her on the oval shape. She went ahead with it and saw a 22 percent increase in sales in the first six months after the new design was introduced.

This interviewee demonstrates his presentation skills as he is asked to and shows how he was able to influence his client's decision.

JUST THE FACTS

Always use actual figures to prove your point. If you are talking about increasing sales, raising money, or cutting costs, for example, give the actual dollar amount or the percentage of increase or decrease. For example, say that you increased sales by 20 percent or cut costs by $300,000.

Tell me how you delegate work effectively.

Answer ▶ One of our clients asked us to work on a major project for them. It involved a conference they were holding in six months. They expected thousands of people to attend and they needed us to help them choose a location, get the best rates on hotels, find caterers, and then organize the event. I picked three people on my staff to work on this project with me. One person had a lot of experience in travel, so I asked her to choose the location and work with some hotels in the area to get us the best rates for those who were attending the conference. Another person had worked on an event for a different client and he had done a great job choosing the caterer, so I asked him to arrange for the meals and refreshments. Finally, I picked the most organized person on my staff to collect responses from those who signed up for the conference. She had to assign them to tables for meals and had to figure out who would attend which conference events. I have to say my staff did a great job. I was so proud of them. More than 5,000 people attended the conference and all went well.

This candidate shows how he was able to delegate work to those who were most suitable for each assignment.

SHOULD I MAKE UP EXPERIENCE?

Never lie on a job interview. While having insufficient experience lowers your chances of getting hired, getting caught in a lie pretty much guarantees that you won't get the job. Instead of lying, talk about your related experience and explain how it is similar to what your prospective employer wants.

Give me an example of a time when you used your fact-finding skills to solve a problem.

Answer ▶ I was advisor to a student who needed to request a leave of absence from the university. I didn't know what the proper procedures were to officially do this. I didn't want to have her do it incorrectly and then be inadvertently dropped from the program.

I asked our department secretary if there was a written document that discussed the procedure. He didn't know of one, so I contacted the registrar's office. They referred me to the associate dean's office. I finally got the answer there and was able to tell the student what she needed to do.

The candidate, as asked, demonstrates how she used her fact-finding skills.

Tell me about a time when you had to make an unpopular decision.

Answer ▶ As director of our after-school program, I noticed that parents were often arriving very late to pick up their children. That meant that staff had to stay late too, which meant we had to pay them for their time. We simply didn't have the money to do that. I decided we would have to charge parents if they were late in order to have the money to pay our staff. Many people weren't happy with this, but we really didn't have a choice. This was enough incentive to get most parents to pick up their children on time. As a matter of fact, late pickups decreased by 85 percent right after this program went into effect.

This answer demonstrates that the candidate is willing to make an unpopular decision in order to solve a problem.

Tell me about a project you initiated.

Answer ▶ Last February, my boss took a three-week vacation. He left me some work to do while he was gone, but I finished it by the end of the first week. I had wanted to reorganize our files for a long time, and now I had the time to work on this. First I developed a plan to work on the project. I set up a schedule that included setting goals for what I wanted to complete by the end of each day in order to finish within two weeks. Then I figured out what filing system I wanted to use. I recruited our intern to help me. We finished the project on the Friday before my boss was set to return. He was happy to see what I had done while he was gone.

This answer demonstrates several competencies. The candidate takes initiative when she takes on a project without being asked. She shows that she knows how to plan and schedule a project and also how to delegate tasks.

Describe a big presentation you had to deliver.

Answer ▶ I had to make a big presentation at a national trade show. I was standing in for my supervisor who had to be somewhere else that day. He gave me the assignment two weeks before the show, so I had to prepare the presentation within a pretty tight time frame. First I set goals for completing each part of the presentation. Then I scheduled meetings with the developers of the products I'd have to present at the show so I could make sure I knew everything I could about them. I put together a great presentation. We took orders from 150 retailers that day alone and the sales on the products I presented increased by 15 percent after the show.

The candidate highlights her time management skills when she describes how she put together a presentation within a tight time frame. She also highlights her presentation skills. Notice that she backs up her answers by using real numbers.

How have you convinced your boss that your approach is the best one to take in order to complete a project?

Answer ▶ Before I started working for my current employer, employees rarely worked in teams. I knew of many projects which a team could handle more effectively than an individual could, but I couldn't seem to convince anyone else. Then my boss's supervisor asked him to work on a huge project with a very tight deadline. Even though my supervisor is a talented man, this project clearly needed the talents of many different people to be successful. But I had to make him see that. I put together a list of people in different departments who had the necessary skills to help complete the project. I presented this list to my boss and sold him on the idea of putting together a team. He and his new team completed the project and his boss was extremely happy with it. My supervisor often uses teams to complete projects now.

This job candidate demonstrates how she was able to persuade her boss that her approach was the best one to take and goes as far as discussing the outcome of the project.

PUT YOUR BEST ABILITY FORWARD

When deciding which accomplishments to discuss on a job interview, you should always select those that best demonstrate your ability to do the job for which you are interviewing. For example, if you are interviewing for a job in an accounting firm and you've previously worked at one, use examples from that experience rather than from your experience at an advertising agency.

Explain what you do when you have a conflict with a client.

Answer ▶ Last March I was working on a client's project that required us to hire a researcher. We worked closely with the client to draw up a contract with the researcher, who then completed the work. The client then decided he wanted some additional research done, but didn't want to pay for it. Of course, our researcher couldn't work for free, so we worked out a deal with her. We "loaned" her one of our interns to assist her, and she was able to charge less for the work she did. The client was happy that he got what he wanted and didn't have to pay full price for it. We were happy because he was pleased with our work, which meant that he would probably return in the future.

This interviewee shows how he resolves a conflict with a client by coming up with a solution with which everyone was happy.

Please tell me about a time you had to fire someone.

Answer ▶ One of my employees suddenly started coming into work late every day. When it first started happening, I called her into my office to find out what was going on. I thought she might have some personal problem that was keeping her from getting to work on time. She assured me that she would make sure to get there punctually. The lateness stopped, but it started again a month later. I called her to my office again and reminded her that tardiness was unacceptable. Our company was big on flex-time, so I offered her a later schedule. She turned it down, saying she couldn't work any later in the evening. Again she started arriving on time, but this time it only lasted two weeks. I had to let her go at that point. I explained the situation to her and she didn't seem very surprised.

This answer highlights the candidate's managerial skills.

CHAPTER 27

Special Interview Situations

WHEN IMAGINING WHAT an interview would be like, you may have pictured yourself sitting in an office opposite your interviewer. That is a typical setting for a job interview, but it is not the only option. For example, you may not meet with the employer in his office but in a restaurant. And instead of speaking with someone one-on-one, you may be interviewed by a group or panel of people, or you may be interviewed as part of a group of job candidates. Your interview may not even take place in person, but instead over the telephone or via videoconference. You may even have to travel to a foreign country for your job interview!

Interviewing over a Meal

If you are unfamiliar with mealtime etiquette, you may want to brush up on your skills—you may be invited to join your potential employer for breakfast, lunch, or dinner. Some employers choose to interview job candidates over a meal. This is a real possibility, particularly if you are interviewing for a job out of town.

While sharing a meal with someone may conjure up feelings of familiarity, don't be fooled into thinking the interview is going to take on a more casual tone than it would have if it were taking place in an office. In reality, you have more to think about than how to answer the questions the interviewer is asking. The interviewer will not only be listening to your answers, she will also be judging your behavior. Learning some simple rules of dining etiquette should put you at ease. Then you can concentrate on more important things—like giving answers that make you shine.

Arriving at the Restaurant and Getting Seated

One of the more awkward moments of a mealtime interview could happen at the very beginning—arriving at the restaurant. Of course you are going to be punctual and arrive at the designated time, but that means you may arrive before the interviewer. If you do arrive first, give the interviewer's name to the host or hostess who may have a reservation for him. It is okay to sit down at the table to wait, but don't order anything yet.

When the interviewer arrives at the table, stand up until he sits down. If both of you arrive at the table at the same time, wait for the interviewer and others in your party, if there are any, to be seated before you sit down.

STAND FOR THE INTERVIEWER

Gender rules generally do not apply when you're in a business setting, such as a mealtime job interview. It makes no difference whether you are a man and the interviewer is a woman or vice versa. If you are seated when the interviewer gets to the table, you should stand until he or she is seated.

Perusing the Menu

You may love spaghetti and meatballs, but is that the smartest thing to order when on a job interview? It probably is not. You should stay away from anything that is difficult to eat neatly. You don't want to risk looking like a slob or having to think too much about the process of eating instead of answers to the questions the interviewer is asking you. Also avoid foods that might get stuck between your teeth, like anything with poppy seeds or spinach.

REMEMBER TO FLOSS

Stick a package of dental floss in your purse or jacket pocket. If you suspect that you might have something stuck between your teeth, you can slip into the restroom to remove it. You also might want to carry around some breath mints (not chewing gum).

Avoid consuming any alcoholic beverages even if you can hold your liquor quite well. Alcohol dulls your senses and makes you less inhibited. This is one situation when you want to be at your sharpest. You can order a soft drink or water instead. If wine is being served at the table, to be polite, allow the server to pour you a glass, but sip it very slowly.

Don't order the most expensive thing on the menu. Order a moderately priced item. You don't want to take advantage of the employer's generosity, since it is likely she will be footing the bill. Order a dish that can be prepared as described on the menu. You don't want to have to give the waiter a lot of specifications. ("Can I get that without onions, mushrooms, or peppers, please."). If you order that way you will look too fussy.

PASS THE BREAD, PLEASE

Before you pour yourself water or take a roll from the breadbasket, offer the item to your fellow diners. Ask if you can pour water for anyone else or pass the breadbasket around the table. The same goes for the butter or any other condiment on the table. If there's only one serving of something left, such as the last roll in the breadbasket, offer it to your dining companions before you take it.

Eating

Don't begin eating until everyone at the table has been served. Don't cut up all your food at once—cut off one piece at a time and put your knife down on the edge of your plate between bites. Use your napkin to remove crumbs from your face, remembering to dab at the corners of your mouth, not wipe the napkin across your lips. Put your napkin down on the table neatly. Don't crumple it up.

WHICH FORK?

Unless you've been to several formal dinners, you might be baffled by the number of utensils at your place setting. You may wonder which fork to use first, for example. It's really quite simple. Generally, your salad or appetizer fork is smaller than the other one. Sometimes, though, you end up with two forks that are the same size. A good rule of thumb is to use the fork farthest away from your plate first and work your way in.

Since the whole point of this lunch (or dinner or breakfast) is to conduct a job interview, it is likely that you will have to speak during the meal. It may be obvious to you as you read this that you shouldn't talk with your mouth full. However, you may forget this important rule as you go ahead and try to answer questions the interviewer asks you without looking like you are hesitating. It is always good manners to chew first, swallow, and then speak. Finish answering the question before you continue eating.

Wondering when the meal is over? Follow the interviewer's lead. If she puts her napkin on the table it means the meal is over. Finish chewing, wipe your face, and place your napkin on the table to signal that you are done, too. Don't stand up and get ready to go until the interviewer does, though. She may still have more questions to ask you.

When the interview is done, shake the interviewer's hand. Then thank her for her time and for the meal. Ask when you can expect to hear any further news and reiterate your interest in the job, just as you would at an interview that takes place in an office.

PREPARE FOR SPILLAGE

Even if you try to eat neatly you may end up getting something on your clothes. You don't have to worry about walking around like that all day, especially if you are heading back to the employer's office. There are several products on the market that can instantly remove stains from clothing. These products come in packages that are the size and shape of a pen and can easily fit in your pocket or purse.

Interviewing in a Foreign Country

Today's economy is a global one and it is possible that you might have to travel abroad for a job interview. The job you are pursuing may be located in another country, or a company's headquarters may be located overseas even if your job won't be. Even when an employer based in a foreign country interviews you locally, you should be aware of the rules of etiquette in his homeland. A breach of etiquette, even if it is only in someone else's eyes, can be considered rude and may jeopardize your chance of the employer hiring you. Here are some basic things you should be aware of before you jet off to your job interview.

READ BEFORE YOU MEET

There are entire books devoted to the subject of international etiquette. Many public libraries and bookstores carry these books. Try looking under the following subjects: International Etiquette, Travel Etiquette, and Business Etiquette. Some of these books discuss the rules for many countries, and others focus on a particular country.

Body Language

One's interpretation of someone's body language is influenced by his culture. You are expected in some cultures, for example, to make eye contact with whomever you are speaking to. In other cultures it is considered rude to do so. In many countries people greet one another with a handshake, while in others people bow. Learn what is customary in the country you are visiting. Then train yourself accordingly.

Dining Abroad

If you are traveling to another country for a job interview, there is a good chance you will have to share at least a meal or two with your hosts. You may have faultless table manners by your home country's standards. However, in the eyes of those in the country you are visiting, your manners may be more suitable for a toddler. Learn about proper dining etiquette and, again, practice the rules before you leave home.

While we're on the subject of dining, another issue you may encounter is food with which you're unfamiliar. You may be served things that you never even considered eating. If you are willing to try new foods, then do so. If someone offers you something you find totally repulsive, politely turn it down. Don't make a face or say anything negative. Something you wouldn't touch with a ten-foot fork may be someone else's fantasy meal.

Laws in Foreign Lands

Since you know the laws in your home country, you can probably avoid doing anything that could get you into serious trouble. However, if you don't know the law in the country you are visiting, you may do something inadvertently that can create legal problems for you, perhaps even get you into jail. Nothing will make a potential employer reject you faster than a phone call asking him to bail you out of jail.

RESOURCES FROM STATE

A must-read for Americans traveling abroad is the U.S. State Department website: *http://usembassy.state.gov*. Resources on that site include general tips for traveling abroad, tips for those traveling to specific regions, and a list of U.S. embassies around the world. The State Department advises travelers who get into trouble abroad to immediately contact the nearest U.S. embassy.

Often people think they can get away with doing something in a foreign country because they are under the (false) assumption that the laws are more lenient there. For example, you may think it's okay to carry around marijuana or use it openly. Don't take that chance. Not only could you get into serious trouble, you may be treated more harshly because you are a foreigner. Know the laws and obey them completely.

Gender Differences

Men and women may be treated as equals in your home country. However, in many countries women and men are treated very differently from one another. Often there is one set of rules that applies to men and another one that applies to women. If you are aware of what the cultural norms regarding gender are in the country you are visiting, then you won't be surprised, or offended, when you encounter something that seems odd to you. For example, a woman may be expected to walk a few paces behind a man in some cultures instead of alongside him. In other countries women and men who aren't married to one another may never touch, so a handshake between a man and woman would be entirely inappropriate (and offensive).

Telephone Interview and Videoconference

In some cases your interview may not even take place in person. A potential employer may choose to interview you by telephone or via videoconference. An employer may choose one of these methods if you don't live locally. It is much less expensive than flying a job candidate across the country. If you pass through this first interview, you will eventually need to be interviewed in person. If you are offered a job based only on a telephone or videoconferencing interview, don't accept it without first visiting the office in which you will be working. You definitely will want to see the facilities and meet those with whom you'll be working in person before making your decision.

Telephone Interview

There is a positive side to a telephone interview. It eliminates two sources of worry: what to wear and body language. You do, however, rely on your voice to convey all your emotions, including enthusiasm. Many communications experts advise people to stand up when they are taking part in a telephone interview. It is also a good idea to smile. It will relax you and help make you sound enthusiastic. Although it may seem unnecessary, you should also dress for the interview. That doesn't mean you have to wear your best suit, but you should at least get out of your bathrobe and fuzzy slippers. This will allow you to feel, and therefore speak, more professionally.

DOGS AND CHILDREN NOT ALLOWED

If you have young children or a dog that likes to bark, the busy living room may not be the best place to have your phone interview. Get a babysitter and ask your neighbor to take your dog for a walk for a half hour. If you're worried that you'll be interrupted—or if you actually are interrupted—you'll lose your concentration and become nervous. Make sure you have a relatively quiet, calm atmosphere for your phone interview.

Interviewing via Videoconference

In an interview that takes place by videoconference, you will be at a videoconferencing center while your interviewer, or interviewers, are at another location.

Once there, you will be facing a camera and talking into a microphone as you answer questions, just as you would on a traditional interview. For someone who isn't used to being on camera—and most people aren't—a videoconference can be a nerve-racking situation.

Body language is very important, so remember to sit up straight, place your hands on your lap, and look directly at the camera. More than for any other type of interview, it is essential that you practice for a videoconference interview. Videotape yourself, or ask a friend to videotape you so you become accustomed to "talking" to the camera.

Panel Interview

In a panel interview, a group of people, rather than an individual interviewer, will ask you questions. This group may include managers, human resources personnel, and possibly those with whom you would be working if you get the job. You may also hear this type of interview called a committee interview. Often all of the people participating in the interview will be making the hiring decision.

It is important to stay relaxed during the interview even though you may feel like you are sitting before a firing squad. Your job is to interact with each person on the panel. As you answer each question, make eye contact with the person who asked it. Give each interviewer equal attention, even if you know who is higher up in the company's chain of command and thus will have more say over whether you get the job. The person you snub, even if he is lower down on the corporate ladder, may have a big influence on the person who wields the most power. If you can remember who's who, try to address each person by name.

FORGETTING NAMES

If you can't remember one of your interviewers' names, it is okay to ask her to tell it to you again. Make sure you remember it this time, though. One good way to remember a person's name when you meet her is to repeat the name aloud (as in "It's a pleasure to meet you, Ms. Baker") or to yourself. The repetition will help to keep the name fresher in your mind.

Shake hands with all participants at the end of the interview. Send an individual thank-you note to each person on the panel in which, if your memory is good, you can bring up something regarding a question that person asked. If you forget the names of anyone on the panel after the interview, a quick call to the receptionist or secretary can help you get that information.

Group Interview

When an employer has a lot of applicants to interview they may begin the process of weeding out the less desirable one by conducting group interviews. In a group interview you will be interviewed at the same time as other job candidates. The interviewer or interviewers will address questions to the group as a whole or to individuals within the group.

In all groups there are people who are leaders and people who are followers. Which candidates take on which roles will become evident as the interview progresses. In many instances that is exactly the information the employer needs to help him make his decision. He wants to know who is a leader and who is a follower and will decide who to hire based on this information. All you can do is be yourself. Remember, the job needs to match your personality for you to be successful and happy doing it. With that said, remember to speak up even if your natural tendency isn't to be a leader. You want your voice to be heard, since your goal is to let the employer know more about you.

Behavioral Interviews

An employer wants to know, before they hire you, how you will behave in certain situations that you could potentially face on the job. Everyone possesses attributes that allow her to cope with different situations. These attributes are called competencies. On a behavioral interview you are expected to prove (or disprove) that you have certain competencies by describing circumstances under which you had to use them in the past. The interviewer will use this information to help him determine whether you will be a good employee.

Preparing for a Behavioral Interview

You will need to do a great deal of preparation before a behavioral interview. Begin by trying to figure out what competencies the employer desires. Read the job description thoroughly and try to pick up clues. You can consult your network to see if any of your contacts are familiar with the company. Someone familiar with the company may know what competencies it values. If you can't find out what competencies you might need to demonstrate on a behavioral interview with a particular employer, don't panic. The competencies employers most desire, and therefore the ones they often ask you about on a behavioral interview, are problem-solving, decision-making, organization, time management, interpersonal skills, and the ability to multitask.

Once you have figured out which competencies you will have to demonstrate, it is time to come up with an anecdote for each one. Review all the jobs listed on your resume to refresh your memory. Think about the projects you worked on at each one and what actions you took in order to complete them successfully. You should also consider the problems you may have encountered and how you solved them. Which of your strengths did you draw upon to help you achieve positive results?

NO TALL TALES

Don't make up stories or embellish real ones to make your point. First of all, it's too easy to get caught in a lie. Second of all, you want your stories to be plausible. Most people can spot a lie from a mile away—particularly an interviewer, who has probably heard them all.

You should start by writing down these anecdotes, making sure to include details. Next, you should practice telling your stories out loud. Find a friend who is willing to listen to you, preferably someone who works in a similar job. Find out what your friend thinks of the story and whether it demonstrates the competency and skill you intend it to demonstrate.

Sample Behavioral Interview Questions

Each of these questions asks the job candidate to demonstrate one or a few competencies. The competency or competencies the employer expects you to demonstrate in your answer is shown in parentheses following the question.

- How have you handled being assigned several projects at once? (prioritizing, time management, multitasking)
- Describe a situation where you had to critique someone's performance and offer suggestions to help him do better. (interpersonal)
- Discuss a project you had to complete on short notice. (time management)
- Talk about a time you had to motivate members of a team. (leadership)
- Describe how you dealt with an unforeseen problem. (problem-solving)
- How have you set goals for yourself and achieved them? (goal-setting)
- Talk about a presentation you had to make. (presentation)
- Discuss a time when you had to deal with an unhappy client. (interpersonal)

Of course, these are only a few of the questions you may be presented with during a behavioral interview. You will most likely need to think on your feet in order to come up with an appropriate example for each question. The main way to prepare is to practice, practice, practice. The more situations you prepare for, the better your chances of impressing the interviewer and getting the job.

PART IV

Get the Right Job

The goal of your job search is finding a job you'll be happy with, that you'll grow with, and that will allow you to be yourself.

CHAPTER 28

Negotiate the Best Terms

ONE OF THE MOST nerve-racking steps on the trail to a new job is near the end of the path: deciding whether to accept an offer. If you have been looking for a job for an extended period of time, your instinct may be to accept the offer even if you feel it is lacking in some way. Some job seekers turn down offers because of compensation only, even though the offer may be suitable in other ways. Job seekers can make unnecessary, costly mistakes during this vitally important stage.

Do You Want This Job?

If you're going to consider a job offer seriously, first be sure that it is a job you really want. Are you willing to live and work in the area in question? Is the work schedule and way of life one you would enjoy? If you're just graduating, is the job in the field you'd like to pursue? These are all things you should consider before you make your final decision.

Considering the Work Environment

Another important factor to consider is the kind of environment in which you'll be working. Is the company's atmosphere comfortable, challenging, and exciting? You must look at specifics, including office or workstation setting, privacy, proximity to other staff, amount of space, noise level, and lighting.

Don't automatically reject a job offer if the office is small or run down. Take it into consideration along with all the other factors. The office may look undesirable, but do the people working in it seem lively? The positive may outweigh the negative.

What is the level of interaction among coworkers? Some organizations strongly encourage teamwork and dialogue among staff, while others emphasize individual accomplishment. You should think about which approach works better for you. If you have serious doubts about whether you will like the work environment before you accept the job, you may grow to hate it after you accept the job.

Corporate Culture

Corporate culture encompasses many things. It includes a company's values, practices, and goals and the way it goes about achieving them. If you work for a company, you should feel comfortable with its culture. If you are a staunch environmentalist, for example, and the company you are considering working for is a big land developer that supports deforestation, this may not be the place for you. If your prospective employer expects their staff to put work ahead of family, and if that is something with which you don't feel comfortable, think carefully about accepting a job offer. It is unlikely that the corporate culture will change, and either you will be uncomfortable working within it or you will go against it. Either way, you may soon be looking for another job.

Location

Most people would be thrilled to be able to walk to work, or at least have to deal with only a five-minute ride. Unfortunately many workers don't have such an easy commute to their jobs. Getting to work often involves sitting in traffic or enduring a long trip on public transportation.

Americans spend a lot of time commuting to work. This results in quite a bit of down time for many people—time they can spend doing something more productive. According to the 2000 United States Census, the average travel time to work was almost twenty-six minutes. One thing you must ask yourself before you accept a job offer is "How long will it take me to get to and from work each day?" And then you must ask yourself whether that commute is too long. You may not mind leaving your house at 6:30 every morning, but how will you feel about getting home at 8 o'clock every night?

Can You Work with These People?

When you think about the fact that the majority of your waking hours will be spent on the job, the importance of working with people with whom you get along looms large. While you don't have to love everyone in your workplace, you do have to have decent relationships with your coworkers and your boss.

When you are interviewing for a job, take note of your prospective boss's demeanor. Does she seem like a reasonable person or does she seem like someone who can fly off the handle pretty easily? Listen to her interact with other people—for instance, the receptionist. Is she polite and friendly? As you walk through the office, look at the people there. Do they look content? Do they seem friendly? It's difficult to make these assessments through first impressions, but if something doesn't seem right to you, pay attention to your instincts.

If the boss speaks in a derogatory tone of voice to one of his employees in your presence, think of what he will do when you aren't there. After all, shouldn't he be on his best behavior when there's a guest in the office?

Career Helper or Career Killer

Whether or not a job will help your career progress is ultimately a much more important question than what your starting salary will be. In some organizations, you may be given a lot of responsibility right away but then find your progress blocked. Make sure you know whether you have opportunities for advancement. Find out if you will be able to grow your career with this employer or if you will end up in a dead-end job. Ask about performance reviews and how often they are conducted. Then find out if excellent performance reviews lead to promotions.

After a lengthy job search, you may be tempted to take a job that doesn't fit well with your career goals. If your goals have truly changed based on your re-evaluating your career, then that might be okay. However, if your goals remain the same, consider the impact that going off course could have on your career.

The Money Questions

The questions of salary and benefits strike fear into the hearts of job seekers young and old. But handling the inevitable money questions doesn't have to be difficult, and the more you think about them in advance, the easier they'll be to answer.

First, never try to negotiate salary or benefits until you've gotten an offer. At that point, don't worry about the recruiter withdrawing her handshake and showing you the door if you dare ask about flexibility in the company's offer. The worst case might be that the salary is set by company policy and the recruiter or hiring manager has no power to negotiate. He may not be able to give you an immediate answer and will have to get back to you.

To learn about the opportunities for advancement within a particular company, you can ask for some statistics. Inquire about which members of upper management came from the lower ranks of the company. Does the employer promote from within? Find out what happened to other people who held the position you've been offered. Have they moved up, or have they moved out?

Before You Get the Offer

When it comes to buying a car, you can pretty much bet that the price the salesman gives you is negotiable. You are going to have to bargain. The same can't be said of a job offer. Before you even get an offer, you should have some idea of what salary to expect. That way, when an employer makes an offer, you will know how to respond. You will only know that if you do your homework.

Before you decide to ask for a higher salary you must know what the going rate is in your field. Just how do you know how much you should expect? The answer is the same as in every other step of your job search: Do your homework. Read the trade journals for your industry. Read the newspaper help-wanted ads. If possible, talk to current employees.

Salaries vary by geographic region. For example, a teacher in Wisconsin may earn a lower salary than a teacher in California. In addition to finding out what the average earnings are in your field and industry, you must also find out what those jobs pay where you plan to work. There is generally a relationship between the local cost of living, the salary, and the supply of and demand for workers with a specific set of skills.

There are many salary surveys available on the web. Using your favorite search engine, type in the term "salary survey." Use your network to find out how much others are earning at the same level. Talk to alumni of your college or university in similar positions (or employed by the same organization). They may be an excellent source of information. By doing this research, you will get an idea of the salary level you can realistically expect.

Know Your Own Worth

Setting realistic expectations is especially important for the entry-level job seeker or recent graduate. If you don't have a lot of professional experience, you don't leave the employer with much hard evidence on which to base a decision to offer you more money. Instead, you're asking her to take a leap of faith based on potential you've demonstrated in classes, internships, volunteering, or extracurricular activities. Without a track record of professional experience, your arsenal is missing a powerful weapon. Even so, that doesn't mean you can't give negotiating your salary a try.

On the other hand, if you have some experience under your belt and are looking for a midlevel or executive position, your negotiating power might be much greater. For a lucky (or unlucky) few at the top of the heap, salary and benefit negotiations can be as complex and painstakingly slow as watching the grass grow. Whatever your level of experience, your task is to try to figure out just how high the employer is likely to go.

Deciding to Negotiate

Once you have decided to negotiate salary, you can approach your prospective employer with the confidence of knowing you are presenting a reasonable request, or at least one with which you are comfortable. The idea is to first assure him of your interest. Then give reasons for your proposed increase rather than just saying you need it or want it.

Your financial needs are not a good enough reason for an employer to negotiate with you. They have no reason to offer you more money just because you have bills to pay. Everyone has bills to pay. The employer should be willing to pay you more because you are worth it and because you are asking for a fair salary based on what others doing the same job are earning. An employer may simply tell you they can't negotiate the salary, and then you must either be willing to accept their offer or walk away.

Some salaries are truly non-negotiable due to contractual constraints. In union shops, for example, salaries are set through negotiations between the union and the employer. The employer cannot offer a higher salary to a new employee than he is paying his current workers.

If you can negotiate, this doesn't mean you name a figure and the employer either matches it or doesn't match it. It means you're ready to listen to what she has to offer and give it consideration. To succeed in negotiation, both parties have to reach an agreement with which they're happy.

If you succeed at winning yourself a bigger paycheck but antagonize your future boss in doing so, trouble lies ahead. If, on the other hand, you set realistic expectations and realize that you may not get everything you want, you'll probably do just fine.

How to Negotiate

If, after listening politely to the specifics of the offer, you're left hoping for a higher salary, greater health coverage, or something else, it's okay to (calmly) say so. Find out if the offer is firm. If it seems there may be some room to negotiate, make sure you have a figure in mind, because if the recruiter does have the freedom to barter, she will probably ask you pointblank to supply a figure.

When you're asked that question, rule number one is as follows: Don't tip your hand by giving the interviewer a specific number for which you're willing to settle. You don't want to take yourself out of the running by naming a figure that's absurdly optimistic, and you certainly don't want to risk naming a figure lower than what the employer is ready to offer. Instead of naming your price, say something like, "Based on my experience and skills and the demands of the position, I'd expect I'd earn an appropriate figure. Can you give me some idea what kind of range you have in mind?"

When considering compensation, don't forget to look at the entire package. That includes health insurance, vacation time, sick days, and personal days. If the actual dollar amount you are being offered seems somewhat low, is it being made up for with very generous vacation time or with a paid-in-full health insurance plan? Don't forget that these things are valuable, too.

Of course, the recruiter may come back with "Well, how much were you interested in?" There's a limit to how far you can take this without antagonizing the other person, so if you can't get her to name a range, give in graciously and name your own. Be sure not to make the bottom number too low (because you may be stuck with it) or the range too large, and give yourself enough room at the top without being unrealistic. If you name a range of, say, $25,000 to $30,000, it may be that the company was considering a range of $22,000 to $28,000. Therefore, you should receive an offer in the mid-to-upper end of your range, depending on your experience and qualifications.

When Negotiating May Not Be a Good Idea

Perhaps the salary the employer is offering is fair, based on going rates and your experience. Should you still ask for more money? Your answer depends on what you feel comfortable doing. If you ask for more money even though you think the initial offer is fair, are you willing to walk away from the job if your request isn't met? Worse, are you willing to possibly create tension between yourself and your future boss?

Get It in Writing

If you're somewhat content with the distribution of funds but haven't discussed health insurance and other benefits, like a 401(k) plan and vacation time, do so immediately. Then request everything be outlined in writing, especially if you'll be leaving a job to take the new position. You have rights, and if something looks amiss, it's time to go back to the bargaining table—that is, if you're still interested. Regard with suspicion an employer who won't give you confirmation of the position in writing.

It's about Job Satisfaction

The point of your job search is not salary negotiation; it's finding a job you'll be happy with, that you'll grow with, and that will allow you to be yourself. If your starting salary isn't the one you dreamed about but the job presents the right opportunity, think about how much easier it'll be once you've had a chance to make yourself invaluable to the organization.

Generally, a high salary doesn't buy job satisfaction. It may seem like the person with the BMW parked in the employee lot has the best job, but she may actually be unhappy at work. If you truly feel like a job will give you a lot of satisfaction, and you will be able to live comfortably on the salary being offered even if it isn't as high a salary as you would like, you should consider accepting the offer.

On the other hand, if the salary or benefits fall far short of your realistic expectations, despite all your efforts to negotiate, nothing says you have to take the job. Don't make the mistake of accepting a position with which you're fundamentally unhappy. Trust your instincts—if you're dissatisfied with the employer before your start date, don't bet the situation will get better.

Accepting a Job Offer

After going through the decision-making process and negotiating a salary, you've decided to accept a job offer. Before you tell the employer of your decision, make sure you are one hundred percent committed to it. Ask yourself the following questions one last time before you give your final answer:

- Do I fully understand the job and am I happy with what it entails?
- Will I be comfortable with the corporate culture?

- Will I be, as far as I can tell right now, compatible with my future coworkers and boss?
- Is the work environment one in which I will be happy?
- Is the location of the workplace acceptable? Will I be able to handle my commute?
- Do I understand the employer's expectations and will I be able to meet them?
- Does the employer understand my expectations and will he be able to meet them?
- Does the salary and other compensation seem fair to me? If not, will I be able to live with that?
- Will I have the opportunity for growth in this job?
- Do I believe I will be treated fairly by my new employer?

Of course, no one can predict the future, but if by answering these questions you can assure yourself you are making the right decision, you will at least be getting off to the best start you can.

Letting Your New Employer Know You'll Be Coming On Board

Once you've made your decision, it's time to let your new employer know. You can first do this by calling him on the phone, or by e-mail if that has been your primary mode of communication. Then follow that up with a written letter that states your acceptance of his offer.

No Turning Back Now

Once you've accepted a job offer, you must stick with your decision. If you are having any doubts about it, if you think you may get a better offer from another employer, or if you think your current boss might make a counteroffer, then don't accept yet. Wait until you've heard from everyone involved in your decision before you tell your future boss of your acceptance.

Think about how you would feel if she decided to interview one last candidate after offering you the job and decided that he was the better choice. If the fact that this is just "the right thing to do" doesn't give you enough of a reason not to first accept and then reject an offer, remember that you don't know who you will meet in the future. This person, who may harbor very negative feelings toward you, can end up your future coworker or boss!

Declining a Job Offer

Whatever your reason is for deciding not to take a job offer, you must inform the employer of it. It would be rude to keep her waiting for your answer, just as it would be rude for her to keep you waiting. This advice holds true even if you feel the employer treated you unfairly by not presenting a fair offer or being willing to negotiate. Again, you simply don't know who you will meet again at another point in your career. The cliché "Don't burn any bridges" is certainly true here.

CHAPTER 29

The Mature Job Candidate

OLDER JOB CANDIDATES face special challenges when job searching. Although they usually have more experience than their younger competitors, mature job seekers often find that employers are reluctant to hire them. They are sometimes met with prejudice in the job market due to interviewers' preconceived notions about those over a certain age.

In order to meet your goal—finding a job—you will have to learn how to combat this prejudice, as well as deal with overt age discrimination.

Who Are You Calling Mature?

When you think of a "mature person," you almost certainly think of someone much older than you are. No matter what your current age is, "mature" is always several years ahead of you. If you are in your forties, or fifties, or even in your sixties, you probably feel quite spry. And why shouldn't you? You are in the prime of your life. You are well past the awkwardness of young adulthood—okay, perhaps very well past it. You're settled down, have more than a few years of work experience under your belt, and you are ready to approach your job search with the self-confidence you didn't have when you were in your twenties or even in your thirties.

If you are worried about being the oldest one in the office, don't be. According to the U.S. Bureau of Labor Statistics, the number of people in the labor force who are 55 and older will increase by 49.1 percent through the year 2014.

Then you go on your first job interview and realize the interviewer is several years younger than you are—possibly even half your age. You find that she doesn't look at you and think of all the experience you would bring to the job. The interviewer instead looks at you, mentally calculates your age, and wonders how you will deal with all the "modern" technology in the office. This is in spite of the fact that you have been using computers for many years. She assumes you will resist learning new skills, regardless of your continually taking classes in order to improve your skills. She worries that you will be taking many days off for doctors' appointments although you haven't been healthier in your entire life.

Your interviewer, unfortunately, is afflicted with those prejudices and preconceived notions mentioned in the introduction to this chapter. Note the use of the word "afflicted." The interviewer's inability to recognize and reluctance to take advantage of the talents that mature workers possess can truly be detrimental to the employer, who may miss out on getting a highly qualified job candidate. Of course, it will make your job search difficult since you will have to work very hard to prove that you are the best applicant for the job.

Focus on Your Attributes

The word "experience" means different things to different people. You, as a mature job seeker, may think about the number of years you have spent working and feel confident that you are more qualified for a particular job than your much younger competitors.

Alternatively, a potential employer may look at your lengthy work history and see red flags. He may think, because you are a mature candidate, that you are set in your ways and are unwilling to, or even unable to, adapt to a new job. A younger worker, the employer may reason, can more easily learn new skills. She can be molded into the type of worker he wants.

This is untrue. Older workers are willing and able to learn new skills. It is your job to convince him that you are eager to do this. Also, as an experienced candidate, you will bring many attributes to the job that an inexperienced job seeker cannot. When on a job interview, use anecdotes from your work history to illustrate your attributes.

Skills Come from Experience

Focus on your skills. Your experience has allowed you to fine-tune those skills you acquired through formal training. After all, they say, "Practice makes perfect." You have also acquired skills through hands-on training over the years. In your resume and on job interviews, make sure you highlight all your skills.

Time Efficiency

Your years of experience have taught you how to get work done in a timely manner. You know the fastest routes to getting the best results you can get. After many years of trial and error, you now know which shortcuts result in success and which ones result in a subpar end product.

Workplace Savvy

As an experienced job candidate, you also have workplace savvy that can only be gained from age and experience. This is not something one can be taught, so there is no way your younger competitors can have it yet. You have the ability to deal with most situations that come along—there are few you haven't encountered over the years.

Don't Let Your Age Show

Age equals experience, but you don't want potential employers to automatically label you as an "older worker." You want all the attributes you've earned through your experience to jump out at them, not your age. However, it is impossible to hide your age, both in person and on your resume. For example, you will have to indicate the dates of employment on your resume. While you can choose how far back you want to go when listing prior jobs, you don't want to leave out a job that could set you apart from the other candidates.

Listing the years you attended school on your resume gives away your age. You should include your educational background on your resume, but leave out the dates. In addition, if you attended school more than five years ago, put your education at the bottom of your resume, not near the top.

Your job-search methods can also date you. A typewritten resume, for example, indicates that you may not have looked for a job in a while. Worse than that, it is a dead giveaway that you aren't up-to-date on the latest technology.

Brush up on your computer skills if they are insufficient, and write your resume using word processing software. Get online if you aren't yet. You must be ready to send and receive e-mail since that is how most people communicate. If you don't have an e-mail account, you must get one.

There are some services that offer free e-mail accounts. You should have an e-mail address included in the contact information on your resume.

You may have gotten every job you've ever had using traditional job-search methods like the help-wanted ads in the newspaper. Things have changed, and in order to improve your chances of finding a job, you must use current job-search methods. That means job searching online.

Physically hiding your age would be a challenge for most people. Should you go out and get a face-lift if you are looking for a new job? No, of course not! However, try to avoid letting your appearance date you. If you've had the same hairstyle for the last twenty years, it's time to update your look. Buy a new suit if the only one you have is several years old (even if it looks brand new). If your briefcase was a graduation present (back in 1976) and is now "well-worn," don't bring it on a job interview.

Age Discrimination

Age discrimination is a real problem that comes up for current employees and in the hiring process. Older workers are sometimes denied opportunities employers give to their younger colleagues. When making hiring decisions, employers sometimes don't consider job candidates over a certain age. Refusing to hire someone because of his age is illegal in the United States. The Age Discrimination in Employment Act of 1967 (ADEA) protects individuals who are age forty and above from employment discrimination, including discrimination in hiring. This means that an employer can't refuse to hire you because of your age (as long as you are forty or older).

An employer can't state an age preference in advertisements for most jobs. There are exceptions for jobs for which age is a real issue, such as a modeling or an acting job.

Responding to Age-Related Questions on Job Interviews

Even though an employer can't decide not to hire you because of your age, that might not stop her from inquiring about it on a job interview. And it won't keep you from feeling uncomfortable if the interviewer asks you how old you are. So what should you do if a prospective employer asks your age? You have some choices: You can answer the question honestly, you can lie, or you can refuse to answer it. Even if you normally are untruthful about your age, you are cautioned against lying about anything on a job interview. It will put you in a bad light with the employer—the employer can't discriminate against you because of your age, but he may decide to not hire you if he feels you are dishonest. You can either tell the truth or you can refuse to answer the question.

If you refuse to answer the question, you should do so in a nonconfrontational manner. You might even consider joking about the question—for example, "A lady never reveals her age" (if, in fact, you are a lady).

It is a myth that it is illegal for an employer to ask your age on a job interview or on an employment application. In reality, it is not the question that is illegal. Rather, if the employer decides not to hire you because of your age, that is illegal (see Chapter 25).

What to Do about Age Discrimination

When you are turned down for a job, you will probably try to figure out the reason. It is often easy to jump to the one for which you bear no responsibility—your age. You may make the assumption that you weren't hired because the employer discriminated against you due to your age. Be careful before you take that accusation any further than your own mind. There could be other reasons you were rejected for a job. For example, although you have a lot of experience, it may not be the right experience. Your formal training may not be appropriate. Maybe the interviewer just didn't like you or didn't think you would fit in well in his workplace.

Does Age Discrimination Happen Often?

Age discrimination happens, but people don't always report it. There are also cases in which people claim they've been discriminated against because of age even though they haven't. They might have decided against hiring you for the job for entirely different reasons. In 2005 the U.S. Equal Employment Opportunity Commission (EEOC) received 16,585 claims of age discrimination. Of those claims, 63 percent were deemed nonreasonable.

Your suspicions could be right, though. Maybe the employer didn't hire you because of your age. Ask yourself these questions before you draw a conclusion:

- Did the interviewer ask overt questions about your age?
- Did he make derogatory comments about your age or the number of years you've been working?
- Did the employer turn you down for the job but hire someone a lot younger than you are?

If you do ultimately conclude that you were discriminated against because of your age, you can file a claim with the U.S. Equal Employment Opportunity Commission. You can file a claim by mail or phone with your nearest EEOC office. You can find a list of EEOC offices on the agency's website: *www.eeoc.gov/offices.html*. You can also look for a listing in the government pages of your telephone directory.

According to the EEOC website, you have 180 days from the date of the alleged violation to file your claim. You must provide the EEOC with your name, address, and telephone number, as well as the name, address, and telephone number of the employer who allegedly discriminated against you. You also have to include the date and a description of the violation.

Many states and localities also have age discrimination laws. Agencies within those states and localities are responsible for enforcing those laws. If you file a claim with one of those agencies (referred to as Fair Employment Practices Agencies—FEPAs—by the EEOC), that agency will dual-file your claim with the EEOC. Likewise, if you file your claim with the EEOC, it will dual-file it with your state or local FEPA.

If you think you have been a victim of age discrimination, as defined by the Age Discrimination in Employment Act of 1967, you can file a private lawsuit against the employer. You should be aware that you must file a claim with the EEOC before you file your private suit.

Returning to the Job Market

Out of choice or necessity, many people in midlife find themselves re-entering the job market after a lengthy absence. Their return to the work force may come about because of a change in life circumstances, including:

- "Empty Nest Syndrome"
- Divorce
- Death of a spouse
- Spouse's retirement / job loss

Regardless of one's reasons for returning to the job market, this can be a difficult endeavor, particularly if one is a mature worker. If you are reentering the work force at any age, you must prove that you have kept up with changes in the field in which you want to work. You must show that your skills are up-to-date and that you are knowledgeable about the field.

If you are a mature job candidate who is returning to work, you will have a hard time making the argument that you have work experience that your younger competitors lack. You may in fact have work experience, but since there is a break in your work history, this may not count in your favor.

Make Your Non-Work Experience Count

Since you have spent a significant amount of time away from work, you will have to count on your non-work experience to help you prove you have the skills and other qualifications a potential employer desires. If you've been involved in volunteer work during your hiatus from work, you will definitely have an easier time doing this.

Begin by making a list of any volunteer work you've done since you've stopped working. Leadership positions you've held in various clubs and organizations should be at the top of your list. Also include any projects you've participated in, even if they were a one-time deal. For example, were you on the planning committee for a fundraiser or did you help organize a special luncheon? Don't forget to list committees you've sat on. Think about the skills you used in each of these situations. Were they skills you had from your previous jobs or were they new skills? Determine if a potential employer will find these skills valuable.

If you let your network die during your absence from the work force, you'll be at a disadvantage once you get started up again. It's best to begin to revive it as soon as you make the decision to return to work. Get in touch with some of your old contacts and begin to make new ones.

For more information on networking, see Chapter 3.

Writing Your Resume

Since your work experience probably ranges from a few to many years old, depending on how long you've been away from the work force, you should not use a chronological resume if you are returning to work. A chronological resume focuses on your work history. The last thing you want to do is draw attention to the fact that you were last employed some time ago. You should instead use a functional resume. It will allow you to focus on your skills rather than on your work experience. When you write a functional resume, you list the skills that are relevant to the job for which you are applying. Beneath each skill, you then list accomplishments that are related to that skill. Since you don't have recent work experience, you can draw upon your unpaid or volunteer experience when you list your accomplishments.

Make sure you let your prospective employer know if you took any classes during your hiatus from work. This can show that you kept your mind active and your skills sharp.

Going on a Job Interview

When you're on a job interview, don't be surprised if a lot of the questions the interviewer asks you are about your lack of recent work experience. It is your goal to make him see that a lack of "paid experience" doesn't mean a lack of experience in general. Get the interviewer to think about the fact that you were productive during your time out of the work force.

You improved your skills and gained new ones. As you did on your resume, focus on your unpaid or volunteer work. Discuss any classes you took. Make sure to do a lot of reading about your industry and profession so you can sound knowledgeable during the interview.

After Retirement: A New Career

When past generations retired from work, it usually meant the end of working for a paycheck. Most people spent their retirement years traveling or pursuing their hobbies, or maybe doing some volunteer work. These days, people enjoy better health and live much longer than they did in past decades. While some retirees look forward to not having to go to work every day, others use their retirement as an opportunity to pursue new careers.

Sometimes this decision is precipitated by financial need. Other times it is a choice born of the desire to finally realize a dream career that, for various reasons, he could not chase after earlier.

If you want to have a post-retirement career, it is much easier to choose one for which you can use transferable skills. Transferable skills are skills obtained in one line of work or occupation that you can adapt to another. If you don't have to acquire new skills, you can begin looking for a job in your new field immediately. If you don't have these transferable skills, you will need to retrain for your new career. This can mean anything from completing a degree to simply taking one course.

Whether you are twenty-six or sixty-six, you must have the necessary qualifications before an employer will hire you. Before you choose your new career, you must determine what skills you need and if you are willing to invest money, time, and energy to acquire them. Also take care to choose your career wisely, particularly if you must retrain in order to get hired. This will take extra time and money that you might not have originally planned for.

The bottom line is this: If you want to work in retirement, you absolutely can. Many people find that pursuing a long-lost dream in retirement revitalizes and inspires them. All it takes is a little extra thought and planning to do it right. The time and energy you put in now will contribute to a better experience down the road.

CHAPTER 30

How to Handle Roadblocks

LOOKING FOR A JOB is hard work. It is probably one of the most difficult things you will ever encounter. Most people will, unfortunately, have to embark on this task several times in their lives. Following the advice laid out in this book will greatly increase your chances of succeeding on your job search. However, even the most informed job seeker can meet with failure after failure. This can be extremely discouraging. Don't give up. You will find a job—it just may take longer than you expected when you started out.

What to Do When You Can't Find a Suitable Job

After searching through many job listings, applying for some jobs, and even going on a few interviews, you may still find yourself unemployed. There might be many reasons for this. Some reasons may be within your control and therefore fixable. Others may be outside your control, and your only solution may be making changes that may have a big impact on your life. Other reasons may require that you just keep doing what you're doing until something happens.

Here are possible reasons your job search has been unsuccessful:

- The economy is bad.
- Job opportunities in your field or industry are limited.
- You need more experience.
- Your resume doesn't represent you well.
- You don't represent yourself well on a job interview.

When the economy is bad, job seekers suffer. There's not much you can do about that. Keep looking at job listings. Use all available resources: newspapers, online job banks, your network, and employment agencies. Consider taking a temporary job until you find something you really want.

TRY TEMPING

Temporary jobs are a great way to get experience without committing to a full-time job. You can turn down assignments in order to go on job interviews or when you need to spend more time on your job search. Another big plus? Sometimes temporary assignments turn into permanent ones.

Some fields and industries experience downturns that are not tied to the current state of the economy. For example, American car manufacturers are losing business to foreign automobile makers. Many are laying off workers, causing a slump in the automotive industry. If job opportunities in your field or industry are limited, you may have to consider retraining for a different type of job. Later we will explore ways to find a new occupation. You may find it hard to think about retraining for a new career. After all, you've already made an investment in this one. You may not have a choice, though. Remember that some of the skills you have will be transferable, so you probably won't have to start entirely from scratch.

If you recently changed careers and you are lacking experience, you may have to lower your expectations of getting hired for the type of position you desire. You may have to consider an entry-level job in your field so that you can gain the necessary experience. Temporary work is one way to get more experience. You may consider doing an internship even if you are no longer a student. If you previously attended college, call or visit the career services office of your alma mater or contact the alumni association. You can also try to set up an internship by talking to members of your network.

Have you been slow to get job interviews? Perhaps you do have the experience and skills you need, but your resume doesn't show it. Consider revamping your resume (yes, again). Reread Chapters 9, 10, and 11 to get some tips on how to write a resume that gets results.

If your resume is getting you calls for job interviews, it may not be the problem. Could it be the way you present yourself on the interview? Make sure your answers to interview questions highlight your skills. Don't try to be humble on a job interview. This is one time you want to brag about yourself. You may need more interview practice. Have a friend run through some interview questions with you. Make sure he knows that you are seeking criticism. After all, you do want to improve your interview skills.

Make a Career Change

As discussed earlier, some occupations experience downturns from which they have little chance of recovering. Unfortunately, many workers are caught in the crossfire, leaving them unable to find a job even though they may have years of experience and excellent skills. If you are having trouble finding work in your field, and you've eliminated possible causes like a poor resume or inadequate interview skills, then it may be time for a career change. Changing your career is not something you should do haphazardly. It is a big decision and one that you should take very seriously. Take the time to find the best option for you.

Self-Assessment

Your first step should be to find the occupations that are suitable for you based on a variety of factors. You will learn about these factors—specifically, your personality, values, skills, and interests—while doing a *self-assessment*. You can use a variety of tools to help you learn about these factors. These tools are commonly referred to as career tests, but the word "test" is a misnomer. Tests generally have right and wrong answers. There are no right or wrong answers when you are doing a self-assessment. There is just the process of learning about yourself in order to figure out in what occupation you would be happiest and most successful.

BE HONEST ABOUT YOURSELF

It is important to be as honest as you can when doing a self-assessment. There are no right or wrong answers. You want your results to reflect your personality, skills, and values. You shouldn't go into it thinking that any answers are bad ones.

A career-planning professional can administer these self-assessment tests. This option will be discussed shortly. If money is an issue, you may want to try using a "career test" online. Many of them are available for free. You can find a few listed in the Resources section at the end of this book.

Exploring Your Possibilities

After completing the self-assessment, you should have a list of possible career choices. Now it's time to pare down your list so that it is more manageable. What do you know about some of the occupations on your list? Are there a few you've never heard of? Others you've never considered? Are there some you know only a little about?

It's time to do some research. You should try to gather information about as many of these occupations as you can. Often people discount a particular occupation because they either don't know anything about it or they are misinformed about it. You don't need to start off with in-depth research. Simply get a job description for each occupation on your list. You can use the Occupational Outlook Handbook, published by the Bureau of Labor Statistics of the U.S. Department of Labor. The print version is available in most libraries. It is also online at *www.bls.gov/oco*. The Occupational Outlook Handbook contains information about almost every occupation you can think of and is revised every other year.

LOOK AT WHERE YOU LIVE

While an occupation may be on an upward trend nationally, it could be on a downward slope where you live. You can find information on outlooks for various occupations in most states by visiting their labor offices' websites. The U.S. Department of Labor maintains a list of links to those sites at *www.dol.gov/esa/contacts/state_of.htm*.

Once you have narrowed down your choices based on job descriptions, you can begin to read more about the occupations that seem like good possibilities. Continue using the Occupational Outlook Handbook to find out about salaries, job duties, and educational requirements.

There is one factor that should weigh heavily on your mind, especially if you are making a career change because job opportunities in your current field have dried up. You must look at the employment outlook for any occupations you are considering. This will help you figure out if you will have a good chance of finding work in the future. After all, changing careers every couple of years is probably not something you want to do.

MAKE SURE YOU LIKE THE CAREER

You may be tempted to look at "top careers lists" that give you the expert's predictions of what jobs will have the best outlook in the future. While you should consider occupational outlook when choosing a career, you shouldn't make your decision based only on an occupation's appearance on such a list. You must take into consideration whether you will actually like the work.

Any occupation you are seriously considering deserves even further exploration. Talk to people in the field to learn more about it. You can conduct informational interviews, a formal way to learn about an occupation. Your network (see Chapter 3) will come in handy when you are looking for people to interview. Once you have made a decision, it is time to begin your job search if you already have the necessary skills. If not, you may have to look into getting some training.

Training for a New Career

When they choose a new career, some people pick one for which they don't need a lot of retraining. The skills they currently have can easily be transferred to this new occupation. Other people may pick a career in spite of the fact that they will have to acquire new skills. You may discover that your career change requires a return to school for an additional degree or you may find out that you just need to take a few classes. Since you are making this career change because opportunities in your prior field declined, you may be eligible for retraining provided by the federal government. The Employment and Training Administration of the U.S. Department of Labor provides job training to individuals through One-Stop Career Centers located around the country. America's Service Locator at *www.servicelocator.org* can help you find a local One-Stop Career Center.

Working with a Career Development Professional

Some people are at a loss as to what to do when their job search is failing. They aren't sure if their job-search strategy is at fault or if they need a career change. If that describes what you are thinking right now, don't feel you have to go through this alone. If you're having trouble figuring out what to do as far as your career is concerned, you should consider meeting with a career development professional.

These professionals come with many different titles. There are career counselors, career development facilitators, and job coaches. There are even social workers who specialize in career development. Whomever you choose to work with, do some research to make sure that person is properly licensed and has experience working with people with your particular issues. To find out if the person you want to work with has the proper license, check with your state's department of education. Then ask to interview him as well to make sure you will be able to work with this person.

CHECK OUT YOUR CAREER COUNSELOR

Career counselors, to be licensed in most states, must have a master's degree in counseling. Many career counselors belong to the National Career Development Association. The NCDA has a state-by-state list of members on their website (*www.ncda.org*).

A career development professional can help you figure out what went wrong with your job search. She can assess your resume and your interviewing skills to find out if they are the problem. She can determine whether a career change is needed, and if so, can assist you in making the transition. A career counselor can administer career tests to help you figure out what your options are and then can help you narrow down your choices. She can assist you in getting information about various occupations and can help you decide which one is best for you.

Of course, you will be the one making the final decision. Beware of any career development professional that tries to push you into a particular career. You should make your choice based on the professional's advice (after all that's why you're paying her), but ultimately it is your choice to make.

Career-planning help can be expensive. There are places you can get this service at a low cost, or even for free. Look into the career services provided by your alma mater. Many colleges offer free career counseling to alumni. Also check with your local college. They may provide these services to the community. Some public libraries even offer career-planning assistance, as do some community agencies.

Working with a Resume-Writing Professional

Your job search may be stalled simply because your resume isn't good. This may have nothing at all to do with your skills, experience, or education. Your resume may be poorly written and therefore it doesn't do you justice. If you've tried several times to put together a good resume but find yourself unable to do so, it may be time to hire a professional resume writer.

Many career development professionals, described in the prior section, provide resume-writing services. Other people working as resume writers have training provided by one of several organizations, including the National Resume Writer's Association.

VISIT THE BBB

Before engaging the services of a professional resume writer or any other career development professional, try to check out that business or individual with your local Better Business Bureau. Find out if they have any complaints on file. Visit the Better Business Bureau website (*www.bbb.org*) for a list of local affiliates.

Professional resume writers are not required to be licensed or certified, so when you hire one, you are really on your own. Therefore, you should always ask to see samples of that person's work. You must also ask for references. Call those references to find out if they were successful in their job searches as a result of the resume writer's services.

Dealing with the Stress of a Lengthy Job Search

A job search that lasts for a long time can wear you down. You may have started out with a positive attitude, but if you've been looking for a job for a while, you may no longer be as upbeat. For one thing, rejection can really deflate one's ego. Then there's the frustration of plugging away at something that doesn't seem to be moving forward.

Remember, a job search, on average, takes several months. Depending on the economy, it may take even longer. The best thing you can do is to stay positive. A positive attitude will translate into self-confidence, something you surely need when you go out on job interviews. A negative attitude, in contrast, will make you look defeated. It will not bring you any closer to getting hired. And you certainly don't want to make your job search last any longer than it has to, do you?

If you are currently employed, continue to do your job well. You don't want the stress of job loss to be added to the stress of a job search. If your reason for looking for a new job is that you don't get along with your boss or coworkers, look for ways to improve these relationships. If you simply hate your work, remember that you're doing something proactive so that you will eventually not have to do it any longer. If money is the issue, remember that earning some money is better than earning none.

If you are unemployed and find yourself spending every waking moment on your job search, take a break. You need to set limits on the time you spend looking for a job. Try to stick to working only during business hours, let's say 9 A.M. to 5 P.M. Remember to take a lunch hour halfway through the day. You can even meet friends for lunch—perhaps catch up with your old work buddies. Or you may try doing something a little more productive, like scheduling lunches with your network contacts. Okay, that may feel a little more like work than a break, but you can always take a break at another time.

Get out of the house for a while. A change of scenery may revitalize you. If you have a laptop computer, work outdoors if the weather is cooperative. Some businesses, including coffee shops, have wireless Internet connectivity so you can pretty much work anywhere these days. If you don't have a laptop, find out if your local library has public computers.

DE-STRESS FOR BEST RESULTS

If the stress of your job search is getting to you, consider taking a yoga class. It can help you relax while also keeping you in good physical condition. Eating a healthy diet is also very important when your body is under a lot of stress.

While you're in the library, borrow a book that isn't job-search-related. Reading a good novel after a long day working on your job search will be refreshing. If you can't concentrate on a book, take yourself to a movie. You may be trying to save money, so a matinee may be a better option. Remember, if you spend time away from your job search during the day, you can always make up for it in the evening. Just don't count on contacting any leads by phone after regular business hours.

Coping with Shyness

The job search can be torturous for someone who is extremely shy. We're not just talking about a person who is a little bashful, but instead one who has moderate to great difficulty interacting with others. If you find your shyness is acting as a barrier to your career success, keep reading.

Shyness can impact your job search in many ways. While you may be able to deal with it when interacting with people with whom you are familiar, talking to strangers can be very difficult. And what does the job search consist of more often than anything else? Talking to strangers including interviewers, recruiters, and even receptionists.

One way to combat your shyness is to keep a positive attitude about yourself. Try to refrain from negative self-talk, such as "I'm not good enough." You should be confident that you are worthy of getting hired. Focus on your skills and why they make you a desirable candidate.

THERE ARE LOTS OF SHY PEOPLE

If you consider yourself shy, you aren't alone. According to a study published in the mid-1990s by Lynne Henderson and Philip Zimbardo in the *Encyclopedia of Mental Health*, approximately 50 percent of people surveyed considered themselves to be shy. This represented an increase from those who said they were shy in a study published just twenty years before that one.

Practicing for the interview can also be helpful, but don't just practice your answers. You should also rehearse greeting the interviewer and shaking his hand. Become comfortable with making and maintaining eye contact. Ask someone to practice with you. Once you have these skills down, practice them on strangers. Go shopping and talk to salespeople. Talk to the teller at the bank or the clerk in the post office. The more you talk to people and the more often you make eye contact, the more comfortable you will become.

Networking can be a nightmare if you are shy. Not only do you have to talk to people you may not know well, you have to ask them for advice. As discussed in Chapter 3, networking is an ongoing process and not just something you have to do while you are job hunting. Hopefully you established your network long before you had to look for work. Remember, your contacts aren't total strangers. They may be people you don't know well, but at least you do know them. If someone in your network refers you to someone you don't know at all and you don't feel comfortable calling that person, send an e-mail instead. Once you've established a relationship via e-mail, it should be easier to make that first phone call.

The Basics Of Job Winning: A Condensed Review

STEP 1: DECIDE WHAT YOU WANT

The first step to finding your ideal job is to clearly define your objectives. Choose a career where you will enjoy most of the day-to-day tasks. Keep in mind that you are not merely choosing a career, but also a lifestyle. Ask yourself how you might adapt to the day-to-day duties and working environment that a specific position entails. Then ask yourself how you might adapt to the demands of that career or industry as a whole.

STEP 2: CHOOSE YOUR STRATEGY

The most common job-seeking techniques are:

- Following up on help-wanted advertisements (in the newspaper or online)
- Using employment services
- Relying on personal contacts
- Contacting employers directly (the Direct Contact method)

Each of these approaches can lead to better jobs. However, the Direct Contact method boasts twice the success rate of the others. If you choose to use other methods as well, try to expend at least half your energy on Direct Contact.

STEP 3: SET YOUR SCHEDULE

When outlining your job search schedule, be realistic. If you will be job-searching full-time, your search could take at least two months or more. If you can only devote part-time effort, it will probably take at least four months. In tough economic times, it could last much longer.

Job-hunting is tough work, both physically and emotionally. It is also intellectually demanding work that requires you to be at your best. So don't tire yourself out by working on your job campaign around the clock. At the same time, be sure to discipline yourself.

If you are searching full-time and have decided to choose several different strategies, divide up each week, designating some time for each method. By trying several approaches at once, you can evaluate how promising each seems and alter your schedule accordingly.

STEP 4: DEVELOP YOUR LIST

Develop a checklist for categorizing the types of firms for which you'd like to work. Categorize firms by product line, size, customer type (such as industrial or consumer), growth prospects, or geographical location.

Assemble your list of potential employers. Choose firms where you are most likely to be able to find a job. Try matching your skills with those that a specific job demands. Consider where your skills might be in demand, the degree of competition for employment, and the employment outlook at each company.

STEP 5: CREATE YOUR RESUME

Begin working on your resume. Once it is complete, begin researching your first batch of prospective employers. You will want to determine whether you would be happy working at the firms you are researching and to get a better idea of what their employment needs might be. You also need to obtain enough information to sound highly informed about the company during phone conversations and in mail correspondence. If necessary, tailor your resume to each employer you plan to contact.

STEP 6: DO YOUR RESEARCH

Save your big research effort until you start to arrange interviews. Nevertheless, plan to spend several hours researching each firm on your list. For answers to specific questions, contact any pertinent professional associations that may be able to help you learn more about an employer. Read industry publications looking for articles on the firm. Then look up the company on the Internet or try additional resources at your local library. Keep organized, and maintain a folder on each firm.

Information to look for includes: company size; president, CEO, or owner's name; when the company was established; what each division does; and benefits that are important to you.

STEP 7: ASSEMBLE YOUR NETWORK

Begin with as many people that you know personally as you can. Dig into your personal phone book and your holiday greeting card list and locate old classmates from school. Approach people who perform your personal business such as your lawyer, accountant, banker, doctor, stockbroker, and insurance agent. These people develop a very broad contact base due to the nature of their professions.

STEP 8: CONTACT FOR INTERVIEWS

Now it is time to make Direct Contact with the goal of arranging interviews. The obvious means of initiating Direct Contact are:

- Mail (postal or electronic)
- Phone calls

Prepare a cover letter that says exactly what you want, and, of course, include your resume. Remember that employers receive many resumes every day. Don't be surprised if you do not get a response to your inquiry, and don't spend weeks waiting for responses that may never come. Follow up your letter and resume (or precede them) with a phone call.

STEP 9: PREPARE FOR THE INTERVIEW

As each interview is arranged, begin your in-depth research. You need to know the company's products, types of customers, subsidiaries, parent company, principal locations, rank in the industry, sales and profit trends, type of ownership, size, current plans, and much more. Be familiar with common industry terms, the trends in the firm's industry, the firm's principal competitors and their relative performance, and the direction in which the industry leaders are headed.

Make a list of questions that you think might be asked in each interview. Think out your answers carefully and practice them with a friend. Record your responses to the problem questions. Practice again after your first few interviews. Go over the difficult questions that you were asked.

STEP 9: GO TO THE INTERVIEW

The very beginning of the interview is the most important part because it determines the tone for the rest of it. Those first few moments are especially crucial. Do you smile when you meet? Do you establish enough eye contact, but not too much? Do you walk into the office with a self-assured and confident stride? Do you shake hands firmly? Do you make small talk easily without being garrulous? Make sure your first impression is a good one.

STEP 10: AFTER THE INTERVIEW

Write a follow-up e-mail immediately after the interview, while it is still fresh in the interviewer's mind. If you haven't heard back from the interviewer within a week of sending your thank-you e-mail, call to stress your continued interest in the firm and the position. If you lost any points during the interview for any reason, this letter can help you regain footing. Be polite and make sure to stress your continued interest and competency to fill the position. Just don't forget to proofread it thoroughly. If you are unsure of the spelling of the interviewer's name, call the receptionist and ask.

Last Words

Again and again during your job search you will face rejection. You will be rejected when you apply for interviews. You will be rejected after interviews. Don't let rejections slow you down. Keep reminding yourself that the sooner you go out, start your job search, and get those rejections flowing in, the closer you will be to obtaining the job you want.

Resources

Career Counseling Services and Other Career-Related Instruments

Check your local telephone directory, do web searches, and ask colleagues for recommendations if you're searching for a career professional. Also, the career counseling departments of many colleges and universities offer online information and tests. Lots of relocation businesses and services have long or short quizzes on their web sites that will help you find a place in the country—or the world—that suits you. Remember that many popular career instruments, such as the Myers-Briggs Type Indicator (MBTI), Strong Interest Inventory (SII), and Campbell Skills and Interests Inventory (CSII) can only be administered by people who have completed a qualifying program and can help you interpret your results.

BAY AREA CAREER CENTER
57 Post Street, Suite 804
San Francisco, CA 94104
(415) 398-4881
www.bayareacareercenter.com
Credentialed career counselors and coaches, relevant workshops, job support groups, and an Informational Interview Network help you find your direction and make successful changes in your work life.

DISCOVER YOUR PERSONALITY
www.discoveryourpersonality.com
MBTI tests online and phone consultations.

ELEVATIONS, THE CAREER DISCOVERY TOOL
www.ElevateYourCareer.com
Career assessment, evaluation, networking, and coaching.

EMOTIONAL INTELLIGENCE
www.emotionaliq.com
MSCEIT test measuring emotional intelligence and certification for administering test.

EQ UNIVERSITY
www.equniversity.com
Emotional intelligence assessment, training, and development.

MARK GUTERMAN, MA, CAREER CONSULTANT

www.meaningfulcareers.com

Mark@meaningfulcareers.com

Counseling, books, articles, and other resources for guiding your career.

HOLLAND TYPES

http://facweb.bhc.edu/advising/counseling/services/develop/interests.htm#holland's

Information about Holland Types on website of Black Hawk College.

ROBIN B. HOLT, MA, CAREER CONSULTANT

rholt@bayareacareercenter.com

INTERNATIONAL PERSONALITY ITEM POOL (IPIP)

www.personal.psu.edu/faculty/j/5/j5j/IPIP/

Take the original 300-item IPIP or a shorter version to estimate where you stand on five personality domains and thirty subdomains.

INTERNET CAREER CONNECTION

www.iccweb.com

Online interest inventory.

JANDA, LOUIS, PHD. *CAREER TESTS.* AVON, MA: ADAMS MEDIA, 1999.

Twenty-five tests covering many aspects of the career decision process.

JOBHUNTERSBIBLE.COM

www.jobhuntersbible.com

Website of Richard Bolles, author of *What Color Is Your Parachute?* Berkeley, CA: Ten Speed Press, 2006.

TERRY KARP, MA, CAREER CONSULTANT

tkarp@bayareacareercenter.com

KEIRSEY.COM

www.keirsey.com

Keirsey Temperament Sorter, descriptions of the various temperaments, and some famous people in each category.

KNOCKEMDEAD.COM

Website of Martin Yate, author of *Knock 'em Dead.* Avon, MA: Adams Media, 2009.

LIVECAREER

www.livecareer.com

Free online career interest test.

O-NET RESOURCE CENTER

www.onetcenter.org

Interest profiler and other career exploration instruments on website run by the U.S. Department of Labor.

THE PERSONALITY PAGE

www.personalitypage.com

Personality tests and information

PERSONALITY TEST CENTER

www.personalitytest.net

Personality tests.

PERSONALITYTYPE.COM

www.personalitytype.com

Personality quiz by Paul D. Tieger and Barbara Barron-Tieger, authors of *Do What You Are*. New York: Little Brown and Co., 2007.

QUEENDOM.COM

www.queendom.com

Large website with free and fee-based self-assessment tests in the fields of careers, personality, psychology, relationships, intelligence, and health; also offering advice, community, surveys, and trivia quizzes on many subjects

HELEN M. SCULLY, MA, CAREER CONSULTANT

www.ScullyCareerAssociates.com

SIMILARMINDS.COM

http://similarminds.com/personality_tests.html

Variety of personality tests.

DENA SNEIDER, MA, CAREER CONSULTANT

dsneider@bayareacareercenter.com

TYPEFOCUS CAREERS

www.typefocus.com

Personality assessment and career counseling.

SUSAN URQUHART-BROWN, MA, CAREER CONSULTANT AND BUSINESS COACH
www.careersteps123.com
susanub@careersteps123.com
Help for fledgling business owners who want to build successful, thriving businesses.

YAHOO! GEOCITIES PERSONALITY TESTS
www.geocities.com/lifexplore/tests.htm
Links to lots of different personality tests.

Books

Baron, Renee. *What Type Am I: Discover Who You Really Are.* (NY: The Penguin Group, 1998.)

Bennett, Scott. *The Elements of Resume Style.* (NY: AMACOM, 2005.)

Bixler, Susan, and Nancy Nix-Rice. *The New Professional Image.* Avon, MA: Adams Media, 2005.

Bolles, Richard N. *What Color Is Your Parachute?* Berkeley, CA: Ten Speed Press, 2006.

Eikleberry, Carol, PhD. *The Career Guide for Creative and Unconventional People.* Berkeley, CA: Ten Speed Press, 1995.

McKay, Dawn Rosenberg. *The Everything Practice Interview Book.* (Avon, MA: Adams Media, 2004).

Nadler, Burton Jay. *The Everything® Cover Letter Book.* 2nd Edition. (Avon, MA: Adams Media, 2005.)

Nadler, Burton Jay. *The Everything® Resume Book.* 2nd Edition. (Avon, MA: Adams Media, 2005.)

Noble, David F., PhD. *Professional Resumes for Executives, Managers, and Other Administrators.* (Indianapolis: JIST Works, 1998.)

Parker, Yana. *The Resume Catalog: 200 Damn Good Examples.* (Berkeley, CA: Ten Speed Press, 1996.)

Tieger, Paul D. and Barbara. *Do What You Are: Discover the Perfect Career for You Through the Secrets of Personality Type*. (NY: Little, Brown & Company, 2001.)

U.S. Department of Labor. *Occupational Outlook Handbook* (revised and updated every two years).

Yate, Martin. *Knock 'em Dead: The Ultimate Job Seeker's Guide 2010*. (Avon, MA: Adams Media, 2009.)

Online Resources

These sites are useful for career information as well as job-hunting tips and ideas.

ABOUT CAREER PLANNING

http://careerplanning.about.com
Dawn Rosenberg McKay, the About.com Guide to Career Planning, provides you with the help you need to get your career off the ground.

ABOUT JOB SEARCHING

http://jobsearching.about.com
About.com Guide to Job Searching Alison Doyle takes you through the process of finding a job that's right for you.

ALLBUSINESS

www.allbusiness.com
Information and forms for small businesses

BESTJOBSUSA

www.bestjobsusa.com
General purpose employment site operated by Recourse Communications, Inc.

BIZJOURNALS

www.bizjournals.com
Links to websites of over forty print business journals

CAREERBUILDER.COM

www.careerbuilder.com

CAREER EXPLORER

www.careerexplorer.net